Corporate Social Performance

Paradoxes, Pitfalls, and Pathways to the Better World

A Volume in
Contemporary Perspectives in Corporate Social Performance and Policy

Series Editor
Agata Stachowicz-Stanusch, *Silesian University of Technology, Poland*

Contemporary Perspectives in Corporate Social Performance and Policy

Agata Stachowicz-Stanusch, Series Editor

Corporate Social Performance:
Paradoxes, Pitfalls and Pathways To The Better World (2015)
edited by Agata Stachowicz-Stanusch

For my daughter, Natalie

Corporate Social Performance

Paradoxes, Pitfalls, and Pathways to the Better World

edited by

Agata Stachowicz-Stanusch
Silesian University of Technology, Poland

INFORMATION AGE PUBLISHING, INC.
Charlotte, NC • www.infoagepub.com

Library of Congress Cataloging-in-Publication Data

Corporate social performance : paradoxes, pitfalls, and pathways to the
better world / edited by Agata Stachowicz-Stanusch.
pages cm. -- (Contemporary perspectives in corporate social
performance and policy)
ISBN 978-1-68123-164-8 (paperback) -- ISBN 978-1-68123-165-5 (hardcover) --
ISBN 978-1-68123-166-2 (ebook) 1. Social responsibility of business. 2.
Corporations--Moral and ethical aspects. 3. Corporate governance--Social
aspects. I. Stachowicz-Stanusch, Agata.
HD60.C686 2015
658.4'08--dc23

                              2015020992

ISBN: 978-1-68123-164-8 (Paperback)
       978-1-68123-165-5 (Hardcover)
       978-1-68123-166-2 (ebook)

CONTENTS

PART III: PITFALLS OF CORPORATE SOCIAL PERFORMANCE

PART IV: PATHWAYS OF CORPORATE SOCIAL PERFORMANCE

ACKNOWLEDGMENTS

I thank all chapter authors who met deadlines, engaged ideas, responded to feedback and wrote magnificent chapters that make this book amazing. I am proud to have had the opportunity to work with all them. I am indebted to our reviewers for their valuable and thoughtful suggestions which have enriched this book. I would like to thank PhD Anna Sworowska my research assistant who has been very skillful and supportive in moving the book through into publication. Especially, I would like to thank George Johnson, Publisher of Information Age Publishing for his continuous support.

Agata Stachowicz-Stanusch

Corporate Social Performance:
Paradoxes, Pitfalls, and Pathways to the Better World, pp. xi–xi
Copyright © 2015 by Information Age Publishing

PART I

INTRODUCTION

CHAPTER 1

CORPORATE SOCIAL PERFORMANCE IN THE AGE OF IRRESPONSIBILITY

Agata Stachowicz-Stanusch

The concept of corporate social performance (CSP) has been significantly expanded compared to the historical origins and continues to be the subject of public debate (Bevan, Isles, Emery, & Hoskins, 2004, p. 8). Its opponents and supporters are arguing about fundamental assumptions, while practitioners are searching for the best ways to ensure its effectiveness and are trying to develop the best strategies for its implementation. Modern and responsible business is looking for synergies between economic, environmental and social aspects of the operation, building its comprehensive development based on CSP. Making of voluntary commitments as to the rules of conduct in many cases may allow the abandonment of regulation, thus leading to a reduction of administrative burdens for business. Moreover, from the wider perspectives, activities carried on CSP also lead indirectly to achieve a number of policy objectives, such as: more integrated labor markets, increasing social cohesion, innovation increase and sustainable use of natural resources.

However, we should be aware of some pitfalls that may occur while CSP is being introduced in business practice as such strategies are quite expen-

Corporate Social Performance:
Paradoxes, Pitfalls, and Pathways to the Better World, pp. 3–12
Copyright © 2015 by Information Age Publishing
All rights of reproduction in any form reserved.

sive to be applied. It results sometimes in it abandonment when times are tough or if competitors do not use similar strategies in place. On the other hand some companies provide philanthropy or partnership with nonprofit entities as superficial activity often lacking the expertise. Moreover, firms may be easily manipulated by stakeholders that do not really represent the public.

The last decade had abundant corporate, national and international ethical and financial scandals and crises. After this epoch of moral catastrophes stakeholders expect that corporations which are considered as the most powerful institutions today and which have enormous impact on our planet's ecosystems and social networks will take more active roles as citizens within society and in the fight against some of the most pressing problems in the world, such as poverty, environmental degradation, defending human rights, corruption, and pandemic diseases.

Although corporate social performance (CSP) has been a prominent concept in management literature and in the business world in recent years "it remains a fact that many business leaders still only pay lip service to CSR [Corporate Social Responsibility], or are merely reacting to peer pressure by introducing it into their organizations" (Bevan, Isles, Emery, & Hoskins, 2004, p. 4). So do companies really do "well" by doing "good" or maybe "companies engage in CSR in order to offset corporate social irresponsibility?" (Kotchen & Moony, 2012, p. 4). I hope that we may agree that companies and CSR only by working together guarantee their own survival and we the society and the planet will be much obliged (Thomé, 2009, p. 3).

This volume is a collection of ideas, examples and solutions on CSP implementation and problems that occur in this area of consideration.

The book is organized under three themes. Theme one, "Paradoxes of Corporate Social Performance," opens with Irene Nikandrou and Irene Tsachouridi's chapter, "Does Being 'Good' Pay Off Even During Periods of Crisis?: An Employee Perspective." Authors through their experimental study show that those perceiving higher levels of organizational virtuousness perceive lower levels of breach and violation both when the organization fulfills its obligations (transactional and developmental) and when the organization does not do so. By and large the research indicates that "being good" can pay off, as it can act as a positive frame of reference even during tough times.

In the next chapter "Corporate Social Performance Needs More Competition Not Less: An Idea for a Paradigm Shift in CSP" Athanasios Chymis, Massimiliano Di Bitetto, and Paolo D'Anselmi trace the weakness of theoretical underpinnings of CSP on the long-lasting divide between this concept and economics in general and Friedman in particular. Authors present some first empirical evidence that competition is the driving force behind CSP and they suggest the CSP literature can move forward by incorporating competition in its research agenda. They also propose to broaden the CSP literature and include public enterprises as well as every public administration—since they all consume scarce resources—to be the subject of interest.

Subsequently, Olimpia Meglio in the chapter "Should Acquisitions Perform Well, Good or Both? A Stakeholder Perspective on Acquisition Performance," drawing on the literature streams related to corporate social performance and stakeholder theory, shows how the failure to consider neglected—but relevant—stakes that acquisitions put at risk, such as those of employees and consumers, produces measures of acquisition performance that do not do justice to the multiplicity of outcomes that these deals generally cause. These research streams help to illuminate the possible influences of these stakes on acquisition performance and further our understanding of this complex phenomenon.

Duane Windsor's chapter titled "Identifying Reasons Why Some Firms Maximize Corporate Social Irresponsibility and Some Firms Minimize Corporate Social Responsibility" investigates corporate social irresponsibility (CSI) in comparison to the concept of corporate social responsibility (CSR). Investigation into CSI is more about antecedents and consequences of socially undesirable behaviors than about normative or strategic justifications. Investigation into CSR is more about antecedents and consequences of socially desirable but individually and organizationally avoidable behaviors. The chapter addresses this fundamental, unresolved question to help identify a desirable research program for future scholarship. This chapter undertakes to advance theoretical and empirical understanding of reasons for occurrences of CSI maximization and CSR minimization.

Harry Costin closes Part I with his chapter" Corporate Social Responsibility: A Three-Layer Discussion." He presents the three distinct levels implicit in discussions about CSR are: (1) fundamental values and notions about the appropriate structure of society and the relationships between key actors and stakeholders; (2) CSR as a set of concepts and prescriptive actions; and finally, (3) the most efficient ways to achieve the goals established by CSR. One could add corporate social performance as a fourth layer, a direct resultant of the other three. This discussion focuses primarily upon the first three ones.

Part II, "Pitfalls of Corporate Social Performance" opens with the chapter: "Corporations and Corporate Social Performance—Be Genuine, Simplify, or Leave It …" by Kathrin Köster. In this chapter the author takes a "forward to transform mental models perspective" practicing and arguing for authenticity and simplicity. A transdisciplinary approach enriches the discussion by going beyond existing boundaries of our research conditioning building on the insights of quantum physics and ancient Asian philosophy.

Consciousness, interconnectedness and wholeness in the sense of mind, heart and hands are introduced into the discussion postulating the concept of "individual social responsibility" (ISR). It is the responsibility of leaders to develop their self-consciousness following 6 steps suggested in this chapter. A corporation embarking on the path of ISR will implement the following conclusions drawn in this article: (1) Social responsibility as the heart of CSP needs to be a deeply held belief of the corporation in order to be effective. It needs to be part of the corporation's spirit. (2) The motivation for corporate social performance is intrinsic and genuine—starting with the management team—rather than purely triggered by external factors as an extrinsic motivation. (3) For long-term effectiveness of the corporation, CSP builds an integral part of the corporation's strategy and its implementation. (4) The acknowledgment and conscious use of mental power along with the power of positive feelings can generate positive impact for internal and external stakeholders. This, in turn, means more motivated and committed staff as well as an increasing number of enthusiastic customers. To illustrate Individual Social Responsibility the second half of this chapter is dedicated to corporate examples. Each company is taken to elucidate the impact of ISR on one main stakeholder group: Customers (ColmarBrunton), society and societies in general (LesMills), suppliers and local communities (WE'AR), and staff (Futurice).

In the subsequent chapter, "The Importance of Corporate Social Performance: A Review of the Construct's Evolution and Relation to Financial Performance," Andrew E. Michael distinguishes between various definitions and dimensions of corporate social performance and outlines the concept's evolution. The author notes that interest in corporate social performance has grown partly due to the unethical business practices and corporate fraud that have led to a call for a change in the way organizational leaders manage their companies so that they take into consideration other stakeholders and not only the shareholders. He then reviews the vast literature on the relationship between corporate social performance and corporate financial performance describing the various explanations for the apparent mixed research findings. Andrew E. Michael notes that this research has been partly motivated by researchers' and practitioners' desires to find a positive relationship between corporate social performance and financial performance, evidence that would encourage managers and shareholders to be more willing to divert organizational funds to socially responsible activities. However, the author argues that the existence or not of such a relationship should be irrelevant and that organizational leaders should engage in socially responsible behavior and foster a culture of humanism in their organizations because it is ethically the right thing to do.

Adela J. McMurray, Susan Mravlek, and Claire A. Simmers in their chapter, "Corporate Social Responsibility (CSR) as a Derivative of Capitalistic

Anxieties," examine the complex relationship between corporate social responsibility (CSR) as a social phenomenon and systemic managerial behavior responding to societal and organizational forces. Globalization and the insurgence of social media have redefined public expectations of corporation behaviors putting significant pressures on corporations to "do good" by making contributions to the well-being of society. This logic is arguably altruistic and better fits socialistic ideals, than capitalistic archetypes. Analyzing CSR studies, authors suggest that CSR can provide corporations with the 'illusion' of "doing good." Studies addressing illusion and collusion remain nascent as frameworks, measurements, methods, and theory are underdeveloped and fragmented. This chapter provides a consolidation of the literature to illustrate the interdependence of managerial realities and demands for CSR within a socioanalytic perspective. The chapter provides a conceptual model identifying collusion and illusion as interdependent CSR factors, suggesting that the "sugar coating" in CSR is the cost of doing business. An agenda for additional theoretical and empirical research is discussed.

The next chapter, "Corporate Social Responsibility and Corporate Social Performance: Neither Binary nor Righteous" written by Robert L. Heath and Damion Waymer, is based on the logic and literature review of corporate social responsibility (CSR), which goes back to the 1920s in the United States. The authors argue that CSR standards are socially constructed and applied by stakeholders to judge the quality of performance by organizations, their ability to serve society rather than expecting society to serve them. In that regard, CSR and CSP, should not be considered as binary (either holistically fulfilling stakeholders' expectations or not) or righteous. To the last point, companies which do some social performance activities should not be granted nor expected to be rewarded in some substantial way for what might be fairly inconsequential actions without really being an organization that meets high CSR standards.

This section of my book is closed by Abubakr Suliman and Hadil Al-Khatib's chapter titled "CSR and Employer Branding in Work Organizations." In this chapter they claim that in today's competing markets, more and more companies are seeing the benefit of linking their branding to corporate social responsibility (CSR). Basing on the existing literature, the authors show design step that makes it possible to create an effective synergy between the two notions and emphasize that introducing ethics into brands is critical for all employees and employers. This chapter examines the CSR role in employer branding, synergy between CSR and employer branding, global studies on CSR and employer branding and conclude with some real example on managing CSR and employer branding in some global companies, namely, Nestlé in the Middle East, the Emirates Airlines, and the Gulf Food Trading.

The last part of this book "Pathways of Corporate Social Performance" opens with the chapter "Sustainable Management of Renewable Natural Resources: The Case of Fisheries Management Systems" by Einar Svansson and Stefan Kalmansson. The authors in their chapter notice that an unlimited open access to the ocean resources is not an option in the 21st century; too many fishermen with too much capacity would quickly deplete the stocks through overfishing. The subject of the chapter is to theoretically review management systems for renewable resources. The focus is on fisheries systems based on transferable quotas where the Icelandic system is used as a case. The analytical tool used is the sustainability triangle. Transferable quota systems can be valuable to govern fisheries towards sustainable development with efficient economic result and a fair environmental impact. The social dimension is the most questionable. Einar Svansson and Stefan Kalmansson highlight that there is still need for more research on these systems with more case comparative study between countries and analyze of different versions of government systems. They also argue that the Icelandic system is a complex structure of many important variables where the transferable rights system is an important component. It is important to build stability for seafood industries with a long-term framework for fisheries management. The authors also point out that it is a valid question if social solutions should be internal or external to the system. Overall the transferable quota systems can help to impose more sustainable fisheries. Other industries that are built on renewable resources can possibly learn from the experience of the fisheries management systems worldwide, both from the positive and negative factors.

Marco Tavanti in his chapter "Global Sustainability Reporting Initiatives: Integrated Pathways for Economic, Environmental, Social, and Governance Organizational Performance" highlights the typologies and integration of sustainability reporting. Through a review of various global sustainability reporting initiatives he makes a case for supporting the Global Reporting Initiative (GRI) as the most significant reporting integrating economic, environmental, social, and governance in organizational performance. He reviews and correlates the measurements in nonfinancial reporting, especially exemplified in the "Corporate Social Responsibility Reports," "Global Citizenship Reports," "Corporate Citizenship," and "Environmental, Social and Governance (ESG) Reporting." The examination of the evolution of standards in the GRI is correlated to growing importance in sustainability reporting. In the field of complementary reporting, GRI is emerging as the most authoritative sustainability-reporting framework helping organizations to increase transparency and accountability in nonfinancial reporting. As the number of companies increase in their voluntary sustainability and ESG reporting, the need for integration, harmonization, accountability and transparency is urgent and necessary. The GRI offers such platform for reporting that not only integrates the environmental, social and governance elements on sustainability, but it also encourages a fundamental shift from shareholder reporting into a multistakeholder accountability. As the attention to sustainability will become part of corporation's strategic plans in the years to come, the precise measurements of performance provided by the GRI framework will be crucial for truly integrating sustainability in corporate performance.

In the next chapter, "Sustainability and its Paradigms," Maurice Yolles and Gerhard Fink notice that while today the concept of sustainability is popular, reading the literature is problematic since the collective ideas on sustainability appear to be confused in regard to the nature, definition and application of the concept. The reason is not too frequently recognized: that the different perspective that seem to populate the literature arise from two broadly competing paradigms. These not only maintain contradictory perspectives for sustainability, but also to the related concept of viability. Using cultural agency theory, it is shown how these paradigms arise, and that they have membership of the broader sociopolitical paradigms of *individualism* and *collectivism*. The authors say broader perspective since these paradigms are not singular sets of predefined concepts, but rather they maintain spectral bandwidths that enables paradigmatic variations. Here this variability will be explored, thereby highlighting the operational natures of the sustainability.

Veronica Vecchi, Niccolò Cusumano, and Manuela Brusoni in their chapter "Impact Investing: An Evolution of CSR or a New Playground?", direct our attention to the fact that impact investing is drawing the attention of financial institutions, foundations, governments and increasingly from scholars around the world. However impact investing lacks a common definition and it is often mixed up with other related concepts. So far Impact Investing has been mainly perceived as a way to channel resources into the social enterprise but it may also represent a way to develop CSR in a more impactful approach or strategy, thus bringing enterprises to really embed social value in their core business. The aim of this chapter is (1) to shed the light on the blurred concept of impact investing, trying to understand its background and evolution; (2) discuss the real innovativeness of impact investing as a way to overcome traditional approaches to CSR.

In the subsequent chapter, "Media Responsibility 2.0: A New Responsibility Model in the Media Sector," Lida Tsene and Betty Tsakarestou are examining the correlations between social media values, that are embedded in evolving practices and CSR values with a focus on media companies. How and in what ways have social media been changing the way media industries approach responsibility? Is our hypothesis that social media propose a new organizational, operational, and cultural model for media business, with an orientation to accountable and socially responsible behavior valid and what would the limitations be? Since 2008, that the authors have conducted their empirical qualitative research, they kept following the transformations within the media sector and media organizations. There is being observed the emphasis on open data and entrepreneurial journalism as well as the emergence of not one new dominant journalism and new media model. However, authors emphasize that the ways new possibilities for journalism require new forms of organization. Social media along with traditional media organizations are shaping a new operational model for media industries based on accountability, transparency, stakeholder engagement. It will take time though for this model to be established but social media are not here to replace traditional, but to co-create a more responsible media ecosystem.

Soojin Kim, Laishan Tam and Jeong-Nam Kim in their chapter "Reconceptualizing Corporate Social Responsibility (CSR) as Corporate Public Responsibility (CPR)," propose the reconceptualization of corporate social responsibility (CSR) as corporate public responsibility (CPR) for three reasons. First, organizations are constrained by limited resources, so they should invest strategically for their CSR initiatives. Second, organizations' inability to fulfill their corporate responsibility for their key publics is one of the causes of organization crises. Third, the current approach to treating society as a whole as the beneficiary of corporate responsibility fails to guide organizations, especially small-to-medium-sized enterprises, in planning their efforts in fulfilling their corporate responsibility. Therefore, the authors suggest that organizations first identify their key publics for whom they should prioritize their corporate responsibility before they plan their efforts for other groups. Even if a corporation donates a large sum of money to charitable organizations, it will still be considered socially irresponsible if it mistreats its employees. On the contrary, if it fulfills its responsibility for its employees first and is able to strategically utilize its resources for the benefit of other groups, such as customers and society at large, then it is more likely to be considered socially responsible. Reconceptualizing CSR as CPR will help organizations coordinate their efforts more strategically.

The chapter "Organizational Mindfulness in Corporate Social Responsibility," by Yi-Hui Ho and Chieh-Yu Lin aims to explore the application of the organizational mindfulness concept to CSR. Mindfulness denotes as the ability to update situational awareness on a continuing basis, to cast doubt, and to probe further to resolve doubtfulness. The authors define CSR mindfulness as a way of working during CSR implementation marked by a focus on the present, attention to operational detail, willingness to consider alternative perspectives and an interest in investigating and understanding failures. This chapter suggests that firms require mindfulness thinking in implementing CSR. CSR mindfulness can be conceptualized as a cognitive ability that is reflected by preoccupation with failure, reluctance to simplify interpretations, sensitivity to operations, commitment to resilience, and deference to expertise. The chapter also proposes a conceptual framework of antecedents and consequences of organizational CSR mindfulness. The authors argue that CSR mindfulness is positively associated with external stakeholder focus, organizational learning capability, organizational ethical culture, business strategic proactivity, and firm size. Organizational CSR mindfulness will have a positive effect on corporate social performance and economic performance, and a negative effect on the amount of individual role overload that firm members experience. This chapter sheds light on the importance of organizational mindfulness in CSR.

Peter Odrakiewicz closes the book with his chapter: "The Transformations Through the Teaching of Corporate Social Performance (CSP) Utilizing Case Studies, Interviews, Videos and Social Media in Knowledge Transfer in Tertiary Schools of Management." This chapter seeks to demonstrate the innovative ways by which corporate social performance (CSP) knowledge transfer and corporate social performance teaching in universities and management colleges can improve performance. The author first examines these innovative methods of CSP knowledge transfer and their role in the teaching of CSP integrity (Odrakiewicz, 2014, pp. 402–406). Second, the chapter highlights the importance of this subject in management education at institutions of higher learning, as well in business enterprises. It is an exploration of challenging learning and corporate social performance competences acquisition from innovatively defined and designed case studies, including practical examples (interviews, videoconferencing, web-based meetings, shared workspaces, wikis, virtual meeting spaces, and social and professional web networks). Impediments to CSP skills acquisition in institutions of higher learning can be the result of both poor attention to the issues of CSP knowledge transfer in educational management and can also stem from a lack of consultation with key players on the importance of this subject in colleges and universities. In addition, owners or their representatives/CEO's, company directors, who knowingly or unknowingly perpetrate anti-CSP management environments, as they aim to implement a "bottom line profit" philosophy at all costs, lacking CSP ingredients, are impediments in this process.

This book is authored by a range of international experts with a diversity of backgrounds and perspectives hopefully suggesting some paradoxes and pitfalls of the CSP concept but also pathways for better and effective practical implementation of the corporate social performance.

REFERENCES

Bevan, S., Isles, N., Emery, P., & Hoskins, T. (2004), *Achieving high performance. CSR at the heart of business*. London, England: The Work Foundation.

Kotchen M., & Moon, J.J. (2012). Corporate social responsibility for irresponsibility. *The B. E. Journal of Economic Analysis & Policy, 12*(1)(Contributions), pp. 3–6. Article 55. doi: 10.1515/1935-1682.3308. Retrieved from http://environment.yale.edu/kotchen/pubs/csrcsi.pdf

Odrakiewicz, P. (2014), Challenges of CSP knowledge transfer in educational settings. Retrieved from http://www.en.pwsb.pl/images/WykOtw13_14.pdf

Thomé F. (2009). Corporate responsibility in the age of irresponsibility: A symbiotic relationship between CSR and the financial crisis? *International Institute for Sustainable Development*. Retrieved from http://www.iisd.org/pdf/2009/csr_financial_crisis.pdf

PART II

PARADOXES OF CORPORATE SOCIAL PERFORMANCE

CHAPTER 2

DOES BEING "GOOD" PAY OFF EVEN DURING PERIODS OF CRISIS?

An Employee Perspective

Irene Nikandrou and Irene Tsachouridi

During the past decade organizational virtuousness has begun to attract conceptual and empirical attention (Bright, Cameron, & Caza, 2006; Cameron, Bright, & Caza, 2004; Cameron & Winn, 2012; Chun, 2005; Weaver, 2006). Organizational virtuousness is related to behaviors in organizational settings which have intrinsic positive human impact. Organizational virtuousness (OV) is a construct similar to that of corporate social responsibility (CSR). CSR is related to actions which produce social good (McWilliams, Siegel, & Wright, 2006). As such, CSR can have a positive human impact and can improve the life of community at large. Despite the fact that both corporate social responsibility and organizational virtuousness benefit the others, they are different constructs. CSR is typically explained as motivated by instrumental benefits or exchange relationships while organizational virtuousness goes beyond instrumental concerns (Cameron & Winn, 2012). So, organizational virtuousness extends beyond

Corporate Social Performance:
Paradoxes, Pitfalls, and Pathways to the Better World, pp. 15–36
Copyright © 2015 by Information Age Publishing
All rights of reproduction in any form reserved.

mere self-interested benefit and considers positive human impact an end in itself (Cameron, 2003).

Going beyond instrumental concerns, organizational virtuousness can have a great impact on the cognition, affect and behavior of those who observe it. Perceiving virtuousness can make people imitate the behavior that they received. So, they can act beyond self-interested benefit and behave in a prosocial way (Cameron, 2003). Recent studies have indicated that perceptions of organizational virtuousness are associated with higher organizational performance as well as with increased levels of citizenship behaviors and positive attitudes (Cameron et al., 2004; Rego, Ribeiro, & Cunha, 2010; Rego, Ribeiro, Cunha, & Jesuino, 2011).

Perceptions of organizational virtuousness can also have an impact on the perception of psychological contract. Psychological contract could be defined as individual beliefs regarding an exchange agreement between individuals and their organization (Rousseau, 1995). These beliefs are largely based upon implied or explicit promises of the organization (Morrison & Robinson, 1997), while the preemployment experiences, recruiting practices and early on-the job socialization can also be important for the formation of the psychological contract (Rousseau, 2001). As it is obvious, the formation of psychological contract depends not only on the organization but also on the employees. Psychological contract comprises subjective beliefs and is more or less in the eye of the beholder. As a consequence, employees' subjective perceptions regarding their organizational treatment and the resources received can have a great impact on the psychological contract built between themselves and the organization.

Transactional, developmental and socioemotional resources are considered the three main categories of resources exchanged in the workplace and as such employer obligations towards employees could also be classified as transactional, developmental and socioemotional (Bal, Jansen, van der Velde, de Lange, & Rousseau, 2010b). Organizational virtuousness' perceptions can have a great impact on whether employees consider that their organization fulfills its socioemotional obligations (e.g., support, socioemotional concern, respectful treatment) due to the fact that intended positive human impact and honest empathetic concern are integral parts of organizational virtuousness (Cameron, 2003).

Taking into account that socioemotional obligations are one of the main obligations of the organization towards its employees, we expect that organizational virtuousness can affect employees' global belief that the organization generally fulfills its obligations as well as their subsequent emotional reactions. In other words, organizational virtuousness' perceptions can influence the levels of psychological contract breach and violation expressed by employees. Breach refers to the cognition that the organization has failed to fulfill its obligations, while violation could be defined as a deep emotional response which is the result of blaming the organization for the nonfulfilled obligations (Morrison & Robinson, 1997; Raja, Johns, & Ntalianis, 2004). Breach and violation are the two most well-known constructs of psychological contract theory due to their association with key employee attitudes and behaviors (Cassar & Briner, 2011; Raja et al., 2004; Suazo, 2009; Suazo & Stone-Romero, 2011; Zhao, Wayne, Glibkowski, & Bravo, 2007).

In this study we investigate whether different perceptions of organizational virtuousness (strong, moderate and low) can differentiate the levels of breach and violation expressed by individuals both in conditions without crisis when the organization fulfills its transactional and developmental obligations and in conditions of crisis when the organization cannot fulfill such obligations. Furthermore, we investigate individuals' attribution of intentionality to the organization for the nonfulfillment of its obligations during the period of crisis.

Our study can contribute to the existing literature through three main ways. First, by focusing on breach and violation in conditions without crisis (when the transactional and developmental obligations are fulfilled) we can provide a more clear understanding regarding the importance of organizational virtuousness' perceptions for individuals' levels of breach and violation. In other words, the current study can enable us to gain better insights about whether the socioemotional resources—associated with higher levels of organizational virtuousness—are able to differentiate the levels of breach and violation when the transactional and developmental obligations are fulfilled. As such, we will understand whether low levels of organizational virtuousness can be perceived by employees as a broken promise associated with breach and violation. Focusing on this issue our study contributes to previous research on the antecedents of breach and violation (Dulac, Coyle-Shapiro, Henderson, & Wayne, 2008; Raja et al., 2004).

Second, by focusing on breach and violation in conditions with crisis (when the transactional and developmental obligations are not fulfilled) we contribute to the study of the buffering effects of organizational virtuousness. Preliminary findings have indicated that organizational virtuousness is negatively associated with the long-term effects of downsizing (Bright et al., 2006), as it maintains social capital and prevents the emotional distress usually experienced by employees during downsizing (Cameron, 2003). In this study we extend these findings by examining whether higher organizational virtuousness' perceptions can act as a positive frame of reference associated with better cognitive and emotional individual reactions (lower breach and violation) when the organization cannot fulfill its transactional and developmental obligations during a period of crisis. The study of this issue is of great importance if consider that existing research remains inconclusive regarding the ability of high quality employing relationships to act as a positive frame of reference preventing employees' negative reactions to nonfulfilled obligations (Bal, Chiaburu, & Jansen, 2010a; Dulac et al., 2008; Suazo & Stone-Romero, 2011).

Third, we investigate whether organizational virtuousness' perceptions can differentiate the attribution of intentionality to the organization for the nonfulfillment of its transactional and developmental obligations during a period of crisis. Morrison and Robinson (1997) proposed that employees seek to attribute intentionality when the organization does not fulfill its obligations towards them. Nevertheless, to the best of our knowledge there are no empirical studies investigating the factors affecting the attribution of intentionality from the part of individuals when the organization does not fulfill its obligations.

In order to explore the above issues we chose a scenario experiment. Such type of methodology gave us the ability to precisely manipulate the independent variable (perceptions of organizational virtuousness) as well as enabled us to incorporate to our study the information of crisis and the nonfulfillment of the obligations from the part of the organization. Scenario experiments have also been used by other researchers in the field of organizational behavior (De Cremer & van Knippenberg, 2005; De Cremer, Mayer, van Dijke, Schouten, & Bardes, 2009; Koivisto, Lipponen, & Platow, 2013; Penhaligon, Louis, & Restubog, 2013; Singh & Krishnan, 2008).

THEORETICAL FRAMEWORK AND HYPOTHESES

Organizational Virtuousness

Virtuousness is rooted in the Latin word "virtus" which means strength or excellence. Associated with excellence virtuousness implies an inherent moderation (Arjoon, 2000) and represents Aristotelian grand mean. Virtuousness can be neither excessive nor deficient, as deficiency and excess are qualitatively different (Cameron & Winn, 2012).

In organizational settings, virtuousness relates to the behavior of individuals in organizations as well as to the enablers in organizations that foster and perpetuate virtuousness (Cameron, 2003). Virtuousness serves the moral goals of an organization and goes further from bottom line goals such as profit, power and persistence (Park & Peterson, 2003). Human impact, moral goodness and social betterment are the three key definitional attributes of organizational virtuousness (Cameron, 2003). This indicates that organizational virtuousness is not subservient to any instrumental outcome (Cameron & Winn, 2012) and is an ultimate good in itself. Organizational virtuousness goes beyond normative expectations and aspires to help other flourish (Cameron, 2003). In other words, organizational virtuousness has an inherent value associated with intended positive human impact.

Virtuousness at organizational level differs from individual level virtues as organizational virtuousness refers to a constellation of virtues in the aggregate and is manifested by collectives of people (Cameron & Winn, 2012). From an employee perspective the virtues capturing the construct of organizational virtuousness are those of optimism, trust, compassion, integrity and forgiveness (Cameron et al., 2004).

Of course, organizational virtuousness is not an all-or-nothing situation and organizations are not completely virtuous or nonvirtuous (Cameron, 2003). In other words, organizational virtuousness can have different levels. In this study we focus on these different levels of organization virtuousness. Through the use of different scenarios we are trying to make respondents perceive three different levels of organizational virtuousness (low, moderately and strongly expressed organizational virtuousness) in order to investigate whether such perceptions can differentiate individual responses to our dependent variables. The virtues manipulated in our scenarios—in order to make respondents perceive in the aggregate different levels of virtuousness—are those of optimism, forgiveness, integrity, compassion and trust (Cameron et al., 2004). We have to mention that instead of separately manipulating each virtue, we manipulate their combination, as virtuousness refers to a combination of virtues which seldom occur in isolation (Cameron & Winn, 2012).

HYPOTHESES

Conditions Without Crisis

Organizational Virtuousness and Perceived Breach

According to psychological contract theory employees form some perceptions regarding the mutual obligations that the employees and the employer "owe" to each other (Rousseau, 1989). Currently, psychological contract theory places emphasis on the perceived failure of the organization to fulfill its obligations as it can be associated with negative attitudes and behaviors from the part of the individuals (Bal et al., 2010a; Restubog, Zagenczyk, Bordia, & Tang, 2013; Zagenczyk et al., 2013).

Perceived breach captures the cognition that the organization has failed to fulfill one or more of its obligations (Morrison & Robinson, 1997). As a kind of perception, breach can be the result of personal as well as organizational factors (Dulac et al., 2008; Raja et al., 2004). Generally, the nonfulfillment of employer obligations can be an important factor for individuals' perceptions of breach (Robinson & Morrison, 2000). Transactional, developmental and socioemotional obligations can be crucial for whether employees consider that their organization fulfills its obligations or not (Bal et al., 2010b). Nevertheless, the fulfillment (or nonfulfillment) of obligations per se does not determine the levels of breach perceived by the individuals. People can be more or less prone to realize a discrepancy between what they expect and what they receive from their organization, as their levels of vigilance vary. Vigilance could be defined as the degree to which individuals actively monitor whether their organization fulfills its obligations (Morrison & Robinson, 1997).

In this study we propose that perceptions of organizational virtuousness can differentiate the levels of breach when the organization fulfills its transactional and developmental obligations. This can happen for two mains reasons. First of all, high levels of organizational virtuousness associated with actions which help others flourish (Cameron, 2003) can make individuals emphasize the fulfillment of the organization's socioemotional obligations. This can be associated with lower levels of breach as socioemotional obligations are considered a main category of employer obligations towards employees (Bal et al., 2010b).

Second, different organizational virtuousness' perceptions can differentiate breach by affecting individuals' levels of vigilance. Research until know indicates that the relationship between the organization and its employees can affect employees' vigilance. High quality relationships characterized by support are associated with lower levels of breach (Dulac et al., 2008) as they create a positive bias in the degree to which employees interpret organizational actions and actively monitor for nonfulfilled obligations. As such, those perceiving higher levels of organizational virtuousness are expected to less actively monitor for nonfulfilled obligations. On the contrary, those perceiving lower levels of organizational virtuousness are expected to be more vigilant as they doubt whether their organization is trustworthy. Being more vigilant, they will easily realize the nonfulfillment of socioemotional obligations from the part of the organization and will express higher levels of breach.

Thus, we can expect that:

Hypothesis 1. Organizational virtuousness' perceptions differentiate the levels of breach in conditions without crisis (those perceiving higher levels of organizational virtuousness will report lower breach).

Organizational Virtuousness and Feelings of Violation

Violation is a construct distinct from breach (Morrison & Robinson, 1997). Violation is "a deep emotional response that is more affective and a result of blaming one's organization for a broken promise" (Raja et al., 2004, p. 351). Violation has not only to do with the outcome of employer's actions but also with the reasons why something happened (Robinson & Morrison, 2000). The general view that individuals hold about their organization can affect their levels of violation, as research findings have indicated the negative association between perceptions of support and feelings of violation (Dulac et al., 2008).

In this study we propose that perceptions of organizational virtuousness can differentiate individual feelings of violation in conditions without crisis when the transactional and developmental obligations are fulfilled. Perceiving an honoring relationship with their organization (Cameron, 2003) can make individuals trust their organization and express a better emotional state. Research findings support such view by indicating the positive relationship between organizational virtuousness' perceptions and positive employees' affective state (Rego et al., 2010, 2011). On the contrary, those perceiving lower levels of organizational virtuousness will interpret more negatively the organizational actions—due to their worse working relationship—and will blame their organization for the fact that it expresses lower levels of virtuousness.

Thus, we can expect that:

Hypothesis 2. Organizational virtuousness' perceptions differentiate the levels of felt violation in conditions without crisis (those perceiving higher levels of organizational virtuousness will report lower felt violation)

Conditions of Crisis

Organizational Virtuousness, Perceived Breach, Feelings of Violation and Attribution of Intentionality to the Organization for the Nonfulfilled Obligations

Existing research has brought to light that supporting employees and creating a high quality employing relationship can bring benefits to the organization, as it can make employees react more positively in order to return the benefits received (Baran, Shanock, & Miller, 2012; Byrne, Pitts, Chiaburu, & Steiner, 2011; Dulac et al., 2008). Nevertheless, research findings remain inconclusive regarding whether perceptions of a high quality relationship can act as a positive frame of reference when an organization cannot fulfill its obligations.

On the one hand, research findings indicate that those perceiving high quality relationships with their organizations respond more negatively to nonfulfilled employer obligations (Bal et al., 2010a; Suazo & Stone-Romero, 2011). Perceiving a higher quality relationship can increase employees' expectations regarding their treatment by the organization. Thus, when the organization does not fulfill its obligations they experience a great discrepancy between what they expect and what they actually receive and they experience stronger levels of anger and betrayal. This does not happen in the case of those who perceive a relationship of poorer quality. In this case individuals generally have lower expectations regarding their organizational treatment and as such they are not surprised when the organization breaks its promises. In this case, the support provided by the organization can act as an intensifier making individuals react more negatively to nonfulfilled employer obligations. Based on this view those perceiving high quality relationships are expected to react worse than those perceiving low quality relationships (Bal et al., 2010a).

On the other hand, other research findings indicate that employees in high quality relationships interpret organizational actions more positively and do not blame their organization (Dulac et al., 2008). Good treatment from the part of the organization makes employees form a positive image of their organization based on which they interpret all organizational actions. As such, they view nonfulfilled obligations as a natural lapse which will be rectified. They do not blame the organization for such situation and they attribute it to external circumstances. So, the quality of the relationship can act as a buffer making individuals react less negatively to nonfulfilled employer obligations. Based on this view we expect that those perceiving high quality relationships will react less negatively than those perceiving low quality relationship.

In this study we adopt the buffering hypothesis and we propose that higher organizational virtuousness' perceptions can make individuals view the nonfulfillment of employer obligations during crisis more positively than those perceiving lower levels of organizational virtuousness. Research findings indicate that organizational virtuousness can buffer the deleterious effects of downsizing and can protect the organizations from the negative employee reactions (Bright et al., 2006).

Organizations characterized by high levels of organizational virtuousness show honest empathetic concern towards their people. Consequently, despite the crisis individuals will perceive higher levels of socioemotional support and they will feel confident that the nonfulfillment of transactional and developmental obligations is not a purposeful act from the part of the organization and will be rectified as soon as possible. Believing that their organization really cares about them and goes beyond its self-interested benefit, those perceiving higher levels of organizational virtuousness will not blame their organization for the nonfulfilled obligation and will appreciate the socioemotional benefits provided. On the contrary, those perceiving lower levels of organizational virtuousness perceiving less socioemotional benefits and thinking that the organization seeks for self-interested benefits will interpret the nonfulfillment of transactional and developmental obligations more negatively and will blame their organization for such treatment. They are used to receive low levels of care and concern and thus they may consider the nonfulfillment of transactional and developmental obligations as one more action of disrespect.

Thus, we can expect that:

Hypothesis 3. Organizational virtuousness' perceptions differentiate the levels of breach in conditions with crisis (those perceiving higher levels of organizational virtuousness will report lower breach)

Hypothesis 4. Organizational virtuousness' perceptions differentiate the levels of felt violation in conditions with crisis (those perceiving higher levels of organizational virtuousness will report lower felt violation)

Hypothesis 5. Organizational virtuousness' perceptions differentiate the attribution of intentionality for the nonfulfillment of transactional and developmental obligations in conditions with crisis (those perceiving higher levels of organizational virtuousness will attribute lower levels of intentionality to the organization)

METHOD

Experimental Design and Participants

For the purposes of the current study a laboratory scenario experiment was employed. Laboratory experiments despite lacking the value of "real world" context can enable researchers to exert control over critical variables increasing thus the internal validity of the study (Crano & Brewer, 2002). The manipulation of the independent variable (organizational virtuousness) was made through the use of three different scenarios (strongly expressed organizational virtuousness, moderately expressed organizational virtuousness, low expressed organizational virtuousness). In such type of research individuals are asked to express how they would feel or behave in a certain situation (Greenberg & Eskew, 1993). Scenarios enable researchers to gain access to the thoughts and feelings that mediate behavior (Kelley, 1992, p. 16). The value of scenarios is not limited to whether or not the participants would really do what they say, but they give us important information about what people think is appropriate behavior in certain contexts (Greenberg & Eskew, 1993, p. 232).

In our experiment, 136 participants (students of an organizational behavior course) took part. Experiment was conducted at the beginning of an organizational behavior lecture inside a university classroom. Forty six of the participants were male and 90 of them were female. Respondents had a mean age of 20.67 years and a mean work experience of 1.08 years. Each participant received one of the three scenarios. As a consequence, each participant was exposed to one of the three experimental conditions (between subjects experimental design). More analytically, 46 participants were assigned to the experimental condition of strongly expressed organizational virtuousness, 46 were assigned to the experimental condition of moderately expressed organizational virtuousness and 44 were assigned to the experimental condition of low expressed organizational virtuousness. We need to mention that the scenarios were randomly distributed to participants (randomized experiment). Randomization enabled researchers to presume initial equivalence of the experimental groups (within the limits of chance) (Crano & Brewer, 2002). So, the only systematic difference among experimental conditions was treatment.

In addition, randomization checks (analysis of variance-one way [ANOVA]) performed by the researchers to ensure that demographic characteristics (age, gender, education, years of studies completed, years of work experience) were not differentiated among the three experimental conditions. As such, we can be more confident that respondents were randomly assigned to the experimental conditions and that their demographic characteristics did not confound our results. In other words, we provided additional evidence that the only systematic difference among our three experimental conditions was our independent variable.

Manipulation of the Independent Variable and Procedures

The independent variable (organizational virtuousness) was manipulated with three different scenarios of approximately equal size. Scenarios incorporated four different parts.

First part. All scenarios gave respondents the same general information regarding the described organization. According to the description participants are working for the last five years for the company described.

The company employs 200 employees. Furthermore, they received the information that the organization keeps its promises towards employees, pays them when they exert extra work effort and provides them opportunities for career development.

Second part. The three scenarios—after giving the above general information—provided to the respondents of the three experimental conditions different information about their organization. The first scenario described an organization expressing high levels of organizational virtuousness (strongly expressed organizational virtuousness), the second scenario described an organization expressing moderate levels of organizational virtuousness (moderately expressed organizational virtuousness) and the third scenario described an organization expressing low levels of organizational virtuousness (low expressed organizational virtuousness). The manipulation of the three different levels of organizational virtuousness was made by incidents describing the behavior of the organization toward its employees. The incidents were based on the combination of the five virtues—optimism, trust, forgiveness, compassion and integrity—as proposed by Cameron et al. (2004). Doing so we tried to make participants perceive in the aggregate different levels of organizational virtuousness. The incidents provided are parallel to the items of Cameron and colleagues' scale in order to ensure that we manipulate different levels of organizational virtuousness. Manipulation check—as is mentioned later in the chapter—indicated that our participants indeed perceived in the aggregate three different levels of organizational virtuousness. Below we present a summary of the three scenarios.

Strongly expressed organizational virtuousness:

In this organization all employees do what is expected and find a personal meaning in the job. You feel confident that you will achieve the organizational goals even when the organization faces challenges. Moreover, all employees respect each other and collaborate. When you face personal problems the organization stands by your side and supports you to handle them. The organization forgives mistakes trying to understand why they happened. All these years the organization actively supports its people and there are no conflicts between the organization and its members.

Moderately expressed organizational virtuousness:

In this organization all employees do what is expected. Generally you do not find personal meaning in your job. When the organization faces great challenges, you do not express high levels of confidence that your will achieve the organizational goals. The organizational climate sometimes could be characterized by competitiveness and conflicts. When you face personal problems the organization acknowledges their impact on your psychological state but it does not accept this situation to affect your performance. Mistakes are not immediately punished but there may be long-term consequences. It is generally a trustworthy organization but sometimes conflicts between the organization and its members may arise.

Low expressed organizational virtuousness:

In this organization all employees do what is expected. If you do not do so, you will be punished. When the organization faces challenges you are not confident that you will achieve the organizational goals. Generally, the organizational climate could be characterized by secrecy, competitiveness and conflicts. The organization is not interested whether you face problems or not and it does not permit mistakes. You face immediately the consequences of your mistakes either verbally or financially (lower salary). Generally, this organization avoids scandals but often conflicts between the organization and its members arise.

Third part. After reading the above scenarios the participants of all experimental conditions received the same information that their organization during this period does not face financial crisis and fulfills its transactional and developmental obligations towards employees. Then, participants answered questions regarding their organizational virtuousness' perceptions (manipulation check), as well as their perceptions of breach and their feelings of violation.

Forth part. Participants received the information that the organization during this period faces financial crisis and for this reason it cannot fulfill its obligations. More specifically, the organization finds it difficult to pay employees when they exert extra work effort and to offer them opportunities for training and career development. Moreover, within this climate of insecurity it is difficult for employees to be promoted. Then participants answered some questions regarding perceived breach, felt violation and attribution of intentionality to the organization for the nonfulfillment of its obligations during crisis.

Measures

Organizational virtuousness. For checking the manipulation of our independent variable we used the organizational virtuousness' 15 item scale proposed by Cameron et al. (2004). Sample items included: "We are optimistic that we will succeed, even when faced with major challenges," "A sense of profound purpose is associated with what we do here," "Honesty and trustworthiness are hallmarks of this organization" and "This is a forgiving, compassionate organization in which to work." Responses were measured on a six point scale ranging from 1 (never true) to 6 (always true) (Cronbach a = 0.95).

Perceived breach before and during crisis. We measured breach with four items from the scale proposed by Robinson and Morrison (2000). Sample items included: "Almost all the promises made by my employer during recruitment have been kept so far (reversed)" and "So far my employer has done an excellent job of fulfilling its promises to me (reversed)." Responses were measured with a 7-point scale ranging from 1 (strongly disagree) to 7 (strongly agree) (Cronbach a of breach before crisis = 0.83 and Cronbach a of breach during crisis = 0.88).

Felt violation before and during crisis. We measured feelings of violation with the four item scale proposed by Robinson and Morrison (2000). Sample items included: "I feel betrayed by my organization" and "I feel that my organization has violated the contract between us." Responses were measured with a 7-point scale ranging from 1 (strongly disagree) to 7 (strongly agree) (Cronbach a for violation before crisis = 0.89 and Cronbach a for violation during crisis = 0.93).

Attribution of intentionality for nonfulfilled obligations during crisis. One single item was used to measure attribution of intentionality to the organization for not fulfilling its obligations. Respondents were asked the degree to which they consider their organization responsible for the nonfulfillment of its transactional and developmental obligations towards them. A 7-point scale ranging from 1 (the organization has no responsibility) to 7 (the organizational has full responsibility) was provided to the participants.

To test the convergent and discriminant validity of our multiple item dependent variables (breach before crisis, violation before crisis, breach during crisis, violation during crisis) we conducted a confirmatory factor analysis using LISREL and maximum likelihood estimation. Our results confirmed the convergent and discriminant validity of our measurement model (average variance extracted surpassed 0.5 and was greater than the squared correlation between each couple of constructs) and the fit indices showed an acceptable fit of our measurement model (Normed Fit Index = 0.92, Nonnormed Fit Index = 0.92, Comparative Fit Index = 0.93, Incremental Fit Index = 0.94, Standardized Root Mean Square Residual = 0.072).

RESULTS

The descriptive statistics, correlations and reliabilities of our variables are presented in Table 2.1.

Table 2.1.   Means, Standard Deviations, Correlations and Reliabilities

	Mean	SD	1	2	3	4	5
1.Perceived breach before crisis	2.32	0.95	(0.83)	–	–	–	–
2.Felt violation before crisis	2.2	1.16	0.71**	(0.89)	–	–	–
3. Perceived breach during crisis	3.48	1.36	0.37**	0.41**	(0.88)	–	–
4. Felt violation during crisis	3.39	1.47	0.38**	0.53**	0.76**	(0.93)	–
5. Attribution of intentionality to the organization for the nonfulfillment of transactional and developmental obligations during crisis	4.33	1.47	0.30**	0.26**	0.35**	0.48**	–
5. Organizational Virtuousness' perceptions (1= low expressed org.virtuousness, 2 = moderately expressed org. virtuousness, 3 = strongly expressed org.virtuousness	–	–	–0.39**	–0.49**	–0.41**	–0.50**	–0.28**

Values in parentheses represent Cronbach a

$**p < .01$

Manipulation Check

The results of ANOVA and Duncan post-hoc test indicated that respondents indeed perceived three different levels of organizational virtuousness ($F = 80.81$, $p = 0.000$). More specifically, those exposed to the condition of strongly expressed organizational virtuousness reported significantly higher levels of organizational virtuousness (5.05) when compared to those exposed to the other two conditions. Furthermore, those exposed to the condition of moderately expressed organizational virtuousness reported significantly higher levels of organizational virtuousness (3.66) than those exposed to the condition of low expressed organizational virtuousness (3.35).

Hypothesis Testing

In order to test our hypotheses we conducted two multiple analyses of variance (MANOVA). The first MANOVA was conducted in order to test differences among the experimental conditions in conditions without crisis, while the second MANOVA was conducted in order to test differences in our dependent variables in conditions with crisis. This method of statistical analysis is the most appropriate in order to investigate the impact of an independent variable on several dependent variables simultaneously. Wilks' Lambda was used for testing overall significance among groups, while Duncan post hoc test was used for comparison of different groups (experimental conditions) two by two.

Conditions without crisis. The results of MANOVA (Table 2.2) indicated that there were statistically significant differences in our dependent variables among our experimental conditions (Wilks' Lambda= 0.73, $F = 11.04$, $p = 0.000$). More analytically, those exposed to the condition of strongly expressed organizational virtuousness expressed significantly lower levels of breach (1.76) than those exposed to the condition of moderate (2.54) and low organizational virtuousness (2.66) (Hypothesis 1 supported). The difference in breach between these two conditions (moderate and low) was not statistically significant.

Furthermore, those perceiving higher levels of organizational virtuousness expressed significantly lower levels of violation (1.45) than those perceiving moderate (2.36) and low levels of organizational virtuousness (2.83) (Hypothesis 2 supported). The difference in violation between these two conditions (moderate and low) was statistically significant.

Conditions with crisis. According to the results of MANOVA (Table 2.3) there were statistically significant differences in the dependent variables among experimental conditions (Wilks' Lambda = 0.74, $F = 7.13$, $p = 0.000$). As far as perceived breach during crisis is concerned those perceiving higher levels of organizational virtuousness reported significantly lower levels of breach (2.73) than the participants of the other two conditions (Hypothesis 3 supported). The levels of breach reported by those exposed to moderately expressed virtuousness (3.67) were not significantly lower than those expressed by participants exposed to the condition of low expressed virtuousness (4.09).

Moreover, those exposed to the condition of strongly expressed organizational virtuousness reported significantly lower levels of felt violation

during crisis (2.42) than those perceiving moderate and low levels of organizational virtuousness (Hypothesis 4 supported). The difference between
the other two conditions (moderate and low) was statistically significant
(3.60 and 4.20 respectively).

**Table 2.2.   Perceived Breach and Felt Violation in Conditions
Without Crisis According to the Three Levels of Virtuousness in
Organizations (MANOVA)**

	Strongly Expressed Organizational Virtuousness $n = 46$	Moderately Expressed Organizational Virtuousness $n = 46$	Low Expressed Organizational Virtuousness $n = 44$	F	p value	Partial Eta Squared	Observed Power
Multivariate test: Wilks' Lambda (condition) = 0.73				11.04	.000	0.14	1.00
Perceived breach before crisis	1.76 (0.13)	2.54 (0.13)	2.66 (0.13)	14.57	.000	0.18	1.00
Felt violation before crisis	1.45 (0.15)	2.36 (0.15)	2.83 (0.15)	21.67	.000	0.25	1.00

Values represent means with standard errors in parentheses. Statistics: MANOVA with F, p values,
Partial Eta Squared and Observed Power

Additionally, those perceiving higher levels of organizational virtuousness attributed significantly less intentionality to their organization for the
nonfulfilled transactional and developmental obligations during crisis (3.8)
when compared to those perceiving low levels of organizational virtuousness (4.81) (Hypothesis 5 supported). The levels of intentionality attributed
expressed by those perceiving moderate levels of virtuousness were not
differentiated from those of none of the other conditions (4.39).

DISCUSSION

Our study indicates that "being good" can bring benefits to the organizations as it can affect the way that individuals interpret organizational actions
both during periods without crisis (fulfillment of employer transactional
and developmental obligations) and during periods of crisis (nonfulfillment
of employer transactional and developmental obligations). More specifically, our experimental study indicates that organizational virtuousness'

perceptions can differentiate the levels of breach and violation expressed by individuals when their organization does not face financial crisis and thus fulfills its transactional and developmental obligations. Furthermore, according to our findings higher organizational virtuousness' perceptions can buffer the organization against breach, violation and attribution of intentionality to the organization when the organization cannot fulfill its transactional and developmental obligations during a period of crisis.

Table 2.3.   Perceived Breach, Felt Violation and Attribution of Intentionality to the Organization for The Nonfulfillment of Transactional and Developmental Obligations in Conditions With Crisis According to the Three Levels of Virtuousness in Organizations (MANOVA)

	Strongly Expressed Organizational Virtuousness n = 46	Moderately Expressed Organizational Virtuousness n = 46	Low Expressed Organizational Virtuousness n = 44	F	p value	Partial Eta Squared	Observed Power
Multivariate test: Wilks' Lambda (condition) = 0.74				7.13	.000	0.14	1.00
Perceived breach during crisis	2.73 (0.18)	3.67 (0.18)	4.09 (0.19)	14.11	.000	0.18	1.00
Felt violation during crisis	2.42 (0.19)	3.6 (0.19)	4.2 (0.19)	22.78	.000	0.26	1.00
Attribution of intentionality for non-fulfillment of transactional and developmental obligations during crisis	3.8 (0.21)	4.39 (0.21)	4.81 (0.22)	5.72	.004	0.08	.86

Values represent means with standard errors in parentheses. Statistics: MANOVA with F, p values, Partial Eta Squared and Observed Power.

First of all, our research findings indicate that organizational virtuousness' perceptions can bring benefits to the organizations during periods without crisis, as they can differentiate the levels of breach and violation expressed by respondents. According to psychological contract theory breach and violation constitute employee responses to broken promises from the part of the organization (Morrison & Robinson, 1997; Robinson & Morrison, 2000). Our findings suggest that low levels of organizational virtuousness can be considered by individuals a broken promise associated with higher levels of breach and violation. As such, breach and violation seem to be a response to whether individuals perceive organizational care and concern or not. Such findings underline the importance of socio-emotional benefits provided by the organization as they can differentiate individuals' levels of breach and violation even when the organization fulfills its transactional and developmental obligations.

Furthermore, our results support other findings that high quality relationships can attenuate the negative employee reactions associated with nonfulfilled obligations (Dulac et al., 2008). Indeed, according to our research organizational virtuousness' perceptions can buffer the organization against the negative reactions of individuals during periods of crisis when the organization cannot fulfill its transactional and developmental obligations. Other research findings have indicated that high quality relationships can accentuate the negative employee reactions to nonfulfilled employer obligations due to feelings of anger and betrayal (intensifying hypothesis) (Bal et al., 2010a; Suazo & Stone-Romero, 2011).

Our findings support the buffering hypothesis and indicate that higher organizational virtuousness' perceptions can make individuals express lower levels of breach and violation, while they also attribute less intentionality to their organization for the nonfulfilled obligations when compared to those perceiving lower levels of organizational virtuousness. Probably perceptions of honest empathetic concern from the part of the organization can create emotional reserves to individuals and can render them unable to interpret negatively the organizational actions even during tough times. Despite the fact that the organization seems to be unable to fulfill its obligations individuals perceiving higher levels of organizational virtuousness interpret these nonfulfilled obligations more positively and they do not blame their organization. Such findings extend previous findings about the buffering effects of organizational virtuousness (Bright et al., 2006) by bringing to light the ability of organizational virtuousness to affect the cognitive and emotional reactions of individuals during periods of crisis.

It is important to mention that our findings indicate that moderate levels of organizational virtuousness differentiate the feelings of violation (both in conditions without crisis and in conditions with crisis) when compared to low levels of organizational virtuousness. Nevertheless, they cannot differentiate neither the perceived breach (both in conditions without crisis and in conditions with crisis) nor the attribution of intentionality to the organization for the nonfulfilled obligations during crisis when compared to lower levels of organizational virtuousness. These findings indicate that probably higher levels of organizational virtuousness are necessary in order to buffer the organization from both cognitive and emotional negative reactions from the part of the individuals. More research is needed to better understand employee reactions and feelings during periods of crisis, when the organization cannot fulfill its obligations and employees perceive a breach and violation in their psychological contract.

Our study using experimental methodology has strong internal validity which is about the certainty with which one can attribute a research outcome to the treatment (Crano & Brewer, 2002, p. 22). So, we can be more confident about the "true relationship" between the examined variables. Furthermore, the use of scenarios enabled us to gain access to the thought processes of participants (Kelley, 1992) and simulate the conditions of organizational virtuousness. As a consequence, we "created a more accurate picture" of how individuals interpret organizational actions during periods of crisis as well as during periods without crisis according to the different perceptions of virtuousness. Future experimental studies could further explore such issue, while also field studies could triangulate these findings by providing evidence regarding the generalizability of such findings.

To sum up, our study proposes that "being good" pays off even during periods of crisis. Perceiving an organization expressing interest and concern can make individuals interpret organizational actions more positively. This can be of great importance if consider that such interpretations can affect the subsequent employee attitudes and behaviors (Raja et al., 2004; Restubog, Hornsey, Bordia, & Esposo, 2008; Restubog et al., 2013; Zhao et al., 2007). Focusing on ethical organizational behaviors is not a waste of time and energy. Consequently, constructs which incorporate ethical behaviors—namely, corporate social responsibility, corporate citizenship and organizational virtuousness—need further attention both at the academic and at the business level.

REFERENCES

Arjoon, S. (2000). Virtue theory as a dynamic theory of business. *Journal of Business Ethics, 28*(2), 159–178. doi:10.1023/A:1006339112331

Bal, P. M., Chiaburu, D. S., & Jansen, P. G. W. (2010a). Psychological contract breach and work performance. Is social exchange a buffer or an intensifier? *Journal of Managerial Psychology, 25*(3), 252–273. doi:10.1108/02683941011023730

Bal, P. M., Jansen, P. G. W., van der Velde, M. E. G., de Lange, A. H., & Rousseau, D. M. (2010b). The role of future time perspective in psychological contracts: A study among older workers. *Journal of Vocational Behavior, 76*(3), 474–486. doi:10.1016/j.jvb.2010.01.002

Baran, B. E., Shanock, L. R., & Miller, L. R. (2012). Advancing organizational support theory into the twenty-first century world of work. *Journal of Business and Psychology, 27*(2), 123–147. doi:10.1007/s10869-011-9236-3

Bright, D. S., Cameron, K. S., & Caza, A. (2006). The amplifying and buffering effects of virtuousness in downsized organizations. *Journal of Business Ethics, 64*(3), 249–269. doi:10.1007/s10551-005-5904-4

Byrne, Z., Pitts, V., Chiaburu, D., & Steiner, Z. (2011). Managerial trustworthiness and social exchange with the organization. *Journal of Managerial Psychology, 26*(2), 108–122. doi:10.1108/02683941111102155

Cameron, K. S. (2003). Organizational virtuousness and performance. In K. S. Cameron, J. E. Dutton, & R. E. Quinn (Eds.), *Positive organizational scholarship* (pp. 48–65). San Fransisco, CA: Berrett-Koehler.

Cameron, K. S., Bright, D., & Caza, A. (2004). Exploring the relationships between organizational virtuousness and performance. *American Behavioral Scientist, 47*(6), 766–790. doi:10.1177/0002764203260209

Cameron, K. S., & Winn, B. (2012). Virtuousness in organizations. In K. S. Cameron & G. M. Spreitzer (Eds.), *The Oxford handbook of positive organizational scholarship* (pp. 231–243). New York, NY: Oxford University Press.

Cassar, V., & Briner, R. B. (2011). The relationship between psychological contract breach and organizational commitment: Exchange imbalance as a moderator of the mediating role of violation. *Journal of Vocational Behavior, 78*(2), 283–289. doi:10.1016/j.jvb.2010.09.007

Chun, R. (2005). Ethical character and virtue of organizations: An empirical assessment and strategic implications. *Journal of Business Ethics, 57*(3), 269–284. doi:10.1007/s10551-004-6591-2

Crano, W. D., & Brewer, M. B. (2002). *Principles and Methods of Social Research* (2nd ed.). Mahwah, NJ: Lawrence Erlbaum Associates.

De Cremer, D., & van Knippenberg, D. (2005). Cooperation as a function of leader self-sacrifice, trust, and identification. *Leadership & Organization Development Journal, 26*(5), 355–369. doi:10.1108/01437730510607853

De Cremer, D., Mayer, D. M., van Dijke, M., Schouten, B. C., & Bardes, M. (2009). When does self-sacrificial leadership motivate prosocial behavior? It depends on followers' prevention focus. *Journal of Applied Psychology, 94*(4), 887–899. doi:10.1037/a0014782

Dulac, T., Coyle-Shapiro, J. A.-M., Henderson, D. J., & Wayne, S. J. (2008). Not all responses to breach are the same: The interconnection of social exchange and psychological contract processes in organizations. *Academy of Management Journal, 51*(6), 1079–1098. doi:10.5465/AMJ.2008.35732596

Greenberg, J., & Eskew, D. E. (1993). The role of role playing in organizational research. *Journal of Management, 19*(2), 221–241. doi:10.1177/014920639301900203

Kelley, H. H. (1992). Common-sense psychology and scientific psychology. *Annual Review of Psychology, 43*, 1–24. doi:10.1146/annurev.ps.43.020192.000245

Koivisto, S., Lipponen, J., & Platow, M. J. (2013). Organizational and supervisory justice effects on experienced threat during change: The moderating role of leader in-group representativeness. *The Leadership Quarterly, 24*(4), 595–607. doi:10.1016/j.leaqua.2013.04.002

McWilliams, A., Siegel, D. S., & Wright, P. M. (2006). Corporate social responsibility: strategic implications. *Journal of Management Studies, 43*(1), 1–18. doi:10.1111/j.1467-6486.2006.00580.x

Morrison, E. W., & Robinson, S. L. (1997). When employees feel betrayed: A model of how psychological contract violation develops. *Academy of Management Review, 22*(1), 226–256. doi:10.5465/AMR.1997.9707180265

Park, N., & Peterson, C. M. (2003). Virtues and organizations. In K. S. Cameron, J. E. Dutton, & R. E. Quinn (Eds.), *Positive organizational scholarship* (pp. 33–47). San Fransisco, CA: Berrett-Koehler.

Penhaligon, N. L., Louis, W. R., & Restubog, S. L. D. (2013). Feeling left out? The mediating role of perceived rejection on workgroup mistreatment and affective, behavioral, and organizational outcomes and the moderating role of organizational norms. *Journal of Applied Social Psychology, 43*(3), 480–497. doi:10.1111/j.1559-1816.2013.01026.x

Raja, U., Johns, G., & Ntalianis, F. (2004). The impact of personality on psychological contracts. *Academy of Management Journal, 47*(3), 350–367. doi:10.2307/20159586

Rego, A., Ribeiro, N., & Cunha, M. P. (2010). Perceptions of organizational virtuousness and happiness as predictors of organizational citizenship behaviors. *Journal of Business Ethics, 93*(2), 215–235. doi:10.1007/s10551-009-0197-7

Rego, A., Ribeiro, N., Cunha, M. P., & Jesuino, J. C. (2011). How happiness mediates the organizational virtuousness and affective commitment relationship. *Journal of Business Research, 64*(5), 524–532. doi:10.1016/j.jbusres.2010.04.009

Restubog, S. L. D., Hornsey, M. J., Bordia, P., & Esposo, S. R. (2008). Effects of psychological contract breach on organizational citizenship behaviour: Insights from the group value model. *Journal of Management Studies, 45*(8), 1377–1400. doi:10.1111/j.1467-6486.2008.00792.x

Restubog, S. L. D, Zagenczyk, T. J., Bordia, P., & Tang, R. L. (2013). When employees behave badly: the roles of contract importance and workplace familism in predicting negative reactions to psychological contract breach. *Journal of Applied Social Psychology, 43*(3), 673–686. doi:10.1111/j.1559-1816.2013.01046.x

Robinson, S. L., & Morrison, E. W. (2000). The development of psychological contract breach and violation: a longitudinal study. *Journal of Organizational Behavior, 21*(5), 525–546. doi:10.1002/1099-1379(200008)21:5<525::AID-JOB40>3.0.CO;2-T

Rousseau, D. M. (1989). Psychological and implied contracts in organizations. *Employee Responsibilities and Rights Journal, 2*(2), 121–139. doi:10.1007/BF01384942

Rousseau, D. M. (1995). *Psychological contracts in organizations: Understanding written and unwritten agreements*. Thousand Oaks, CA: Sage

Rousseau, D. M. (2001). Schema, promise and mutuality: The building blocks of the psychological contract. *Journal of Occupational and Organizational Psychology, 74*(4), 511–541. doi:10.1348/096317901167505

Singh, N., & Krishnan, V. R. (2008). Self-sacrifice and transaformational leadership: mediating role of altruism. *Leadership & Organization Development Journal, 29*(3), 261–274. doi:10.1108/01437730810861317

Suazo, M. M. (2009). The mediating role of psychological contract violation on the relations between psychological contract breach and work-related attitudes and behaviors. *Journal of Managerial Psychology, 24*(2), 136–160. doi:10.1108/02683940910928856

Suazo, M. M., & Stone-Romero, E. F. (2011). Implications of psychological contract breach. A perceived organizational support perspective. *Journal of Managerial Psychology, 26*(5), 366–382. doi:10.1108/02683941111138994

Weaver, G. R. (2006). Virtue in organizations: Moral identity as a foundation for moral agency. *Organization Studies, 27*(3), 341–368. doi:10.1177/0170840606062426

Zagenczyk, T. J., Cruz, K. S., Woodard, A. M., Walker, J. C., Few, W. T., Kiazad, K., & Raja, M. (2013). The moderating effect of machiavellianism on the psychological contract breach–organizational identification/disidentification relationships. *Journal of Business and Psychology, 28*(3), 287–299. doi:10.1007/s10869-012-9278-1

Zhao, H., Wayne, S. J., Glibkowski, B. C., & Bravo, J. (2007). The impact of psychological contract breach on work-related outcomes: A meta-analysis. *Personnel Psychology, 60(3)*, 647–680. doi:10.1111/j.1744-6570.2007.00087.x

CHAPTER 3

CORPORATE SOCIAL PERFORMANCE NEEDS MORE COMPETITION NOT LESS

An Idea for a Paradigm Shift in CSP

Athanasios Chymis,
Massimiliano Di Bitetto, and Paolo D'Anselmi

INTRODUCTION

It has been almost 30 years since Ullman's (1985) widely cited article "Data in Search of a Theory: A Critical Examination of the Relationships Among Social Performance, Social Disclosure and Economic Performance of Us Firms." Yet, corporate social performance (CSP) (and corporate social responsibility [CSR] at large) is still in the search of such a theory (Margolis, Elfenbein, & Walsh, 2007; Orlitzky, Schmidt, & Rynes, 2003; Van der Laan, Van Ees, & Van Witteloostuijn, 2008; Wood, 2010).

Despite the large literature on the relationship between social performance (SP) and financial performance (FP) it is intriguing that the CSP literature still lacks a solid theory. More than 40 years have elapsed since

Corporate Social Performance:
Paradoxes, Pitfalls, and Pathways to the Better World, pp. 37–56
Copyright © 2015 by Information Age Publishing

the famous Friedman's aphorism[1] which signaled the beginning of an extensive research regarding the SP-FP relationship. This research was productive in the way that it examined many levels of social responsibility (i.e., toward various stakeholders, see Wood (2010) for a comprehensive review), irresponsibility (Frooman, 1997) as well as a variety of measures of SP. It gave birth to the very interesting stakeholder theory (Freeman, 1984) and different theories on what it actually means for a firm to be socially responsible as well as why a firm would be socially responsible.

However, the issue with this large literature is that is still lacks a strong theoretical support. Data seem to support the idea of a positive relation between SP-FP even though not unanimously (Margolis et al., 2007). Questions regarding the potential misspecification problem of the correlation have been raised (McWilliams & Siegel, 2000) as well as other issues such as the measurement problem (Graves & Waddock, 1994). Suggestions on different types of stakeholders such as primary and secondary (Agle, Mitchell, & Sonnenfeld, 1999) tried to look deeper in the SP-FP relation and the literature also proposes that the causal relation between SP-FP needs more attention (Brammer & Millington, 2008) while some have argued that there seems to be no causal relation (Nelling & Webb, 2009).

The purpose of this chapter is to go beyond the current literature on the relationship between social and financial performance and search for the incentives for being socially responsible. Why would someone be willing to be socially responsible? In order to do so we revisit the fundamentals of economic theory and we argue that the origins of economic theory, which is philosophy itself, can shed light on this important question. By doing so, we also find common ground between CSP and M. Friedman.

We understand that Milton Friedman is a controversial figure in the sustainability world and here lies our attempt, contribution and provocation: we make the point Milton is less of a devil and more a friend when we take his thinking seriously and take the time to think about how the world of free competition, a la Friedman, would look like. It may indeed look much different from the world we see around us today. More importantly, it may be a more socially responsible world.

We show that a basic but often forgotten theoretical pillar of CSP is competition, a simple yet powerful concept. A concept that could be used to bridge the long-lasting divide between CSP and economics, a divide that stems from the aforementioned Friedman's quote. We argue that the lack of solid theory behind CSP may be related to the created divide between CSP and economics. Trying to prove Friedman wrong gave birth to an, indeed, rich and diverse literature on the relationship between social and financial responsibility. However, by discarding Friedman CSP literature may have deprived itself a valuable resource, a real friend in its quest of a solid theory behind CSP.

Although the concept of competition has been referred to in the literature (Campbell, 2007) as a factor—among many others—affecting SP of firms or, more specifically, as a control variable in the empirical analyses of the SP-FP relationship (Berman, Phillips, & Wicks, 2005) we claim that competition should draw our attention not only as one of the many factors affecting SP but as the primary factor.

We explain that Friedman was largely misread and misunderstood and we argue that he is not against social responsibility but he rather assumed it in the price mechanism of a free market. Indeed, in this chapter we make the point that, contrary to the CSP conventional wisdom, Friedman is not an enemy for CSP literature. He is not the annoying guy whom the literature has been striving to prove wrong for the last four decades. We explain why this attitude has been a pitfall for CSP literature, a pitfall we need to avoid in the future. CSP literature may actually *need* Friedman to boost its theoretical background. CSP needs Friedman if it is to leave paradoxes and pitfalls behind and curve a pathway to a better world.

In the following sections we develop the fundamentals of economics, the relation between economics and ethics, we reconcile Friedman with CSP and we show that competition is the driving force behind CSP.

ECONOMICS: THE FUNDAMENTALS (VOLUNTARISM, FREEDOM, RESPONSIBILITY AND ETHICS)

Economics, as every social science, was born from philosophy. Adam Smith, the father of modern economics was a moral philosopher before he became an economist and created the new branch of science (i.e., economics) from the tree of philosophy. It is notable that Smith had in much higher esteem his, mostly philosophical (unfortunately much less famous), book *The Theory of Moral Sentiments* rather than his (famous) economics treaty on the *Wealth of Nations* (Wight, 2001).

Adam Smith (1776) based on philosophers' teachings, describes that humans have needs. In order to fulfill these needs and increase their level of happiness (or utility, satisfaction, well-being) people develop skills and produce goods and services. By developing skills people realized that it is easier to focus on the production of a limited number of goods and acquire other goods from their fellow men rather than trying to cover all their personal needs by themselves. This is called division of labor.

At the same time the intrinsic need for social contact drove people to interact with their fellow men and to exchange goods, services and ideas.[2] The concept of the market (Agora, in Greek) was born. The market is the place where people come together, interact and engage in transactions. This procedure takes place *voluntarily*. No one is forced to come to the market, to interact and transact with other fellow citizens.

Voluntarism is a key concept in both economics and CSP. Voluntarism means that each individual takes the full *responsibility* for his/her own actions, that is, takes the cost and benefit of the action. We see that the concepts of voluntarism and responsibility are related. It is expected, we could say it is *ethical*, for an individual who voluntarily takes any action to be responsible for that action (Hazlitt, 1964/2012). The opposite would be considered as unethical and immoral: imagine a case where one is forced by someone else to take an action of which s/he will bear the full responsibility. Or, imagine the case where one takes an action voluntarily but s/he passes the responsibility of this action to someone else.

A simple but illustrative example would be the following: One would like (voluntarily) to buy a good or a service from the market but s/he does not want to assume the responsibility of bearing the cost of this purchase. We can hardly imagine anyone disagreeing that this is unethical behavior and sounds more like a theft. Of course our analysis pertains to adults and not children or adolescents (minors) who are not responsible for their actions and for this reason their parents are responsible for them.

Voluntarism has a central role in economics. The underlying reason for this is that only voluntarism can guarantee that the responsibility of a decision (or action) would fall squarely on the person who voluntarily makes the decision (or takes an action). It is the concept of voluntarism behind the idea of *freedom* and consequently of *free market* (Hazlitt, 1964/2012; Mises, 1949/1998). Unless someone is free there is no room to decide and act voluntarily. If one cannot decide and act voluntarily the concept of responsibility evaporates. How can anyone be responsible for anything s/he does involuntarily (under coercion)? The responsibility is now assumed by those who practice the coercion and there is no responsibility left for the coerced one. This is exactly what happens in the case of parents and children. Parents are responsible for their children behavior and actions because children are told what to do by their parents.

Philosophy as well as psychology suggests that one major prerequisite of happiness is freedom[3] (Thucydides, 1936; Veenhoven, 2000). Indeed, history is full of examples of people willing to pay any cost, even die, for freedom. Economics science as a branch of philosophy could not disregard the crucial concept of freedom. Voluntarism needs freedom. There is no voluntary transaction, the key economic principle, without freedom. People should be free to interact in the market in order to voluntarily exchange goods, services and ideas and, consequently, cover their physical, emotional and intellectual (physical, mental, and spiritual) needs (Friedman, 1962/2002).

It is the freedom to decide, to choose and to act that brings responsibility. Continuing the above argument on the relation between voluntarism and responsibility, it is freedom the prerequisite of responsibility. We do not require responsibility from minors (although we teach them how to be responsible and that responsibility is a noble and ethical characteristic of a free person) because they are not completely free; they are under their parents' supervision.

Once economics has established that for people to be able to maximize their happiness freedom is a necessary condition in order for them to voluntarily engage in transactions with other fellow people, it goes a step further to explain how this free market should operate in order to allow for people to maximize their well-being. Under what conditions the self-interest and the interest-for-others can be better aligned? Adam Smith is crystal clear on that: We need *Competition*. As Milton Friedman (1970, p. 176) puts it, we need "open and free" competition.

Adam Smith asks the question: how can a person cover his/her needs the best? In other words, how can one maximize one's utility or satisfaction or, ultimately, happiness? We mentioned before that people's needs motivate them to develop skills. They use these skills to produce goods, services and ideas that they are going to exchange in the free market voluntarily for the goods, services and ideas they need. This means that what people will produce using their skills and their endowments such as labor and capital (time included) need to be *useful to other people* so they can exchange them. Unless they produce goods and services, which can make other people happy (i.e., increase their utility, satisfaction or well-being), they will not be able to increase their own happiness (utility, satisfaction or well-being).

This is the point which Adam Smith (1776) illustrates using the famous quote on the butcher, the brewer, and the baker.[4] Smith realized that a free market provides a venue where one's self-interest can be aligned with the other's interest. A branch of economics called agency theory specifically addresses the issue of interest alignment (Tosi, Katz, & Gomez-Mejia, 1997).

And we arrive at the question which lies in the heart of economics: Who is going to decide whether a specific good, service or idea is useful for the public? In other words, who can allocate the resources (capital, labor, land, and skills-entrepreneurship) the most efficient way, that is, the way that maximizes social welfare at the minimum cost?

Economics science has long answer this question: no central planning can do this job better than the free market (Hayek, 1944/1994; Friedman, 1962/2002; Smith, 1776). This is Smith's (1776) "invisible hand" and Hayek's (1944/1994) "spontaneous order." No authority no matter how knowledgeable it is, how wise it is and how well-intentioned it is can have all the knowledge and information that is integrated in hundreds, thousands, millions or even billions of people who transact in the free market (Hayek, 1945). No one can be more efficient than all of them voluntarily interacting in a free market.

We established that ethics has meaning when people voluntarily behave ethically. It is meaningless to claim I am ethical when I am forced by someone else to be. A choice can be judged as ethical or not only if it is a free choice. If I do something under the coercion of, say, a dictator there is no much room for me to be judged based on this choice. It is only the free choice that can allow me to assume the responsibility of this choice and bear the full cost and benefit of that particular choice.

Adam Smith (1976) and economics as a science conclude that ethics have meaning in a free society (Hazlitt, 1964/2012). We also conclude that ethics is important and directly related to economics. Once we strive for the social welfare maximization we want to align as much as we can the self-interest with the interest for the others. Adam Smith showed that this can be best achieved in a free market where a self interested individual maximizes his/her own well-being only by offering the best goods and services to his/her fellow people and thus maximizing their utility (i.e., welfare).

It is the never ending human needs which have to be satisfied using scarce resources that introduce the concept of competition. It is the needs that make humans develop skills (i.e., entrepreneurship) in order to address these needs. It is the skills which people implement in order to meet the needs of their fellow people that make them excel by being competitive, assuming full responsibility of their actions and, consequently, receive a payment (in the form of money, product, service, glory, social or psychological support, etc.) for this excellence. The whole operation of human society is based on voluntarism. The alignment of self-love (i.e., self-interest) and love-for-others (i.e., interest-for-others) is the key for a sustainable, responsible and just world.

For the economic science free competition is the key for the achievement of an ethical society which maximizes its welfare. It is competition the driver for ethics maximization in a society. Competition is the mechanism that brings forth the best qualities of every human being, the best skills and the highest level of entrepreneurship. It is competition that improves the incentives alignment among individuals and groups of people.

Now, here is a fine point we have to explain. One may ask: well, not all people are ethical and for sure some try to exploit their fellow people in order to maximize their benefit. Hence, the alignment of self-interest and interest-for-others is not perfect. Indeed, nobody believes human societies are perfect. Perfection is always a procedure, a tendency, an ultimate goal. It is not a static situation and there is always room for something better.

Comparing an ideal situation with a pragmatic one is not the best way to find a solution to a problem. New institutional economics (NIE) has an expression to describe the comparison between reality and utopia: nirvana fallacy (Furubotn & Richter, 2005).

It is meaningless to compare a real situation to an ideal one. Always the ideal will prevail. Following Popper (1963) we could say there is no falsifiable hypothesis to test. The proposition that the ideal situation is the best is not falsifiable. The key point is that we should compare a real situation with another real one. This is a major insight of NIE. It is the futile effort of groups of people to move from a real situation to an ideal one—forgetting that freedom is a necessary condition for happiness—that made things worse. Examples abound. A look at the past iron curtain regimes can show us what a society may look like when people decided to impose a "paradise" on earth and they failed miserably. Hayek (1944/1994) explains how this happens even when the governors have the noblest intentions.

It is true that not all people are ethical and definitely the level of ethics among individuals varies considerably. Competition is the only mechanism that can bring forth the best level of ethics of each individual (Friedman, 1962/2002; Hayek, 1944/1994; Hazlitt, 1946/2007, 1964/2012). It is the only mechanism that can elevate the level of personal ethics of each. Striving to maximize one's own happiness shows and teaches (by trial and error) that improving one's own personal ethics may be the best way to do it. By trying to offer society the best one can maximize his own well-being. It is not the benevolent dictator who will tell someone how to behave and act. It is meaningless to improve one's ethics this way because it does not contain his/her own personal effort.

According to the NIE one major prerequisite for free markets to successfully drive societies to social welfare maximization is institutions (North, 1990, 2005). Thucydides (1936), the ancient historian of the Peloponnesian war begins his historical account describing that the transition from a tribal society to a well organized city-state was based on institutions such as protection of property rights and a judicial system that could guarantee the protection of such rights.

Economic science (philosophy as well) supports—and history shows—that the institutional framework a society needs in order to better align the self-interest with the interest-for-others, is going to emerge within a free society where free people (the citizens) voluntarily come together and discuss the commons. Democracy is born. And democracy (free citizens) first creates the necessary institutions in order to protect itself and boost economic activity that will maximize the social benefit (Bergh & Lyttkens, 2014).

What every individual needs for making an educated decision regarding every socioeconomic activity is information. Hayek (1945) has elaborated extensively on this important issue. No central authority is capable of acquiring all available information in order to decide on the price of a good, a service, an entrepreneurial activity, even of a simple idea. The only mechanism that is able to better transmit the information of millions of people is the price mechanism of the free market. It is the market the point of meeting of all free people willing to maximize their own happiness. It is the market the milieu of meeting of every bit of information, tacit knowledge and entrepreneurial skills. All this information gets integrated in the price and reflects at the best and most efficient, fair and ethical (at the humanly possible level of course) way all the available information in society. Institutions necessary for the protection of rights and the organization of the market also emerge from the free interaction of free people (Rothbard, 1962/2009).

For more information on how voluntary interaction of people can create and shape institutions and organizational arrangements that produce successful outcomes we refer the reader to the outstanding work of the Nobel laureate Elinor Ostrom (1990) *Governing the Commons*. Ostrom has done magnificent work through the use of a plethora of case studies and demonstrates how communities around the world can reach viable outcomes through institutions that are inherently shaped. Ostrom's path-breaking work shows how the usual problem of the commons (e.g., fisheries, pastures, etc.) can have a happy rather than a tragic end—to allude to Hardin's (1968) "tragedy of the commons"—without the intervention of either the state (nationalization of the commons) or a private agent (privatization) alien to the local community and often imposed by the state.

Having all the aforementioned analysis in mind we move to our next step which is to show that M. Friedman and CSP can be bridged and CSP literature needs him.

HOW CSP AND FRIEDMAN CAN BE BRIDGED

Friedman's View

Friedman's (1970) argument against what he calls social responsibility is supported on the grounds of "principle and consequences" (p. 122). For Friedman it is unethical for a manager, who is liable to the shareholders, to engage in what may be considered as social performance such as donations to the local community because the manager spends not his own money but the shareholders money. Consequently, on the grounds of principle the manager is irresponsible and unethical. Hardly could anyone disagree with this argument. But Friedman did not say he is against such a policy *if* the shareholders are aware and agree with the community donation. Indeed, in an interview in 1989, Friedman clarifies this point. Addressing the issue of philanthropy he argues that as long as philanthropic activities have the consent of the shareholders they are perfectly acceptable and legitimate.

Regarding the grounds of consequences Friedman (1989) argues that spending for any social causes the firm will suffer losses. This is actually the argument that triggered the emergence of the vast and productive literature on the relationship between social and financial performance. However, if we take into consideration Friedman's economic thinking we will realize that Friedman *assumes* that the price mechanism has already incorporated all information, preferences and values of the people is such a way that *currently the firm is maximizing profits*. Consequently, any deviation from this situation, that is, *any* extra spending-investment from the manager will only lead to losses. Friedman abides to the neoclassical economics (NCE) principle of the perfectly competitive firm which is price taker and the only thing it needs to do in order to maximize profits is to just apply the price mechanism to its decisions.

Ronald Coase (1937) and the new institutional economics showed that the NCE assumption of perfect competition does not apply in reality. Moreover, before the NIE it was the Austrian school of economic thought (Menger, von Böhm Bawerk, von Mises, Hayek) who showed there is no equilibrium the way NCE describes simply because real life is much more complicated and dynamic than the static perfect competition ideal (Boettke, 2010).

An interview Friedman gave in 1972 (McClaughry, 1972) can help us better understand that he, in fact, assumes social performance of firms. He assumes it as already existent in the price mechanism. Friedman was asked regarding the Henry Ford case. Henry Ford back in 1914 doubled the wages of his employees. Ex post it was proved that this was a wise thing to do. The company thrived. Friedman was asked if this decision was a socially responsible decision as the CSR scholars would argue. Friedman replied that Henry Ford made that decision because he could make more money, not because he felt it is a social responsible thing to do (McClaughry, 1972).

Friedman's answer has a weak point that the NIE comes to support: He does not explain why Ford did not maximize profits before this decision while following the market wages. However, the Austrian school of economic thought as well as the NIE provides the answer: the price mechanism much like *every* humanly devised mechanism is not perfect and it is subject to continuous improvement (Furubotn & Richter, 2005; Hazlitt, 1946/2007; Mises, 1949/1998).

What is the driving force behind this eternal improvement? Entrepreneurship (Mises, 1949/1998). Indeed, Friedman in this interview says that Ford's decision was simply "good management," nothing more and nothing less (McClaughry, 1972). For Milton Friedman any entrepreneurial activity that can be considered socially responsible and is proven, ex post, that it enhances financial performance it is called good management. It is the market the ultimate judge of any managerial decision. If the decision increases profits it is good management, otherwise it is not. There is a fine yet crucial point here that Friedman dismisses: Time.

Before we develop the time perspective, let us come back to Friedman's (1970) famous quote

> that responsibility is to conduct the business in accordance with their [shareholders] desires, which generally will be to make as much money as possible while conforming to their basic rules of the society, both those embodied in law and those embodied in ethical custom. (p. 32)

Archie Carroll (1999), a leading CSR scholar defines CSR as a 4-level construct. A socially responsible firm is the one which is responsible in economic, legal, ethical and discretionary level. We observe that Friedman's aforementioned aphorism really incorporates the three out of the four levels. As Treviño and Nelson (1995) have noted, Friedman's view on CSR "tacitly embraces two out of the three additional components of the CSR pyramid: legal and ethical responsibilities" (p. 29, cited in James & Rassekh, 2000). Indeed, Friedman wants the free and open competition to work in order to make firms economically responsible. If the firm is not economically responsible it will exit the market sooner or later.

The last level of Carroll's (1999) pyramid—the discretionary level—is nothing more than entrepreneurship (Porter & Kramer, 2002, 2006, 2011). This is Friedman's "good management" (McClaughry, 1972). Friedman calls for more competition (free and open) in order for the price mechanism to better reflect all information, preferences and values so that any firm maximizing its profits maximizes social welfare. Milton Friedman assumes CSR. Following the philosophical roots of economics he understands that the most ethical and just system for humans to maximize their welfare, a system that best aligns self-interest with interest-for-others (social interest) is the system of price mechanism under free and open competition.

Friedman urges for more competition because free and open competition is the necessary condition for the alignment of firm's profits with social welfare (Friedman, 1962/2002, 1970). It is competition the catalyst which will guarantee that when a firm maximizes its profits it ultimately maximizes the social welfare. Friedman is not against CSR, he simply assumes it in his economic theory. For Friedman social responsibility is a byproduct of the operation of the firm. If we could rephrase Friedman's aphorism we could say: "if a firm operates in free and open competition and abides by the rules of the game (i.e., formal and informal laws and customs) it most probably maximizes social benefit and consequently maximizes social performance."

For Friedman, in particular and, economics, in general, the social benefit incorporates social responsibility and performance of firms.

The Cause for Misunderstanding Friedman: The Time Perspective

An interesting detail that also helps to explain why Friedman was misunderstood is that his argument does not have the time perspective. However it is generally accepted that time plays significant role (Becker, 1965). So, when we talk about profit maximization under the NCE perspective (i.e., the ideal of perfect competition) of the firm as a price taker time has no much significance. However, in real life time has great significance.

An investment always reduces short term profits of a firm but we must allow for some time for the investment to come to fruition. When Ford doubled his employees' wages he reduced firm's short term profits but he increased the long term profits. In economic terms we could say that Ford was willing to forgo part of his present utility (profits) in order to increase his future utility (profits). Similarly, a consumer decides to forgo current consumption in order to increase future consumption by either saving his money or investing it and looking forward to a higher future value of his asset.

For the economist Friedman (1966), what counts is the result (profit maximization), not the process (how you achieve such a maximization). If being socially responsible (a process of management discretionary decisions, firm's policy and governance, etc.) ultimately maximizes profits, it is perfectly fine (Ford's example). Friedman does not look at the process, he does not examine the way a manager makes decisions, in short he is a neoclassical (NC) economist who does not enter firm's black box, that is, the inner workings of the firm. NIE deals with the time issue and Ronald Coase (1937) was the first who tried to open this black box and examine the functions and the procedure that take place within governance structures and hierarchies (Williamson, 1975, 2000). Management scholars of course also care about the time perspective as the whole management activity is a process in time. Wood in her 1991 famous article clearly refers to the "processes of corporate social responsiveness" as a fundamental part of the CSP model.

Friedman (1966) as a NC economist cares only about the outcome, the bottom line. He knows that if competition works freely and openly then a firm that maximizes its profits, also maximizes social welfare, thus social performance! Friedman does not care to talk about specific actions regarding social performance because looking at the big philosophical picture of economics he is assured that to the extent competition works to the same extent society aligns self-interest with social interest. Consequently, the duty of governments is to create conditions witch improve and secure free and open competition.

The Competition-CSP Relationship

Following the above analysis we propose that CSP literature embraces the concept of competition and shifts the research attention from the SP-FP link to the issue of competition and how competition affects CSP. In order to add some empirics in our theoretical argument we use data from the World Economic Forum (WEF, 2013) to show a very simple yet indicative correlation between the level of competition and firms' ethical conduct for the 31 OECD high income countries group[5] (Figure 3.1).

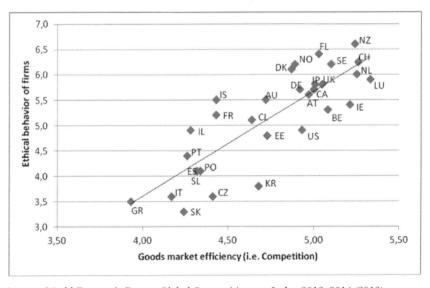

Source: World Economic Forum, Global Competitiveness Index 2013–2014 (2013).

Figure 3.1. The relation between "goods market efficiency" (i.e., competition) and "ethical behavior of firms."

There is no particular reason why we chose the specific group of countries except for reasons of diagram clarity. We could have chosen all 148 countries included in the WEF study but 148 dots in a diagram would be very cumbersome for the reader. WEF is an international organization[6] that publishes reports regarding global competitiveness. Every year they publish the global competitiveness index (GCI) report. They use an array of subindices grouped in 12 pillars to construct the competitiveness index of each country.

GCI captures, specifically, market competition through a series of subindices under the pillar "Goods market efficiency" which is composed by 16 subindices. It also has a subindex for CSP called "ethical behavior of firms." The specific subindex is part of another group of subindices which form the pillar "institutions." "Institutions" is composed by 21 subindices divided in public and private institutions. "Ethical behavior of firms" belongs to the private institutions group. The way GCI report measures the performance in each index is mostly by questionnaires to various stakeholders at a national economy level and mostly business people.[7]

We use "goods market efficiency" as a proxy for competition because the largest part of this pillar directly reflects competition of the market (WEF, 2013, p. 50). A minor part of the pillar refers to quality of demand conditions which also is related to and affects competition in the market. Specifically, the pillar "goods market efficiency" is composed by two subcategories (a) "competition" representing 67% of the pillar, and (b) "quality of demand conditions" which represents the rest 33%.

"Competition" is composed by 14 subindices, 8 of which refer to domestic competition and the rest 6 to foreign competition. "Domestic competition" is captured by the following subindices: (1) "Intensity of local competition," (2) "extent of market dominance," (3) "effectiveness of anti-monopoly policy," (4) "effect of taxation on incentives to invest," (5) "total tax rate," (6) "number of procedures required to start a business," (7) "time required to start a business" and, (8) "Agricultural policy costs." The "foreign competition dimension" is captured by (9) prevalence of trade barriers, (10) trade tariffs, (11) prevalence of foreign ownership, (12) business impact of rules on foreign direct investment, (13) burden of customers procedures and, (14) imports as a percentage of GDP.

At this point we need to elaborate more on the concept of competition. In the SP-FP literature there has been some work although limited on how competition affects this relationship (Berman, Phillips, & Wicks, 2005). Campbell (2007) and Van de Ven and Jeurissen (2005) theoretically predict a curvilinear relationship explaining that low competition levels gives monopoly power to the firm which means a low pressure from various stakeholders groups, while fierce competition reduces significantly the financial resources, thus limiting the ability of firms to invest in socially responsible activities. Moderate competition levels are those related to higher social performance. Chymis (2008) empirically tested this prediction and found support by the data.

However, there is a difference between "competition," as conceptualized and measured in the aforementioned literature, and "competition" as we conceptualize and measure in Figure 3.1. The extant literature measures competition at the industry level (intraindustry competition) using measurements such as the Herfindahl-Hirschman index (HHI) or the CR4[8] which are indeed very good measures for competition in the industry.

What we describe here is a broader meaning of competition, closer to the Friedman description, such as the competitive conditions at the whole market. This makes an important difference and can, in part, explain why in Figure 3.1 there seems to be a positive linear relationship between firm's ethics and competition while the extant literature predicts a curvilinear relationship. While the two kinds of competition are not conceptually different we could say that the intraindustry meaning is narrower while the general competitive conditions in the whole economy at a national level offer a broader meaning to competition as defined in this chapter.

Another explanation for the differentiation of our result to that of the literature is the time horizon as discussed previously. The way WEF measures competition gives it a relatively long-run macroeconomic level perspective while the HHI or the CR4 refer mostly to microeconomic relatively short-run industry level. At the microeconomic level, firms striving to survive under fierce intraindustry competition shoot for the short term survival rather than the long term profit (which entails social performance investments).

On the other hand, the macroeconomic level of competition in a country is mostly related to the long term, rather than the short term within industry, competition. Higher competitive macroeconomic environment increases efficiency of the economy overall which means it enhances the transmission of information to the price mechanism. This means firms know their practices will be known in the long term and they have a strong incentive to be socially responsible in order to keep legitimacy in the long run.

Finally we should not forget the measurement as well as model specification problems of the SP-FP literature recognized by many (Berman et al., 2005; McWilliams & Siegel, 2000; Wood, 2010). The not clearly defined causality between SP-FP may also affect the way the model needs to be specified. Of course our little empirics here are far from complete and specified. Rather, our point is to indicate an unexplored area for the CSP literature to discover.

Future Research

CSP literature has mostly focused on the for-profit private companies. The recent debt crises in many countries bring to the surface the question of responsible public management. How do public companies, financed by citizens taxes perform socially? How do they perform even financially (recall the first level of Carroll's (1999) pyramid of social responsibility: economic level)? Do they bring what they promise to the tax payers?

The recent credit-financial crisis which in many countries has evolved in a major economic crisis also challenges CSP scholars to address important questions regarding the responsibilities of public organizations in general and public administration in particular. We should pay attention on the words of T. Geithner (then President and Chief Executive Officer of the Federal Reserve Bank of New York) during a speech on September 5, 2008: "some [of the causes of the crisis] were the result of *incentives created by policy and regulation*" (as cited in Souto, 2009, p. 37, emphasis added). What are the social responsibilities of nonmarket organizations such as bureaucracies and public administrations, even the central banking system, which is private but closely related to governments and policymakers and thus not subject to competition?

These questions bring Friedman again on the scene. Based on the analysis of economic theory, the relation between economics and ethics as well as the explanation of Friedman's (1962/2002) view we could borrow from Friedman to say the following proposition: *we need free and open competition if it is to maximize social performance*, social performance of not only for-profit private enterprises but of all human organizations.

Recently some scholars have tackled some of the above questions (D'Anselmi, 2011; Di Bitetto, Gilardoni, & D'Anselmi, 2013; Di Bitetto, Chymis, & D'Anselmi, 2015). It is a brand new unfathomed area for research. The SP-FP literature has been very useful so far and it is time to go a step forward. It is time to embrace Friedman and take the research on CSP beyond the simple private for-profit firm and cover both private and public firms. Not only that but the social performance literature can make a big step forward to cover every organization (private and public) that absorbs scarce resources.

Every organization private and public has the moral duty to its constituents, tax payers, investors, consumers (to mention a few of the stakeholders) to be accountable and give back to society. Every economic agent has a moral duty to be transparent and to reveal the consequences of its activity, the social and economic footprint of the scarce resources it uses. Friedman is clear on how this can be achieved: Competition. Competition can be a litmus test for the legitimacy of every organization that consumes scarce resources in order to produce something.

In a globalized world every bit of resources used for some activity is a foregone resource for another activity. The recent credit-financial and economic crises revealed the irresponsible behavior, at a national level, of both private and public firms as well as public administrations and central banks. The long-run well-being of future generations was undermined for the benefit of the short-run well-being of the current generations. Friedman is more relevant now than ever before. Free and open competition is a necessary condition for a more responsible world.

CONCLUSION

Using the fundamentals of economic theory we showed the relation between economics and ethics and we examined M. Friedman's view on social responsibility. We demonstrated that there is no need for the CSP literature to be haunted by Friedman and try to prove him wrong by narrowly focusing on the SP-FP relationship. We illustrated that competition seems to be a key concept in the whole social performance literature that needs our special attention. Competition can boost social performance. M. Friedman urges for "free and open competition." It follows that M. Friedman can be a friend of CSP literature. A valuable friend that the CSP scholars can use in order to build a better and more solid theory for SP, a theory that has been recognized that is missing (Berman et al., 2005; Ullman, 1985; Wood, 2010).

It is time for the CSP literature to rethink its relationship with Friedman. We showed that it is a simple misunderstanding. Even though this misunderstanding was very fruitful, producing a large literature on the relationship between social and financial performance, we believe it is time to take CSP a step further, to reconcile CSP with Friedman and to enhance the CSP theoretical foundations based on him and on economics in general.

We also call for a need to include in our studies all organizations, private and public as well as for-profit and not-for-profit. Organizations that consume scarce resources are accountable to various stakeholders who offer the necessary resources for their operation. This opens a brand new research area for the social responsibility literature. To allude to the title of this book, it is a paradox that CSP literature has been considering Friedman an enemy for so long whereas he offers an answer on how to maximize social welfare. At the same time it will be a pitfall to deprive ourselves from such a valuable source of theoretical advancement. Friedman's theory on competition can be used to boost CSP theory. CSP literature has grown significantly during the last decades. It is now at a crossroad where it can move forward by incorporating economics and M. Friedman in its theoretical construct and escape from the pitfall of the no longer productive antithesis with economics.

We close with a quote of M. Friedman (1970) from his famous *New York Times* magazine article where he praises competition: "It [competition] forces people to be responsible for their own actions and makes it difficult for them to 'exploit' other people for either selfish or unselfish purposes. They can do good, but only at their own expense" (p. 33).

NOTES

1. "The Social Responsibility of Business is to Increase Its Profits" M. Friedman, *New York Times* magazine, September 13, 1970.
2. We use the expression "goods, services and ideas" in order to better reflect *all* human needs, physical, mental, and spiritual.
3. To quote Thucydides (1936), the ancient historian of the Peloponnesian war, "the secret of happiness is freedom and the secret of freedom is courage."
4. "It is not from the benevolence of the butcher, the brewer, or the baker that we expect our dinner, but from their regard to their own interest." Adam Smith (1776).
5. These are: Australia, Austria, Belgium, Canada, Chile, Czech Republic, Denmark, Estonia, Finland, France, Germany, Greece, Iceland, Ireland, Israel, Italy, Japan, Korea, Luxembourg, Netherlands, New Zealand, Norway, Poland, Portugal, Slovak Republic, Slovenia, Spain, Sweden, Switzerland, United Kingdom, and United States.
6. More information regarding WEF here: http://www.weforum.org/
7. For more information on the construct and opperationalization of each index we refer the reader to the GCI report of 2013-2014. Retrieved from http://www3.weforum.org/docs/WEF_GlobalCompetitivenessReport_2013-14.pdf
8. Concentration Ratio 4: The market share of the four top firms in a specific industry.

REFERENCES

Agle, B. R., Mitchell, R. K., & Sonnenfeld J. A. (1999). Who matters to CEOs? An investigation of stakeholder attributes and salience, corporate performance, and CEO values. *Academy of Management Journal, 42*(5), 507–525.

Becker, G. (1965). A theory of the allocation of time. *The Economic Journal, 75*(299), 493–517.

Bergh, A., & Lyttkens, C. H. (2014). Measuring institutional quality in ancient Athens. *Journal of Institutional Economics, 10*(2), 279–310.

Berman, S. L., Phillips, R. A., & Wicks, A. C. (2005, August). *Resource dependence, managerial discretion and stakeholder performance.* Paper presented in the Academy of Management meetings, Honolulu, Hawaii.

Boettke, P. J. (2010). What happened to "efficient markets." *The Independent Review, 14*(3), 363–375.

Brammer, S., & Millington, A. (2008). Does it pay to be different? An analysis of the relationship between corporate social and financial performance. *Strategic Management Journal, 29*(12), 1325–1343.

Campbell, J. L. (2007). Why would corporations behave in socially responsible ways? An institutional theory of corporate social responsibility. *Academy of management Review, 32*(3), 946–967.

Carroll, A. B. (1999). Corporate social responsibility: Evolution of a definitional construct. *Business and Society, 38*(3), 268–295.

Chymis, A. (2008). *Reconciling Friedman with corporate social responsibility: How market competition affects corporate social performance.* Saarbrücken, Germany: VDM Verlag Dr. Muller.

Coase, R. H. (1937). The nature of the firm. *Economica, 4*(16), 386–405.

D'Anselmi, P. (2011). *Values and stakeholders in an era of social responsibility: Cut-throat competition?* London, England: Palgrave Macmillan.

Di Bitetto, M., Gilardoni, G., & D'Anselmi, P. (Eds.). (2013). *SME's as the unknown stakeholder: Entrpreneurship in the political arena.* London, England: Palgrave Macmillan.

Di Bitetto, M., Chymis, A., & D'Anselmi, P. (Eds.). (2015). *Public management as corporate social responsibility: The economic bottom line of government.* Cham, Switzerland: Springer International Publishing.

Fernández-Feijóo Souto, B. (2009). Crisis and corporate social responsibility: Threat or opportunity? *International Journal of Economic Sciences and Applied Research, 2*(1), 36–50.

Freeman, R. E. (1984). *Strategic management: A stakeholder approach.* Boston, MA: Pitman/Ballinger.

Friedman, M. (1966). *Essays in positive economics.* Chicago, IL: University of Chicago Press.

Friedman, M. (1970, September 13). The social responsibility of business is to increase profits. *New York Times Magazine*, 32–33, 122–126.

Friedman, M. (1989). Freedom and philanthropy: An interview with Milton Friedman. *Business and Society Review, 71*, 11–18.

Friedman, M. (2002). *Capitalism and freedom.* Chicago, IL: University of Chicago Press. (Original work published 1962)

Frooman, J. (1997). Socially irresponsible and illegal behavior and shareholder wealth: A meta-analysis of event studies. *Business and Society, 36*(3), 221–249.

Furubotn, E. G., & Richter, R. (2005). *Institutions & economic theory.* Ann Arbor, MI: University of Michigan Press.

Graves, S. B., & Waddock S. A. (1994). Institutional owners and corporate social performance. *Academy of Management Journal, 37*(4), 1034–1046.

Hardin, G. (1968). The tragedy of the commons. *Science, 162*(3859), 1243–1248.

Hayek, F. A. (1945). The use of knowledge in society. *The American Economic Review*, 519-530.

Hayek, F. A. (1994). *The road to serfdom.* Chicago, IL: University of Chicago Press. (Original work published 1944)

Hazlitt, H. (2007). *Economics in one lesson.* Auburn, AL: Ludwig von Mises Institute. (Original work published 1946)

Hazlitt, H. (2012). *The foundations of morality.* Auburn, AL: Ludwig von Mises Institute. (Original work published 1964)

James, H. S., Jr., & Rassekh, F. (2000). Smith, Friedman, and self-interest in ethical society. *Business Ethics Quarterly, 10*(3), 659–674.

Margolis, J. D., Elfenbein, H. A., & Walsh, J. P. (2007). Does it pay to be good? A meta-analysis and redirection of research on the relationship between corporate social and financial performance. Ann Arbor, 1001, 48109-1234.

McClaughry, J. (1972). Milton Friedman responds. *Business and Society Review, 1,* 12–16.

McWilliams, A., & Siegel, D. (2000). Corporate social responsibility and financial performance: Correlation or misspecification? *Strategic Management Journal, 21*(5), 603–609.

Mises, L. von (1998). *Human action.* Auburn, AL: Ludwig von Mises Institute. (Original work published 1949)

Nelling, E., & Webb, E. (2009). Corporate social responsibility and financial performance: the "virtuous circle" revisited. *Review of Quantitative Finance and Accounting, 32*(2), 197–209.

North, D. C. (2005). *Understanding the process of economic change.* Princeton, NJ: Princeton University Press.

North, D. C. (1990). *Institutions, institutional change and economic performance.* Cambridge, England: Cambridge University Press.

Orlitzky, M., Schmidt F. L., & Rynes, S. L. (2003). Corporate social and financial performance. *Organizational Studies, 24*(3), 403–441.

Ostrom, E. (1990). *Governing the commons.* Cambridge, England: Cambridge University Press.

Popper, K. R. (1963). Science as falsification. *Conjectures and Refutations,* 33–39.

Porter, M. E., & Kramer, M.R. (2006). Strategy and society: The link between competitive advantage and corporate social responsibility. *Harvard Business Review, 84*(12), 77–92.

Porter, M. E., & Kramer, M. R. (2011). Creating shared value. *Harvard Business Review, 89*(1/2), 62–77.

Porter, M., & Kramer, M. (2002). The competitive advantage of corporate philanthropy. *Harvard Business Review, 80*(12), 57–68.

Rothbard, M. N. (2009). *Man, economy, and state.* Auburn, AL: Ludwig von Mises Institute. (Original work published 1962)

Smith, A. (1776). *An inquiry into the nature and causes of the wealth of nations: A selected edition.* Retrieved from http://www.econlib.org/library/Smith/smWN.html

Thucydides. (1936). *The history of the Peloponnesian war.* Athens, Greece: Papyros.

Tosi, H. L., Katz, J. P., & Gomez-Mejia, L. R. (1997). Disaggregating the agency contract: The effects of monitoring, incentive alignment, and term in office on agent decision making. *Academy of Management Journal, 40*(3), 584–602.

Treviño, L. K., & Nelson K. A. (1995). *Managing business ethics: Straight talk about how to do it right.* New York, NY: John Wiley and Sons.

Ullmann, A. A. (1985). Data in search of a theory: A critical examination of the relationships among social performance, social disclosure, and economic performance of U.S. firms. *Academy of Management Review, 10*(3), 540–557.

Van de Ven, B., & Jeurissen, R. (2005). Competing responsibly. *Business Ethics Quarterly, 15*(2), 299–317.

Van der Laan, G., Van Ees, H., & Van Witteloostuijn, A. (2008). Corporate social and financial performance: An extended stakeholder theory, and empirical test with accounting measures. *Journal of Business Ethics, 79*(3), 299–310.

Veenhoven, R. (2000). Freedom and happiness: A comparative study in forty-four nations in the early 1990s. *Culture and Subjective Well-Being*, 257–288.

Wight, J. (2001). *Saving Adam Smith: A tale of wealth, transformation, and virtue*. New York, NY: Pearson Education.

Williamson, O. E. (1975). *Markets and hierarchies*. New York, NY: Free Press.

Williamson, O. E. (2000). The new institutional economics: Taking stock, looking ahead. *Journal of Economic Literature, 38*, 595–613.

World Economic Forum. (2013). Global Competitiveness Report 2013–2014. Retrieved from http://www3.weforum.org/docs/WEF_GlobalCompetitivenessReport_2013-14.pdf

Wood, D. J. (1991). Corporate social performance revisited. *Academy of Management Review, 16*(4), 691–718.

Wood, D. J. (2010). Measuring corporate social performance: a review. *International Journal of Management Reviews, 12*(1), 50–84.

CHAPTER 4

SHOULD ACQUISITIONS PERFORM WELL, GOOD, OR BOTH?

A Stakeholder Perspective on Acquisition Performance

Olimpia Meglio

INTRODUCTION: READING THE MULTIDIMENSIONALITY OF ACQUISITION PERFORMANCE THROUGH A STAKEHOLDER'S LENS

The conventional discourse about acquisitions is primarily concerned with understanding how they perform (e.g., Capron, 1999; Cording, Christman, & King 2008; Fowler & Schmidt, 1988). To the community of acquisition scholars, acquisition performance represents a central construct, and a huge amount of empirical studies aim to identify variables that explain or predict acquisition performance (e.g., King, Dalton, Daily, & Covin, 2004; Larsson & Finkelstein, 1999).

Corporate Social Performance:
Paradoxes, Pitfalls, and Pathways to the Better World, pp. 57–77
Copyright © 2015 by Information Age Publishing
57

Meglio and Risberg (2011) conduct a narrative review of 101 articles that measure acquisition performance and uncover a multitude of conceptualizations and indicators used to measure performance under the unitary label of acquisition performance. The existence of a profusion of measures for acquisition performance explains not only the difficulty of summarizing research results through meta-analyses (Datta, Pinches, & Narayan, 1992; King et al., 2004) but also the widespread feeling that we know very little about acquisition performance (Bower, 2004).

From Meglio and Risberg's (2011) review, it also emerges that despite the multitude of acquisition-performance measures, most articles use one that is market-based. The underlying assumption seems to be that both of the merging companies are monoliths and that shareholders are the primary—and often the sole—actors with an interest in the deal.

I believe that this portrait is simplistic and misleading because it does not account for several interests affected by acquisitions. A partially different reading of these deals is offered by newspapers, economic and financial magazines, and press releases, which generally report effects on employees (see Exhibit 1). The prior research indicates that the discourse and framing techniques used by the media and executives help us to make sense of how mergers and acquisitions are perceived by various stakeholder groups (Risberg, Tienari, & Vaara, 2003; Vaara & Tienari, 2002; Vaara, Risberg, Søderberg, & Tienari, 2003). As an example, I analyze how Christina Roger (2014) describes the FIAT Chrysler deal in the January 1, 2014, edition of the *Wall Street Journal* (see Exhibit 1).

Exhibit 1.   Fiat to Get Full Control of Chrysler

DETROIT—Chrysler, the smallest of the three American automakers, is set to be completely absorbed by an Italian company, Fiat.

 "The unified ownership structure will now allow us to fully execute our vision of creating a global automaker that is truly unique in terms of mix of experience, perspective and know-how—a solid and open organization that will ensure all employees a challenging and rewarding environment," Sergio Marchionne, chief executive of Fiat and chairman and chief executive of Chrysler Group, said in a statement Wednesday....... The merger will help both companies operate with a single set of financial statements, said Jack R. Nerad, the executive editorial director at Kelley Blue Book. "Their ability to move capital around is going to be a big advantage for them," Mr. Nerad said......

The deal that awarded Fiat a 58.5 percent stake in Chrysler and the remainder to the union's voluntary employee benefits association was a cornerstone of the Obama administration's restructuring of the American auto industry in the recession.

"I have been looking forward to this day from the very moment that we were chosen to assist in the rebuilding of a vibrant Chrysler back in 2009," said John Elkann, chairman of Fiat.....

Christina Rogers, retrieved from wsjonline.com.

In the article, Roger (2014) provides the audience with main features of the deal, thus allowing us to see the relevant stakes. Both the financial terms and corporate governance implications play key roles, followed closely by the strategic vision driving the deal. Sergio Marchionne, the Chief Executive of the FIAT group, discusses the future of the organization as a whole, including the employee perspective, thus showing how a top management team attempts to mobilize human resources towards the attainment of strategic goal. The article explicitly refers to unions taking part in negotiations because they have an interest in a public offering that cashes out their shares. Other details about the agreement's financial terms are provided in a subsequent paragraph.

The article closes by reporting facts about geographical markets and product lines. The complementarity of product lines and geographical markets represents an important strength of the new entity because different areas enjoy different market trends. However, sales and profits remains the focus, whereas less attention is paid to models and innovation. All these factors, along with new leadership, are expected to improve FIAT Chrysler's capability to better serve its markets.

Although the article refers to a single case, its content resembles one of many such articles that describe acquisitions. Prominent roles are played by some stakeholders—that is, shareholders, employees, and consumers— although the role of consumers is indirect. Shareholders and employees generally receive a great deal of attention, whereas there is scant research on the effect of consumers' issues on performance. In general, acquisition research prioritizes business-to-business consumers over end consumers (cf. Öberg, 2013).

In the academic literature, employees and consumers are often treated as means to pursue acquisition goals. Overall, there is a lack of consideration of both internal and external stakeholders. In turn, that lack of consideration produces an incomplete assessment of the possible actions and reactions that influence acquisition performance. For this reason, I join the Nordic scholars who have recently advocated for employing a stakeholder approach to analyze these deals, and I argue that it is fruitful to introduce the notion of stakeholders into the acquisition discourse (Anderson, Havila, & Nilson, 2013). The consideration of several stakes in an acquisition helps me to overcome the narrow view that acquisitions should only serve shareholders' interest—an interest that is satisfied by performing well. This implies a shift from corporate financial performance to corporate social performance that involves considering all an acquisition's outcomes throughout the stakeholder network (Borglund, 2013). These notions overcome the limitations suffered by current measures of acquisition performance and provide a new view of the debate on performance measurement.

The goal of this chapter is to analyze how corporate social performance can inform current measures of acquisition performance. I achieve this goal by integrating different research streams—specifically, the acquisition performance measurement, stakeholder analysis, and corporate social performance literatures. Identifying the different stakeholders behind different dimensions of performance is a new way to understand the multidimensionality of acquisition performance. Specifically, I focus on employees and consumers, both of whom are primary stakeholders, with the former internal and the latter external to a merging company's boundaries. Cording, Harrison, Hoskisson, and Jonsen (2014) have recently outlined how these stakes, although different, are intertwined and influence each other, thus lending support to my choice to examine them together.

This chapter intends to contribute to the research on both acquisition performance and corporate social performance. It contributes to the acquisition research by reading the multidimensionality of acquisition performance through the stakeholder's lens. It contributes to the corporate social performance research by contextualizing performance measurement in the acquisition context. From a managerial standpoint, this chapter highlights first that acquisition performance is the result of different, often conflicting, stakes that an acquisition puts at risk and second that executives must achieve a balance among these pressures.

The remainder of this chapter is organized as follows. In the next section, I describe the current understanding of acquisition performance measurement and advocate for including stakeholder analysis in the study of acquisition performance. Next, I analyze acquisitions from a stakeholder perspective in an attempt to investigate the impact of acquisitions on both acquiring and target companies' stakeholders. Then, I put the spotlight on employees and consumers and discuss how top management teams can address these stakeholders. Implications for research and practice are illustrated in the concluding section.

Measuring Acquisition Performance

Organizational performance is a recurrent research focus in a variety of disciplines, including management. Organizational performance is conceived as a benchmark to gauge the effectiveness of managerial decisions because many management scholars define organizational performance as the dependent variable to identify what variables may explain or predict its variance (March & Sutton, 1997).

In a similar vein, acquisition scholars have long been interested in understanding whether acquisitions perform well. However, even meta-analyses have not provided conclusive results (Datta et al., 1992; King et al., 2004). A narrative review of the articles that measure acquisition performance is provided by Meglio and Risberg (2011) and Zollo and Meier (2008). These scholars highlight the multiplicity of meanings attached to acquisition performance that is reflected in a multitude of measures, variables and indicators found in the existing literature under the unitary label of acquisition performance. Specifically, Meglio and Risberg place acquisition performance measures into two performance domains—financial and nonfinancial. They include market and accounting measures of performance in the financial domain and operational and overall measures of performance in the nonfinancial domain. Market performance measures reflect two different dimensions: the market value of the company, often at the time of announcement, which is measured in terms of CAR (cumulative abnormal returns) or CAAR (cumulative average abnormal returns); and the risk the company faces, expressed as Jensen's Alpha or Beta coefficient. Accounting measures may reflect three different dimensions. The first dimension is profit, which is measured by ROA (return on assets), ROS (return on sales), or net income. The second dimension is growth, which is measured by, for example, sales growth. The third dimension is liquidity and leverage, which is measured by, for example, cash flow.

The nonfinancial domain comprises both operational and overall performance. Operational performance measures reflect three dimensions. The first is the marketing dimension, measured by market share. The second dimension is innovation, measured by number of patents or patent frequency. The third dimension is productivity, measured by cost synergies. Overall, performance measures reflect two dimensions: success and survival. Success is measured by the degree of attainment of acquisition goals. Survival is often measured by divestiture within a chosen time interval.

The majority of the articles under review, according to Meglio and Risberg (2011), measure acquisition performance as financial performance, that is, as a market reaction to the announcement of the deal. CAR is the most frequently used indicator for acquisition performance. If I must the identify stakeholders behind different measures, following Meglio and Risberg, I conclude that shareholders have a primacy over all stakeholders because shareholder value is a common measure of performance (e.g., Capron, 1999). One reason for this focus can be found in the classical claim that an acquiring firm's shareholders lose value from acquisitions and an acquired firm's shareholders gain (Jensen & Ruback, 1983), although there are studies that aim to falsify this claim. What is even more important is the array of justifications offered by scholars to support the usage of their chosen measures of acquisition performance. For example, Lubatkin and Shrieves (1986) justify the use of market-based measures by asserting that compared to accounting measures, market-based measure are direct and objective measures of stockholder value. From this justification, one can understand the underlying belief that market-based measures approximate true performance better than other types of measures. Over time, this belief has been taken for granted by the use of citations because many scholars justify their choice of method by referring to past studies. This is a way to argue that a type of measure has passed the test of time—if previous studies have used it, then it must be a reliable measure (Corvellec, 1997).

The less-frequently used accounting-based measures are generally measured by growth. In my view, accounting-based measures can reflect the interest of top management, whose pay is generally linked to this indicator. In addition, if we study nonfinancial measures of acquisition performance, success and survival do generally reflect the interests of top management. Survival could also reflect employees' interests because survival may imply that employees retain their jobs.

These considerations allow me to argue that accounting or market measures for acquisition performance tend to privilege the perspectives and interests of top management and shareholders. If many scholars use market and accounting data, top management and shareholders receive a disproportionate amount of attention. Acquisitions do typically have goals other than increasing shareholder value because they influence the network of stakeholders that are both internal and external to the merging companies. Exclusively focusing on what is measurable can result in overlooking other stakes of acquisition processes that are likely to affect acquisition outcomes. Building on and extending these ideas, I contend that another possibility for capturing all the possible effects of acquisitions involves acknowledging the existence of outcomes, other than economic or financial outcomes, brought about by these deals. To achieve this aim, I introduce the notions of corporate social responsibility (CSR) and corporate social performance into the debate on acquisition performance measurement.

CORPORATE SOCIAL RESPONSIBILITY AND PERFORMANCE

The preceding discussion highlights that current discourse about acquisition performance measurement has not been addressed by a popular debate within the management field—the idea that companies should be socially responsible. The concept of corporate social responsibility (CSR) has steadily evolved since it was first introduced a century ago. Lee (2008) argues that the first instance of a CSR attitude appeared in 1917 in Henry Ford's conception of business as a service. At that time, society was unready for such a conception of business. However, from then until now, the concept of CSR has undergone a process of progressive rationalization that has moved the discussion from the societal to the organizational level of analysis. Despite its prominence in the management discourse, there is still no agreed upon definition, and CSR remains a contested concept (Okoye, 2009). From this, I conclude that CSR has become an umbrella concept under which different conceptualizations coexist (Hirsch & Lewin, 1999), and that much of the debate centers on CSR's contribution to business success (Scherer & Palazzo, 2007). Baden and Harwood (2013) contend that this can be explained by the association of the term "CSR" with anti-Friedmanite views. Milton Friedman (1962) fiercely opposed the idea that companies should be socially responsible and claimed that CSR is an unnecessary burden on shareholders that imposes unfair costs on companies. Conversely, Freeman (1984) draws attention to companies' responsibilities towards all stakeholders. Consequently, much of the literature has addressed the reconciliation of these opposing views by emphasizing the business case for CSR (Vogel, 2005). Moreover, the CSR concept has been coupled with strategic choices, and its relationship with financial performance has been the subject of a great deal of investigation. Despite the popularity and longevity of the CSR concept, it is still ambiguous and its relationship with corporate financial performance remains controversial (Wood, 2010).

According to Wood (2010), the intellectual roots of CSP (corporate social performance) scholarship are found in the general systems theory that gained consensus in the 1950s. Specifically, Boulding (1956) observes that an organization is an open system, meaning that it is connected to its larger environment, which includes the social, cultural, legal, political, economic, and natural dimensions. Seeing corporations as open systems, embedded within a large environment, leads to the questions about to whom corporations are responsible, the content of that responsibility and what responsibility means to a corporation. Carroll (1979) first attempted to offer a conceptual model for CSP. He outlined the difficulties of measuring responsibility and suggested introducing the concept of CSP because it was easier to operationalize. He further identified four domains for CSR, which he referred to as economic, legal, ethical, and discretionary responsibilities. His model has been the starting point for further refinements—for example, Wood who revises Carroll's model to add dynamism. Her primary contribution is to identify the principles that guide managerial choices and the processes of social responsiveness that produce outcomes and have an impact on performance.

Although empirical evidence about the relationship between CSP (corporate social performance) and CFP (corporate financial performance) is ambiguous, the idea that companies should be socially responsible is now widely accepted, if not taken for granted. However, this shift has not been an easy one. Wood's (1991) depiction of CSP views the business organization ("corporate") as the locus of actions that have consequences for stakeholders and society as well as for itself ("social performance") … Corporate social performance … is a set of descriptive categorizations of business activity, focusing on its impacts and outcomes for society, stakeholders and the firm. Types of outcomes are determined by linkages, both general and specific, defined by the structural principles of CSR. (Wood, 2010, p. 54)

Therefore, in Wood's (1991) model, there is a relationship between processes and outcomes. Moreover, social performance encompasses financial performance, which constitutes one dimension of an overall measure for performance, not for a competing type of performance. This position contrasts the dichotomous view of CSP as something that a firm should do in addition to achieving its economic goals.

These opposing views explain the investigation of the relationship between CSP and CFP, which has attracted a considerable deal of attention and produced a huge number of empirical analyses (e.g., Cochran & Wood, 1985; Griffin & Mahon, 1997; Margolis & Walsh, 2001; Orlitzky, Schmidt, & Rynes, 2003). The results of these studies, taken together, indicate that the relationship should be recognized as complex, ambiguous and nuanced, which renders generalizations difficult and most likely useless. Additionally, reviews have surfaced showing that there remains a lack of understanding of the direction of causality between a firm's financial performance and its social behavior, that is, whether CSP is an independent or a dependent variable in the CSP-CFP relationship (Callan & Thomas, 2009). Additional drawbacks arise from the use of different methods to measure social and financial performance, incomparability among different periods, problems in sampling procedures and the importance of testing new mediating or moderating variables.

Although these issues indicate that the measurement process deserves careful attention and that more research is needed, I note that a more thorough investigation of the drivers of CSP is also essential to improve the measurement process. Awareness of the drivers of CSP performance is strictly linked to the identification of the domains and dimensions of CSP and therefore, it is essential for improving the measurement process. To achieve this aim, I adopt a stakeholder perspective, which is, in my view, the most suitable to achieve a better grasp of the performance outcomes of CSR. As Perrini, Russo, Tencati, and Vurro (2011) outline, a stakeholder-theory perspective allows us to understand CSR's influences and effects on financial performance. With these considerations in mind, I move on to apply a stakeholder lens to acquisitions.

ACQUISITIONS AND STAKEHOLDERS

From Freeman (1984) onward, stakeholder theory has gained consensus among scholars. Stakeholder theory describes companies as constellations of cooperative and competitive interests that possess intrinsic value (Donaldson & Preston, 1995). The notion of stake is central to a stakeholder approach and requires distinguishing claimants from influencers. According to Mitchell, Agle, and Wood (1997,), claimants are "groups that have a legal, moral or presumed claim on the firm,' whereas influencers are "groups that have an ability to influence the firm's behavior, direction, process, or outcomes" (p. 859). From these definitions, it emerges that the distinction is subtle, which helps us to understand why the concept of stakeholder itself remains vague and ambiguous. Stakeholder scholars provide us with a variety of definitions of the term stakeholder that range from narrow to broad and identify a set of dimensions to build typologies (Mitchell,et al., 1997).

According to Freeman (1984), "a stakeholder in an organization is (by definition) any group or individual who can affect or is affected by the achievement of the organization's objectives" (p. 460). This is a broad definition compared to that offered by Clarkson (1995), who defines a stakeholder as one who bears some risk resulting from an investment of capital into a company. This latter view presupposes that resources—and time and attention, in particular—are scarce and that managers are required to focus their efforts on managing the relationships with those who bring resources to the company.

Applied to the acquisition context, it is easy to understand that acquisitions radically influence the network of the relationships of acquiring and target firms with their respective internal and external stakeholders (Halinen, Salmi, & Havila, 1999). Many actors play a role in the acquisition process, from investment banks to advisors, from employees to customers. All of these actors, whether individual actors or coalitions, have legitimate and powerful claims to stakes. They are affected by the deal and in turn, they affect acquisition performance. In some cases, their influence is based on a contract that links an individual or a company to the acquiring or merging company. This is the case with employees, suppliers, or business-to-business customers. However, power and therefore influence can be legitimated by a superior, often collective, interest to protect, as in the case of governmental bodies that may have input into whether a deal will take place. Building on this definition, an acquisition can be analyzed as a multistakeholder deal, with the number of stakeholders magnified over the course of the acquisition process for the simple reason that two companies are involved (Anderson, et al., 2013), with acquiring and the target companies almost never holding equal positions and with often-divergent stakes.

It is also important to recognize that all stakes are neither alike nor constant. For instance, during the pre-merger phase, top management and company owners play a critical role, whereas the remaining stakeholders are relatively inactive. A deal announcement expands the number of stakeholders. Some stakes are instantaneous, as in the case of investment banks interested in earning the transaction fee, and other stakes change over time. This means that some stakeholders may have different goals and are able to exert either more or less influence over time.

These considerations drive a process approach to the analysis of the roles played by stakeholders during the acquisition process and the power that they exert over acquisition performance (Meglio & Risberg, 2010). To make sense of the stakeholding actors during an acquisition process, I positioned each stakeholder along the acquisition process (see Table 4.1). The acquisition process is depicted as a linear flow of three different phases, which therefore does not include the recursive or alternate paths that actually comprise the entire process. As shown in Table 4.1 some stakeholders (such as the top management team) influence all phases, whereas other stakeholders' (such as consumer) influence is limited to single phases.

Table 4.1. Stakeholders in Acquisitions: A Process Perspective

Stakeholder	Preacquisition	Closing the Deal	Postacquisition
Shareholders	√	√	√
Top management	√	√	√
Middle Managers			
Consulting firms	√	√	
Investment banks	√	√	
Employees			√
Suppliers			√
Customers			√
Competitors	√	√	
Government		√	
Unions		√	

The definition of process employed here takes a historical, developmental perspective and focuses on sequences of incidents, activities, and actions unfolding over time, taking into account enabling and constraining influences from the firm's inner and outer contexts (Pettigrew, 1992). Applied to the analysis of stakeholders, a process approach enables recognition of the importance of several contextual factors that shape stakeholders' influence on acquisition performance. In the case of acquisitions, several contextual factors affect the influence that stakeholders actually exert on acquisition performance, such as the nature of the deal (either friendly or hostile) or the degree of relatedness between the merging parties or industries involved. In the case of a friendly acquisition, we expect employees to have a more positive attitude toward the deal compared to the case of a hostile takeover. In this latter case, we expect that employees will exhibit negative reactions towards the acquisition, such as sabotage or an increased absenteeism rate. If the deal involves knowledge-intensive firms, scientists play a more important role than other employees because innovative performance is heavily dependent upon them (Ranft & Lord, 2000). With these considerations in mine, I move onto the analysis of two primary stakeholders—employees and consumers—and discuss the influence of their stakes on acquisition performance. The interest in considering these stakeholders arises concurrently from the awareness that what happens to one stakeholder influences the reactions of other stakeholders. Specifically, Cording, Harrison et al. (2014) highlight how employees and consumers influence each other and how this influence in turn affects financial performance. Top management teams may play a crucial role in reaching a balance among conflicting stakes, thus favoring an alignment of different stakes.

ACQUISITIONS AS MULTISTAKEHOLDERS DEALS

Employees as Stakeholders in Acquisitions

There already exists an abundant literature on the topic of employees' reactions to acquisitions. However, the majority of those studies have primarily investigated the effects of acquisitions on morale and productivity (Larsson & Finkelstein, 1999). Here, my aim is instead to establish a link between the stake of employees generally put at risk by an acquisition, identifying the possible facets/dimensions of this stake neglected by the current research and analyzing their consequences on acquisition performance. Notably, I refer to acquisition performance as an overall construct that acknowledges all the possible outcomes generally produced by these deals.

Acquisitions are traumatic events for the organizations involved because they bring uncertainty to employees' career paths and disrupt work routines, morale and social connections (Larsson, Driver, Holmqvist, & Sweet, 2001). Consequently, there can be episodes of active and passive negative reactions, such as sabotage and an increased absenteeism rate, resulting in decreased productivity. This scenario has a direct implication for acquisition performance because it is likely to result in more time-consuming and costly integration. The managerial implication is that executives should remember that the achievement of expected synergies from eliminating redundancies and duplications can be hindered, offset or at least slowed by this chain of events. This consideration may actually change the conditions under which an acquisition is an effective strategic option.

The magnitude of employees' reactions as along with the effect of those reactions on acquisition performance vary a great deal depending on several contextual factors, such as the degree of relatedness, the size similarity/asymmetry and the nature of the deal (i.e., whether it is friendly or hostile). The degree of relatedness determines how much the two companies overlap, thus determining the degree of integration. The greater and more pervasive the integration, the higher the risk of negative employee reactions. The nature of the deal influences how the acquiring company is seen within the target company. The degree of hostility, along with a lack of prior business relationships, can produce turmoil and low morale among employees. An analogous line of reasoning applies when the target company is significantly smaller than the acquiring one. In such a circumstance, it is very likely that the target company's top management will be replaced by the top management of the acquiring company. In this situation, the target company's employees are likely to experience (metaphorically) a feeling of being eaten, which predicts a negative chain of actions and reactions that may negatively affect acquisition performance. In high-technology industries, scientists, inventors and knowledge workers may represent an exception to this scenario. High-tech deals are generally pursued to appropriate and leverage knowledge from the target firm. These goals emphasize the importance of retaining talented people and create the best conditions for their productivity. Many studies, however, signal how difficult it is to achieve these aims. Ernst and Vitt (2000) show that key inventor productivity slows after an acquisition. This is explained by key inventors' relative loss of standing in the acquired company (Paruchuri, Nerkar, & Hambrick, 2006). Moreover, Kapoor and Lim (2007) find that the productivity of all inventors, regardless of their status, is lower than that of inventors at nonacquired firms.

An alternative scenario occurs if employees at different hierarchical levels welcome an acquisition as an opportunity. This may happen in the case of a white knight or when the target is a family business with no second generation willing to replace the founder. In those circumstances, in which the company's survival could be at risk, the acquirer is seen positively and employees are more willing to cooperate. Another possible example is that of an acquisition inspired by acquirer diversification. In that case, the need for change within the target company is expected to be low. Assurance of future career prospects should preserve morale and encourage employees' cooperative efforts, thus reinforcing the idea that an acquisition alone does not assure that intended goals will be achieved.

An effective tool to address such sensitive issues is to assure that people are treated fairly during the postacquisition phase. This leads me to introduce the concept of organizational justice in the postacquisition context. Organizational justice represents an established area of research (Strom, Sears, & Kelly, 2014). The existing literature distinguishes between two distinct forms of justice—*distributive justice*, referring to employees' views that the rewards distributed by their organization are fair, and *procedural justice*, referring to employees' views that the processes by which their organizations decide to distribute rewards are fair (Cohen-Charash & Spector, 2001). Organizational justice has established a reputation of predicting a wide range of organizational and personal outcomes such as job satisfaction, organizational citizenship behavior, organizational commitment, counterproductive work behaviors, organizational withdrawal, and job performance (Cohen-Charash & Spector, 2001). Most relevant to the acquisition context, two recent studies have empirically supported the idea that organizational justice is one of several antecedents of work engagement (Moliner, Martinez-Tur, Ramos, Peiro, & Cropanzano, 2008; Saks, 2006), which is crucial during the integration process. In such a context, integration leaders may play a key role in maintaining a positive work environment that promotes norms for employees' constructive efforts in realizing integration between merging companies (Meglio, King, & Risberg, 2013).

Consumers as Stakeholders in Acquisitions

Existing research outlines how business-to-business customers experience acquisitions. Acquisitions encompass a broad spectrum of changes that actually cause the dissolution of business relationships with customers. The departure of key personnel, dissatisfaction produced by failure to meet customer requirements, an acquiring company's poor reputation or financial difficulties, less-favorable business conditions, and product replacement may all be reasons to terminate a business relationship (Öberg, 2013). This suggests the importance of carefully scrutinizing customers with the goal of reassuring them and using customer relationship management strategies to nurture the business relationship.

End consumers have received little attention in the acquisition-related literature, which is quite surprising because a frequently advocated rationale for pursuing a deal is to acquire the target company's customers. Many acquisitions are driven by the aim to "buy" the target company's market share, as though the acquisition of such market share was an automatic benefit of an acquisition. There appears to be an underlying assumption that could explain the lack of an empirical investigation of consumer behaviors following an acquisition in both industrial and service industries, such as the automotive and banking sectors. From the acquiring company's perspective, there is often a hidden belief that the acquisition will result in better conditions for consumers, which will assure greater postbuying satisfaction. This discourse seems to emphasize a passive role played by consumers during the postacquisition period, when it is very likely that those consumers will experience the negative consequences of organizational turmoil. However, consumers do have a voice, albeit only during the postacquisition phase and through their choices—e.g., exit choices—they may directly influence the merging companies' financial performance through consumers' buying behavior. Schuler and Cording (2006) outline how marketing scholars have attempted to investigate the relationship between CSP and consumer buying intention and behavior (e.g., Brown & Dacin, 1997; Creyer & Ross, 1997; Sen & Bhattacharya, 2001). Taken together, these studies support the idea that CSP enters the evaluation process that precedes buying acts. Information regarding CSP can influence consumers' choices depending on several contextual factors. First, information regarding CSP must be readily available and must originate from a third party. Schuler and Cording (2006) refer to this factor as information intensity. A different issue relates to the nature of information, which can be either positive or negative, thus either magnifying or hindering company reputation. Information has an impact on consumers' moral values, subjective norms and attitudes toward a brand.

The proposed model, which Schuler and Cording (2006) suggest best fits goods and services that require an effortful and nonroutine decision, can be applied to the acquisition context. As discussed above, acquisitions are not neutral events for a variety of actors and for society as a whole. Instead, acquisitions have many consequences that can actually alter a company's reputation in the market. For example, we consider some industries—for example, the banking and automotive industries—that are deeply involved in merger waves. They both serve end consumers and therefore, they are best suited to our analysis. The banking sector has been interested in extensively reorganizing regional branches, closing many of them to cut costs and avoid duplication. This strategy has produced significant layoffs but also has disrupted relationships between consumers and front-line employees. This latter issue has not received scholarly attention, as though consumers were not affected by it. For example, questions about how consumers are sold on or react to a different banking experience have yet to be answered.

Another example is offered by the automotive industry. In Italy, for example, FIAT has progressively moved its interests from Italy to the United States. It is a reasonable possibility that the decreasing number of FIAT automobiles sold in Italy can be explained by Italians' sense that the company has betrayed them. This argument finds support in Cording, Harrison et al. (2014), who contend that an important assumption of stakeholder theory is the concept of generalized exchange. Generalized exchange, as advanced by Ekeh (1974), implies that the attitudes and behaviors of one stakeholder (in our case, end consumers) are influenced by the company's behavior towards a different stakeholder (in our case, employees).

Consumers' attitude towards CSP may vary a great deal depending on their country of origin and other demographic variables. There are empirical studies measuring consumers' sensitivity to CSP in the United States (Paul, Zalka, Downes, Perry, & Friday, 1997) and in other Western countries such as the Netherlands (Meijer & Schuyt, 2005) that suggest that this sensitivity is affected by geographical conditions and common demographic variables. These findings have interesting implications for acquisitions involving companies from different countries, especially when Eastern and Western cultures are required to blend. Under such circumstances, consumers' differing sensitivities to CSP should be carefully scrutinized and their effects on sales assessed.

Alternative Scenarios and the Role of Top Management Team

The preceding discussion highlights that acquisition performance is influenced by two primary stakeholders put at risk by an acquisition. Although their stakes are different, according to the generalized exchange theory, they should be treated as intertwined (Ekeh, 1974). The postacquisition phase, as described above, disrupts existing relationships and causes great uncertainty. One way that employees and consumers can reduce the uncertainty is to make sense of the new company's organizational authenticity, that is, the degree of consistency between a company's espoused values and its realized practices (Cording, Harrison et al., 2014). In an acquisition context, what is important is the organizational authenticity exhibited by the acquiring company during the postacquisition integration; that is, the degree of consistency between declaration of intent and actual decisions. In this situation, employees scrutinize how the acquiring company treats consumers, and consumers scrutinize how the acquiring company treats employees. Conversely, the top management team, which has a key role in handling conflicting stakes, should rely on organizational justice, as described above. The argument that I advance here is that the important factors in the postmerger phase are not only how the process is handled (procedural justice) but also the consistency between what is communicated and what is actually done. Because there are several contextual factors that shape postmerger integration, I identify two alternative scenarios. Specifically, I analyze how convergence or divergence among stakes produces different outcomes.

As specified above, the top management team's stake is prestige and pay, both of which are assured by growth. Growth can show convergence or divergence with employees' and consumers' stakes.

The first scenario—which I label convergence—materializes if growth assures job security and career prospects. This is the case of unrelated acquisitions, when the need for restructuring is limited or when the target company is a family business with no rising second generation. Under these circumstances, employees welcome the acquisition because the deal is likely to produce limited changes. The reaction from end consumers should also be positive, unless the acquiring company has a worse reputation than that of the target.

Convergence assures a complementarity of goals among different stakeholders and a positive effect on financial performance. Under these circumstances, the role of organizational authenticity and organizational justice is limited because the postacquisition phase is not very traumatic.

A second scenario—which I label divergence—materializes when an acquisition requires layoffs, as in the case of horizontal or hostile acquisitions. Under these circumstances, the top management team faces a huge dilemma: whether to lay people off or retain them. The first choice allows the achievement of expected cost benefits; although the latter preserves employees' morale and productivity, it scarifies the exploitation of synergies. Conversely, if the top management team lays people off without providing any type of support or "parachute," attainment of the acquisition goal is slowed down due to turmoil and forms of resistance. When layoffs are inevitable, I suggest that the way in which the process is handled makes a difference. Organizational justice is an effective a tool to handle these conflicting goals. Organizational justice can also alleviate consumers' concerns about the acquiring company's CSP profile. Organizational authenticity augments organizational justice because it is essential that the top management team does not break its promises while it integrates the two companies.

DISCUSSION AND CONCLUSION

In this chapter, I attempt to provide a fresh perspective on the analysis of acquisition performance and to extend the focus of the existing literature beyond shareholder interests, which are reflected in the prevailing use of market-based measures for acquisition performance in the premier academic journals (see Meglio & Risberg, 2011). The belief underlying the use of market-based measures is that acquisitions are neutral events for stakeholders other than shareholders. The conventional portrait of these deals is as a battleground where opposing shareholder groups compete for the best return, which depends on the price set. The question posed in the title can now be answered by the response that performing well and performing good are not mutually exclusive goals. The arguments provided in this chapter highlight that performing good is an effective route to performing well.

Within the management field, the current debate about acquisition performance measurement has generally discarded the idea that acquisitions should also perform good. The idea advanced in this chapter builds on the premise that whether inside or outside of their boundaries, merging companies are not monoliths. Instead, both companies can be seen as networks of relationships with stakeholders (whether internal and external to their boundaries) legitimated by a contract or other interests that require protection. Acknowledging the existence of different stakes recognizes that no single performance measure can do justice to every stake. This is a new way to conceive the multidimensionality of acquisition performance, frequently evoked by scholars, but generally underplayed in theoretical and empirical research. Therefore, I suggest that one way to grasp such multidimensionality is to acknowledge that underlying the dimensions of an acquisition process, several stakes and stakeholders play a role.

In this chapter, although I recognize the multiplicity of stakes, I focus my analysis on two stakeholders: employees and consumers. My choice is driven by their relevance and ability to influence how an acquisition actually performs. These stakeholders are different in many respects: employees are internal to the companies involved in an acquisition, whereas consumers are external. Employees have a stake to protect—that is, work security and career prospects—which we can immediately grasp. Consumers' stake is more subtle because it relates to the factors that influence buying behaviors and how they are affected by an acquisition.

My analysis has also managerial implications because failing to employee and consumers' stakes may produce increasing costs or reduced revenues that influence the acquiring company's bottom line. Seeing employees and consumers as stakeholders enables us to overcome the view that depicts them as a means to an end. They may actually play a relevant role in the postacquisition context because they have relevant stakes to protect. A more thorough understanding of what these stakes look like, along with their behavioral consequences, is instrumental in identifying possible tools to address these issues. In addition, the top management team is in the best position to achieve a convergence or balance among the different stakes put at risk by an acquisition. Thus, I suggest that the best way to assess the influence of employees on acquisition performance is by recognizing their stake in an acquisition: work security and career prospects. Consumers' stakes are linked to the moral values that influence their buying behaviors. Their behaviors are also influenced by how the acquiring company treats employees. In a similar vein, the way that consumers are treated influences employees' reactions. This means that the two stakes do influence each other and deserve a comprehensive assessment from the top management team to improve financial performance. Organizational authenticity and organizational justice are key concepts in this multi-stakeholder relationship.

REFERENCES

Anderson, H., Havila, V., & Nilsson, F. (Eds.). (2013). *Mergers and acquisitions: The critical role of stakeholders.* New York/Oxon: Routledge.

Baden, D., & Harwood, I. A. (2013). Terminology matters: a critical exploration of corporate social responsibility terms. *Journal of Business Ethics, 116*, 615–627.

Borglund, T. (2013). The growing importance of corporate social responsibility in mergers and acquisitions. In H. Anderson, V. Havila, & F. Nilsson (Eds.), *Mergers and acquisitions: The critical role of stakeholders* (pp. 17–39). New York/Oxon: Routledge.

Boulding, K. E. (1956). General systems theory: The skeleton of science. *Management Science, 2*, 197–208.

Bower, J. L. (2004). When we study M&Awhat are we learning. In A. L. Pablo & M. Javidan (Eds.), *Mergers and acquisitions: Creating integrative knowledge* (pp. 235–244). Oxford, England: Blackwell.

Brown, T. J., & Dacin, P. A. (1997). The company and the product: Corporate associations and consumer product responses. *Journal of Marketing, 61*, 68–84.

Callan, S. J., & Thomas, J. M. (2009). Corporate financial performance and corporate social performance: an update and reinvestigation. *Corporate Social Responsibility and Environmental Management, 16*(2), 61–78.

Capron, L. (1999). The long-term performance of horizontal acquisitions. *Strategic Management Journal, 20*, 987–1018.

Carroll, A. B. (1979). A three-dimensional model of corporate social performance. *Academy of Management Review, 4*, 497–505.

Clarkson, M. B. E. (1995). A stakeholder framework for evaluating corporate social performance. *Academy of Management Review, 20*(1), 92–117.

Cochran, P. L., & Wood, D. J. (1985). Corporate social responsibility and financial performance. *Academy of Management Journal, 27,* 42–56.

Cohen-Charash, Y., & Spector, P. E. (2001). The role of justice in organizations: A meta-analysis. *Organizational Behavior and Human Decisions Processes, 86,* 278–321.

Cording, M., Christman, P., & King D. (2008). Reducing causal ambiguity in acquisition integration: Intermediate goals as mediators of integration decisions and acquisition performance. *Academy of Management Journal, 51,* 744–767.

Cording, M., Harrison, J. S., Hoskisson, R. E., & Jonsen, K. (2014). Walking the talk: a multistakeholder exploration of organizational authenticity, employee productivity, and post-merger performance. *Academy of Management Perspectives, 28*(1), 38–56.

Corvellec, H. (1997). *Stories of achievement-narrative features of organizational performance.* New Brunswick, NJ: Transaction.

Creyer, E. H., & Ross, W. T., Jr. (1997). The influence of firm behavior on purchase intention: Do consumers really care about business ethics? *Journal of Consumer Marketing, 14,* 421–432.

Datta, D. K., Pinches G. P., & Narayan, V. K. (1992). Factors influencing wealth creation from mergers and acquisitions: a meta-analysis. *Strategic Management Journal, 13*(1), 67–84.

Donaldson, T., & Preston, L. E. (1995). The stakeholder theory of the corporation: concepts, evidence and implication. *Academy of Management Review, 20*(1), 65–91

Ekeh, P. P. (1974). *Social exchange theory.* Cambridge, MA: Harvard University Press.

Ernst H., & Vitt J. (2000). The influence of corporate acquisitions on the behaviour of key inventors. *R&D Management, 30*(2), 105–118.

Fowler, K. L., & Schmidt D. R. (1988). Tender offers, acquisition, and subsequent performance in manufacturing firms. *Academy of Management Journal, 31,* 962–974.

Freeman, R. E. (1984). *Strategic management: A stakeholder approach.* Boston, MA: Pitman.

Friedman, M. (1962). *Capitalism and freedom.* Chicago, IL: University of Chicago Press.

Griffin, J. J., & Mahon, J. F. (1997). The corporate social performance and corporate financial performance debate: Twenty-five years of incomparable research. *Business & Society, 36,* 5–31.

Halinen, A., Salmi, A., & Havila, V. (1999). From dyadic change to changing business networks: An analytical framework. *Journal of Management Studies, 36*(6), 779–794.

Hirsch, P. M., & Levin D. Z. (1999). Umbrella advocates versus validity police: A life-cycle model. *Organization Science, 10*(2), 199–212.

Jensen, M. C., & Ruback R. S. (1983). The market for corporate control. *Journal of Financial Economics, 11*(1), 5–50.

Kapoor, R., & Lim, K. (2007). The impact of acquisitions on the productivity of inventors at semiconductor firms: A synthesis of knowledge-based and incentive-based perspectives. *Academy of Management Journal, 50*(5), 1133–1155.

King, D., Dalton, D., Daily, C., & Covin, J. (2004). Meta-analyses of post-acquisition performance: Indications of unidentified moderators. *Strategic Management Journal, 25,* 187–200.

Larsson, R., & Finkelstein, S. (1999). Integrating strategic, organizational, and human resource perspectives on mergers and acquisitions: A case survey of synergy realization. *Organization Science, 10*(1), 1–26.

Larsson, R., Driver, M., Holmqvist, M., & Sweet, P. (2001). Career dis-integration and re-integration in mergers and acquisitions: Managing competence and motivational intangibles. *European Management Journal, 19*(6), 609–618.

Lee, M.-D. P. (2008). A review of the theories of corporate social responsibility: its evolutionary path and the road ahead. *International Journal of Management Reviews, 10,* 53–73.

Lubatkin, M., & Shrieves, R. E. (1986). Towards reconciliation of market performance measures to strategic management research. *Academy of Management Review, 11*(3), 497–512

March, J. G., & Sutton, R. I. (1997). Organizational performance as a dependent variable. *Organization Science, 8*(6), 698–706.

Margolis, J. D., & Walsh, J. P. (2001). *People and profits: The search for a link between a company's social and financial performance.* Mahwah, NJ: Lawrence Erlbaum Associates.

Meglio, O., King, D. R., & Risberg, A. (2013). *Improving acquisition performance with contextual ambidexterity: The role of integration leadership and mechanisms* (Working paper).

Meglio, O., & Risberg, A. (2010). Mergers and acquisitions-time for a methodological rejuvenation of the field. *Scandinavian Journal of Management, 26*(1), 87–95.

Meglio, O., & Risberg, A. (2011). The (mis)measurement of M&A performance: A systematic narrative literature review. *Scandinavian Journal of Management, 27*(4), 418–433.

Meijer, M. M., & Schuyt, T. (2005). Corporate social performance as a bottom line for consumers. *Business & Society, 44*(4), 442–461.

Mitchell, R. K., Agle, B. R., & Wood, D. T. (1997). Toward a theory of stakeholder identification and salience: Defining the principle of who and what really counts. *Academy of Management Review, 22*(4), 853–886.

Moliner, C., Martinez-Tur, V., Ramos, J., Peiro, J. M., & Cropanzano, R. (2008). Organizational justice and extrarole customer service: The mediating role of well-being at work. *European Journal of Work and Organizational Psychology, 17,* 327–348.

Öberg, C. (2013). Why do customers dissolve their business relationships with the acquired party following an acquisition? In H. Anderson, V. Havila, & F. Nilsson (Eds.), *Mergers and acquisitions. The critical role of stakeholders* (pp. 185–202). New York/Oxon: Routledge.

Okoye, A. (2009). Theorising corporate social responsibility as an essentially contested concept: Is a definition necessary? *Journal of Business Ethics, 89*(4), 613–627.

Orlitzky, M., Schmidt, F. L., & Rynes, S. L. (2003). Corporate social and financial performance: A meta-analysis. *Organization Studies, 24,* 403–442.

Paruchuri, S., Nerkar, A., & Hambrick, D.C. (2006). Acquisition integration and productivity losses in the technical core: Disruption of inventors in acquired companies. *Organization Science, 17*(5), 545–562.

Paul, K., Zalka, L. M., Downes, M., Perry, S., & Friday, S. (1997). U.S. consumer sensitivity to corporate social performance. *Business & Society, 36*(4), 408–418.

Perrini, F., Russo A., Tencati, A., & Vurro, C. (2011). Deconstructing the relationship between corporate social and financial performance. *Journal of Business Ethics, 102*(1), 59–76.

Pettigrew, A. M. (1992). The character and significance of strategy process. *Strategic Management Journal, 13*(1), 5–16.

Ranft, A., & Lord, M. (2000). Acquiring new knowledge: the role of retaining human capital in acquisition of high-tech firm. *Journal of High Technology Management Research, 11,* 295–319.

Risberg, A., Tienari, J., & Vaara, E. (2003). Making sense of a transnational merger: Media texts and the (re)construction of power relations. *Culture & Organization, 9*(2), 121–137.

Roger, C. (2014). *Fiat to get full control of Chrysler*. Retrieved from http://www.wsj.com/articles/SB10001424052702303640604579294631534003954

Saks, A. M. (2006). Antecedents and consequences of employee engagement. *Journal of Managerial Psychology, 21,* 600–619.

Scherer, A. G., & Palazzo, G. (2007). Toward a political conception of corporate responsibility: business and society seen from an habermasian perspective. *Academy of Management Review, 32*(4), 1096–1120,

Schuler, D. A., & Cording, M. (2006). A corporate social performance-corporate financial performance behavioral model for consumers. *Academy of Management Review, 31*(3), 540–558.

Sen, S., & Bhattacharya, C. B. (2001). Does doing good always lead to doing better? Consumer reactions to corporate social responsibility. *Journal of Marketing Research, 38,* 225–243.

Strom, D. L., Sears, K. L., & Kelly, K. M. (2014). Work engagement: the role of organizational justice and leadership style in predicting engagement among employees. *Journal of Leadership and Organization Studies, 21*(1), 71–82.

Vaara, E., & Tienari, J. (2002). Justification, legitimization and naturalization of mergers and acquisitions: A critical discourse analysis of media texts. *Organization, 9*(2), 275–304.

Vaara, E., Risberg, A., Søderberg, A.-M., & Tienari, J. (2003) The construction of national stereotypes in a merging multinational. In A.-M. Søderberg & E. Vaara (Ed.), *Merging across borders: People, cultures and politics*, Copenhagen, Denmark: Copenhagen Business School Press.

Vogel, D. (2005). *The market for virtue: the potential and limits of corporate social responsibility*. Washington, DC: Brookings Institution Press.

Wood, D. J. (1991). Corporate social performance revisited. *Academy of Management Review, 16,* 691–718.

Wood, D. J. (2010). Measuring corporate social performance: A review. *International Journal of Management Reviews, 12*(19), 50–84.

Zollo, M., & Meier, D. (2008). What is M&A performance? *Academy of Management Perspective, 22*(3), 55–77.

CHAPTER 5

IDENTIFYING REASONS WHY SOME FIRMS MAXIMIZE CORPORATE SOCIAL IRRESPONSIBILITY AND SOME FIRMS MINIMIZE CORPORATE SOCIAL RESPONSIBILITY

Duane Windsor

There is increasing focus by scholars on corporate social irresponsibility (CSI), which they explicitly distinguish from corporate social responsibility (CSR). Some firms may maximize CSI: recent illustrations include Enron and Siemens. Social welfare would be improved directly by reducing CSI (Armstrong, 1977; Armstrong & Green, 2013) toward strict legal compliance. The focus on CSI reveals a significant gap between CSI and CSR. A case against CSI is not automatically a case for CSR (see Campbell, 2007; Carroll & Shabana, 2010); rather a case against CSI is simply a case for strict legal compliance. Encouraging CSR may be less socially valuable than discouraging CSI. CSR has been subjected to various criticisms (see Okoye, 2009), and scholars have proposed various alternatives (see Schwartz & Carroll, 2008). There are essentially no normative or strategic

Corporate Social Performance:
Paradoxes, Pitfalls, and Pathways to the Better World, pp. 79–101
Copyright © 2015 by Information Age Publishing
79

cases for CSI because of the social harms caused, unlike the situation of proposed normative and strategic cases (however disputed) for CSR defined broadly as including strict legal compliance and voluntary corporate citizenship behaviors beyond legal duties. There are thus anti-CSI, pro-compliance, and procitizenship arguments. In contrast to Campbell (2007), the interest here is on why some firms may minimize CSR through citizenship avoidance and lowest-cost legal compliance although avoiding CSI maximization. Investigation into CSI is more about antecedents and consequences of socially undesirable behaviors and how to discourage such behaviors than about normative or strategic justifications. Investigation into CSR is more about antecedents and consequences of socially desirable but individually and organizationally avoidable behaviors. An argument for procitizenship behavior is that it may be an organizational and societal hedge (or insurance) against CSI practices by individuals.

What is particularly desirable is improved systematic understanding of individual motives, organizational settings, and public policy issues in influencing anti-CSI and pro-CSR choices. The term "firm" as used here can mean quite different scenarios. There may be a corrupt organizational culture supporting CSI or an organizational culture focused on profit seeking that while not promoting CSI also promotes CSR minimization. There may be an important set of executives, directors, and employees who engage in CSI or avoid CSR. Public policy may be limited or expansive, permissive or restrictive. The chapter addresses this fundamental, unre-solved question to help identify a desirable research program for future scholarship. This chapter undertakes to advance theoretical and empiri-cal understanding of reasons for occurrences of CSI behaviors and CSR avoidance. Scholarly understanding of the antecedents or determinants of CSI practices or CSR avoidance is particularly far from well devel-oped presently, despite prior theoretical and empirical investigation. The chapter does not formally explicate a fully developed framework, but does emphasize throughout the importance of more research into the roles of individual motives, organizational settings, and public policy issues in affecting anti-CSI and pro-CSR behaviors.

The concept of irresponsibility has emerged in the literature as what has been characterized as an interesting theoretical move for questioning whether businesses are always or necessarily socially responsible (Jones, Bowd, & Tench, 2009). One recent definition of CSI is a socially harmful action that a manager would not knowingly undertake acting for his or her own welfare, or that a reasonable person would expect to cause substantive net harm when considering all parties (Armstrong & Green, 2013). The key point made in this proposed theoretical move is that the historical conception of responsibility tended to presume that managers should practice CSR (Carroll & Shabana, 2010), whereas there seem to be instances suggesting that managers practice CSI (actions) or produce social harms (consequences) whether intentionally or inadvertently. The present author adds that there is reason to consider whether firms not practicing CSI nevertheless try to minimize CSR.

There is continuing controversy over whether the empirical evidence supports a positive or negative relationship between corporate social performance (CSP), or CSR, and corporate financial performance (CFP) (see dramatically contrasting findings in Flammer, 2013a; Godfrey, Merrill, & Hansen, 2009; Griffin & Mahon, 1997; McWilliams & Siegel, 2000; Orlitzky, Schmidt, & Rynes, 2003; Orlitzky & Swanson, 2008). However, while evidence of a positive relationship arguably supports CSR strategy, evidence of a negative relationship does not support CSI strategy but only serves to limit CSR initiatives. CSI involves social harm; CSR involves private cost inhibiting strict legal compliance and additional citizenship behaviors. It is also possible that there is no strong average relationship among CFP, CSI, and CSR (Barnett & Salomon, 2006, 2012, propose a curvilinear relationship to address this difficulty); and that instead motives, actions, and results vary greatly by firm (Wood, 1991). Measurement of multi-dimensional CSP involves significant problems in operationalization, data collection, and weighting (Epstein & Yuthas, 2014; Wood, 2010). One possibility is that CSI is somehow better suited to a shareholder-oriented business model, while CSR is somehow better suited to a stakeholder-oriented business model (Jones, Bowd, & Tench, 2009). Hillman and Keim (2001) reported empirical findings that shareholder value was promoted by effective stakeholder management but not by social issues management. Jones, Bowd, and Tench thus advance a CSI-CSR model or theoretical framework for improving empirical research.

The idea and terminology of CSI is not strictly new (Armstrong, 1977; Mitchell, 2001). What is new is the scholarly interest in irresponsibility and the emphasis on theoretical development of the approach and empirical research linked to that report (Murphy & Schlegelmilch, 2013; Tench, Sun, & Jones, 2012). This scholarly interest should be linked to research into CSR avoidance. While reducing CSI implies improved legal compliance, that improvement does not necessarily affect CSR avoidance.

The rest of this chapter is organized as follows. In the next section, following a brief literature review, the author explicates a theoretical framework or conception for the relationship between CSI and CSR. In the subsequent section, the author provides an interpretation of what the empirical literature on CSI appears to find. In the next section, the author discusses what is known about reasons for corporate social irresponsibility. The concluding section summarizes the chapter's arguments and implications.

A THEORETICAL CONCEPTION FOR
UNDERSTANDING CSI AND CSR

One reason for renewed interest in CSI may be the developmental history of CSR scholarship. A large literature concerning CSR traces back to at least the early 1950s with some earlier foundations (Carroll & Shabana, 2010). The CSR idea does not seem to be a unified theoretical paradigm. One recent interpretation of CSR's developmental history identifies evolving phases by decades (Moura-Leite & Padgett, 2011). In this interpretation, the 1950s focused on business responsibilities to society and good deeds; the 1960s concerned dramatic social changes; the 1970s featured business managers applying traditional management functions to CSR issues; the 1980s emphasized stakeholder responsiveness; the 1990s saw almost universal approval of CSR (with dissents); the 2000s then saw CSR become an important strategic issue. The extant CSR and related CSP literatures are layered one upon another over time in shifting phases; and there are partly complementary and partly substitute approaches such as business ethics, corporate citizenship, stakeholder management, and sustainable development (Schwartz & Carroll, 2008). One might charitably understand a view that there is chaos in CSR literature and practice.

There are thus divided opinions on how CSR has developed to the present. In the 2000s, the literature shifted to strategic CSR, in which CSR activities support the longer-term reputation and success of the firm. One may point out that criticism of CSR as corporate altruism and criticism of CSI as social harm do both presume legal compliance by managers. No one advocates violation of law in the conventional sense (leaving aside the special topic of civil disobedience). However, there is a considerable difference between critics of CSR who also advocate minimal governmental intervention in the economy (there are critics of voluntary CSR who advocate expanded government intervention) and critics of CSI who advocate expanded government regulation. There is also some growing sentiment that strategic CSR in the 2000s has led to CSR initiatives being undertaken for strictly profit-maximization motives and is now essentially a business-supporting ideology (Demmerling, 2014; Fleming & Jones, 2013). There is also some growing sentiment that anti-business activists have seized control of the CSR agenda and are pressuring companies unduly (Chatterji & Listokin, 2007). CSR has become, in this latter view, a combination of enticing or bullying firms into more and more initiatives on behalf of various causes such as employee pay, environmental protection, labor conditions in developing countries, U.S. on-shoring, diversity, inner-school education, and healthier food (Chatterji & Listokin, 2007). CSI appears to be a possible path out of this thicket through focusing on more readily identified and criticized illegal and unethical behaviors rather than on inducing what some may characterize as difficult to limit altruistic behaviors.

A second reason, articulated by Armstrong (1977), is that responsibility is apparently difficult to define while irresponsibility is apparently easier to define. Armstrong explained the definition problem as follows. Promoting responsibility requires specifying what a manager should do. Deterring irresponsibility requires specifying what a manager should not do. Prohibition is easier to address than exhortation. Armstrong defined social irresponsibility as a decision to accept an alternative that the decision maker thinks is inferior to some alternative when considering the effects upon all parties. A typical instance would be when one party gains at the expense of the whole system or set of other parties. This instance, one may note, violates Pareto's efficiency standard which requires that no party lose when another party gains. Armstrong also pointed out that the stockholder-oriented business model may encourage socially irresponsible acts not because managers violate duty but rather precisely because managers seek to do their duty understood as fiduciary. The difficulty is that the fiduciary responsibility approach may occur at the expense of society. How the manager should implement the shareholder-oriented business model or achieve CSR outcomes seems much more difficult to define in contrast. Armstrong pointed out that not being irresponsible might be much more of a contribution to social welfare than trying to be responsible.

A third reason lies in the long-lived controversy over whether voluntary CSR (interpreted as corporate altruism) is sound policy for a firm. The case against voluntary CSR is put as normative: a violation of agent fiduciary responsibility. The case permitting voluntary CSR is strategic. CSR may simply prove to be a contested terrain without theoretical solution (Okoye, 2009). Rather scholars and managers have reasons for supporting or opposing CSR as typically defined in the literature. The available empirical evidence, cited earlier, is not sufficient to overcome these reasons strongly in either direction; some authors find a negative relationship and some authors find a positive relationship. Barnett and Salomon (2006, 2012) propose a curvilinear relationship in which both negative and positive findings can be explained. In addition to the ideological criticism of CSR noted above, there is a theoretical objection to voluntary CSR based on agency. The manager is supposed to be a fiduciary agent of the owners, and CSR construed as altruism is arguably a violation of that duty. This violation argument cannot overcome a strategic rationale for voluntary CSR to build firm reputation and thus future performance success. There is a sense, however, in which purely altruistic CSR is a problem, particularly if it is difficult to define responsibility as noted by Armstrong. There is possibly a tendency to view CSR as profit-reducing (Reinhardt & Stavins, 2010, seem to take this perspective concerning environmental stewardship), while

CSI may be viewed as profit-enhancing (at least in the short run for both CSR and CSI). The strategic rationale for voluntary CSR is long run, so the time horizons do not match.

This section now explicates a theoretical conception or framework for explaining the relationship between CSI and CSR. The author separates corporate behavior into responsible and irresponsible categories. Each category requires more careful definition. CSI may have been promoted by emphasis on profit seeking and agency theory in business education promoting a culture of greed relative to character virtues such as honesty and trustworthiness involving sacrifice of material gain (Gintis & Khurana, 2007). A survey of 401 financial executives, supplemented by in-depth interviews with another 20, reports that 78% would trade economic value to maintain smooth earnings (i.e., would engage in earnings management). Some 55% would avoid initiating a very positive net present value (NPV) project if the result was to miss current quarter consensus earnings (Graham, Harvey, & Rajgopal, 2005).

A first step here is to isolate the arguments for and against both CSI and CSR. Table 5.1 provides a layout of the arguments. In a simple two-by-two framework, the horizontal stub distinguishes between a case for and a case against. The vertical stub distinguishes between CSR and CSI. The case for CSR is a combination of a normative or ethical rationale and a strategic or prescriptive rationale. The two rationales may be reinforcing: the ethically right action is the strategically correct action. If the two rationales are in conflict, such that the right action is costly strategically, then the decision problem is which rationale is superior in particular circumstances or over time. The case against CSR is the shareholder model: voluntary CSR or corporate altruism is a diversion of corporate resources. Even the case against CSR (which cannot overturn a strategic rationale for CSR) is not a case for CSI. While the boundary between for and against in the framework of Table 5.1 has to do with profitability, the boundary between CSR and CSI is legal compliance. CSR is here action beyond legal requirements, while CSI involves violation of law or where the law is permissive the generation of social harm that is morally wrong. There is no viable case for legal and ethical violations (disregarding special conditions for civil disobedience). The case against CSI is thus a combination of the ethical and strategic rationales for CSR and also the shareholder model to which CSI is likely to be costly. There is no viable case for CSI, unless one wants to argue something like laissez-faire Darwinism amounting to ruthless competition without rules beyond survival of the fittest. The burden of proof is on the proponent of a case for CSI. The dividing line in Table 4.1 between CSR and CSI along the vertical stub is legal compliance. CSR requires at least minimal compliance.

Table 5.1.   A Simple Framework for the CSI-CSR Relationship

	Case	
	For	*Against*
CSR	Ethical Rationale	Shareholder Model
	Strategic Rationale	
CSI	[there is no defensible case]	Ethical Rationale
		Strategic Rationale
		Shareholder Model

A responsible firm complies strictly with just law (criminal and civil) as a minimum standard. (Just law implies an exception for civil disobedience situations, as illustrated by Google in China.) A responsible firm also complies strictly with ethical norms against doing wrong and imposing harm even if not legally mandatory obligations; but this case is more difficult to demonstrate. While one can argue a case for responsibility exceeding legal and ethical compliance, this case becomes a set of issues in philanthropy (altruism) and stakeholder engagement contributing to strategic success over time. This philanthropy/engagement case is separable from compliance.

Irresponsibility is violation of legal and/or strong ethical norms. Irresponsible behavior can be traced to a number of reasons and associated conditions. A causal framework should include individual motives, organizational settings, and public policy issues. A corporation as such (an artificial person at law) does not have motives. (The purpose of profit seeking is attributed to the investors organizing the firm. But the investors hire executives as agents to operate the firm.) The individuals within the corporation do have motives and choices. One can differentiate between intentional and inadvertent irresponsibility; and among organizational culture, executive irresponsibility, and employee irresponsibility. CSI occurs within a public policy framework, including a governmental license (or corporate charter) to operate—which some have argued should be revocable (Noonan, 2012, applied to BP North America).

Intentional irresponsibility involves one or more individuals engaging in some form of violation of legal and/or ethical norms for personal gain in some form (direct or indirect, immediate or longer term). Executive fraud or employee theft, or bribery or kickbacks, involve intentionality. Inadvertent irresponsibility involves an error of judgment or action by someone. Negative externalities, unanticipated or unrecognized, often involve inadvertence (for instance, accidental pollution). Whether intentional or inadvertent, corporate irresponsibility involves a claim by some other party that a policy or an act is socially irresponsible. For instance, labor unions may argue that employees should not voluntarily work on a holiday even for additional compensation, because base compensation should be raised. Whether a particular argument demonstrates corporate irresponsibility is typically disputable: in the instance cited, consumers and stockholders as well as volunteering employees arguably benefit. Defining a policy or action as socially irresponsible thus involves a judgment. In contrast, voluntary corporate citizenship is a business decision.

Figure 5.1 provides a more detailed depiction of the relationship between CSI and CSR in a regulated market economy. Regulation has the broad sense of criminal law, civil law, and public policy affecting a firm (Wilson, 1989). The level and distribution of social welfare are determined by the interaction of the market economy and government action. This chapter is not concerned with the theory of the optimal level and content of such regulation, which might be limited or expansive; or of the optimal level and composition of public goods provided by government. The vertical axis only defines strict legal compliance by firms with extant regulations, whether limited or expansive, given the market economy and public goods provision. The point at which the vertical axis intersects the horizontal axis measures change in social welfare resulting from strict legal compliance as 0, because that point reflects the social welfare jointly determined by the market economy and government action. There is no change in social welfare due to strict legal compliance. The horizontal axis then measures change in social welfare due to CSI or CSR relative to this zero point. Viewing the figure on the page, the region left of the vertical axis measures social harm (additional negative effects on social welfare) due to CSI. Such harm can arise from legal violations or ethical misconduct even if permitted by extant regulations. The region located to the left of the vertical axis concerns business ethics, defined in terms of strict compliance with the letter of the law and also ethical conduct reflecting the spirit of the law. The region located to the right of the vertical axis measures social benefit (additional positive effects on social welfare) from corporate citizenship conduct beyond legal requirements. A firm or executive cannot add to social welfare by strict legal compliance, but can add to social welfare by citizenship actions. The dashed vertical line to the right of the vertical axis suggests some likely limited to citizenship costs that a firm or executive can or will agree to bear. CSR has the meaning of strict legal compliance (meaning no CSI) and corporate citizenship beyond such compliance.

The vertical axis is explicitly positioned to the right side of the framework, rather than in the center of the framework. (Windsor, 2013, provides an earlier and more general exposition in which the vertical axis is located at the center of the framework.) In Figure 5.2, social harm and social benefit are not equidistant from the zero point at which the vertical axis intersects the horizontal axis. The distance along the horizontal axis thus

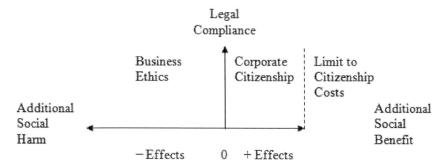

Figure 5.1.   A restatement of CSI and CSR.

explicitly reflects differential impact on social welfare. Following Armstrong (1977), CSI arguably has considerably greater and negative impact on social welfare. To reduce CSI is to improve social welfare correspondingly. Minimization of CSI is thus desirable: private benefit is irrelevant. CSR has considerably less if positive impact on social welfare. There is some debate in the literature over whether voluntary CSR—whether practiced on ethical or strategic rationales—has much discernible effect on social welfare. Voluntary CSR has some limit in private cost to the firm.

It should be noted that the deeper issue is the relationship between firm cost and social benefit. For voluntary CSR, some limited social benefit greater than limited firm cost is still some contribution to social welfare. Rising firm cost will at some point exceed and thus limit social benefit. For CSI, the likely relationship is always social harm greater than the firm's financial gain, such that moving to zero CSI is socially desirable (unless a social opportunity cost rationale is stated).

The relationship between CSI and CSR involves defining the role of legal compliance. CSI has the typical meaning of violation of law, or at least of strong ethical norms. CSR is frequently treated as voluntary altruism or strategically motivated action beyond legal obligation. This definition of CSR was advanced basically to force the idea of CSR into purely voluntary altruism as a violation of the shareholder model and not a legal obligation. There is however a separation in CSR between immediate costs to the firm and long-term benefits to the firm.

Figure 5.1 depiction adopts specific language to help clarify these issues. The vertical axis is a market economy operating on a foundation of laws with which businesses should comply. Effectively, the vertical axis is the institutional structure of a country. As long as a firm complies with the law, then the firm is free to operate in the market economy. The horizontal axis concerns impact of business actions on social welfare. The vertical axis is anchored as a zero point along the horizontal axis. At this point is measured directly the social welfare produced by lawful functioning of the market economy. That point is set to zero when measuring the effects of CSI or CSR beyond legal compliance. Left of the vertical axis is additional social harm (that is, some negative impact on social welfare) and right of the vertical axis is additional social benefit (that is, a positive impact on social welfare) beyond the benefit generated by functioning of the market economy. CSI can arise from violation of laws; such violation generates some social harm. CSR can be defined as voluntary altruism beyond legal requirements. However, CSI can also arise from violation of ethical norms beyond legal standards—in a mirror image formulation that is the opposite of voluntary altruism. There are strategic rationales for voluntary CSR. The horizontal axis left of the vertical axis is the region of business ethics (suggesting a strong prohibition against social harm) and the horizontal axis right of the vertical axis is the region of corporate citizenship (suggesting some expectation of social benefit). Given this conceptualization, then CSI takes definition as violation of legal standards and ethical norms resulting in social harm. CSR takes definition as the combination of legal compliance and corporate citizenship. The vertical axis in Figure 5.1 corresponds to the boundary between CSI and CSR in Table 5.1: that boundary is anchored on legal compliance. An irresponsible firm may violate laws or be in legal compliance but violate ethical norms beyond the law. A responsible firm may be in legal compliance and also practice corporate citizenship.

The private equivalent of legal compliance is the business code of conduct. As Chatterji and Levine (2006) point out, major customers (e.g., Gap, Levi-Strauss, & Nike) and certifying organizations (e.g., Fair Labor Association, ISO 14000, and SA 8000) may require "social responsibility" of third-world suppliers in apparel manufacturing. However, it should be noted that customer-imposed codes are by voluntary contract and certification codes are by voluntary consent. These codes may combine CSI (prohibitions) and CSR (aspirations). Business codes in this context may combine features that in government might be separated into criminal law, civil law, and public policy (Wilson, 1989). In any case, the content in such codes is more likely weighted against CSI. Similarly, ratings may involve some dimensions that are CSI as well as CSR under the overall rubric of corporate social responsibility (see Chatterji, Levine, & Toffel, 2009; Chatterji & Toffel, 2010). One may expect that if social ratings do not accurately reflect CSR, then social ratings may not accurately reflect CSI. The question would be whether CSI is more readily defined and measured than CSR.

INTERPRETING EMPIRICAL EVIDENCE ON CSI

This section adapts the curvilinear findings of Barnett and Salomon (2006, 2012) as an approach to interpreting empirical evidence on CSI. In 2006, those authors argued for moving beyond dichotomous findings—socially responsible investing (SRI) is good or bad for financial returns—to a curvilinear interpretation. The study measured the financial performance —social performance relationship within mutual funds practicing socially responsible investing (SRI). SRI fund managers can use a number of social screening strategies. The authors tested a panel of 61 SRI funds over the period 1972–2000. The findings suggest that as the SRI fund increases the number of social screens used, financial returns first decline and then rebound as the number of screens approaches a maximum. (The likely logic is that more screens initially eliminate more higher-yield stocks, while approaching a maximum assembles a more profitable portfolio.) Within these findings, community relations screening increased financial performance while environmental and labor relations screening had the opposite effect. The study thus shifts the debate from SRI to the merits of different social screening strategies. Expressed somewhat differently, some SRI approaches may be better than other SRI approaches; and a comparison of average SRI and average non-SRI financial performance may conceal as much information as it reveals. The 2012 study found a curvilinear effect for firms (using KLD information for CSP measures). The authors found that firms with low CSP measures and firms with high CSP measures have higher CSP than firms with moderate CSP; and that firms with high CSP have higher CFP than firms with low CSP. The theoretical argument for the study is that firms can benefit from CSR as a function of the firm's stakeholder influence capacity.

A different study reinforces the general findings of Barnett and Salomon. The authors (Oikonomou, Brooks, & Pavelin, 2014) point out that typically firms are a mix of positive and negative CSP indicators. (As a result, characterizing a particular firm's CSP profile can be difficult.) Stakeholders evaluate positive indicators in the context of negative indicators, and negative indicators in the context of positive indicators. A U.S. panel study finds the following curvilinear relationship: firms exhibiting solely positive or solely negative indicators outperform firms exhibiting both positive and negative indicators. The authors infer, in this instance, that stakeholders reward CSR uniformity—in either direction.

Figure 5.2 depicts the Barnett and Salomon curvilinear hypothesis in general form. The vertical axis is some measure of CFP. There are accounting based and market based measures. Market value effects may be separated from cash flow results by shareholder reactions in turn possibly influenced by other stakeholder reactions; shareholders and other

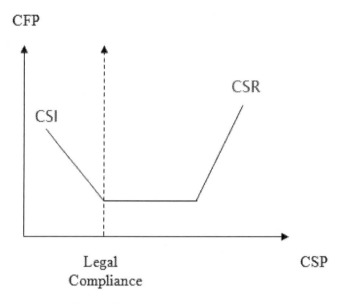

Figure 5.2. A generally curvilinear relationship between corporate financial performance (CFP) and corporate social performance (CSP) mMeasures.

stakeholders may have anti-CSI and pro-CSR preferences (Mackey, Mackey, & Barney, 2007). The horizontal axis is some measure of CSP. (How to operationalize and measure CSP or CSR is a matter of continuing debate. Here CSP can be conceptualized in terms of effect on social welfare. Thus CSR still has the sense of legal compliance and corporate citizenship in some combination.) In general, the hypothesis shown in Figure 5.2 is that CSI can be profitable—at least in the short run, while CSR can be profitable—at least in the long run. And ignoring presently how the short run and long run relate, long-run CSR is more profitable than long-run CSI, even if short-run CSI is more profitable than short-run CSR. By construction, the relationship between CSI and CFP can be positive (i.e., CSI can be profitable) and more profitable than moderate CSP; but the relationship between CSR and CFP can be positive and even more profitable than the relationship between CSI and CFP.

The reader can observe that the general curvilinear hypothesis of Figure 5.2 can be directly superimposed on the vertical and horizontal axes of Figure 5.1. It is necessary only to move the vertical axis of Figure 5.2 to the right; and then the depiction is of Figure 5.1. Rather than providing an additional figure for this limited purpose, the shift is shown by the dashed vertical line in Figure 5.2 which is strict legal compliance as defined in Figure 5.1. Thus the CSI profitability of a firm by construction occurs at social harm, while the CSR profitability of a firm occurs at social benefit as does moderate CSP. However, CSR profitability must be separated into legal compliance and voluntary altruism undertaken for ethical and/or strategic rationales.

There is some empirical evidence suggesting that CSI may be punished in the short run, while CSR may be rewarded only in the long run—and for CSR as an accumulation of stakeholder support over time (Barnett & Salomon, 2012). Arnold and Engelen (2007) reported findings that stock prices react negatively on the announcement date of corporate misconduct. This negative reaction may be temporary, but the findings suggest the reaction is present (see Shiau, Li, & Yang, 2012). A similar finding has been reported for the U.S. banking industry (Zeidan, 2013). For a sample of 128 publicly traded banks subjected to enforcement actions by U.S. regulatory authorities over a 20-year period, there was a significant negative market reaction pursuant to the violations. Market reaction did not vary meaningfully in accordance with the severity or repetitiveness of the violation. This finding partly supports and partly contradicts Baucus and Baucus (1997), discussed immediately below. Those authors found that severity did not matter, but multiple convictions did. However, the Baucus and Baucus study did not focus on the banking industry.

There has been some evidence that corporate illegality shows longer-term negative performance effects. Older findings indicated that following a conviction firms experienced lower accounting returns over five years and slower sales growth in the third, fourth, and fifth years (Baucus & Baucus, 1997). The seriousness of a specific illegality was not a significant matter—the conviction itself was sufficient, but multiple convictions caused strong stakeholder responses affecting accounting returns and sales growth. Relevant to this chapter's inquiry into reasons for CSI, the authors did not find that reduced financial performance deterred subsequent illegal behavior. (Indeed, it is plausible that reduced financial performance might stimulate future illegal behavior as a means of financial recovery.)

An event study of announcement of corporate environmental news announcements for all U.S. publicly traded firms during 1980–2009 finds a significant positive stock market reaction to responsibility news and a significant negative stock market reaction to irresponsibility news (Flammer, 2013b). These findings are in line with previous evidence. The study argues further that the value of environmental CSR depends on a set of external and internal moderators. External pressure to behave responsibly increases punishment for irresponsible behavior and reduces reward for responsible behavior. This argument reinforces the idea expressed in this chapter that CSI is more damaging than CSR is beneficial. Flammer finds that the negative stock market reaction has increased over time, while the positive stock market reaction has decreased over time. Flammer further argues that environmental CSR is a resource with decreasing marginal returns and insurance-like features. Thus the positive or negative stock market reaction to events is smaller for companies with higher levels of environmental CSR. That is to say, the higher the environmental CSR performance, the smaller the stock market reaction whether positive or negative. But for purposes of this chapter, higher environmental CSR performance is preferred and provides a kind of buffer or insurance against CSI at the firm level.

REASONS FOR CORPORATE SOCIAL IRRESPONSIBILITY

In keeping with the depiction in Figure 5.1, CSI can be decomposed into illegal violations (non-compliance with law) and unethical violations—both having the consequence of imposing social harm. Inquiry into causes of illegal and unethical behaviors has a long history (Alexander & Cohen, 1996). However, it is not yet clear that there is a robust and sufficient theory of reasons explaining CSI.

The proposed institutional theory of CSR (Campbell, 2007) seeks to identify conditions under which corporations are likely to behave in socially responsible ways. The theory mediates the relationship between basic economic conditions and corporate behavior through institutional conditions. Such institutional conditions may include public and private regulation, nongovernmental and other independent organizations monitoring corporate behavior, institutionalized norms for corporate behavior, associative behavior among corporations, and organized dialogues with stakeholders—as examples (see Brammer, Jackson, & Matten, 2012). One study suggests, drawing on experimental evidence, that public policies to encourage responsible behavior and discourage irresponsible behavior are likely to increase social welfare only if firms freely adopt such policies and without government subsidy. Mandated CSR is arguably distorting and might increase likelihood of CSI decisions. CSR policies can provide firms with opportunities for profit. Relatively free markets, civil law (torts and contracts), and business codes of ethics emphasizing fair treatment of stakeholders and long-term profitability can reduce the likelihood of CSI decisions (Armstrong & Green, 2013).

A study of clearly illegal corporate behavior tested for a 19-year period using event history analysis and data found that large firms operating in dynamic and munificent environments were most likely to commit illegal acts (Baucus & Near, 1991). In contrast, firms with poor performance were least likely to do so. This contrast depended partly on industry and the firm's history of prior violations which increased the likelihood of illegal behavior. Some industries and firms are more prone to misbehavior. (These findings suggest that illegal behavior in large firms is induced by opportunity, while poorly performing firms may not have opportunity.)

The early research tradition suggested that external and internal factors pressure a firm in ways that lead managers to commit illegal acts rationally as a calculus of expected benefits and costs. Baucus (1994) pointed out that there are also conditions of opportunity and predisposition on the one hand, and unintended consequences of otherwise apparently appropriate decisions on the other hand. The author proposed a multivariate model of illegal behavior in which the situational factors of pressure, opportunity, and/or predisposition lead to unintentional or intentional illegality. Thus a predisposition in combination with an opportunity under pressure may increase likelihood of illegal behavior—with the possibility that the outcome is unintentional. Characteristics of the individual actor affect likelihood of illegality.

Based in the developing field of behavioral ethics (see Ashkanasy, Windsor, & Treviño, 2006; Tenbrunsel, Diekmann, Wade-Benzoni, & Bazerman, 2010; Tenbrunsel & Smith-Crowe, 2008), a recent meta-analysis of over 30 years of research in multiple literatures looks at the relationship among three kinds of antecedents of unethical choices (Kish-Gephart, Harrison, & Treviño, 2010). The three antecedents are characterized as "bad apple" (the individual), the "bad case" (a moral issue), and the "bad barrel" (the organizational environment). One might think of the relationship among the three antecedents as accumulating likelihood of unethical behavior: bad apple within bad case within bad barrel will maximize likelihood; removal of one or more antecedent conditions will reduce and then minimize likelihood. There will thus be mixed results. The authors argue the meta-analysis and structural equation modeling provide empirical support for complex multidetermined choices. The analysis also isolated "ethical impulse" as well as "ethical calculus" perspectives. The study sheds new light on arguments concerning ethical climate and ethical culture in organizations. Behavioral ethics research suggests that individuals think of themselves as more ethical in intention than they are in actual choices.

An organizational culture, or climate, may be disposed to irresponsible conduct (or responsible conduct) at all levels. Culture, or climate, is not the same as arguing that a firm (an artificial person) is irresponsible: rather, all individuals within the firm have basically the same disposition. Irresponsibility (or responsibility) may occur among executives; or among employees below the executive levels. Causes for CSI may be separated into failure of managerial or employee values and cognition (understanding), failure of institutional pressures (law enforcement and stakeholder activism), and profit-oriented pressures (internally and externally). These causes (or factors) may bear differently on different individuals.

There is an interesting question as to whether senior executives alone are the appropriate target in promoting CSR or deterring CSI (Mackey, Mackey, & Barney, 2008). Personal commitment to CSR or personal

CSI misconduct may increase likelihood of such activities. However, the authors argue that such executive-level involvement is neither necessary nor sufficient. Reformers can target executive preferences or different firm stakeholders.

Irresponsibility can be analyzed in terms of motives, actions, and consequences (Wood, 1991); and also specific circumstances of a violation. There is a crucial difference between rational calculation to violate civil law norms on expectation that benefits outweigh fines (Wokutch & Spencer, 1987); and irrational predisposition to violate criminal law norms. How to link these dimensions together is not well studied. What defines irresponsibility most clearly are socially bad consequences: someone (a stakeholder) suffers, and for no good reason. A bad culture inclines executives and employees to irresponsible actions generating such socially bad consequences. (The term social includes specific stakeholder groups.) A typical claim (Mitchell, 2001) is that focus on short-term profits leads to actions that generate stakeholder harms (including long-term harms to stockholders through repercussions.) The claim involves the marked difficulty of getting individuals to appreciate short-term versus long-term results.

An analysis of senior executive fraud draws on fields of psychology, sociology, economics, and criminology to identify antecedents at societal, industry, and firm levels to individual differences affecting likelihood and degree of fraud (Zahra, Priem, & Rasheed, 2005). This approach illustrates the complexity of identifying reasons for CSI. There are multiple fields and several levels of antecedents. One might think of a funnel of causality operating vertically from society through industry and firm to individual, with some factors promoting and other factors inhibiting fraud.

Enron has been characterized as a prototypical instance of corporate fraud (Beenen & Pinto, 2009). The Beenen and Pinto (2009) analysis is of mechanisms resulting in pervasive organization-wide corruption capable of involving even ethical individuals (Bansal & Kandola, 2003). The authors propose a four-part approach for helping prevention and resistance by individuals. The four components are perceive, probe, protest, and persist. Another analysis of antecedents attributes those mechanisms to problems in organizational design: bonus plans promoting reported earnings; mark-to-market accounting approved by the U.S. Securities and Exchange Commission (SEC) increasing those reported earnings; and permitting the chief financial officer to make the finance function into a profit center. These antecedents were put in place some 5 to 10 years before the December 2001 bankruptcy reorganization filing (Stewart, 2006). Aggressive earnings targets result in bad capital commitments. In 1999, the international energy division requested funding for a plan involving $100 million profit on capital of $7 billion (a nominal return of less than 1.5%). Such commitments involved a pattern of economic profit losses over time. In consequence, the chief financial officer was under increasing pressure to use fraud and deception to postpone the inevitable outcome. Performance measures and internal control failures were as important as ethical failures.

A matched sample of 103 firms convicted of issuing fraudulent financial statements during 1992–1996 found that likelihood of conviction increased with concentration of power by insiders (Dunn, 2004). Insiders controlled the top management team and the board of directors, including through ownership interest.

An interesting finding is that firms may engage in CSR to offset CSI (Kotchen & Moon, 2012). This finding may link back to arguments about how positive and negative dimensions of CSP are related. The study uses a 15-year panel of nearly 3,000 publicly traded companies to support this finding. The study also finds evidence of heterogeneity among industries. The effect—engaging in CSR to offset CSI—is stronger in those industries where CSI is subjected to greater public scrutiny. The authors investigate degree of substitutability between categories of CSR and CSI. There is a strong within-category relationship for community relations, environment, and human rights. The within-category relationship for corporate governance is weak. CSI related to corporate governance increases CSR in most other categories. The authors infer that firms appear to offset corporate governance problems with CSR in other categories rather than trying to reform corporate governance. An early study of organizational performance pointed out dimensions of philanthropic and illegal activity—illustrating the possible relationship of CSR and CSI (Wokutch & Spencer, 1987).

CONCLUSION

The available literature does provide some useful guidance to identifying reasons for CSI maximization and CSR minimization. But this guidance is in disjointed fragments, as scholars work to develop a systematically tested multivariate model of antecedents, mechanisms, and consequences of CSI. A more coherent research agenda is desirable, as CSI investigation becomes more widely embraced. It is also important to understand CSR minimization. Some basic elements are sketched below in this concluding section.

The framework sketched in this chapter includes individual motives, organizational settings, and public policy issues. Individuals—executives, directors, and employees—make choices; organizations do not. Organizational settings can range from corrupt climates encouraging individual misconduct to more ethical climates that may discourage misconduct but not necessarily foster citizenship. Public policy, treated in this chapter as various approaches to regulation, may or may not be particularly effective in helping to foster socially desirable organizational climates and/or discourage individual misconduct.

Lange and Washburn (2012) note that CSR literature tends to emphasize broader social structures such as value systems, institutions, and stakeholder relations. Those authors draw on attribution theory to focus on the social reality of external expectations rooted in the perceptions of the individual observer. They argue that attributions of CSI draw on the individual observer's subjective assessments of the undesirability of an effect, culpability of the firm for that effect, and non-complicity of an affected party. They suggest further that the observer also perceives firm characteristics and may have some degree of social identification with ether the affected party or the corporation. The observer is thus framing CSI attributions. (An observer may frame CSR similarly, but the empirical evidence cited earlier tends to suggest that CSI is more strongly affecting than is CSR.)

The literature, emphasizing CSR to date, has tended to focus on development and testing of a multidimensional (and perhaps time-phased) model of antecedents and outcomes of ethical or CSR behavior (Baker, Hunt, & Andrews, 2006). Those authors tested for antecedents conceptualized as corporate ethical values, organizational justice, and organizational commitment; and also examined organizational citizenship behaviors. They gathered data from a regional chapter of the National Association of Purchasing Managers (NAPM) ($N = 489$). The antecedents seemed to have influence on, in this instance, ethical behavior outcomes. In parallel, future scholarship can continue to develop and test a multidimensional (and perhaps time-phased) model of antecedents and outcomes of CSI behavior. Behaviors and mechanisms are arguably even more important in CSI than in CSR. The former involves violation of legal and ethical standards, while the latter concerns compliance and voluntary action beyond prevailing requirements.

A problem for predictive models of CSR and CSI is the levels of analysis involved in considering societal, organizational, and individual factors. Personal traits may place a given individual at high risk of misconduct (Price & Norris, 2009). Demographic factors may also affect alternative modes of rationalizing choices concerning CSI. One study of a sample of 312 fraud-committing and control firms finds support for predictions that younger, less functionally experienced CEOs and CEOs without business degrees are more likely to rationalize accounting fraud as acceptable. CEO stock options also predict fraud; and this prediction is not moderated by demographics (Troy, Smith, & Domino, 2011).

The organization itself is still a sort of "black box" for either CSR or CSI behaviors. Not much is understood as yet about the intermediate mechanisms that link corporate ethics (or its absence) to CFP (Chun, Shin, Choi, & Kim, 2013). Those authors use institutional theory and strategic human resource management literature to hypothesize that internal collective processes based on employees' collective organizational commitment and interpersonal organizational citizenship behavior function as mediators. They test hypotheses on data for 130 South Korean companies and 3,821 of their employees. The authors find support for those hypotheses. The findings, as the authors note, indicate that microprocesses within an organization are important. The same point may be relevant to CSI.

There is a lack of evidence concerning the effect of legislation and law enforcement on CSI. Harte (2012) conducted a study of Fortune 500 firms using data for 1990-2007 and sampling, analyzing the Sarbanes-Oxley Act of 2002 as an event with a 5 year preperiod and a 5 year postperiod. The approach permits the author to see whether prior violations and CSR behavior affected future illegal corporate behavior. The author did find some moderating effect due to the act. The effect may be a result of increased punishments and harsher penalties.

There are likely variations across types of misbehavior and between individuals and firms. Karpoff, Lee, and Martin (2008) tracked all 2,206 individuals who were responsible parties for all 788 SEC and Department of Justice enforcement actions for financial misrepresentation during a multiyear period (January 1, 1978–September 30, 2006). The authors report that 93% lost their jobs; 28% faced criminal charges and penalties with prison sentences averaging 4.3 years. The same authors report on U.S. Foreign Corrupt Practices Act (FCPA) enforcement actions (1978 to May 2013) (Karpoff, Lee, & Martin, 2004). They estimate that 22.9% of Compustat-listed firms with foreign sales engaged in prosecutable bribery at least once during the sample period with a 6.4% probability of a bribery charge. Firms commingling financial fraud and bribery charges faced reputational losses as well as large fines and investigation costs; but firms facing bribery charges only did not suffer reputational losses, while paying significant fines and investigation costs. These findings suggest a separation in some way between bribery misbehavior and financial fraud affecting reputation differently (although firms may have faced different levels of fines and investigation costs).

In terms of the proposed framework—individual motives, organizational settings, and public policy issues—a possibility for persistence of CSI is that legal enforcement simply replaces one set (or cohort) of individuals with another set (or cohort) of individuals. The next set of business managers may have learned nothing about consequences of misconduct or may invent new ways of attempting misconduct. This problem is particularly pronounced if legal enforcement lags new ways of misconduct. Individual consequences and organizational reputation may be separated. Scholarship is just beginning to delve into these various possibilities for how CSI maximization and CSR minimization occur. A role for CSR is as a kind of hedge (or insurance)—useful to organizations and society—against CSI practices by individuals.

REFERENCES

Alexander, C. R., & Cohen, M. A. (1996). New evidence on the origins of corporate crime. *Managerial and Decision Economics, 17*(4), 421–435.

Armstrong, J. S. (1977). Social irresponsibility in management. *Journal of Business Research, 5*(3), 185–213.

Armstrong, J. S., & Green, K. C. (2013). Effects of corporate social responsibility and irresponsibility policies. *Journal of Business Research, 66*(10), 1922–1927.

Arnold, M., & Engelen, P.-J. (2007). Do financial markets discipline firms for illegal corporate behaviour? *Management & Marketing, 2*(4), 103–110. Retrieved from http://www.managementmarketing.ro/pdf/articole/86.pdf

Ashkanasy, N. M., Windsor, C. A., & Treviño, L. K. (2006). Bad apples in bad barrels revisited: Cognitive moral development, just world beliefs, rewards, and ethical decision making. *Business Ethics Quarterly, 16*(4), 449–473.

Baker, T. L., Hunt, T. G., & Andrews, M. C. (2006). Promoting ethical behavior and organizational citizenship behaviors: The influence of corporate ethical values. *Journal of Business Research, 59*(7), 849–857.

Bansal, P., & Kandola, S. (2003). Corporate social responsibility: Why good people behave badly in organizations. *Ivey Business Journal, 67*(4), 1–5.

Barnett, M. L., & Salomon, R. M. (2006). Beyond dichotomy: The curvilinear relationship between social responsibility and financial performance. *Strategic Management Journal, 27*(11), 1101–1122.

Barnett, M. L., & Salomon, R. M. (2012). Does it pay to be *really* good? Addressing the shape of the relationship between social and financial performance. *Strategic Management Journal, 33*(11), 1304–1320.

Baucus, M. S. (1994). Pressure, opportunity, and predisposition: A multivariate model of corporate illegality. *Journal of Management, 20*(4), 699–721.

Baucus, M. S., & Baucus, D. A. (1997). Paying the piper: An empirical examination of longer-term financial consequences of illegal corporate behavior. *Academy of Management Journal, 40*(1), 129–151.

Baucus, M. S., & Near, J. P. (1991). Can illegal corporate behavior be predicted? An event history analysis. *Academy of Management Journal, 34*(1), 9–36.

Beenen, G., & Pinto, J. (2009). Resisting organizational-level corruption: An interview with Sherron Watkins. *Academy of Management Learning & Education, 8*(2), 275–289.

Brammer, S., Jackson, G., & Matten, D. (2012). Corporate social responsibility and institutional theory: New perspectives on private governance. *Socioeconomic Review, 10*(1), 3–28.

Campbell, J. L. (2007). Why would corporations behave in socially responsible ways? An institutional theory of corporate social responsibility. *Academy of Management Review, 32*(3), 946–967.

Carroll, A. B., & Shabana, K. M. (2010). The business case for corporate social responsibility: A review of concepts, research and practice. *International Journal of Management Reviews, 12*(1), 85–105.

Chatterji, A., & Levine, D. (2006). Breaking down the wall of codes: Evaluating non-financial performance measurement. *California Management Review, 48*(2), 29–51.

Chatterji, A., Levine, D., & Toffel, M. (2009). How well do social ratings actually measure corporate social responsibility? *Journal of Economics and Management Strategy, 18*(1), 125–169.

Chatterji, A., & Listokin, S. (2007). Corporate social irresponsibility. *Democracy: A Journal of Ideas,* (3) Winter, 52–63, http://www.democracyjournal.org/3/6497.php

Chatterji, A., & Toffel, M. (2010). How firms respond to being rated. *Strategic Management Journal, 31*(9), 917–945.

Chun, J. S., Shin, J., Choi, J. N., & Kim, M. S. (2013). How does corporate ethics contribute to firm financial performance? The mediating role of collective organizational commitment and organizational citizenship behavior. *Journal of Management, 39*(4), 853–877.

Demmerling. T. (2014). *Corporate social responsibility overload? Intention, abuse, misinterpretation of CSR from the companies' and the consumers' point of view.* Hamburg, Germany: Anchor Academic.

Dunn, P. (2004). The impact of insider power on fraudulent financial reporting. *Journal of Management, 30*(3), 397–412.

Epstein, M. J., & Yuthas, K. (2014). *Measuring and improving social impacts: A guide for nonprofits, companies and impact investors.* Sheffield, England: Greenleaf.

Flammer, C. (2013a). Corporate social responsibility and shareholder reaction: The environmental awareness of investors. *Academy of Management Journal, 56*(3), 758–781.

Flammer, C. (2013b, October). Does corporate social responsibility lead to superior financial performance? A regression discontinuity approach. Retrieved from http://ssrn.com/abstract=2146282, http://dx.doi.org/10.2139/ssrn.2146282

Fleming, P., & Jones, M. T. (2013). *The end of corporate social responsibility: Crisis and critique.* Thousand Oaks, CA: Sage.

Gintis, H., & Khurana, R. (2007). Corporate honesty and business education: A behavior model. In P. J. Zak (Ed.), *Moral markets: The critical role of values in the economy* (pp. 300–327). Princeton, NJ: Princeton University Press.

Godfrey, P. C., Merrill, C. B., & Hansen, J. M. (2009). The relationship between corporate social responsibility and shareholder value: an empirical test of the risk management hypothesis. *Strategic Management Journal, 30*(4), 425–445.

Graham, J. R., Harvey, C. R., & Rajgopal, S. (2005). The economic implications of corporate financial reporting. *Journal of Accounting and Economics, 40*(1–3), 3–73.

Griffin, J. J., & Mahon, J. F. (1997). The corporate social performance and corporate financial performance debate: Twenty-five years of incomparable research. *Business & Society, 36*(1), 5–31.

Harte, B. K. (2012). Illegal corporate behavior: Analyzing the effectiveness of the 2002 Sarbanes-Oxley Act. *The International Journal of Management and*

Business, 3(2). Retrieved from   http://www.iamb.net/IJMB/journal/Vol_3/IJMB_Vol_3_2_Harte.pdf

Hillman, A. J., & Keim, G. D. (2001). Shareholder value, stakeholder management, and social issues: What's the bottom line? *Strategic Management Journal, 22*(2), 125–139.

Jones, B., Bowd, R., & Tench, R. (2009). Corporate irresponsibility and corporate social responsibility: Competing realities. *Social Responsibility Journal, 5*(3), 300–310.

Karpoff, J. M., Lee, D. S., & Martin, G. S. (2004, January 23). The economics of foreign bribery: Evidence from FCPA enforcement actions. Retrieved from http://ssrn.com/abstract=1573222, http://dx.doi.org/10.2139/ssrn.1573222.

Karpoff, J. M., Lee, D. S., & Martin, G. S. (2008). The consequences to managers for financial misrepresentation. *Journal of Financial Economics, 88*(2), 193–215.

Kish-Gephart, J. J., Harrison, D. A., & Treviño, L. K. (2010). Bad apples, bad cases, and bad barrels: Meta-analytic evidence about sources of unethical decisions at work. *Journal of Applied Psychology, 95*(1), 1–31.

Kotchen, M., & Moon, J. J. (2012). Corporate social responsibility for irresponsibility. *The B.E. Journal of Economic Analysis & Policy, 12*(1), Article 55, DOI: 10.1515/1935-1682.3308

Lange, D., & Washburn, N. T. (2012). Understanding attributions of corporate social irresponsibility. *Academy of Management Review, 37*(2), 300–326.

Mackey, A., Mackey, T. B., & Barney, J. (2007). Corporate social responsibility and firm performance: Investor preferences and corporate strategies. *Academy of Management Review, 32*(3), 817–835.

Mackey, A., Mackey, T. B., & Barney, J. (2008). Senior management preferences and corporate social responsibility. In A. Crane, A. McWilliams, D. Matten, J. Moon, & D. S. Siegel (Eds.), *The Oxford handbook of corporate social responsibility* (pp. 532–542). Oxford, England: Oxford University Press.

McWilliams, A., & Siegel, D. (2000). Corporate social responsibility and financial performance: Correlation or misspecification? *Strategic Management Journal, 21*(5), 603–609.

Mitchell, L. E. (2001). *Corporate irresponsibility: America's newest export.* New Haven, CT: Yale University Press.

Moura-Leite, R. C., & Padgett, R. C. (2011). Historical background of corporate social responsibility. *Social Responsibility Journal, 7*(4), 528–539.

Murphy, P. E., & Schlegelmilch, B. B. (2013). Corporate social responsibility and corporate social irresponsibility: Introduction to a special topic section. *Journal of Business Research, 66*(10), 1807–1813.

Noonan, K. (2012). Note: The case for a federal corporate charter revocation penalty. *The George Washington Law Review, 80*(2), 602–631.

Oikonomou, I., Brooks, C., & Pavelin, S. (2014). The financial effects of uniform and mixed corporate social performance. *Journal of Management Studies, 51*(6), 898–925.

Okoye, A. (2009). Theorising corporate social responsibility as an essentially contested concept: Is a definition necessary? *Journal of Business Ethics, 89*(4), 613–627.

Orlitzky, M., Schmidt, F. L., & Rynes, S. L. (2003). Corporate social and financial performance: A meta-analysis. *Organization Studies, 24*(3), 403–441.

Orlitzky, M., & Swanson, D. L. (2008). *Toward integrative corporate citizenship: Research advances in corporate social performance.* London, England: Palgrave Macmillan.

Price, M., & Norris, D. M. (2009). White-collar crime: Corporate and securities and commodities fraud. *Journal of the American Academy of Psychiatry and the Law, 37*(4), 538–544.

Reinhardt, F. L., & Stavins, R. N. (2010). Corporate social responsibility, business strategy, and the environment. *Oxford Review of Economic Policy, 26*(2), 164–181.

Schwartz, M. S., & Carroll, A. B. (2008). Integrating and unifying competing and complementary frameworks: The search for a common core in the business and society field. *Business & Society, 47*(2), 149–186.

Shiau, S.-J., Li, C.-A., & Yang, D.-Y. (2012). Illegal corporate behavior and the value of firms. *Investment Management and Financial Innovations, 9*(4). Retrieved from http://businessperspectives.org/journals_free/imfi/2012/imfi_en_2012_04_Shiau.pdf

Stewart, B. (2006). The real reasons Enron failed. *Journal of Applied Corporate Finance, 18*(2), 116–119.

Tenbrunsel, A. E., Diekmann, K. A., Wade-Benzoni, K. A., & Bazerman, M. H. (2010). The ethical mirage: A temporal explanation as to why we aren't as ethical as we think we are. *Research in Organizational Behavior, 30*, 153–173.

Tenbrunsel, A. E., & Smith-Crowe, K. (2008). Ethical decision making: Where we've been and where we're going. *The Academy of Management Annals, 2*(1), 545–607.

Tench, R., Sun, W., & Jones, B. (Eds.). (2012). *Corporate social irresponsibility: A challenging concept.* Bingley, England: Emerald.

Troy, C., Smith, K. G., & Domino, M. A. (2011). CEO demographics and accounting fraud: Who is more likely to rationalize illegal acts? *Strategic Organization, 9*(4), 259–282.

Wilson, J. Q. (1989). Adam Smith on business ethics. *California Management Review, 32*(1), 59–71.

Windsor, D. (2013). Corporate social responsibility and irresponsibility: A positive theory approach. *Journal of Business Research, 66*(10), 1937–1944.

Wokutch, R. E., & Spencer, B. A. (1987). Corporate saints and sinners: The effects of philanthropic and illegal activity on organizational performance. *California Management Review, 29*(2), 62–77.

Wood, D. J. (1991). Corporate social performance revisited. *Academy of Management Review, 16*(1), 691–718.

Wood, D. J. (2010). Measuring corporate social performance: A review. *International Journal of Management Reviews, 12*(1), 50–84.

Zahra, S. A., Priem, R. L., & Rasheed, A. A. (2005). The antecedents and consequences of top management fraud. *Journal of Management, 31*(6), 803–828.

Zeidan, M. J. (2013). Effects of illegal behavior on the financial performance of US banking institutions. *Journal of Business Ethics, 112*(2), 313–324.

CHAPTER 6

CORPORATE SOCIAL RESPONSIBILITY

A Three-Layer Discussion

Harry Costin

As one examines *Corporate Social Performance: Paradoxes, Pitfalls,* that is, the key issues covered in this book, there is an implicit assumption that such corporate social performance (CSP) is the result of the exercise of what has been commonly called corporate social responsibility (CSR).

CSR is 60 years old as a field or issue of academic concern, and Howard Bowen's 1953 seminal book *Social Responsibilities of the Businessman* is widely considered as the opening salvo of the field (Carroll, 1991, 1999, 2008; Garriga & Melé, 2004; Lee, 2008; Preston, 1975; Wood, 1991a, 1991b).

As a mature field of theory of practice, with a rich literature, CSR provides us with interesting possibilities to look at it as a whole using new perspectives. This is the purpose of this chapter, which will argue that some of the vagueness often attributed to CSR (Carroll, 1999; Davis, 1960) may stem from the fact that discussions concerning CSR occur at three different levels that are often mixed together. This insight may also help clarify the question of corporate social performance, which means different things depending upon the level the discussion is at.

Corporate Social Performance:
Paradoxes, Pitfalls, and Pathways to the Better World, pp. 103–119
Copyright © 2015 by Information Age Publishing

CSR: RIGHT OR WRONG? A THREE-LAYER DISCUSSION

The three distinct levels implicit in discussions about CSR are: (1) fundamental values and notions about the appropriate structure of society and the relationships between key actors and stakeholders; (2) CSR as a set of concepts and prescriptive actions; and finally, (3) the most efficient ways to achieve the goals established by CSR. One could add corporate social performance as a fourth layer, a direct resultant of the other three. This discussion will focus primarily upon the first three ones.

THE STRUCTURE OF SOCIETY: ALTERNATIVE VIEWS

Advocates of CSR take the normative view that CSR is the right thing to do, a view disputed by some prominent critics, such as the 1976 winner of the Nobel Prize in economics, Milton Friedman (1962, 2002). If CSR is self-evident, how can highly articulate and respected thinkers such as Friedman be opposed to it? The answer may lie in the level at which Friedman criticizes CSR, since for him advocating CSR is paramount to endorsing socialism.

For Friedman (2002)

> the discussions of the "social responsibilities of business" are notable for their analytical looseness and lack of rigor. What does it mean to say that "business" has responsibilities? Only people can have responsibilities. A corporation is an artificial person and in this sense may have artificial responsibilities, but "business" as a whole cannot be said to have responsibilities. (p. 33)

As for managers, according to Friedman (2002, pp. 33–35) they are simply agents for the owners and their mandate is straightforward, that is, to manage the corporation so as to maximize profits while abiding by the law. Managers and owners, that is, stockholders, are free to give away to charities or other purposes their own money, but managers cannot give away money that is not theirs for CSR purposes, whatever these may be. Friedman goes further and argues that a few owners or shareholders should not force the other shareholders to accept that the corporation engages in CSR projects.

For Friedman (2002) it is up to the law to define what is right or not for society as a whole, since in a democratic free society laws are made and voted by representatives of all citizens. Therefore, if for example pollution levels are considered too high, new legislation should set and enforce appropriate new standards.

In a certain way Friedman's view of society may be seen as utopian: a free society of conscientious individuals with a fully working democracy, and efficient market forces that optimize the distribution of available goods.

Those familiar with economic history will recognize Friedman's kinship with the ideas of the Austrian economist Friedrich von Hayek, who in his classic 1944 book *The Road to Serfdom* warned against the threat of tyranny that inevitably results from government control of economic decision-making through central planning. Further, these ideas are not just Friedman's but also representative of the Chicago School to which Friedman belongs, headquartered at the department of economics of the University of Chicago.

The discussion of Friedman's criticism of CSR provides us with a platform to contrast his views with those of Bowen (1953), discussed in detail in a recent paper by Acquier, Gond, and Pasquero (2011).

The authors emphasize the importance of Bowen's (1953) background and his historic context to fully understand the ideas of Bowen, considered by many as the founding father of CSR. By contrast to Friedman, who followed in von Hayeks (1944) footsteps, Bowen was a follower of Keynes ideas. After receiving his PhD in economics from the University of Iowa he did postdoctoral work at Cambridge University and the London School of Economics and Political Science, where he was exposed and became interested in Keynes (1936) recently published *General Theory*.

Bowen's (1953) ideas should not only be interpreted in the context of welfare economics, but also as an expression of a protestant interpretation of capitalism. Bowen's book was one out of six in a series on "Christian Ethics and the Economic Life," started in 1949 by the Federal Council of the Churches of Christ, and funded by the Rockefeller Foundation. "Therefore religion—rather than academia—provided the impetus behind the book considered the landmark of the 'modern' era of CSR" (Acquier et al., 2011, p. 613).

A return to religious roots, like exemplified by Bowen (1953), implies going beyond simple reason; it is a realm where values are often derived from principles based upon faith or dogmas. It is in this sense that this paper suggests that it is important to recognize the values and assumptions about the appropriate and just structure of society and the relationships between its members as a distinct conceptual level. At this level there may be a fundamental clash of religious beliefs and political ideologies that goes beyond a "reasoned discourse."

Religion matters and the values of a particular religion are reflected in the legal systems of societies. For example, polygamy, has long been abolished in the legal system of Western societies (when Utah became a member of the United States of America, its Mormon majority had to renounce polygamy, which became illegal). However, polygamy is still legal in countries that include Burkina Faso, Pakistan, Afghanistan (a frequent occurrence), Singapore (husbands need to demonstrate that they have the financial means to support their up to four wives) and Iran, among others.

By contrast to capitalism, which has been interpreted in different nuanced ways by the followers of Keynes and von Hayek, socialism (we use the term "socialism," although it is misleading, because it is specifically used by Friedman and also Bowen, and include communism under the same term) is based upon different principles: for example, socialism advocates collective ownership and central planning of the economy, both supported by principles of equity and rational use of the means of production.

It should be noted that this chapter intends to provide a map of the layered discussion around CSR and CSP, rather than a critique of the relative validity of different social paradigms. Suffice it therefore to say that at the very least three distinct views of society underlie any discussion of CSR and CSP: capitalism, with quite different interpretations of whether CSR makes any sense at all, following the ideas of Keynes (1936) or von Hayek (1944) (a full taxonomy would recognize more views than simply these two, but these are the most influential ones); and socialism, where a form of CSR would be practiced by state-owned corporations, for example, to protect the environment for the common good.

Goals and Aspects of CSR

Having discussed the assumptions that will frame any discussion on CSR, it is now possible to move to the more traditional way of conceptualizing CSR; first, the diverse definitions of CSR and its scope, as well as related concepts that can still be seen as belonging to the "CSR family." At this second level of analysis in our framework, CSR is defined as a set of goals to be achieved with the active participation of corporations as key actors. These goals can be conceived as *effectiveness* or the "right thing to do for businesses in their interactions with society.

Further, even if agreement may exist concerning the CSR goals to be achieved, the means or appropriate ways to accomplish them so are in dispute. For example, should government be the key actor legislating CSR goals and targets or is industry self-regulation a more effective tool. This constitutes the third level in our framework, to be discussed later.

Finally, these three levels of CSR provide the background for CSP, that is, measuring the results of CSR.

In brief:

Values→Goals of CSR→Means of CSR→CSP measurable results

This simple linear model suggests that there may be different paths to achieve a particular set of CSP results. It also raises other interesting questions such as:

1. If results are the fundamental measure, may these be achieved by non-CSR means, e.g., strictly enforced legislation that sets high targets, e.g., for the reduction of the carbon foot print?
2. May the alleged fuzziness of CSR goals (e.g., that corporations should care about their employees) be compensated by specific implementation means and targets?
3. How do different values and distinct historic differences, e.g., between the United Kingdom and the United States (both built upon a protestant Anglo Saxon heritage) and continental Europe, translate into different conceptions of appropriate CSR goals?

CSR: A FAMILY OF CONCEPTS AND DEFINITIONS

Bowen (1953) spoke of the social responsibilities of business and suggested that these had "become not only acceptable in leading business circles, but even fashionable" (p. 44). Stated in other terms, businesses had responsibilities that went beyond achieving profit maximization for their owners and abiding by the laws.

In 1960 Davis, a leading writer on CSR, wrote that CSR related to "businessmen's decisions and actions taken for reasons at least partially beyond the firm's direct economic or technical interest" (p. 70).

Writing in 1971, George Steiner, a follower of Davis (1960) said:

Business is and must remain fundamentally an economic institution, but ... it does have responsibilities to help society achieve its basic goals and does, therefore, have social responsibilities. The larger a company becomes, the greater are these responsibilities, but all companies can assume some share of them at no cost and often at a short-run as well as a long-run profit.

The assumption of social responsibilities is more of an attitude, of the way a manager approaches his decision-making task, than a great shift in the economics of decision making. It is a philosophy that looks at the social interest and the enlightened self-interest of business over the long run as compared with the old, narrow, unrestrained short-run self-interest. (p. 164)

A few years after Friedman dismissed CSR as nonsensical and even dangerous. Davis (1973) offered the following definition that shows the specific ways in which CSR advocates differed from the prominent Chicago economist:

> For purposes of this discussion it [CSR] refers to the firm's consideration of, and response to, issues beyond the narrow economic, technical, and legal requirements of the firm. (p. 312)

> It is the firm's obligation to evaluate in its decision-making process the effects of its decisions on the external social system in a manner that will accomplish social benefits along with the traditional economic gains which the firm seeks. (p. 313)

> It means that social responsibility begins where the law ends. A firm is not being socially responsible if it merely complies with the minimum requirements (p. 313)

Arguing that the public policy process played a critical role, in 1975 Preston and Post suggested to replace the word "social" by "public," when discussing CSR. However, their valuable suggestion did not become mainstream.

In 1980 Jones emphasized that CSR pertained only to voluntary behavior:

> Corporate social responsibility is the notion that corporations have an obligation to constituent groups in society other than stockholders and beyond that prescribed by law and union contract. Two facets of this definition are critical. First, the obligation must be voluntarily adopted; behavior influenced by the coercive forces of law or union contract is not voluntary. Second, the obligation is a broad one, extending beyond the traditional duty to shareholders to other societal groups such as customers, employees, suppliers, and neighboring communities. (pp. 59–60)

Epstein (1987), a prominent scholar of CSR defined it in the following terms:

> *Corporate social responsibility* relates primarily to achieving outcomes from organizational decisions concerning specific issues or problems which (by some normative standard) have beneficial rather than adverse effects on pertinent corporate stakeholders. The normative correctness of the products of corporate action has been the main focus of corporate social responsibility. (p. 104)

Epstein (1987) also integrated corporate social responsiveness with business ethics in what he called the "corporate social policy process" (p. 106).

In 1991 Carroll decided to highlight in specific terms the philanthropic aspect of CSR, suggesting that it embraced "corporate citizenship:"

For CSR to be accepted by the conscientious business person, it should be framed in such a way that the entire range of business responsibilities is embraced. It is suggested here that four kinds of social responsibilities constitute total CSR: economic, legal, ethical and philanthropic. Furthermore, these four categories or components of CSR might be depicted as a pyramid. To be sure, all of these kinds of responsibilities have always existed to some extent, but it has only been in recent years that ethical and philanthropic functions have taken a significant place. (p. 40)

He also stated unambiguously that "the CSR firm should strive to *make a profit, obey the law, be ethical, and be a good corporate citizen*" (Epstein, 1987, p. 43, emphasis in original).

Narrowing and Defining the Scope of CSR

The sample definitions listed above show how critics of CSR have had ample opportunity to take on such a noble, but undoubtedly vague concept. It is in this sense that even Friedman (2002) suggested that corporations might decide to engage in activities such as contributing to upgrade the skill level of members of their local communities, and that this was perfectly reasonable and in the companies' self-interest. However, he strongly objected to referring to these activities as CSR.

The vagueness of CSR broadly conceived as the responsibility corporations have toward society, thereby exemplifying ´good corporate citizenship´ begins to fade, as concrete CSR efforts and actions are identified.

Two models that define corporate excellence (one American and the other European), one international initiative fostered by the United Nations, and one legal principle that underpins European environmental legislation, may be useful to define the goals of CSR, and ways to implement them.

Models of Corporate Excellence: Total Quality Management

Following the oil shock of 1979 the world found itself in recession in the early 1980s. In 1980 Ronald Reagan became the president of the United States and embraced a message of optimism of the greatness of America. However, key industries, such as the automotive sector, were hit hard by Japanese car imports. These cars, built with a focus on fuel efficiency and reliability competed strongly against those made by giants such as Ford and GM, and Honda and Toyota became household names in the country where Ford had launched the modern mass production of industrial goods.

Many searched for an answer to the question how the Japanese were able to beat the Americans at their own game. One of the answers found lied in what became known as *Total Quality Management* or TQM (Costin, 1994), a set principles and tools that were seen as the key to the excellence of Japanese products. The statistical tools on which Japanese evolved TQM had been introduced around 1950 by two prominent Americans, D. Edwards Deming and J. Juran.

During the Reagan era the importance of the principles embodied in TQM was not only recognized, but in 1987 the Malcolm Baldrige National Quality Award, the only award given by the U.S. President and recognizing organizational excellence (both private and public, and embracing today diverse sectors including manufacturing, service, health care and education) was established. The Baldrige Award, given out annually is still administered by the U.S. Department of Commerce and the National Institute for Standards and Technology (NIST), with input from the private sector professional organization the American Society for Quality (ASQ).

The Baldrige Award defines what an "excellent company or organization" is, in a way that could be compared to Peters and Waterman's best-seller *In Search of Excellence* published in 1982.

It is interesting to contrast the award guidelines from different periods, showing the *mores* of each time period. The examples chosen are from the years 1992 and 2006 (NIST, 1992, 2006):

1. The 1992 section on *Core Values and Concepts* speaks of "public responsibility" (p. 2); the 2006 guidelines use the term "social responsibility" (p. 1).
2. The same section discusses the need for a "focus on the future" in 2006, but not in 1992:

    In today's competitive environment, creating a sustainable organization requires understanding the short- and longer-term factors that affect your organization and marketplace. Pursuit of sustainable growth and market leadership requires a strong future orientation and a willingness to make long-term commitments to key stakeholders—your customers, employees, suppliers, partners, stockholders, the public, and your community. (p. 3)

3. The 2006 results section (one of out the seven that are included in the Baldrige Model of Organizational Excellence) includes a subsection absent in 1992, and titled "Leadership and Social Responsibility Outcomes," which asks specifically for evidence of " 'ethical behavior,' fiscal accountability, legal compliance, and organizational citizenship" (p. 33).

The European Model for Total Quality Management

Europe has her own version of the Baldrige, the EFQM Award, managed by the European Foundation for Quality Management. EFQM was founded in 1988 by 14 leading European companies including giants such as Fiat, Ollivetti, Volkswagen, and Electrolux who formed a foundation "dedicated to increasing the competitiveness of European business." Today, EFQM has more than 500 member organizations.

Like the Baldrige Award, EFQM uses an explicit model of organizational excellence. Of particular interest is the fact that the results component of the model highlights four distinct types of results (EFQM):

- *Customer results:* "Excellent organizations achieve and sustain outstanding results that meet or exceed the need and expectations of their customers."
- *People results:* "Excellent organizations achieve and sustain outstanding results that meet or exceed the need and expectations of their people."
- *Society results:* "Excellent organizations achieve and sustain outstanding results that meet or exceed the need and expectations of relevant stakeholders within society."
- *Business results:* "Excellent organizations achieve and sustain outstanding results that meet or exceed the need and expectations of their business stakeholders."

Both in the Baldrige Award as in the EFQM Award there is an explicit acknowledgment that organizations have responsibilities to a diverse set of stakeholders that includes stockholders, customers, employees, and society. This not only demonstrates the kinship between CSR and stakeholder theory (Freeman, 1984), but also addresses implicitly the problem of vagueness of CSR goals. In specific settings such as, for example, a school in a poor neighborhood with high dropout rates, low skill levels, and high unemployment, the Baldrige Award guidelines for Education would ask an institution applying for the award to define specific goals, chosen means, and measurable results.

The Polluter Pays Principle

To wrap up the discussion on CSR goals, that is, the effectiveness dimension, it may be useful to cite an example of a powerful principle that guides environmental legislation in the European Union, the United States, and Japan: *the polluter pays*!

In simple terms *the polluter pays principle* "demands that the polluter bear the burden of remediating the waste it generates" (Larson, 2005, p. 541).

This concept was originally a guiding principle of environmental legislation within the European community, but has since spread to other regions.

A White paper of the European Commission (2000) on environmental liability explains the scope and need for this principle:

> Liability for damage to nature is a prerequisite for making economic actors feel responsible for the possible negative effects of their operations on the environment as such. So far, operators seem to feel such responsibility for other people's health or property—for which environmental liability already exists, at the national level—rather than for the environment. They tend to consider the environment "a public good" for which society as a whole should be responsible, rather than an individual actor who happened to cause damage to it. Liability is a certain way of making people realize that they are also responsible for possible consequences of their acts with regards to nature. This expected change of attitude should result in an increased level of prevention and precaution.

An economist would refer to these negative side effects of industrial activity as negative externalities, such as a river polluted by a mill next to it, a common occurrence during the industrialization era. Strictly speaking, *the polluter pays* principle would fall outside of the domain of CSR, if enacted as legislation. But it could also fall within the domain of CSR in countries where it is used as a guiding principle, that is, in countries where strict legislation to enforce it does not exist. In any event, it represents an excellent example of a principle that is broad in scope, but quite specific in particular applications. CSR principles and goals may be similar in the sense that their scope tends to be quite broad, to the point of being considered by some as fuzzy. But once specific stakeholders are identified (e.g., employees of a corporation, or the local community in which the business operates) it is quite easy to identify specific actions that would fall within the domain of CSR or corporate citizenship. The U.S. Baldrige and European EFQM awards discussed earlier provide good examples on how principles can be translated into actions with measurable outcomes that are context specific (for a further discussion of how the U.S. interpretation of CSR differs from the European one (see Matten & Moor, 2008).

CSR: EFFICIENCY CONCERNS

Our discussion now turns to the question of the efficiency of alternate means to achieve the same goals. In a curious manner the discussion about means will bring us back to the initial discussion about the appropriate structure of society.

Let us begin with an example from the influential British journal *The Economist* (2014a, 2014b), discussing environmental targets adopted by the members of the European Union (EU) January 22, 2014 in an editorial and related article.

The Economist reports that the current EU policy calls for 20-20-20, that is, by 2020 EU members "should reduce greenhouse-gas emissions by 20% (relative to levels in 1990), with 20% of the mix produces from renewable sources and a 20% improvement in energy efficiency." On January 22 the European Commission proposed a 40% reduction of emissions by 2030 with a EU-wide "binding" target of at least 27% for the relative share of renewables.

The criticism from *The Economist* journal of the EU Commission proposal illustrates some of the complexities inherent in the relationship between goal setting and implementation. The argument goes as follows:

1. Global warming is a fact and the reduction of carbon emissions is essential.
2. The EU may have set ambitious targets, but other great pollutants such as China and the United States are not following suit.
3. The two primary EU policies to achieve the goal of reducing carbon emissions, "a carbon market to raise the price of pollution" and generous subsidies to increase the proportion of renewable sources of energy have failed.
4. The primary renewable sources of energy growing, such as wood, may not be of the right kind.
5. Energy costs (electricity) are consequently artificially high and "the 20 largest European energy utilities have lost a jaw-dropping €500 billion in market value since 2008."
6. *The Economist* calls for scraping targets for renewable energy sources altogether. Here lies the key of the disagreement between *The Economist* and the EU. Both share the concern and goal of dealing aggressively with the human causes of global warming, but *The Economist* does not see the need for a strong investment in renewables, considering that fossil fuel sources are finite, and will eventually have to be replaced, independently of the possibility that new oil and gas fields may be found, or that, e.g., "a switch to shale gas cut American emissions by 12% in 2007–12, more than in Europe."

One may tempted to ask in what way the discussion above relates to CSR? In many ways! Impact upon society is often interpreted as impact upon the environment, and "reduction of the carbon foot print" has become an explicit goal of many corporations.

The United Nations Global Compact

The United Nations Global Compact represents a particularly interesting global initiative to achieve CSR goals (Rasche, Waddock, & McIntosh, 2012). As of April 2012 over 10,000 business and nonbusiness participants had joined the Global Compact, a UN voluntary corporate responsibility initiative.

According to Rasche et al. (2012) the Global Compact, launched in 2000, endorsed by the United Nations and covering over 130 countries embraces a number of ambitious goals:

> The underlying idea of the Global Compact is that business participants—in partnership with other actors including NGOs, organized labor, UN agencies, and governments—advance broader UN goals (e.g., the Millennium Development Goals) as well as 10 universal principles in the areas of human rights, labor rights, the environment, and anticorruption. (p. 7)

One of the unique opportunities provided by the Compact is the formation of multiple alliances to pursue the goals of the Compact. The goals themselves may be unrealistic in their scope, but the pursuit of some of them by multistakeholder groups brings the dreams of CSR advocates to a new level. It also embraces one of the key concepts of many definitions of CSR that stress that CSR relates to voluntary actions by corporations that go beyond the minimum required by the law, in a spirit of corporate citizenship.

If common goals voluntarily embraced are at the heart of the Global Compact initiative, other international approaches have focused on standards and processes. These include the ISO 9000 series of international quality standards (Costin & Dargie, 1993), which provided a base for the 14000 series of environmental standards (Perkins & Neumayer, 2010). Both sets of standards focus on process, that is, good practices and systems to consistently ensure quality and appropriate environmental management.

Societal Values and the Implementation of CSR

Earlier in the paper it was suggested that the discussion about the appropriate means to achieve CSR needs to refer back to fundamental societal and ideological views to be fully understood. What appears often a discussion about *efficiency concerns* may hide a priori views about what is right or wrong.

Friedman (2002) suggested that in free societies free market mechanisms and collective choice embodied in national legislation provided the appropriate framework for corporate action. He further stated that actions that many would describe as CSR (e.g., helping the local community) could be perfectly appropriate in the corporation's self-interest, and that it was not the actions that represented a problem, but the hypocrisy of claiming that they were performed in the name of CSR principles.

Most definitions of CSR discussed earlier in the chapter focus on process rather than content, one of the reasons they seem often vague. Corporations embracing CSR are said to voluntarily acknowledge the needs of different key stakeholders besides the owners, such as employees and society, and to translate these into a series of initiatives to benefit these constituents, going beyond existing legal and contractual commitments. However, one could argue that a focus on specific content (e.g., the polluter pays principle) might clarify goals that might be achieved through different means: for example, corporate efforts to significantly reduce the carbon footprint, independent upon whether one does so voluntarily (the traditional CSR perspective), or is forced to do so by law or by public pressure (the reputational impact of CSR related actions). In other words, corporations may become "good corporate citizens" following different paths.

Industry experience may provide a template for situations where a corporation may be forced to embark upon a certain path to its own benefit. And once some of the benefits are realized by the managers, they may themselves become advocates of the new way.

This is suggested by the experience of the quality movement in the 1990s (Costin, 1994). Many first tier suppliers of the automotive industry were required by GM and Ford to implement the Q-1 quality standards, which applied TQM tools and principles to systems built upon the ISO 9000 series of international quality standards. Many corporations became significantly more competitive in the process. In other words: many who were forced to apply quality management principles became strong advocates for the same when they realized their benefits. It is not too adventurous to suggest that something similar may occur in the environmental arena, where companies such as GE are discovering that being first in reducing the carbon foot print may enable them to be leaders in the merging environmental industries.

INTEGRATING THE LEVELS

In practice, the three different levels discussed in this chapter are intertwined in complex and intriguing ways. South Africa's efforts to move beyond *apartheid* provide a good example.

Since 1994 the South African government has implemented a series of CSR oriented regulations, specifically "directed at the empowerment of historically disadvantaged Black people" (Arya & Bassi, 2011 p. 674).

In 2003 the Broad-Based Black Empowerment Act was released and in 2007 the Department of Trade and Industry completed the Codes of Good Practice intended for public, private and foreign corporations operating in South Africa.

These measures were intended to counteract the policies of the apartheid era that brought about enormous income and wealth disparities between the White and Black population and perpetuated a low skill level of Black workers (Butler, 2004).

After the end of the apartheid era, and since 1994, the African National Congress passed a number of CSR laws intended to redress historic imbalances (Employment Equity Act, 1998; Skills Development Act, 1998; Promotion of Equality and Prevention of Unfair Discrimination Act, 2000), one of the widest affirmative action efforts we are aware of. South Africa's efforts and laws were informed by voluntary initiatives such as the United Nations Global Reporting Initiative (GRI), which encourages corporations to report corporate performance in areas of social investment, the environment, ethics and occupational health and safety (Hansen & Ryan, 2006; Visser, 2005).

Some of the features of the broadly-based and strongly supported CSR initiatives of South Africa that illustrate important aspects of the discussion in this chapter were:

1. CSR was defined in a narrow way as "the economic empowerment of historically disadvantaged Black people."
2. Government legislation encompassing a long-term vision from 1994 until 2007, when the Codes of Good Practice came into being has been complemented by industry self-regulation initiatives. In other words we have a clear example of "CSR by law" supplemented by significant voluntary CSR efforts from industry, which correspond to the earlier definitions of CSR that emphasized "going beyond" strictly legal requirements by companies.
3. The general goal articulated in the Codes of Good Practice was translated in some industries into more specific goals and targets. For example the Financial Sector Charter (FSC) that came into effect in January 2004 recognized seven social indicators with measurable targets to be achieved in 5 and 10 years :

   - The management indicator called for 33% of the board of directors to be Black people.
   - The employment equity indicator defined targets for Black people at different levels of the organization: 20–25% at the senior management level, 30% Black people at the middle management level, and 40–50% at the junior management level by 2008.

- A skill development indicator defined as the target level to spend on the training of Black employees a 1.5% of total basic payroll.
- In the Mining Sector Charter an ownership goal of 26% by 2012 was defined.
- Preferential procurement from Black-owned companies was set at 50% of the supplies of companies subscribing to the FSC charter by 2008.
- Targets for socioeconomic development projects benefitting Black communities were set at 0.5% of net income by the FSC.

4. To measure the achievement of the goals of the Codes of Good Practice a number of government regulatory bodies were created. These were supplemented by other professional organizations such as auditing consulting organizations that provided their services to companies wishing to move along the implementation of the Codes of Good Practice.

CONCLUSION

This paper suggests that it is useful to conceptualize CSR as a discussion that occurs at three distinct levels, and that effectiveness and efficiency concerns often disguise fundamental differences closely related to values and normative views of how society and its various stakeholders should be organized and should interact.

As an example let us refer to differences between the United States and continental European countries. In the United States the appropriate role of the federal government in guiding the economy is seen as marginal, with a stronger focus on monetary than fiscal policy. In France, by contrast, the reverse is true. The central government has always played a strong role guiding the economy, and is still a major shareholder in large corporations.

The above may have an impact on diverging definitions of CSR. Traditional definitions of CSR by American scholars have emphasized that CSR *is* or *should be* a voluntary effort by corporations. Europeans, by contrast, have placed a greater emphasis on the *must* of CSR initiatives. It is therefore not surprising that in Europe mandatory environmental regulations for corporations are seen as eminently within the scope of CSR.

Finally, if it is clearly important to distinguish the level at which a discussion concerning CSR occurs, it should be noted that in practice the three levels are intertwined. In other words, it is likely to be more appropriate to describe the interactions between the three levels as three interpenetrating circles rather than as strictly *orthogonal* categories, as a statistician would say.

REFERENCES

Acquier, A., Gond, J. P., & Pasquero, J. (2011). Redescovering Howard R. Bowen's legacy: The unachieved agenda and continuing relevance of social responsibilities of the businessman. *Business & Society, 50,* 607–646.

Arya, B., & Bassi, B. (2011). Corporate social responsibility and broad-based Black economic empowerment legislation in South Africa: Codes of good practice. *Business & Society, 50*(4), 674–695.

Bowen, H. R. (1953). *Social responsibilities of the businessman.* New York, NY: Harper.

Butler, A. (2004). *Contemporary South Africa.* New York, NY: Palgrave Macmillan.

Carroll, A. B. (1991, July/August). The pyramid of corporate social responsibility: Toward the moral management of organizational stakeholders. *Business Horizons, 34,* 39–48.

Carroll, A. B. (1999). Corporate social responsibility: Evolution of a definitional construct. *Business & Society, 38,* 268–295.

Carroll, A. B. (2008). A history of corporate social responsibility: Concepts and practices. In A. Crane, A. McWilliams, D. Matten, J. Moon, & D. Siegel (Eds.), *The Oxford handbook of corporate social responsibility* (pp. 19–46). Oxford, England: Oxford University Press.

Commission of the European Communities. (2000). *White paper on environmental liability.* Brussels, Belgium: Authors.

Costin, H., & Dargie, P. (1993). *ISO 9000 and strategies to compete in the single European Marke.* Methuen, MA: GOAL/QPC.

Costin, H. (1994). *Readings in total quality management.* Forth Worth, TX: The Dryden Press.

Davis, K. (1960, Spring). Can business afford to ignore social responsibilities? *California Management Review, 2,* 70–76.

Davis, K. (1973). The case for and against business assumption of social responsibilities. *Academy of Management Journal, 16,* 312–322.

The Economist. (2014a). European climate policy: Worse than useless. Retrieved from http://www.economist.com/news/leaders/21595002-current-policies-are-mess-heres-how-fix-them-worse-useless

The Economist. (2014b). Charlemagne: Europe's energy woes. Retrieved from http://www.economist.com/news/europe/21595018-storm-over-new-european-union-climate-change-targets-europes-energy-woes

Epstein, E. M. (1987). The corporate social policy process: Beyond business ethics, corporate social responsibility, and corporate social responsiveness. *California Management Review, 29,* 99–114.

Freeman, R. E. (1984). *Strategic management: A stakeholder approach.* Boston, MA: Pitman.

Friedman, M. (1962). *Capitalism and freedom.* Chicago, IL: University of Chicago Press.

Friedman, M. (2002). The social responsibility of business is to increase its profits. In T. Donaldson, P. Werhane, & J. Van Zandt (Eds.), *Ethical issues in business: A philosophical approach* (7th ed., pp. 33–38). Upper Saddle River, NJ: Pearson Education.

Garriga, E., & Melé, D. (2004). Corporate social responsibility theories: Mapping the territory. *Journal of Business Ethics, 53*(1–2), 51–71.

Hansen, A. R., & Ryan, V. (2006). Following the rising polestar: An examination of the structures governing corporate citizens in South Africa. In W. Visser, M. McIntosh, & C. Middleton (Eds.), *Corporate citizenship in Africa* (pp. 43–53). Sheffield, England: Greenleaf.

Jones, T. M. (1980, Spring). Corporate social responsibility revisited, redefined. *California Management Review,* 59–67.

Keynes, J. M. (1936). *The general theory of employment, interest and money.* Cambridge, England: Macmillan Cambridge University Press.

Larson, E. T. (2005). Why environmental liability regimes in the United States, the European Community, and Japan have grown synonymous with the polluter pays principle. *Vanderbilt Journal of Transnational Law, 38*(2), 545–550.

Lee, M.-D. P. (2008). A review of the theories of corporate social responsibility: Its evolutionary path and the road ahead. *International Journal of Management Review,* 53–73.

Matten, D., & Moon J. (2008, April). "Implicit" and "explicit" CSR: A conceptual framework for a comparative understanding of corporate social responsibility. *Academy of Management Review,* 404–424.

National Institute for Standards and Technology. (1992). Malcolm Baldrige National Quality Award: 1992 Award Criteria. Washington, DC.

National Institute for Standards and Technology. (2006). Baldrige National Quality Award: Criteria for Performance Excellence. Washington, DC.

Perkins, R., & Neumayer, E. (2010). Geographic variations in the early diffusion of corporate voluntary standards: Comparing ISO 14001 and the Global Compact. *Environment and Planning A, 42,* 347–365.

Peters, T. J., & Waterman, R. H. (1982), *In search of excellence.* New York, NY: Harper & Row.

Preston, L. E. (1975). Corporation and society: The search for a paradigm. *Journal of Economic Literature, 13,* 334–354.s, *10*(1), 53–73.

Preston, L. E., & Post, J. E. (1975). *Private management and public policy: The principle of public responsibility.* Englewood Cliffs, NJ: Prentice-Hall.

Rasche, A., Waddock, S., &McIntosh, M. (2012) The United Nations Global Compact: Restrospect and prospect. *Business & Society, 52*(1), 6–30.

Steiner, G. A. (1971). *Business and society.* New York, NY: Random House.

Visser, W. (2005). Corporate citizenship in South Africa: A review of progress since democracy. *Journal of Corporate Citizenship, 18,* 29–38.

Von Hayek, F. (1944). *The road to serfdom.* Chicago, IL: University of Chicago Press.

Wood, D. J. (1991a). Social issues in management: Theory and research in corporate social performance. *Journal of Management, 17,* 383–406.

Wood, D. J. (1991b). Corporate social performance revisited. *Academy of Management Review, 16,* 691–718. Retrieved February 12, 2014, from http://www.efqm.org/about-us/our-history

PART III

PITFALLS OF CORPORATE SOCIAL PERFORMANCE

CHAPTER 7

CORPORATIONS AND CORPORATE SOCIAL PERFORMANCE—

Be Genuine, Simplify, or Leave It ...

Kathrin Köster

INTRODUCTION

This chapter takes a kind of "back to the roots view" or "forward to transcend mental models perspective" practicing and arguing for authenticity and simplicity. In the context of conventional research, this might seem unusual at first sight. Provided an open mind, it is self-explanatory and straightforward, though. It enriches the discussion by going beyond existing boundaries of our research conditioning building on the insights of quantum physics and ancient Asian philosophy. Numerous practitioners are longing for a simple approach, but find it difficult to implement. Why is this so? It requires deeper insights into the complex interrelatedness of any individual, corporation and society. Obtaining and living these insights is connected with the development of self-consciousness which seems to be

Corporate Social Performance:
Paradoxes, Pitfalls, and Pathways to the Better World, pp. 123–149
Copyright © 2015 by Information Age Publishing
All rights of reproduction in any form reserved.

a daunting task for many people. It takes courage and discipline to change mental models that have been adhered to since centuries. Corporate social responsibility (CSR) ultimately is individual social responsibility (ISR). It takes personal efforts to change one's own values and habits. There is no shortcut, although big (and successful) corporations tend to think that they can maintain their legitimacy (Davis, 1973) and prove public responsibility (Preston & Post, 1975) by investing resources to build up a CSR façade (cf. Figure 7.1). Given the fact that social responsibility lies in the realm of the individual, mainly the executives of a corporation, referred to as managerial discretion (Carroll, 1979), these individuals have to develop their self-consciousness further in order to *be* socially responsible.

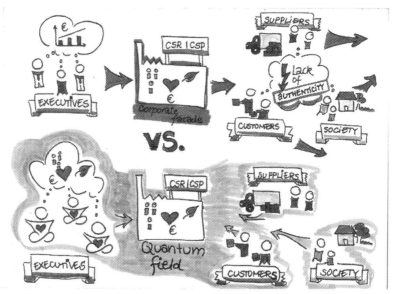

Figure 7.1

CORPORATE SOCIAL PERFORMANCE— AN APPROACH EMBEDDED IN THE VALUES OF THE SCIENCE ERA

Today's Western societies are based on the philosophy of René Descartes and Francis Bacon, and the physics of Isaac Newton. Especially after World War II these Western societies have witnessed progress in terms of growth and technological developments. They have also seen an accelerating trend that mainly big publicly listed companies enjoyed more and more power while rejecting responsibility for their business environment, in the widest sense the society they operate in and the planet they operate on. Corporations multiplied their profits decade after decade. Successful lobbying campaigns targeted at international governments led to further expansion of power of (big) business increasingly operating on a global scale. As Saul (1992) puts it provocatively: "The multinational, with its anational managers, is an attempt to escape any responsibility, thus retaining the power to treat each community according to the corporation's interests"(p. 389) The underlying business principles were an integral part of the overall world view of the science era: The promotion of absence of emotions within a strict objective and mechanistic world, separation and compartmentalization of spheres, specialization, standardization, determinism and reductionism. It is no wonder that the ideal of an organization against such a philosophical background was a "well-oiled machine" based on hierarchies and extensive rulebooks that were regarded as precise, dependable, and universally applicable. Most of the organizations were modeled by the military and incorporated its structure and principles.

Over time, there have been organizational theory developments, for instance towards project-based and network-based organizations, but the fundamentals with deeply held mental models remained largely unchanged: The dominance of the mind and intellect, especially the left-part of the brain associated with "masculine values" such as ambition, aggression, competitiveness, dominance, assertiveness and individualism (Billing & Alverson, 2000). Abstraction and method became the ruling principles resulting in a growing detachment between managers and their organizations. Managers found it entirely legitimate to pursue self-interest, mainly consisting of an increase in power and money, for themselves and their shareholders.

Researchers were intrigued and concerned by this development. The field of social responsibility emerged—soon discussed under the over-arching theme of corporate social performance (CSP) (cf. Clarkson, 1995; Cochran & Wood, 1984; Dentchev, 2004; Orlitzky, 2003; Wood, 1991, 2010). In a certain way, this research continues the long history of discussion of the mutual influence of ethics and economic behavior. Be it the ancient Greek, the Christian philosophers, Adam Smith or David Hume: "Distinctions between economic and ethical questions were rarely ever made" (Sedlacek, 2011, p. 252).

Embedded in the mental models and the deeply held beliefs of the science era, the field of CSP aims to shed light on what corporate social responsibility consists of, how it works, and how it can be measured. Increasingly, it contains normative elements drawn from business ethics research. Wood (1991) provides a rather comprehensive definition of CSP as "a business organization's configuration of principles of social responsibility, processes of social responsiveness, and policies, programs, and observable outcomes as they relate to the firm's societal relationships" (p. 993). The following explanations on CSP as such are referring to this definition.

Corporate social responsibility (CSR) is a part of CSP, namely the above mentioned principles. In the context of this chapter, CSR refers to societal and environmental sustainability on top of and in line with economic considerations (cf. Elkington, 1997). In alignment with the new approach taken in this article, CSR also comprises the mutually beneficial relations to a wider range of stakeholders, focusing on staff, customers, suppliers, local communities and societies in general that are based on and dominated by consciousness and (higher) purpose (see Section 3).

The conventional academic discussion revolves around defining and clarifying the complex phenomenon of CSR in order to fully understand it intellectually, to reduce ambiguity, to clearly determine what is within the scope of research and what is not, and to provide integrative models and guidance for practitioners with respect to the methods of implementation and measurement. This approach follows what science in the science era is supposed to do: "The scientific era has tried to demystify the world around us, to present it in mechanical, mathematical, deterministic, and rational garments" (Sedlacek, 2011, p. 171) We gained numerous insights into CSR, its implementation and outcome. Yet, one has to concede that many corporations do not use the results of this research and continue to do business as usual although they *know* better. Intellectual capacity and capability does not seem to suffice to change (corporate) behavior.

After all, CSR is still regarded by many decision makers as a set of business tools like many others. It is often seen as a compromise they need to strike to abide by the law and to accommodate stakeholders' requests, a compromise between their self-interest and the interest of their stakeholders (cf. Swanson, 1995). Corporations invest large financial resources to "dress up" in CSR clothes, to erect a façade conveying the message to external stakeholders that they do care about their interests and act accordingly. Behind the façade, though, business continues as usual, frequently with the major goal of profit maximization (cf. Figure 7.1).

The main reason for this unwillingness to incorporate CSP in an effective way is the deeply held belief that CSR does not contribute to the betterment of the business and therefore is not needed. Business education at most business schools and executive rewards have been in synch with this mental model until recently.

Following a statement ascribed to Albert Einstein, that "The world we have created today as a result of our thinking thus far has problems which cannot be solved by thinking the way we thought when we created them" (Anonymous, 2014, para.10), researchers and practitioners alike need to put their thinking into a different context.

If one leaves this world of separateness (a company positions itself against stakeholders), if one transcends the constraints formed by the reductionist value set of the science era, the whole area of CSP emerges from an entire different angle. The logic of interconnectedness becomes obvious. This logic transforms (corporate) social responsibility into a basic value any (economic) engagement revolves around.

QUANTUM PHYSICS APPLIED TO
CORPORATE SOCIAL PERFORMANCE

The findings of quantum physics and the related fields have turned our world upside down. To date the majority of people has chosen to ignore these insights and to cherish their deeply held mental models. As if there was a 180-degree-rule, many things seem to be the opposite of what most people believed them to be. The most fundamental new insight concerns the dichotomy between matter (or material) and awareness (or spirit): Not matter is the governing principle of what is perceived as "reality," but awareness. For the sake of simplicity, awareness shall be defined as the entirety of thoughts and feelings a human being has. A look at the human brain provides a better understanding of this view. Conventional wisdom says that the human brain as a physical entity is "in command." Now there is evidence that human thoughts (as part of the awareness) trigger biochemical reactions (as part of matter) in the brain. Thus, neurotrans-mitters, neuropeptides, and hormones are produced that all function as kind of "translators" of our thoughts into physical reactions (cf. Dispenza, 2012). Of course, matter also has an impact on awareness. Both poles are intertwined, with awareness in the "driver seat." In light of these cause-and-effect relations, it makes sense to include consciousness in (managerial) concepts such as CSP. Transferring these insights to the corporation, one needs to first locate consciousness in the organization.

Departing from a mechanic world view as outlined above, the analogy of a human organism seems to be helpful (Morgan, 1997). In extension of this view, let us envisage corporations consisting of the following parts (Stanford, 2013):

- Body: Organizational design and structure, (technological) systems, processes, policies
- Mind: Strategy (including vision and mission), mental models, values, concept of corporate culture, (higher) purpose (derived from consciousness)
- Spirit: Consciousness of all organizational members (leaders and team members) and their conscious behavior (among others re-

garding social responsibility) derived from this accumulated awareness. This includes the feelings of all organizational members.

While the body and mind part of the analogy sound familiar, the integration of the spirit is an additional step that can be considered "the missing
link." Why? Because all matter ultimately follows human consciousness.
Extending the view of the organization by the area of spirit brings in the
causal force to all observable outcomes, outcomes that are also measured
by CSP.

The causal chain is as follows: Only if social responsibility is deeply
ingrained in the awareness of the organization, it can materialize itself
in consistent and effective action. The consciousness of the organization
is usually dominated by the consciousness of the executives. If their true
thoughts are inconsistent with the principles of CSR the organization pos-
tulates, the outcomes are suboptimal at best. The implementation of CSR
and the outcomes of the taken measures lack consistency and credibility.
The thoughts and feelings of the executives and other influential members
of the organization ultimately create everything visible in the external
environment, be it the corporation's products and services itself, or special
CSR projects.

If the executives of the corporation think of CSP in terms of the incum-
bent system of the science era, they tend to see it mechanically: It is a
set of principles, policies, and rules, applied with the intent to maintain
legitimacy. As long as the executives and the corporation owners' interests
deviate from their main stakeholders' interests regarding individual and
social responsibility, there are inherent contradictions between the spirit,
and the mind and body level of the organization. Given the relation of
matter following consciousness, underperformance of the mind and body
part of the corporation is the logical consequence.

The movement of conscious consumerism, one of the external trig-
gers for CSR, underpins the appropriateness of the new research context
extended by the consciousness-factor. There is evidence that younger generations across the societies of industrialized countries and more reluctantly
in the emerging markets are pushing for more transparency regarding
the products they consume (Aburdene, 2005). These consumers expect
responsibility towards the ecosystem and the societies they live in. Their
buying decisions are increasingly driven by self-consciousness regarding
values and deeply held mental models. With this level of consciousness,
customers tend to detect corporations with a mechanical approach to social
responsibility easily. They expect corporations they can trust and do not
accept being "greenwashed," that is, inconsistencies in values and activities
as explained above (Rotherham, 2014).

Let us now come to another finding of quantum physics: The fact that everything is interconnected with everything (Wheeler, 2000). This is true on the subatomic level, where the quantum realm resides. It is a phenomenon called quantum-entanglement. Contrary to common belief, matter is nonlocal. Nonlocality means subatoms being everywhere and nowhere at once. From this perspective, all human beings are not only connected with each other, but also with their environment, our planet. To make this notion easier to conceive, one can imagine that all human beings have an electromagnetic field around them. This field is even perceptible using special measurement equipment. Human beings communicate through this field via the exchange of electromagnetic frequencies. If this classical physics view is extended by quantum physics, so-called quantum fields, that is, nonlocal fields, are added to the picture. The consequence is that people all over the planet, regardless of their location, regardless of their personal acquaintance, and regardless of their intent to interact, constantly exchange information (cf. Broers, 2012).

Coming from the field of biology, Sheldrake (2008) discovered the phenomenon of information exchange between animal populations that could not be explained by conventional science. He discovered so-called morphic fields through which behavior and experience was shared across locational boundaries. Quantum fields could be an explanation of this information exchange resulting in similar behaviors of populations over large distances. In later studies these phenomena were also observed with human populations.

Against this background of new science insights, deeply held beliefs of one individual being separated from other individuals and from nature need to be revised. Ahead of his time, Albert Einstein (1950) seemed to be aware of these relations:

> A human being is part of a whole, called by us 'Universe," a part limited in time and space. He experiences himself, his thoughts and feelings, as something separated from the rest—a kind of optical delusion of his consciousness. (para. 1)

Let us dissolve this optical delusion cherished during the science era and see which insights this new perspective generates with respect to CSP. The true values and behaviors of a corporation eventually transcend through. Due to nonlocality and quantum-entanglement, information is passed on to customers and other external stakeholders, whether intended or not. Real thoughts and feelings spread across the world through the morphic fields inside and outside the boundaries of a corporation.

Many corporations as of today have acknowledged the fact that their stakeholders expect them to act as social responsible units in terms of sustainability for the environment and societies. They increasingly invest resources to craft CSR strategies and derive appropriate activities from them. If the consciousness of the leaders as the most influential members or cells within this corporate organism is not consistent with this strategy, customers and other external stakeholders will pick up on these contradictions, consciously or unconsciously. Inconsistency means lack of authenticity. Lack of authenticity means lack of credibility and trust, leading to fading legitimacy. In a midterm range, the external stakeholders, mainly the customers, will abandon this corporation and feel attracted by authentic organizations that demonstrate social responsibility, that is, true concern for their stakeholders, in this case the customers.

Figure 7.1 illustrates the conventional versus the new perspective on CSP.

The two insights from quantum physics outlined above, the omnipresence and omnipotence of consciousness and the nonlocality and total interconnectedness, lead to the following conclusions:

Social Responsibility as the heart of CSP needs to be a deeply held belief of the corporation in order to be effective. It needs to be part of the corporation's spirit. Ideally, ALL members feel socially responsible, at least the executives that are most influential with their thoughts and feelings.

The motivation for corporate social performance is intrinsic and genuine—starting with the management team—rather than purely triggered by external factors as an extrinsic motivation. Anything else would contradict the self-interest of all organizational members.

For long-term effectiveness of the corporation, CSP builds an integral part of the corporation's strategy and its implementation.

Let us turn to another important area of consciousness, the feelings. Part of the mental models of the science era was the suppression of feelings in the business context. They were considered as unpredictable, unprofessional, and counterproductive. The area of marketing, though, was an exception. (Positive) emotions were deliberately used to influence customers, a reflection of a mechanistic approach.

In the new context of consciousness, it is understandable why the suppression or mechanistic use of feelings deprive human beings from an important source of energy and effectiveness. Mentally and physically, feelings can be seen as 'amplifier'. They boost the power of thoughts. Hence, it is crucial not only to aim at consistency of thoughts and corporate policies, programs and rules, but also at alignment of thoughts and feelings (cf. Dispenza, 2012).

Acting in a way that is socially responsible boosts positive feelings. Since all human beings are interconnected, acting in a way that is good for a person's colleagues or ecosystem is equally conducive for the person performing social responsibility. If this knowledge can be translated consistently into appropriate behavior, positive feelings emerge and function as a kind of positive reinforcement. The organizational team member has more energy at his or her disposal that can flow into the development of sustainable and creative products and services with positive impact on the society.

As described above, the science era has unilaterally focused on the left part of the brain. The active inclusion of the emotional side shifts the focus to the right part of the brain, thus contributing to a balance and cross-fertilization of mind and heart. Ancient Asian philosophies such as Daoism and Confucianism or the Indian Baghavad Gita have postulated the importance of such a balance since thousands of years (Hawley, 2001; Nisbett, 2003; Schmidt, 1996). It is time to incorporate this knowledge into corporations again in order to make them as effective as possible.

Going back to the analogy of the organization as an organism with a body, mind, and spirit, it becomes obvious that only a holistic approach can result in effective CSP.

Ignoring the spirit deprives the organization from its most powerful source of positive impact on the society and the planet. As stated before, if there is inconsistency between the true thoughts and feelings of organizational members, the spirit, on one hand, and the mind and body on the other hand, the entire corporation loses effectiveness due to misalignment. It tries to efficiently implement a CSR strategy that its mind has crafted, and uses its body to measure its outcome. Unconsciously, though, the spirit is "sabotaging" all these efforts. The corporation resembles a sick patient as it aims at doing things half-heartedly. Even if there are no outright inconsistencies, the organization could use its spirit more intensively by acknowledging it with full self-consciousness. It could use it as the center piece of its strategy and implementation through consistent behavior of ALL organizational members. The spirit can be regarded as the corporation's "energy source" amplified by positive feelings.

In addition to the three conclusions derived from quantum physics, a fourth conclusion can be drawn from abandoning reductionist materialism of the science era and applying a truly holistic approach to the organizational context:

4. The acknowledgment and conscious use of mental power along with the power of positive feelings can generate positive impact for internal and external stakeholders. Thus, the genuine thought and feeling of social responsibility is linked to an increase of vitality within the corporation that can translate into stronger attractive-

ness of the organization. This, in turn, means more motivated and committed staff as well as an increasing number of enthusiastic customers.

Any individual that fully comprehends the implications of what is outlined above, will not only intellectually understand, but simultaneously feel his or her dependence on the planet, the people (here the organizational members) and the society with all important stakeholders like customers. Against this background, being sustainable and socially responsible is a compelling integral part of any organization's strategy and its implementation.

It is a reflection of the science era that many corporations handle CSR and consequently CSP as something that can be entrusted to a dedicated subunit of the overall entity, typically the CSR department, the human resource department or the public relations department. This organizational architecture implies that the "'rest" of the corporation is unaffected by CSR or CSP. It is the mental model of specialization that has paved the way for the modern organization. It lured us into the notion that it is appropriate to have some dedicated team members in the company that can deal with yet another set of external stakeholder expectations, such as the "greenies" and others out there who put pressure on the company to receive money or any other concession. Following a mechanistic approach, communication experts professionally convey messages about the 'good' the corporation is doing in order to meet the requests of external stakeholders. This is a typical form of how the organization interacted with its environment in the past. It is not the adequate approach for CSR in times where the insights derived from quantum physics are absorbed by an increasing number of people—employees and customers alike (cf. Aburdene, 2005). Numerous global citizens start to hold corporations accountable for what they are doing across their entire value chain. The paradigm shift in science as outlined above is accompanied by a value shift towards heightened consciousness regarding an individual's and a corporations' responsibility in the world societies.

SUSTAINABLE SUCCESS THROUGH BEING SOCIALLY RESPONSIBLE

In the light of the power of awareness and the interrelatedness and interconnectedness, antisocial thoughts and feelings as well as the pursuit of individual or corporate interests with negative impact on the society cannot be hidden or disguised in the mid- to long-term. If an organization still has the deeply held mental model of profit and/or power maximization as its ultimate purpose, it should be clear and straightforward about it.

The only concession it needs to make is complying with legal regulations in order not to lose its legitimacy and with it its right of existence. Solely and whole-heartedly committed to the purpose of profit or power maximization, should this corporation claim to be socially responsible for the negative impact it has caused, that is, assume public responsibility, or go further and engage in philanthropy (Wood, 1991)?

Not judging ethically but applying pure economic rational from the science era, it is a suboptimal investment to go beyond the minimum legal requirements provided that the executives and owners are not intrinsically motivated by this approach. If they do not fully believe in it and use CSP as a mere method to increase their competitiveness, they will ultimately lose it. Why? With mental models from the science era, they operate in global societies that have an increasingly changed perception of life (or reality) based on the insights derived from quantum physics. Over time, these companies will be marginalized and lose their brand value as described above. They will not be sustainable and ultimately lose their legitimacy. As unauthentic CSP will boomerang and undermine trust, it might be wiser or at least authentic to not engage in any CSR activities beyond the strict legal requirements. Against this background, it may be better to not engage in any form of CSP, as hinted in the title of this chapter: "Corporations and Corporate Social Performance—*Be* Genuine, Simplify, **Or Leave It ...**".

Having discussed the extreme on one side, let us turn to the extreme on the other side, namely an organization that *is* genuinely socially responsible. As corporate executives have the greatest influence in and on the organization, we use the individual executive as starting point for a journey embarking the corporation towards fully effective corporate social performance. What are the requirements for proceeding on this path?

It is self-consciousness on the side of the executives who turn into transformational leaders during their own "metamorphosis." A transformational leader with strong self-consciousness can turn his own individual social responsibility (ISR) to effective CSP via the organizational team members who also embark on the journey of developing their self-consciousness and using in turn their ISR to enforce the organizational Corporate Social Performance. It is a self-reinforcing process ultimately turning the organization into a strong attractor of customers, potential new employees, media and research attention, adequate suppliers, and so forth. In other words: ISR assumed by a self-conscious management team leads to organizational effectiveness including monetary success mid- to long-term. Empirical evidence for this causal relationship is provided by the study of Mackey, Sisodia, and George (2013).

At first glance, one might be clueless where to start the journey and what concretely to do. The ancient Chinese philosopher Confucius offers advice:

The ancients who wished to illustrate illustrious virtue throughout the kingdom, first ordered well their own states. Wishing to order well their states, they first regulated their families. Wishing to regulate their families, they first cultivated their persons. Wishing to cultivate their persons, they first rectified their hearts. Wishing to rectify their hearts, they first sought to be sincere in their thoughts. (Legge, 2001, p. 357)

Translated into a modern organizational context, authenticity and consistency starting with oneself could be seen as the critical success factor for an effective organization, an organization that displays virtue, or, that performs CSR.

With hindsight, an incremental approach taken by each individual as described below seems to be adequate. As we are all different, there are numerous deviations and adaptations of this spiral process summarized in Table 7.1 and visualized in Figure 7.2.

1.   *Questioning deeply held mental models and beliefs.*

A starting point can be reading this article without discarding its underlying mental models immediately but remaining open and curious about a world that functions differently.

2.   *Assuming unconditional responsibility for one's actions.*

Responsibility is a personal matter. Executives cannot repudiate the responsibility for the impact of a decision they have taken. The moral standards of the world of the science era, though, facilitate this disconnect between decisions and their consequences. They promote mechanistic, compartmentalized thinking focusing on separateness. These standards often lead to contradictory behavior. An executive can be very caring for his partner and children, dismissing 10,000 employees in a very inhuman manner without batting an eyelash. Another executive can see his daughter dying from leukemia and continue allowing his company to pour toxic sewerage into a lake in South America. Obviously, these individuals do not act in a socially responsible way in their roles as company heads which stands in stark contrast to their family roles. As a matter of fact, such individuals—still many managers of big corporations—have not yet tapped into the full potential of their consciousness. Their mental models from the science era led them to measure with different yards. Since everything is interrelated, any negative impact an organization has on its environment reversely has a negative impact on this organization—admittedly with a time lag, though. Hence, there is only one yardstick that is applicable to all situations. It starts with the truth, the truth to oneself, the truth that is the basis for unconditional responsibility taking (cf. Senge, 1990).

3. *Willingness for acknowledging and taking responsibility for feelings.*

Leaders need intellectual *and* emotional capability to apprehend the logic outlined above. They need to take stock of their emotions, to address the root-causes of them in order to masters them instead of being ruled by their emotions (cf. Goleman, 1995). The biggest constraint is the feeling of fear, or even "angst." Not many individuals are as courageous as daring to question their entire world view.

4. *Overcoming ego constraints.*

The path towards fully developed consciousness might be cumbersome. It means overcoming the ego that stands in any individual's way. The ego is a residual of the old era, loaded with strong inertia. It aims at maintaining the "optical delusion" of separateness. It puts human beings in a competition and 'fighting' mode. The ego with its power maximization tendencies has been fueled by the values of the science era. It is rather persistent and takes continuous efforts to be balanced off and overcome.

5. *Adopting new mental models and transferring them to the organizational context.*

If executives transcend the mental models of the science era, they gradually abandon thoughts and feelings that would result in negative impact on others, be it internal or external stakeholders. This is the logical consequence from the insight of interconnectedness. Any damage inflicted on staff, customers, the broader society, will return to the source of the damage. This insight commands the moral imperative (without any underlying dogma) to constantly act in a way that oneself would most appreciate. All organizational action takes place within a reference frame. This is the vision along with the (higher) purpose of the organization as outlined in section three. The purpose is strongly intertwined with consciousness. Why does the corporation exist at all? What is its raison d'être? Here comes a fundamental challenge regarding self-consciousness for any executive: Is the purpose of the organization beneficial to its main external stakeholders, namely the customers and ultimately its end consumers, but also for the societies the corporation operates in? Executives of corporations with a heavy negative impact on various stakeholders such as tobacco companies or armament firms might find it difficult to find an honest answer. Depending on the state of development of their self-consciousness, they may decide to switch industries.

6. *Leading and shining by example.*

The image that an organization is an organism rather than a mechanism, leads to the acknowledgment that ALL cells of the body are equally important. If any single cell turns sick the rest of the body starts to suffer. Against this background, the leaders implement social responsibility within their organization. As a "primus inter pares" they treat their staff in a way they themselves want to be treated. They vitalize the organization with their positive feelings and the power of their thoughts. Their consciousness is linked to the consciousness of all employees, whether they are aware of this linkage or not. Depending on the state of consciousness development, the organizational members might just feel appreciated and spread on the good mood, without exactly knowing the root-cause of their feelings. Leaders instill mental and emotional energy in their organization which translates into a creative and positive organizational culture. Whether values as respect or joy are formalized or not, they prevail and unleash innovative power. Over time, the attitude of each organizational member conveys the message: We do like what we are doing, and we do care for our customers, the environment, and the communities we operate in. This requires constant strong efforts by the leaders and the basic open-mindedness of staff.

   7.   *The journey is the reward.*

   The work to develop one's own consciousness is tedious—and rewarding. It goes in spirals and presumably never ends. Short-term, leaders might not even see any progress except from an increasing personal contentment. Formed by the values of the science era like "time is money" executives need to be very persistent and manage to transform the old paradigm. They have to be courageous just to think and act differently from their peers. They have to be patient and rely on strong self-confidence to allow for the time the process of consciousness development takes to travel across the organization. After all, this is a radical change process, maybe the most radical we can imagine.
   Table 7.1 summarizes the journey towards organizational effectiveness through ISR that can be regarded as a spiral process that differs from organization to organization.
   The seven steps outlined above encompass a road towards genuine and simple CSP revolving around ISR. At the end, electromagnetic frequencies transmitted by the leaders linked through the morphic field send strong messages of social responsibility towards the staff. Depending on the organization, team members also might send corresponding messages due to their advanced self-consciousness. Socially responsible thinking and feeling spreads through the entire organization. The reference frame is the organization's purpose that bonds all members together.

Table 7.1.	The Journey Towards Organizational Effectiveness Through ISR
Step 1	Questioning deeply held mental models and beliefs
Step 2	Assuming unconditional responsibility for one's actions
Step 3	Willingness for acknowledging and taking responsibility for feelings
Step 4	Overcoming ego constraints
Step 5	Adopting new mental models and transferring them to the organizational context
Step 6	Leading and shining by example
Step 7	The journey is the reward

Figure 7.2

Strong consciousness levels along with a clear and articulated purpose and the amplifier of positive feelings function as a magnet. Aligned consciousness attracts customers and other external stakeholders. They feel drawn to the corporation due to its authenticity. They do appreciate the products and services of this corporation because they emanate trust. Word of mouth and social media will help to attract more stakeholders, mainly customers, and help the company to thrive. This process is visualized in Figure 7.3.

The journey of CSP built on ISR is a fundamental change project that takes years. Obviously, it is easier for corporations that are built from scratch with a strong spirit and self-consciousness of their members. They tend to naturally *be* socially responsible and have a simple and effective CSP system in place due to their developed consciousness and their organizational purpose. There is a trend, for instance in Berlin (Germany), where a few of such organizations are emerging.

As is true for all major change initiatives, the crucial success factor is the intrinsic motivation of the (transformational) leaders. It is mainly them who have to follow the seven steps. In contrast to conventional change initiatives, the will to develop one's self-consciousness cannot be imposed on anyone. If a team member refuses to open up towards new mental models, acceptance is the only response. Depending on the position of such a person it might be wise to go separate paths to avoid an 'interfering

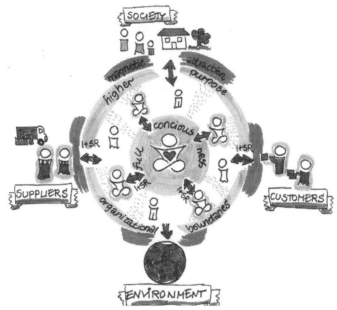

Figure 7.3

transmitter' causing inconsistencies in the message of social responsibility. For people who are willing to take step one (cf. Table 7.1), the corporation can tailor offers to train self-consciousness, either provided by external parties, or by staff members who take on this additional responsibility as part of their job enrichment.

In general, it is easier to introduce genuine, simple CSP centered on ISR as outlined above in a small and medium sized enterprise where leaders have a more direct leverage. To this effect, genuine corporate social performance that leads to an increase of effectiveness may be considered a strategic competitive advantage of small and medium sized enterprises.

EXAMPLES OF GENUINE AND SIMPLE CSP BASED ON ISR

As stated above, the transformation to *genuine* and simple corporate social performance starts with the acceptance of ISR. Against this background it is compelling that the leader of a truly socially responsible organization has embarked on the journey visualized in Figure 7.3. Hence, the examples below will revolve around the leaders and their basic attitudes (ISR). With strengthened self-consciousness and consistent behavior, organizations align themselves increasingly towards their (higher) purpose and increase their internal and external effectiveness.

A few companies have started to embark on this journey to build CSP through ISR, without being familiar with the concept of ISR as outlined in this chapter. They are often taking this route intuitively, without having explicit concepts in place to document their social responsibility. This is not needed either. Following the route of simplicity, they are just acting in the interest of their main stakeholders, guided by their consciousness and purpose, and serve their staff, their customers, their suppliers, and the communities they operate in.

The following company examples aim at providing a deeper under-standing of "ISR at work." Each company is taken to elucidate the impact of ISR on one main stakeholder group: Customers (ColmarBrunton), society and societies in general (LesMills), suppliers and local communi-ties (WE'AR), and staff (Futurice). All these companies with their different team members are at different stages on their spiral journey to extend their spheres of activities and increase their organizational effectiveness as depicted in Figure 7.3. All are economically successful measured in rampant, profit-based growth, environmentally friendly, have satisfied and enthusiastic employees shown in low fluctuation rates and long tenure, increasing numbers of loyal customers, and positive resonance from the communities they operate in.

Three of the corporations are headquartered in New Zealand, the fourth originates from Finland. They are operating in different industries, namely in the service industry (market research, fitness programs), apparel indus-try (fashion and accessories), and in the information technology sector. Sisodia, Wolfe, and Sheth (2014) provide more comprehensive and sys-tematic empirical evidence about the effectiveness of self-conscious socially responsible corporations than the rather anecdotal selection below that is based on the author's own empirical research.

ColmarBrunton—ISR and Customers

Founded in 1981, ColmarBrunton is a market research company with offices in Auckland (HQ) and Wellington. As of 2014, it employs approxi-mately 100 full time and roughly 150 part time staff. The majority of the shares are held by Millward Brown, the minority by senior management and Dick Brunton, co-founder and executive chairman of the company. (Jayne, 2013)

As part of his own personal development and emergence of self-con-sciousness Brunton realized the crucial role of his genuine will to support the customers in the sense of making their lives better. Brunton is fully con-vinced that his (higher) purpose of serving the customer in terms of great customer experiences makes business sense, because the business world is about an "experience economy," it is about authenticity and genuine commitment to serve others. This is fully in line with the holistic approach of ISR outlined above. The mission of ColmarBrunton is to provide a voice to the consumers, the society in the wider sense, to make them really heard by the decision takers, ColmarBrunton's direct customers.

To live up to his commitment, Brunton is aware of the fact that he has to tune into his customer's needs and wishes. He uses his emotional intelligence to do so: "I speak from the heart, and people respond to it" (Brunton, 2014). In his experience, most CEOs he has worked with are extremely intelligent and well educated. However, they are heading soul-less businesses. This is no wonder given the mental models of the science era explained in section two. Brunton is convinced of the equation that ethical business is better business, in monetary terms and beyond. (Brunton, 2011; Jayne, 2013)

This awareness is also reflected in the company's vision "Better world, better business" that was rephrased to "Better business, better future" in 2014 (ColmarBrunton, 2014). Jacqueline Ireland, ColmarBrunton's CEO, is very clear about what this vision means to her: "As a business, we must not impact and ruin social structure.... To me, sustainability is just good, it is the right thing to do, and it is very dear to my heart" (Ireland, 2014).

Since 2008, the market research company has used its set of core competences to conduct a survey among New Zealanders investigating changes of consumer behavior in favor of sustainability in the widest sense. According to the monitor of 2013, there are strong indications that the younger the people, the more demanding they are in terms of all aspects of sustainability. This customer group holds organizations increasingly accountable for their behavior and negative effects on society and planet. In general, the study observed a shift in mental models, with the expansion of focus from the individual towards the concern for the society in general (Ireland, 2013), a finding that is in line with the explanations in section three. The annual sustainability survey is conducted as part of ColmarBrunton's social responsibility at their own expenses. Ireland uses the results in customer workshops to raise customers' awareness regarding these societal trends focusing on the necessity to recognize sustainability as an integral part of their brands (Ireland, 2014).

In his client workshops, Brunton confronts his customers on the issue of honesty and authenticity. As a kind of check list, he uses the whole range of touch points, the so-called "moments of truth," covering the entire value chain, from how the company introduces itself to a potentially new customer, how a contract is negotiated, training is provided, to the ongoing account management, invoicing and price increases. In Brunton's opinion, an organization really serves customers to their needs if it is flexible and savvy to spontaneously correspond to customer's wishes, and to be willing to go beyond the rulebook. Brunton speaks of intuition leading to genuine customer experience (Brunton, 2014), an attitude that displays a holistic approach as described above.

LesMills—ISR and Society in General

LesMills was founded by Olympic champion Les Mills together with his wife in 1968 as a fitness gym in Auckland. In the 1980s, their son Philipp Mills was inspired by the combination of music and fitness flourishing in the United States and started his own program called "Pump" in New Zealand. International demand for the program grew steadily. As of 2014, fitness clubs in about 80 countries are buying licenses for LesMills-programs. The fitness programs can be regarded as the "software," while the gyms the company solely operates in New Zealand can be considered the "hardware," The programs are designed to motivate people to improve the fitness of their body through sophisticated choreography along with energizing music. Quarterly updates ensure attractiveness and fun. As of 2014, LesMills is a family owned company with two independent legal entities, LesMills New Zealand and LesMills International that employ overall more than 1,000 people. The majority of shares of both companies are held by the Mills family, with an increasing minority of shares owned by senior managers and key personnel (LesMills International, 2013a; Mills, 2014).

The company's leader and CEO Philipp Mills is a strong advocate of ISR, starting with the self-responsibility for one's body. An active and passionate sportsman himself, he leads by example, engaging in sports activities inside and outside the company. His (higher) purpose is to transform mental models and habits, particularly the sedentary lifestyle of many people in the (Western) world, partially the consequence of the values of the science era.

Mills' logic is as follows: The health of each individual is connected to the health of our societies and to the health of the entire planet. He regards the global phenomenon of obesity, referred to as "globesity," as a major global challenge societies need to address. The phenomenon is spreading like a pandemic across the world, led by the United States with 30% of the overall population being heavily obese and 70% overweight (Mills & Mills, 2007). Not only does this cause unhappiness and discomfort at the side of the affected individuals, but induces heavy cost for the health systems due to the numerous diseases inflicted by obesity. This capital cannot be invested in measures to protect the environment and preserve natural resources. (Mills & Mills, 2007)

LesMills aims at reversing the "globesity" trend by attracting as many customers as possible who engage in losing weight and increase their personal fitness. The company's formula is: Mass movement against mass phenomenon. "Now, with millions of members supporting us, we're dedicated to creating a fitter planet. We aim to help others around the globe by increasing awareness, fundraising and putting energy into important causes" (LesMills International, 2013a, para. 2) The ISR of the leaders and staff of LesMills seems to catch other individuals worldwide to take self-responsibility and indirectly becoming part of the bigger group of people helping all human beings by freeing resources in our societies that can be used to preserve our planet.

The logic outlined above illustrating how ISR results in corporate social performance is boiled down in LesMills's motto "Fitter people, fitter planet" (LesMills International, 2013a).

WE'AR-ISR, Suppliers, and Local Communities

WE'AR is the perfect example of a new category of companies that could be called the "Ethical Mini Multinational." Such organizations have entirely transcended the mental models of the science era. WE'AR was established in 2005 by the New Zealander Jyoti Morningstar. In 2014, the company, with two independent legal entities in Indonesia and New Zealand, has approximately 35 full-time employees. Turnover saw a year on year increase of more than 50% in 2013. Morningstar's (higher) purpose is to combine sustainable development with needs of yoga practitioners and conscious consumers who look for trendy, yet comfortable and ethical clothes in the West. With her fashion Morningstar offers an alternative for consumers who want to spend their money on ethical *and* fashionable *and* natural products. She states that all individuals contribute to the world they desire through their buying decisions. WE'AR offers a choice for those who like to help to transform the world into a more responsible and sustainable place. Besides online sales, the company distributes its products through its four shops, two in New Zealand and two on Bali, known as an international yoga hot spot (Morningstar, 2014; Rotherham, 2014; WE'AR, 2014a; WE'AR, 2014b).

Morningstar, a long-time yoga practitioner and teacher, has a very strong self-consciousness. She has embarked on the journey depicted in Figure 7.3 at an early stage of her life. She sees her spirit and values fully reflected in her company. Compassion, generosity, adaptability, integrity, and fearless in the face of complexity—these are the values that form the spirit and mind of WE'AR (Morningstar, 2014).

Production was deliberately chosen to be located in a developing country to empower local people to have a better living through sustainable employment. Bali was close to Morningstar's heart due its culture strongly shaped by Hinduism and yoga principles. On Bali, she established relations with some family-run manufacturing houses. As of 2014, WE'AR provides employment to around 150 Balinese in a number of small home workshops and factories in the Chang Gu area. Although Morningstar does not own the manufacturing houses that serve as WE'AR's suppliers, she regularly inspects them and makes sure that all employees are paid a decent wage, have a health care insurance and a pension. Due to her personal relations to her suppliers she is reluctant to grow the business too fast as this would demand the establishment of a supervision system to ensure adherence to WE'AR's moral standards.

The company also invests heavily in education which is a business need. In order to have the required skills on site among suppliers and staff, she needs to train and enable local people. Usually, Morningstar hires an expert from a Western country who is willing to take the challenge and come to Bali for about six months. Within this period of time, these specialists are supposed to contribute to the business solving technical issues and to transfer their expertise to local staff and suppliers. This skill transfer has been established very successfully. New options are explored: There has been small series with hand-woven cotton that is dyed with natural colors. With the support of external advisers, the method is continuously refined. The local manufacturing houses are encouraged to make investments such as buying an electricity-powered shredder that helps with color extraction on a bigger scale. Advice is also provided regarding the cradle-to-cradle process in order not to waste any resources. To summarize, WE'AR's Balinese suppliers have to provide fair labor conditions. In return, they are supported by WE'AR regarding competence development and product and process innovations mainly aiming at sustainable production (Morningstar, 2014; WE'AR Moving Pictures, 2011).

Beyond WE'AR's socially responsible commitment to its Balinese suppliers, the company has a positive impact on the local communities. By setting an example, implementing fair labor conditions and *being* socially responsible, other companies on Bali, domestic and foreign-invested, are encouraged and even indirectly pressurized to change their way of doing business and treating people. The local communities also benefit from Morningstar's commitment to spend one New Zealand Dollar per garment on a social project (WE'AR, 2014a). So far, there has not been a comprehensive plan or scheme on how to use this money apart from the guideline to give money directly to the people using it rather than donating it to any institution. As the company is growing, Morningstar plans to channel her social investment into three areas, two of them targeting local communities on Bali, and one aiming at the communities in New Zealand: On one hand, WE'AR will support the fight against the abduction and displacement of Balinese children, commonly referred to as "sex-slavery." On the other hand, the company will continue to invest in initiatives to improve schooling on Bali which is also in the best self-interest of businesses operating on the island. In New Zealand, Morningstar aims at a special part of the community, namely prisoners. There is growing evidence that yoga can have strong transformative effects on disadvantaged and underprivileged people such as prison inmates (Mansel, 2013).

Futurice—ISR and Staff

The software service company that builds user driven web and mobile devices was established in 2000. Headquartered in Finland with operations in Germany and the United Kingdom, the company employed 160 people in 2013. Futurice's main customers are international operators, device manufacturers and media companies. Its revenues grew from 7.7 m Euros in 2009 to 11.6 m Euros in 2011 (Great Place to Work Institute, 2013; Kervinen, 2012).

Futurice's leadership team has consciously left the mental models of the science era exemplified by organizational control systems and hierarchies which they experienced as counterproductive to their corporate performance (Nevanlinna, 2014). Instead, they fully built on ISR starting with their staff. With the strong belief in empowerment of the individual and the power of mutual trust, the leaders established full transparency in the organization with the goal that all information including strategy details and budgets are accessible by the entire workforce. Each individual team member was encouraged to take decisions on his or her own and was given full freedom to do so. The decisions are guided by one simple thumb rule called "3 x 2" : "3" stands for people in terms of colleagues (1), customers (2), and numbers in terms of business results (3). '2' symbolizes the present and the future alike. In other words, team members should act in the best interest of their colleagues, their customers, and the overall business (Kervinen, 2012). Put in the context of this article, the leaders, deliberately or not, trust in the alignment forces of consciousness and the field as described in section two. They emulate the total interconnectedness and availability of information by implementing full information transparency in their organization. In addition, they have gone through a lengthy process to build the (higher) purpose along with their vision, mission, and strategy together with all organizational members to make sure that the common reference frame, the "magnet" as depicted in Figure 7.3, is known and fully endorsed by the entire workforce. A major part of the purpose can be summarized as follows: "We believe software is the backbone of the societies of tomorrow. We believe that in order to have a healthy society, we need software of exceptional quality that solves the right problems" (Saarinen, 2013, para. 5)

Within this frame of purpose to help societies in general with their software solutions and designs, the company acknowledges the importance of feelings and actively integrates them in the overall business. This basic attitude is reflected in the first of Futurice's four values: "caring." "The people of Futurice are always considered as unique persons, not only employees" (Kervinen, 2012, p. 4). Special rituals such as the "weekly smile" session demonstrate how feelings are part of the business. Organizational members draw their own smiley face on a board, accessible to their peers, and share their mood and thoughts, happy or sad, business-related or generic, with their team members. The overall well-being of their members, including harmonious relations with their families, builds the centerpiece of Futurice's raison d'être. This interrelation is nicely elucidated in a simple circle: Happy people, happy customers, happy end-users (Nevanlinna, 2014). The example of Futurice clearly shows the logic of genuine and simple CSP: There is authentic and true care for staff and customers alike, the main stakeholders. Enthusiastic employees and loyal customers lead to monetary business success. There is no need for additional metrics that would measure CSP: Simple and straightforward employee and customer surveys suffice.

SUMMARY, IMPLICATIONS, AND FUTURE RESEARCH

Extending the "playing field" of research, this chapter transcended the mental boundaries of the science era and introduced consciousness as a crucial factor influencing the (business) world. This approach is strongly interdisciplinary transferring insights from quantum physics to the world of corporations and their impact on our societies. The corporation is seen as an organism consisting of the consciousness of all its team members, aligned by their (higher) purpose that is usually instilled by the leaders. WE'AR provides a perfect example for conscious leadership. If this organism is aware of the fact that everything is interconnected, it will have a purpose that has a positive impact on stakeholders as exemplified by the purpose and vision of LesMills, and it will allocate resources automatically in a way that *is* socially responsible. No additional measures related to the implementation of corporate social performance are needed because the inbuilt intelligence of the organization based on continuously developing consciousness (if the leaders embark on the journey described in Table 7.1 and Figure 7.2) results in high staff satisfaction, enthusiastic customers, and *consequently* in growing profits. These key performance indicators can be monitored and evaluated with conventional controlling approaches seen as means for continuous improvement. The example of Futurice is a good illustration case. The critical success factor is individual social responsibility

(ISR), the center-piece of well-known ancient Asian philosophy traditions such as Confucianism or Daoism.

Due to an increasing number of people with awakening or fully developed consciousness, the fact whether companies act in a socially responsible way or not will soon be reflected in brand value. This is clearly shown in the ColmarBrunton example. If a corporation does not live up to its postulated values, and acts in a way that negatively impacts its main stakeholders, the customers will increasingly exert their right of choice and ignore this firm. A decrease in brand value will be the consequence. Corporations need to become aware of the fact that their main stakeholders, employees, customers and suppliers, are becoming increasingly demanding regarding their expectations towards the role of an organization. It is neither a money printing mechanism nor a power maximization vehicle for executives and owners. It is a network of people that come together linked by their consciousness, attracted by a common purpose. Guided by their self-consciousness they engage in serving themselves by serving customers and their environment, namely our planet and our societies.

The concept of ISR is based on extended mental models in synch with insights from natural sciences and ancient philosophies. Mental models are shaped and conveyed through education. Hence, ISR calls for modified business and leadership education on an undergraduate, graduate, and post-graduate level. Priority should be on executive training due to the fact that top management needs to take a leading role in implementing ISR. Following the trend of extending the conventional syllabus of business administration studies by sustainable management and CSR, there needs to be an additional subject on "Consciousness Development" along with offers of meditation and other techniques enhancing the journey towards greater awareness with the aim of enabling people to understand AND practice ISR. Some renowned business schools already offer such elements as part of their overall business administration studies. As stated, courses on awareness building need to be electives to respect the free will of any individual. Not everybody is prepared to transcend his or her mental models. Tutors could be transdisciplinary providing students and executives with insights from their respective fields, be it quantum physics, ancient philosophies, business ethics, or consciousness-based management approaches.

Future research on ISR clearly focusses on the broadening of empirical evidence which is extremely limited to date. So far, there seems to be only a small number of organizations practicing ISR at different stages. World-wide "stock-taking" projects would be highly valuable, starting with a qualitative approach, adding more quantitative elements over time. The nature of the phenomenon calls for longitudinal studies. As ISR is easier to implement in start-up companies or small and medium sized enterprises, there is the difficulty of identifying such organizations that might not even have their ISR-approach documented. Hence, a collaborative effort among world-wide academics similar to the GLOBE study would be an adequate approach to search for "ISR at work" on a global scale and discover "hidden shining examples of ISR." Content-wise the concept of ISR is strongly linked with the movement and research efforts of conscious capitalism, nontraditional innovation management, and to some extent integral theory.

REFERENCES

Anonymous. (2014). Albert Einstein. In *Wikipedia*. Retrieved March 28, 2014, from en.wikiquote.org/wiki/Albert_Einstein

Aburdene, P. (2005). *Megatrends 2010. The rise of conscious capitalism*. Charlottesville, VA: Hampton Roads.

Billing, Y., & Alverson, M. (2000). Questioning the notion of female leadership: A critical perspective on the gender labelling of leadership. *Gender, Work and Organization*, 7(3), 144–157.

Broers, D. (2012). *Das Geheimnis des Matrix Code* [The secret of the matrix code] (2nd ed.). Munich, Germany: Trinity.

Brunton, D. (2011, April 26). Successful customer service has to come from the heart. *New Zealand Herald*, p.11.

Brunton, D. (2014). Interview with Dick Brunton, Executive Chairman of ColmarBrunton. Conducted on January 21, 2014, 15.00–18.00 in Whenuapai, Auckland, New Zealand, by Kathrin Köster

Carroll, A. B. (1979). A three-dimensional conceptual model of corporate performance. *The Academy of Management Review*, 4(4), 497–505.

Clarkson, M. (1995). A stakeholder framework for analyzing and evaluating corporate social performance. *Academy of Management Review*, 20, 92–117.

Cochran, P. L., & Wood, R. A. (1984). Corporate social responsibility and financial performance. *Academy of Management Journal*, 27(1), 42–56.

ColmarBrunton. (2014). Homepage. Retrieved April 3, 2014, from http://www.colmarbrunton.co.nz/

Davis, K., (1973). The case for and against business assumption of social responsibilities, *Academy of Management Journal*, 16, 312–322.

Dentchev, N. (2004). Corporate Social Performance as a Business Strategy, *Journal of Business Ethics*, 55, 397–412

Dispenza, J. (2012). *Breaking the habit of being yourself: How to lose your mind and create a new one*. London, England: HayHouse.

Einstein, A. (1950). Letter to Robert S. Marcus dated February 12, 1950. Retrieved March 27, 2014, from http://blog.onbeing.org/post/241572419/einstein-sleuthing-by-nancy-rosenbaum-associate

Elkington, J. (1997). *Cannibals with forks*. Oxford, England: Capstone.

Goleman, D. (1995). *Emotional intelligence. Why it can matter more than IQ*. New York, NY: Bantan Books.

Hawley, J. (Ed.). (2001). *The Bhadavad Gita. A walkthrough for Westerners.* Novato, CA: New World Library.

Great Place to Work Institute. (2013). The 100 best workplaces in Europe 2013. Retrieved April 2, 2014, from http://www.greatplacetowork.net/storage/documents/Publications_Documents/2013_europe_publication.pdf

Ireland, J. (2013). Consumer trends and attitudes to sustainable business in 2013. Retrieved February 23, 2014, from http://vimeo.com/81745328

Ireland, J., (2014). Interview with the CEO of Colmar Brunton, conducted on February, 21, 2014, 10.30-12.00, in Takapuna, Auckland, New Zealand, by Kathrin Köster.

Jayne, V., (2013, April). Nurturing the noble business. *NZ Management*, 42–45.

Kervinen, A. (2012). The decision to trust boosts performance. Retrieved April 2, 2014, from: http://www.futurice.com/the-decision-to-trust-boosts-performance.pdf

Legge, J. (2001). *The Chinese classics* (Vol. 1, Reprint). Safety Harbor, FL: Simon Publications.

LesMills International. (2013a). About Les Mills. Retrieved February 2, 2014, from http://www.lesmills.com/global/about-les-mills/about-les-mills.aspx?_ga=1.3 0165631.196020309.1396872047

LesMills International. (2013b). Changing the world. Retrieved February 2, 2014, from http://w3.lesmills.com/global/en/about-les-mills/changing-the-world/

Mackey, J., & Sisodia, R. (2013). Conscious capitalism. Liberating the heroic spirit of business. Boston, MA: Harvard Business Press

Mansel, T. (2013). How yoga is helping prisoners stay calm. Retrieved February 19, 2014, from http://www.bbc.co.uk/news/magazine-24272978

Mills, P. (2014). Telephone interview with the CEO of LesMills, conducted on February 10, 2014, 11.30-12.00, by Kathrin Köster

Mills, P., & Mills, J. (2007). *Fighting globesity. A practical guide to personal health and global sustainability.* Auckland, New Zealand: Random House.

Morgan, G. (1997). *Images of organizations* (2nd Ed.). Thousand Oaks, CA: Sage.

Morningstar, J. (2014). Interview with the managing director of WE'AR, conducted February 18, 2014, 11.00–13.00, Auckland, New Zealand, by Kathrin Köster

Nevanlinna, H. (2014). With openness and trust. Retrieved April 3, 2014, from https://tapahtumat.tekes.fi/uploads/06409158/Nevanlinna-3161.pdf

Nisbett, R. E. (2003). *The geography of thought. How Asians and Westerners think differently … and why.* New York, NY: Free Press.

Orlitzky M. (2003). Corporate social and financial performance, a meta-analysis, *Organization Studies, 24*, 403–441.

Preston, L. E., & Post, J. E. (1975). *Private management and public policy: The principle of public responsibility.* Englewood Cliffs, NJ: Prentice-Hall.

Rotherham, F. (2014). Yoga ethic behind new store. Retrieved February 18, 2014, from http://www.stuff.co.nz/business/small-business/9722848/Yoga-ethic-behind-new-store

Saarinen, V. (2013). Why does Futurice exist? Retrieved April 3, 2014, from http://blog.futurice.com/why-does-futurice-exist

Saul, R. J. (1992). Voltaire's bastards: The dictatorship of reason in the West. Harmondsworth, London: Penguin.

Schmidt, K. O. (Ed.). (1996). *Lao-Tse. Tao The King.* Hammelburg, Germany: Drei Eichen Verlag.

Sedlacek, T. (2011). *Economics of good and evil: The quest for economic meaning from Gilgamesh to Wall Street.* Oxford, England: Oxford University Press.

Senge, P. M. (1990). *The fifth discipline. The art & practice of the learning organization.* New York, MU: Currency Doubleday.

Sheldrake, R. (2008). Das schöpferischeUniversum, Munich: Nymphenburger [Original English version: *A New Science of Life* (1981): London: Blond & Briggs]

Sisodia, R., Wolfe, D., & J. Sheth (2014). *Firms of endearment. How world-class companies profit from passion and purpose* (2nd ed.) Upper Saddle River, NJ: Pearson.

Stanford, N. (2013). *Organizational health. An integrated approach to building optimum performance.* London, England: Kogan Page.

Swanson, D. (1995): Addressing a theoretical problem by reorienting the corporate social performance model, *Academy of Management Review, 20*, 43–64

WE'AR. (2014a). Philosophy. Retrieved April 3, 2014, from http://wearyogaclothing.com/pages/philosophy

WE'AR. (2014b). Shop locations. Retrieved February 3, 2014, from http://wearyogaclothing.com/pages/shop-locations

WE'AR Moving Pictures. (2011). WE'AR eco clothing: How to make natural dyes. Retrieved April 2, 2014, from http://vimeo.com/31170688

Wheeler, J. A. (2000). *Geons, black holes, and quantum foam: A life in physics.* New York, NY: W.W. Norton.

Wood, D. J. (1991). Corporate social performance revisited. *The Academy of Management Review, 16*(4), 691–718.

Wood, D. J. (2010). Measuring corporate social performance: A review. *International Journal of Management Reviews, 12*(1), 50–84.

CHAPTER 8

THE IMPORTANCE OF CORPORATE SOCIAL PERFORMANCE

A Review of the Construct's Evolution and Relation to Financial Performance

Andrew E. Michael

Corporate social performance has been defined, modeled, and measured in various ways. A plethora of research on corporate social performance and in particular its relationship to corporate financial performance has been carried out during the last 40 years (Margolis, Elfenbein, & Walsh, 2009; Peloza, 2009; Wood, 2010). This interest partly derives from researchers' and practitioners' desires to show that if corporate social performance has a positive impact on corporate financial performance, then it is more likely that managers and shareholders will be willing to divert organizational funds to socially responsible activities (Barnett, 2007). Research findings on this relationship appear to be mixed due to different units of analysis and measurements of the construct, as well as different methods of analyses. Some studies have found a positive relationship, others a negative relationship,

Corporate Social Performance:
Paradoxes, Pitfalls, and Pathways to the Better World, pp. 151–177
Copyright © 2015 by Information Age Publishing
All rights of reproduction in any form reserved.

while others have found no relationship or inconclusive evidence. Interest in corporate social performance has also been fuelled by unethical business practices and corporate fraud that have resulted in a call for a change in the way organizational leaders manage their companies so that they take into consideration other stakeholders and not only promote the interests of the shareholders (Michael, 2012, 2014). This chapter looks at various definitions and dimensions of corporate social performance and outlines the concept's evolution. This is followed by a review of the literature on the relationship between corporate social performance and financial performance and concludes with thoughts regarding the importance of this relationship arguing that the existence or not of such a relationship should be irrelevant and that organizational leaders should engage in socially responsible behavior and foster a culture of humanism in their organizations.

DEFINING CORPORATE SOCIAL PERFORMANCE

Corporate social performance (CSP) is a complex and multidimensional construct that has been extensively researched since the mid-1970s (e.g., Carroll, 1979; Graves & Waddock, 1994; Margolis, Elfenbein, & Walsh, 2009; Mitnick, 2000; Rowley & Berman, 2000; Stanwick & Stanwick, 1998a, 1998b; Wartick & Cochran, 1985; Wood, 1991a, 1991b). It is closely linked to the theme of corporate social responsibility (CSR). A review of the literature shows that in various studies, the two constructs have been used interchangeably. However, although they are closely related, they are not the same.[1] De Bakker, Groenewegen, and den Hond (2005) suggest that some researchers (e.g., Frederick, 1994), see CSR as pertaining to principles whereas CSP is more about the outcomes of firms' actions. For others (e.g., Wartick & Cochran, 1985; Wood, 1991b) CSP is a more comprehensive concept that includes responsibilities and responsiveness, as well as policies and action. The CSR construct itself has evolved since the 1950s when the modern era of CSR began (Carroll, 1999). Although a review of the development of the CSR construct is beyond the scope of this chapter, due to the close connection between CSR and CSP, a consideration of some definitions of CSR will help to better understand the relation between the two constructs.

One of the first to comment in the modern era on businesses' social responsibilities was Howard Bowen (1953) who argued that businessmen had an obligation to "pursue those policies, to make those decisions, or to follow those lines of action which are desirable in terms of the objectives and values of our society" (p. 6). In describing businesses' social responsibilities, William Frederick (1960) wrote that "social responsibility ... implies a public posture toward society's economic and human resources and a willingness to see that those resources are used for broad social ends and not simply for the narrowly circumscribed interests of private persons and firms" (p. 60). Harold Johnson (1971) wrote: "A socially responsible firm is one whose managerial staff balances a multiplicity of interests. Instead of striving only for larger profits for its stockholders, a responsible enterprise also takes into account employees, suppliers, dealers, local communities, and the nation" (p. 50). Eells and Walton (1974) stated that "corporate social responsibility represents a concern with the needs and goals of society which goes beyond the merely economic" (p. 247). Numerous definitions of CSR were presented up until the 1970s and a few more in the 1980s (Carroll, 1999). These definitions are important because they reflect the multidimensionality, complexity and normative nature of the construct which in turn, as one might expect, also characterize CSP, a construct that partly aims to measure businesses' socially responsible behavior.

Whereas various references to business social responsibility had been made during the 1950s and 1960s, the term CSP began to be increasingly used in the 1970s (Carroll, 1977). Sethi (1975) argued that CSR lacked an internal structure and content and proposed a framework that would facilitate the analysis of corporate social activities. He distinguished between three broad and general dimensions that could be used to define and measure CSP and that could be applied to a particular firm or industry. The underlying criterion for evaluating CSP within this framework is legitimacy (Suchman, 1995). Under this prism, corporate behavior is described as a three-state phenomenon related to a notion of legitimacy that ranges from narrow to broad.

> Legitimization involves not only the type of corporate activities, but also the process of internal decision making; the perception of external environment, the manipulation of external environment … to make it more receptive to corporate activities; and the nature of accountability to other social institutions in the system. (Sethi, 1975, p. 60)

Using this criterion, corporate behavior is defined in three ways: social obligation, social responsibility, or social responsiveness.

Social obligation is a firm's behavior in response to market forces or legal constraints. Such behavior satisfies legitimacy criteria that are economic and legal. However, these criteria alone are insufficient to confer corporate legitimacy (Dowling & Pfeffer; Epstein, both as cited in Sethi, 1975). Corporate behavior that satisfies market place and legal criteria (social obligation) does not suffice because firms may not always meet social expectations. Hence, Sethi defined social responsibility as corporate behavior that goes beyond social obligation "bringing corporate behavior up to a level where it is congruent with the prevailing norms, values and expectations of performance" (p. 62). However, for Sethi (1975), even social responsibility is not an adequate expression of corporate behavior. Thus corporations must not only change their behavior according to the social concerns that are associated with their current business activities. Rather, they should also anticipate potential problems and likely changes in the social system and put into effect policies and programs that will minimize potentially detrimental effects of their current and future activities. Sethi called this type of anticipatory and preventive corporate behavior social responsiveness.

In 1979, Carroll proposed that "the social responsibility of business encompasses the economic, legal, ethical, and discretionary expectations that society has of organizations at a given point in time" (p. 500). This four part definition of CSR was embedded in Carroll's conceptual model of CSP in which CSP is a three-dimensional integration of corporate social responsibility, corporate social responsiveness, and social issues. Carroll's dimension of corporate social responsibility embodies the economic, legal, ethical, and discretionary responsibilities of businesses. However, in contrast to Sethi (1975), CSR is not a response but rather a reflection of a moral stance or belief. Carroll sees corporate social responsiveness as the business philosophy, strategy and managerial responses to social issues which may range from no response to a proactive response. The model recognizes social issues as an important aspect of CSP but stresses that these issues change over time and are different for different industries.

Wartick and Cochran (1985) reframed Carroll's (1979) three dimensions presenting a CSP model that "reflects an underlying interaction among the principles of social responsibility, the process of social responsiveness, and the policies developed to address social issues" (p. 758). Social responsibility concerns principles that are based upon moral agency and the social contract between businesses and society. Social responsiveness is considered a process reflecting the approach to realizing social responsibility, and social issues management is the method for operationalizing social responsiveness. The three dimensions conceptually integrate corporate social involvement (Wartick & Cochran, 1985).

In 1991, Donna Wood modified Wartick and Cochran's (1985) model defining CSP as "a business organization's configuration of principles of social responsibility, processes of social responsiveness, and policies, programs, and observable outcomes as they relate to the firm's societal relationships" (Wood, 1991a, p. 693). The model articulates three principles of corporate social responsibility (the institutional principle of legitimacy, the organizational principle of public responsibility, and the individual principle of managerial discretion) emphasizing that principles motivate human and organizational behavior. The principle of legitimacy is Davis's (1973) Iron Law of Responsibility. "Society grants legitimacy and power to business. In the long run, those who do not use power in a manner which society considers responsible will tend to lose it" (p. 314). The principle of public responsibility is derived from Preston and Post (1975). "Businesses are responsible for outcomes related to their primary and secondary areas of involvement with society" (Wood, 1991a, p. 697). The principle of managerial discretion is based on the idea that managers are moral actors. "Within every domain of corporate social responsibility, they are obliged to exercise such discretion as is available to them, toward socially responsible outcomes" (Wood, 1991a, p. 698).

Wood's CSP model also identifies specific responsive processes (not *a* process, as presented in Wartick and Cochran's 1985 model) to show the channels through which organizations engage with their external environment. These processes include environmental assessment, stakeholder management, and issues management. The importance of incorporating into the model the outcomes of corporate behavior (namely the social programs, policies, and impacts) is also stressed. According to Wood (1991a), the CSP model can accommodate a "wide variety of motives, behaviors, and outcomes actually found in business firms" (p. 693); "it permits CSP to be seen ... as a construct for evaluating business outputs that must be used in conjunction with explicit values about appropriate business-society relationships" (pp. 693–694). Moreover, it reestablishes a broken link between social responsibility and social responsiveness, therefore "allowing CSP to serve as a central organizing concept for research and theory in business and society" (p. 713).

A common theme that characterizes the various definitions of CSP is that a socially responsible organization is one that takes into consideration not just stockholders but also other stakeholders. Building on stakeholder theory and the idea that firms should attend to all stakeholders (Freeman, 1984), Clarkson (1991, 1995) developed a stakeholder management model that could be used as a framework for "describing, evaluating, and managing corporate social performance" (p. 349). This model can be used to support social auditing because it helps to systematically evaluate social issues, determine specific measures of performance, and compare performance data between firms within and across industries (Davenport, 2000).

Diane Swanson (1995) argued that Wood's (1991a) CSP model did not integrate the economic and duty-aligned perspectives of the business and society fields and this created problems for theory development. The main idea of the economic perspective is that the firm's economic responsibility is to produce goods and services for society in an efficient and profitable way. The primary interest of the duty-aligned perspective is to create rules for corporate moral behavior and express them as rules and obligations. Swanson reframed the principles, processes, and outcomes in Wood's model so that it "formulates decision making in terms of ethical and value processes that are linked across the individual (executive, manager, employee), organizational, and societal levels" (p. 56). The reoriented model provides a conceptual framework to explore whether the "field's economic and duty-aligned perspectives can be integrated into an adequate normative theory of corporate social performance" (p. 60).

Kim Davenport (2000) noted that until the 1990s, CSP had been measured mainly by assessing discrete dimensions of the construct and only few attempts had been made to develop a composite picture of an organization's overall social performance. In her study, she identified 20 principles (measures) that stakeholders use to judge the social responsibility of corporations. The study suggested that the defining characteristics of good corporate citizenship are ethical business behavior, environmental commitment, and the management of the company for the benefit of all stakeholders. An encouraging sign related to this finding is that since the time when Freeman (1984) expressed his stakeholder approach to strategic management, many companies have defined their responsibilities and obligations to their shareholders, employees, customers and other important constituencies (Clarkson, 1995; Davenport, 2000). The aforementioned criteria of corporate citizenship can be mapped into Wood's (1991a) CSP model, thus operationally linking stakeholder theory and CSP theory by facilitating the measurement from a variety of stakeholder perspectives of the principles, processes, and outcomes of CSP (Davenport, 2000).

Husted (2000) defined CSP as the "ability of the firm to meet or exceed stakeholder expectations regarding social issues" (p. 27) and proposed a contingency theory in which CSP is determined by the fit between the social issue and the firm's corresponding strategies, structures and responses. Thus, corporate social responsiveness should depend on the nature of the social issue which in turn depends on the expectational gaps between the actual corporate performance and stakeholders' perceptions of what ought to be the firm's corporate performance (Husted, 2000; Wartick & Mahon, 1994). The use of an appropriate strategy and structure to address these gaps can help to satisfy stakeholder expectations leading to higher CSP.

Husted (2000) proposed four strategies with their corresponding structures to deal with different types of social issue situations. The *computation* strategy is a programmed or routine response that is appropriate when there is no expectational gap. A *discovery* strategy accompanied by collegial structures (whereby all relevant experts share all relevant information) can be used to find solutions to achieve agreed-upon goals when there is a disagreement involving the nature of the facts pertaining to a particular situation. An *inspiration* strategy should be used to realign the firm with its stakeholders when a gap exists "between what is and expectations about what ought to be" (p. 37). This can be achieved using a structure of "organized chaos" in which the organization and its stakeholders creatively and collaboratively try to create new linking values and develop a new vision. A *bargaining* strategy using a representative structure should be used to align the organization and its social environment by jointly resolving problems that arise from differing perceptions of the firm's corporate social responsibilities that inevitably lead to conflicting interests, goals and objectives. According to Husted, since organizations are likely to face all the aforementioned social issues at one point or another, all four strategies and structures are necessary.

The preceding brief review of various definitions of CSR and CSP indicate the multidimensionality of social performance and suggest why it is difficult to reach a consensus as to what should be part of an organization's social responsibility (Beurden & Gössling, 2008). De Bakker et al. (2005) contend that no consensus has been achieved regarding the extent of progress made in the CSR/CSP literature. They distinguish and analyze three views regarding the evolution of the constructs. According to their *progressive view*, "the CSR/CSP literature has developed from conceptual vagueness, through clarification of central constructs and their relationships, to the testing of theory … [with the whole] process aided by the application of increasingly sophisticated research methods" (p. 284). The "variegational view" argues that progress in the literature regarding the social responsibilities of business has been obscured and even hampered by the continuous introduction of new constructs (Carroll, 1999; Mohan, as cited in De Bakker et al., 2005). The "normativist view" which is also the most pessimistic one, holds that very little progress has been made or can be made due to the inherently normative nature of the constructs (Matten, Crane, & Chapple, as cited in De Bakker et al., 2005).

The results of De Bakker et al.'s (2005) bibliometric text analysis provided support for both the progressive and variegation views but not the normativist view. One can view the emergence of the CSP as a separate construct and resulting literature dedicated to it as an early example of progression into a specific subfield. However, there have also been an increasing number of differentiated concepts that are associated with CSR and CSP. This suggests that two processes are occurring simultaneously in the CSR/CSP research. "There is a tendency to build on each other's work, to develop propositions, and to test theories. But at the same time, new constructs and new linkages are continually being proposed" (De Bakker et al., p. 312).

These conclusions offered by De Bakker et al. (2005) contrast sharply with the normativist view held by Rowley and Berman (2000) who argue that the CSP construct has not developed into a "viable theoretical and operational construct" because, as such a construct, it is fatally flawed. Rowley and Berman argue that there are four problematic areas that inhibit the creation of a body of CSP literature. The first problem is that the objectives pursued by the researchers are not the research objectives that should be pursued. The second problem is that although CSP is a multidimensional construct, many researchers use a one dimensional proxy (e.g., illegal activity or air pollution) when operationalizing CSP. Thus, any generalizations on the CSP-CFP relationship based on one dimension are likely to reduce the validity and reliability of the findings. The third problem arises from the use of composite CSP measures that aggregate several CSP dimensions. Rowley and Berman argue that with such aggregation, "much of the meaning and richness in the data is lost, and comparison across firms (and studies) is more difficult" (p. 403). Additionally, it is not clear what weight each of the dimensions that comprise a composite measure should be. Moreover, different studies often use different dimensions raising the question as to what are the appropriate dimensions that should be used to construct a comprehensive, valid CSP measure. The fourth problem perceived by Rowley and Berman is that the CSP research is not based upon a strong theoretical foundation. Similar views were expressed earlier by other researchers. For instance, Ullman (1985) argued that CSP research is nothing more than "data in search of theory." Mitnick (1993) wrote that the CSP models "are little more than heuristics or graphical displays of lists ... [that] are not conceptually operational" (as cited in Rowley & Berman, 2005, p. 405). In contrast to these views, other researchers believe that CSP research since the mid-1990s has satisfactorily been supported by a theoretical foundation that is based on stakeholder theory and the resource-based view of the firm, good management theory, and slack resources theory (Boaventura, da Silva, & Bandeira-de-Mello, 2012). However, a review of the literature suggests that the validity of the CSP construct is still contested and that it "has proven to be one of the most difficult constructs to measure in management research" (Simerly, 1999, p. 253).

IN SEARCH OF THE CSP-CFP LINK

The issues that have been raised by Rowley and Berman (2000) are important concerns that many researchers are aware of and that have begun to be addressed. Despite these theoretical and methodological issues, most researchers involved with CSR and CSP still believe that CSP should be measured "because it is an important topic to business and to society" (Carroll, 2000, p. 473). As Carroll (2000) and other researchers suggest, the challenge is to develop valid comprehensive measures of CSP that really measure "social" performance. Three important questions need to be considered. First, should research aim to identify a relationship between CSP and CFP? Second, can CSP measures actually be validly linked to CFP measures? If the answers to both of these questions are affirmative, then investigating the third question regarding the existence of a relationship between CSP and CFP becomes more meaningful. Before considering the desirability and utility of researching the CSP-CFP link, the nature of the CSP-CFP relationship is briefly discussed.

The relationship between CSP and CFP has been studied extensively during the past 40 years. Much of this research has been motivated to find evidence to support the business case for CSP (Carroll & Shabana, 2010). More than 270 studies have been carried out including a number of meta-analyses (Griffin & Mahon, 1997; Orlitzky, Schmidt, & Rynes, 2003; Margolis et al., 2009). The majority of studies have found a positive relationship while others have found no significant relationship or inconclusive evidence. A small number of studies have found the two constructs to be negatively related. Thus, research findings are mixed but overall there may be a positive relationship (Beurden & Gössling, 2008; Boaventuraet al., 2012). According to Davenport (2000), "the CSP body of literature produces ambiguous results largely because the studies have not chosen variables and predicted relationships appropriate to a stakeholder/CSP framework" (p. 212). The contradictory results may be due to inaccurate model specifications, differences in the ways that social and financial performance have been conceptualized (Miller, Washburn, & Glick, 2013) and operationalized (Van der Laan, Van Ees, & Van Witteloostuijn, 2007), and the use of different methodologies.

A variety of measures have been used to conduct empirical research on CSP (Davenport, 2000; Margolis et al., 2009; Peloza, 2009). Many studies have used perceptual based ratings of a company's social performance such as Fortune's annual ratings of the largest U.S. corporations and Kinder, Lyndenberg, Domini (KLD) ratings (Beurden & Gössling, 2008; Johnson & Greening, 1999; Wu, 2006). Some of the social performance dimensions included in the KLD ratings are employee relations, community, product, environment, and diversity. Similarly, a number of measures have been used to represent a firm's financial performance. These include accounting based measures such as return on equity (ROE) and return on assets (ROA), and market based measures such as the firm's stock returns.

The empirical link between CSP and CFP does appear to depend on the operational definition of financial performance with CSP being more highly correlated with accounting-based measures of CFP than with market-based indicators (Orlitzky et al., 2003, p. 403). However, Marom (2006) argues that stakeholder reactions to CSP initiatives are mainly observed in the long run. Since accounting measures tend to reflect short-term past performance, they may not provide meaningful measures of performance, thus limiting the conclusions that can be drawn from research findings on the CSP-CFP relationship (Baird, Geylani, & Roberts, 2012). Without ignoring all of the caveats pertaining to the potential research design problems, a review of the main research findings regarding the CSP-CFP relationship is outlined below.[2]

Using a sample of 110 Fortune 500 firms, Coffey and Fryxell (1991) found a positive correlation between the number of women represented on the firm's board of directors and the level of the firm's stocks owned by institutional investors. However, despite the expectation that institutional ownership would encourage more CSP, no significant relationship was found between charitable giving and institutional ownership. Also, surprisingly, evidence of firms' effective social issues management was found to be negatively related to the level of institutional ownership.

Griffin and Mahon (1997) reviewed 51 articles that included 62 research results regarding the relationship between CSP and CFP. Sixteen studies were published in the 1970s, 27 in the 1980s and 8 in the 1990s. The majority of research results (33) showed a positive relationship between CSP and CFP but a sizeable minority of 20 results indicated a negative relation. Nine research results showed no effect or inconclusive evidence. Certain important issues emerged from their analysis. The first was that most of the articles were large cross-sectional studies that incorporated many industries and thus the results may hide individual differences regarding the measurement of CSP and CFP in a particular industry. Firms operating in different industries may face different social issues and have stakeholders whose needs vary in importance. Many researchers have argued that studies on the CSP-CFP relationship should be conducted within specific industries matching each industry's stakeholders with appropriate financial and social measures to enhance internal validity and reduce potential confounding effects (Carroll, 1979; Chand, 2006; Wokutch & Spencer, 1987; Wood & Jones, 1995). Moreover, some argue that the use of accounting measures is inappropriate in large cross-sectional comparisons across industries (Davidson & Worrell, as cited in Griffin & Mahon, 1997).

The second key issue was that 80 different measures of CFP were used but over 70% of these measures were used only once. This means that there was insufficient use of repeated measures that would have facilitated the development of validity and reliability checks for these financial measures. The most widely used financial measures were ROA and ROE. Perceptual based ratings of CSP such as Fortune and KLD ratings were found to be related to financial performance. In contrast, performance based measures, such as the toxic release inventory (TRI)[3] and corporate philanthropy, despite being able to differentiate between high and low social performers, were not found to be related to financial performance.[4]

Using a dataset that included most of the S&P 500 firms, Waddock and Graves (1997) found CSP to be positively related with future financial performance. CSP was measured using the eight dimensions of corporate social performance determined by KLD. Three accounting measures

(ROA, ROE, and return on sales) were used to reflect the firms' financial performance.

Roman, Hayibor, and Agle (1999) revised and reconstructed Griffin and Mahon's (1997) review. They concluded that many of the early studies did not provide valid evidence of the CSP-CFP relationship. They also argued that other studies were erroneously categorized. Overall, 26 of Griffin and Mahon's (1997) 62 research results were either reclassified or removed. Eleven results were removed; nine were categorized as showing a positive relationship instead of a negative one; and six results were moved from either negative or positive to inconclusive. Four newly published studies were also added. As a result of this reclassification, 33 studies showed a positive relationship between CSP and CFP, 14 studies showed no effect or were inconclusive, and only five studies showed a negative relation. This led the authors to conclude that "at the very least, good social performance does not lead to poor financial performance" (p. 121).

Ruf, Muralidhar, Brown, Janney, and Paul (2001) found that change in CSP (determined using the KLD database) was positively related with sales growth for the current and subsequent year suggesting that CSP can yield short term benefits. Also change in CSP was positively related to return on sales for the third financial period under study indicating that improved corporate social performance may also result in long-term financial benefits. The results showed that the controlled variables (firm size, industry type, and previous year's financial performance) explained a significant amount of the variation in CFP.

In a study of the U.K. supermarket industry, findings showed contemporaneous social and financial performance to be negatively related (Moore, 2001). However, prior financial performance was found to be positively related with subsequent social performance providing support for the slack resources theory view pertaining to CSP. The results also showed age and size of the firm to be positively related to social performance.

In their meta-analytic review of 52 studies, Orlitzky et al. (2003) found that social responsibility and to a lesser extent environmental responsibility are positively related to financial performance but the operationalizations of the two constructs moderate the relation. For instance, CSP reputation indices were more highly correlated with CFP than other CSP indicators and CSP appeared to be more highly correlated with accounting-based CFP measures than with market-based measures. Findings also provided support for a bidirectional causality in which firms that are socially responsible perform financially better and firms that are financially successful can afford to spend more money on social issues.

Margolis and Walsh (2003) conducted a meta-analysis of 127 empirical studies published between 1972 and 2002. In 109 of these studies, CFP was the dependant variable and CSP the independent variable. A positive relationship was found in 54 of these studies. However, no relationship was found in 20 studies, a negative relationship was found in 7 studies, and in 28 studies the relationship was not significant.

Cox, Brammer, and Millington (2004) investigated the pattern of institutional shareholding in 500 U.K. companies. They found that overall CSP as well as three dimensions of CSP (employee relations, environment and community) were positively related to long-term institutional investment. The magnitude of the effect and the degree of statistical significance was largest for the employee-relations component of CSP. The relationship between CSP and charitable holdings was also positive but not significant.

Wu (2006) conducted a meta-analysis of 121 empirical studies to investigate the relationship between CSP, CFP and firm size. The findings showed a weak, positive average effect size (p. 166) between CSP and CFP. Studies that used market-based measures had smaller effect sizes than those that used other CFP measures such as profitability, and Fortune ratings had stronger effect sizes than KLD ratings. Similarly to the findings of other meta-analyses (Griffin & Mahon, 1997; Orlitzky et al., 2003), a stronger CSP-CFP relationship was found in studies that used perceptual-based measures of CSP rather than performance based measures. One possible explanation for this recurring finding is that perceptions may be biased and not accurately reflect an organization's actual social performance. Alternatively, performance based measures based on cross sectional studies do not accurately reflect the inter-temporal effects and thus underestimate the long term effects of CSP that perceptual based measures may more accurately reveal.

Brammer, Brooks, and Pavelin (2006) found a negative relation between a composite social performance indicator and stock returns for a sample of U.K. firms in their cross-sectional study. The poor financial return offered by these firms was mainly attributed to their good social performance on the environment and to a smaller extent the community aspects. However, the employment performance indicator was weakly but positively related to returns. Investors holding on to a portfolio comprised of the least desirable stocks earned considerable abnormal returns.

Brammer and Millington (2008) looked at the impact of one component of CSP, charitable giving, and found that firms with both unusually high and low CSP performed financially better than other firms. Unusually poor charitable givers did best in the short run but unusually good social performers did best over longer time periods. This finding along with the results obtained in another study by Barnett and Salomon (2012) provide support for the view that the relationship between CSP and CFP may not be linear but U-shaped (Barnett, 2007; Barnett & Salomon, 2006). This nonlinear relationship suggests that important intertemporal effects associated with the firm's stakeholder influence capacity (SIC), that is, its ability to "identify, act on, and profit from opportunities to improve stakeholder relationships through CSR" (Barnett, 2007, p. 803) may need time to be experienced providing additional support for longitudinal studies.

Beurden and Gössling (2008) conducted a meta-analysis of 34 quantitative studies published between 1990 and 2007. They found a positive relationship between CSP and CFP in 23 (68%) of the studies, no significant relationship in nine (26%) of the studies, and a negative relationship in two studies. Twenty studies used corporate reputation ratings such as Fortune and KLD to measure CSP. Market-based and/or accounting-based measures were used in 20 of the studies to measure CFP. Firm size was found to be a confounding variable in 11 studies, type of industry in 6, and R&D and risk in 3 studies.

In their study of 441 large U.S. firms, Callan and Thomas (2009) found a positive relationship between CSP and CFP in support of the stakeholder theory view. CFP was measured using return on assets (ROA), return on sales (ROS), return on equity (ROE) and Tobin's q. CSP was measured using an index based solely on the KLD scores for qualitative issue areas such as corporate governance and human rights. A separate index of the KLD indicators for controversial business issues (such as association with fire arms or tobacco products) was also created. Results show that a firm's participation in controversial business issues has a much stronger effect on its returns than do changes in qualitative areas. This implies that studies that use a combined index of both types of indicators may yield biased results that do not distinguish between the two types of issues. Also type of industry, firm size and R&D were found to be statistically significant control variables.

Lee, Faff, and Langfield-Smith (2009) used the "best of sector" (BOS) corporate sustainability ratings methodology as a CSP metric to measure the relative performances of leading and lagging CSP firms. The BOS screening approach selects companies perceived to be industry leaders with respect to social, environmental and economic performance. Both accounting and market-based measures of CFP were used. In contrast to the findings of most of the other studies, no relationship was found between CSP and CFP using the accounting measures, and a negative relationship was found using market-based measures. Similarly, in another study by Fauzi (2009) that used data obtained from the corporate annual reports of companies listed on the New York Stock Exchange, CSP had no effect on CFP.

In examining the business case for CSP, Peloza (2009) reviewed 159 studies and found that the majority (63%) showed a positive relationship between CSP and CFP, 22% found a neutral or mixed relationship, and 15% of the studies reported a negative relationship. Similar to the findings of other reviews, he found that accounting based measures were more often positively related to CSP than market based measures. Peloza argues that this is evidence that financial performance has a greater impact on CSP than CSP has on financial performance because accounting based measures reflect a firm's past performance whereas market based measures reflect a firm's future performance. He concludes that the business case for CSP is unclear because the relationship is weak, the direction of causality is undetermined, and the measures used to investigate the relationship are inconsistent.

Margolis et al. (2009) conducted a comprehensive meta-analytic review of 251 studies and found an overall small positive effect between CSP and CFP. The effects are stronger in the more recent time period. The small positive effect suggests that firms' financial performance is not negatively affected by engaging in CSP.

Choi, Kwak, and Choe (2010) studied the relation between CSR and CFP in Korea during 2002–2008. The firms selected for this study were large and exhibited superior financial performance. Corporate social responsibility was measured using both an equal-weighted and a stakeholder-weighted CSR index. Corporate financial performance was measured using ROE, ROA, and Tobin's q. A significant positive relationship was found between CFP and the stakeholder-weighted CSR index but not the equal-weighted measure highlighting the importance for firms of determining which aspects of its CSR are most important to their main stakeholders.

Kapoor and Sandhu (2010) examined the impact of CSR on CFP in 93 companies in India and found a significant positive relation between CSR and corporate profitability but an insignificant positive effect of CSR on corporate growth.

Surroca, Tribo, and Waddock (2010) examined the potential mediating effect of a firm's intangible resources using data on 599 industrial firms from 28 countries. The data was obtained from the Sustainalytics Platform database. Based on the results of their study, they concluded that there is no direct relationship between corporate responsibility performance and financial performance and that intangibles such as innovation, human capital, culture and reputation mediate the relationship. Moreover, they found the mediation effect to be stronger in growth industries.

Soana (2011) investigated the relationship between CSP and CFP using two separate samples involving 16 Italian banks and 21 other international banks. The ethical rating of the international banks was determined by Ethibel and that of the Italian banks by AXIA. Results did not show a statistically significant relationship between the "global" ethical rating and the accounting or marketing ratios that were used to measure CFP.

Baron, Harjoto, and Jo (2011) estimated a simultaneous equation model for a panel of over 1600 firms. They found CFP to be positively correlated with CSP for firms in consumer markets but negatively correlated for firms in industrial markets. CSP increased with CFP in consumer markets in line with the slack resources theory. As expected, CSP was also found to be responsive to social pressure.

In their empirical analysis that was based on an extensive longitudinal dataset, Oikonomou, Brooks, and Pavelin (2011) concluded that overall, higher levels of CSP in terms of support for local communities, good employee relations, higher levels of product safety and quality can lead to improved credit quality, lower perceived credit risk and risk premiums associated with corporate bonds and thus a lower cost of corporate debt.

Baird et al. (2012) empirically tested the extent to which the systematic variation in the intrinsic value of a firm's stock price was related to CSP. A firm's inclusion in the Domini 400 Social Index (DS400) indicated a firm's positive social performance. The results show that there is a statistically significant relationship between CSP and CFP. However, this relationship is conditioned by the industry context and thus the relationship varies across industries. With respect to the industry specific effects, results show that firms had higher stock prices when they exhibited strong community relations, better employee relations, and demonstrated positive environmental performance in industries with high environmental impact.

Wang and Choi (2013) used a sample of 622 firms to investigate the moderating roles of temporal and interdomain consistency in the CSP-CFP relationship. Five KLD dimensions were used to reflect CSP and Tobin's q (estimated from the firm's market-to-book ratio) was used as a measure of CFP. Their empirical results suggest that the level of CSP as well as the two types of consistency in CSP both have a positive influence on the financial performance.

Using good management theory, Tyagi and Sharma (2013) examined the relationship between CSP and CFP for 297 Indian firms during the period 2005–2011. The study used the environment social governance (ESG) scores of Indian firms as a proxy for CSP.[5] Corporate financial performance was measured using mainly accounting measures. Overall the results suggest a neutral to modest negative relationship that is significant only with respect to return on assets and return on net worth. As found in other studies (e.g., Andersen & Dejoy, 2011), the findings show that the type of industry, firm size, risk, and levels of R&D significantly affect the relationship.

A review of the literature highlights certain important issues pertaining to the measurement of CSP and its relationship to CFP. First, there is no consensus on what is the best way to measure CSP and CFP (Soana, 2011). For instance, many studies use composite measures of social performance at the organizational level despite their potential for averaging out the effect of different stakeholder groups whose needs and importance differ across firms (Van der Laan et al., 2007). Inconsistencies in how firm performance is conceptualized can create problems in effectively interpreting research (Miller et al., 2013).[6] Second, the relationship between CSP and CFP varies across industries. This supports the view that a contingency approach should be used in measuring CSP and its association with CFP. Studies should be industry-specific and use a variety of CFP measures. Also, more longitudinal studies are needed to better understand the temporal lag in the relationship between CSP and CFP (Boaventura et al., 2012). Third, potential moderating variables and mediating effects should be properly specified to avoid bias (Andersen & Dejoy, 2011; Callan & Thomas, 2009; Peloza, 2009). There is a need for greater awareness regarding the potential for model misspecifications (McWilliams & Siegel, 2000). Baird et al. (2012) succinctly summarize the complexity regarding the CSP-CFP relationship. "Whether CSP leads to better or worse financial performance depends on the interaction of a number of factors: managerial motives, industry environment, the firm's capabilities and limitations, and the particular modes of social performance the firm chooses to pursue" (p. 368).

At the beginning of this section, three questions were raised. One concerned whether CSP measures can actually be validly linked to CFP measures. Although there is no consensus regarding this issue, the evidence appears to allow for an optimistic view held by the majority of researchers that despite methodological challenges, progress has been made in defining and measuring both constructs more appropriately thus allowing for meaningful investigations regarding the relationship between them.

Another question concerned whether CSP and CFP are significantly related. The majority of studies since 1990 including meta-analyses suggest that CSP is positively related to CFP. However, evidence suggests that findings are likely to be more meaningful if obtained from longitudinal studies on specific industries as opposed to cross sectional studies involving many industries. Moreover, a number of studies have identified important moderating variables and other studies show that the relationship between CSP and CFP is indirect, influenced by various mediating variables.

A third question posed at the beginning of this section concerned whether research *should* aim to identify a relationship between CSP and CFP. For instance, should the existence or not of such a relationship determine managers' corporate responsibility decisions and their firms' behaviors? This chapter concludes by discussing this question and the importance of CSP in the next section.

THE DESIRABILITY OF CSP—A HUMANISTIC VIEW

The relationship between CSP and CFP and the potential business case for social responsibility remain controversial areas of studies in the business and society field (Perrini, Russo, Tencati, & Vurro, 2011). The overall positive (direct or indirect) relationship between CSP and CFP that is arguably supported by the empirical evidence reviewed in the previous section suggests that organizations do not need to view profitability and social responsibility as competing goals (Callan & Thomas, 2009). At the very least, firms can promote specific types of socially responsible behavior within their respective industries and not worry that they will be less competitive. However, should the desirability or not of CSP depend on a positive or neutral relationship between CSP and CFP? Moreover, what is the most appropriate way to judge firm performance?

Porter and Kramer (2006) have argued that "the prevailing approaches to CSR are so fragmented and so disconnected from business and strategy as to obscure many of the great opportunities for companies to benefit society" (p. 80). According to Porter and Kramer (2011), most firms view value creation narrowly, trying to optimize their short-term financial performance while not attending to the most important customer needs and ignoring the broader factors that determine their long-term success. Perrini et al. (2011) call for a broader definition of business success stating that the "narrow and exclusive focus on short-term monetary results has led to counter-productive and negative consequences for business and society" (p. 59). Jensen (2002) also argues that a firm's objective should be to maximize its long run value. Porter and Kramer (2011) believe that for most companies, societal issues are not part of their core strategy and that many firms have developed corporate responsibility programs as a reaction to external pressure to improve their reputations. These programs are viewed as a necessary expense instead of an opportunity.

Porter and Kramer (2011) argue that companies must reconnect their success with social programs by creating shared value, a concept defined as "policies and operating practices that enhance the competitiveness of a company while simultaneously advancing economic and social conditions in the communities in which it operates" (p. 66). By creating shared value, firms can address societal issues without necessarily experiencing higher costs because they will be more innovative and productive. Hence, CSP and CFP are not antagonistic but interrelated in a way that creates a win-win situation. This idea is also supported by stakeholder theory and good management theory, theories that have provided the theoretical foundation for the research relating to CSR, CSP, and CFP. It is important to note, however, that for Porter and Kramer, creating shared value "is not philanthropy but self-interested behavior [that aims to] create economic value by creating societal value" (p. 77). This will help companies to view capitalism in a broader way that does not see business as contributing to society *only* by making a short-term profit which in turn creates employment, income, consumption, investment and taxes. When companies' roles in society are determined only by their profitability and responsibilities to shareholders, then during times of growing competition and reduced profitability, they may lay off workers, lower wages, and relocate to lower-cost regions (Porter & Kramer, 2011). Such decisions and behaviors are in contrast to a more humanistic management approach. Moreover, when managers are only focused on their firms' financial performance, they may experience pressure to act irresponsibly engaging in fraudulent and unethical behavior that results in corporate social irresponsibility (CSI or CSiR).

Armstrong and Green (2013) see corporate social irresponsibility (CSI) as being "concerned with whether firms undertake harmful actions that managers would be unwilling to undertake for themselves" (p. 1922). Examples of CSiR include violating human rights of workers, deceiving customers, cheating the government or damaging the environment (Lin-Hi & Müller, 2013). Various societal, industry and company level factors can create pressures that may lead top managers to commit fraud (Zahra, Priem, & Rasheed, 2005). Evidence suggests that the attitudes, values and traits of organizational leaders determine the extent of a firm's CSR and CSiR activities (Christensen, Mackey, & Whetten, 2014).

Corporations have the responsibility of not only behaving in a socially desirable way. They must also avoid CSiR. They should not feel that doing "good" justifies doing "bad." Interestingly, in an archival study of 49 Fortune 500 Firms, Ormiston and Wong (2013) found that prior CSR is positively related with subsequent CSiR. This relationship is stronger when the firms' CEOs exhibit high moral identity symbolization, meaning that they outwardly express their morality to the public through actions and behavior. Furthermore, the relationship between CSR and CSiR appears to be bidirectional. Using an extensive 15-year panel dataset covering almost 3000 publicly traded companies, Kotchen and Moon (2012) found that more CSiR leads to more CSR with the effect being stronger in industries where there is a greater public scrutiny of CSiR. Corporate social irresponsibility with respect to community relations, the environment and human rights leads to greater CSR with respect to each of these dimensions. However, firms seem to try to offset the negative effects of CSiR related to corporate governance not by reforming governance but by engaging in CSR in other dimensions.

The above findings are of concern because they suggest that the CSP of many organizations may not be based on a genuine belief and commitment to be ethical and to engage in humanistic management practices. Responses from 111 executives of FTSE 100 and other All-Share companies suggest that businesses engage in CSR activities to have a competitive advantage and pursue their commercial interests. Executives perceive CSR as a necessity integrating it in all of their firms' operations and activities.

They also believe that it is possible for a firm to be both profitable and respectful to its stakeholders (Varenova, Martin, & Combs, 2013).

Perrini et al. (2011) have developed a multilevel framework of the CSP-CFP relationship. They believe that by integrating CSR efforts into specific management domains (e.g., internal organization, customers, supply chain, society, corporate governance, and the natural environment) a firm can benefit from both revenue-related outcomes (e.g., growth opportunities) and cost-related outcomes (e.g. greater operational efficiency and lower cost of capital). Echoing Porter and Kramer's (2006, 2011) views, Perrini et al. contend that "CSR supports firms in the process of intangible assets' accumulation, strengthening company ability to identify, protect and give value to inimitable resources, such as skills and competencies, knowledge and innovation, values, legitimacy, trust, and reputation in the stakeholder network" (p. 68).

Although the pursuit of firms' commercial interests should be expected (Campbell, 2007), from a humanistic management perspective, one may still be concerned about the decisions and actions that managers may take when they are not able to create a shared value or when CSP and financial performance are perceived to be at odds. The decision by managers to engage in socially responsible behavior and to attain high levels of corporate social performance should not be determined solely on the basis of economic reasoning and whether such outcomes lead to better financial performance. Windsor (2001) argues that much of the discourse in support of CSR is purely economic or based on the idea that it should be instrumental to wealth creation. In contrast to this cost-benefit conception of responsibility, Windsor argues that corporate responsibility must have a normative base. This view may sound utopian but it is important to understand its implications.

If we accept the view that firms should seek to attain high levels of CSP only if they result in higher CFP (an instrumental view of CSR), then we will be sending the wrong message to existing managers, business school students, and society in general. This is not to say that managers should engage in irresponsible behavior that drives their businesses into bankruptcies. The message that must be made clear is that business owners and managers have a *responsibility* to respect and take into consideration all stakeholders when setting their strategic goals and planning their strategies (Freeman, 1984). One of the principle functions of corporations is to serve the social good (Swanson, 1995). Relying only on an instrumental stakeholder theory approach is a type of second-best solution because the normative purposes associated with CSR are not guaranteed by a firm's instrumental activities (Scott & Hart, as cited in Swanson, 1999).

According to the normative approach to CSP (Swanson, 1999) the existence or not of such an instrumental relationship should not be the factor that determines the legitimacy of a firm's existence and operations in society. Businesses are part of society. They are organizations that are comprised of people who assume various managerial and employee roles. They survive because they make use of these employees to produce goods and provide services that their customers purchase. The firm and stakeholders exist in symbiosis in their communities. If firms are socially irresponsible, detrimental effects associated with the destruction of the environment, workforce exclusion, high levels of unemployment, poverty, discrimination and corruption will destroy this symbiosis and in the end hurt not only the employees, suppliers, and customers, but the business owners as well. Hence, the legitimacy of firms can be earned only by proactively engaging in socially desirable behavior that helps to sustain this symbiosis (Suchman, 1995).

Despite all the methodological limitations plaguing the studies that have investigated the CSP-CFP relationship, many researchers have concluded that CSP does not appear to negatively affect financial performance, thus providing an argument in support of socially responsible behavior. Although this may be true, the more appropriate argument that we should be making to our business students and organizational decision makers is that managers and owners of businesses should engage in socially responsible behavior because it is the right thing to do. This is more than just obeying the law. Many years ago, dumping toxic waste in rivers was not illegal. Was it still not wrong? Did it not negatively affect society and the environment? Likewise today, there may be activities that are not illegal but that are harmful. Alternatively, certain behaviors such as discrimination may be illegal but difficult to prove. Should businesses foster such behavior because their financial performance is not negatively impacted even if in reality it is but this is not immediately obvious? Arguably, most people would not contend that it is wrong for organizations and their managers to treat organizational stakeholders as they would have themselves treated.

CONCLUDING REMARKS

Interest in social issues management and the relation between business and society, has partly contributed to the numerous studies that have been conducted on CSR, CSP and CFP. Corporate social performance is a multidimensional construct. However, as a result of the extensive and ongoing research, our understanding of its complex relation to CFP has grown providing important insights for the academic community and business practitioners. Although our knowledge of the subject is still incomplete, and there is no generally accepted consensus regarding the relationship between CSP and CFP, an argument has been made that the instrumental stakeholder argument, despite its potential merits, should not be the deciding motive for CSR. Corporate social performance is aligned with a humanistic management perspective and should thus be supported by normative arguments. A humanistic organizational culture fosters engaging relations between organizational stakeholders (Fey & Denison, 2003; Maignan, Ferrell, & Hult, 1999). In such a culture, the organization's mission is aligned with the values and beliefs of its members and managers and employees show concern for others and cooperate with all stakeholders. It is therefore not a surprise that in his study of 295 Fortune 500 American companies, Melo (2012) found a humanistic culture to have a positive effect on CSP. Therefore, a commitment to promoting humanism in business and management should lead to improved corporate social performance and a better society.

NOTES

1. To identify relevant literature for the purposes of this study, an electronic search was conducted of various databases including ProQuest, Sage Journals Online, Taylor & Francis Online, and EBSCO Business Source Complete. Initially, the keyword search of the titles and abstracts involved the terms corporate social responsibility, corporate social performance and corporate financial performance. The term "corporate social irresponsibility" was used in the final search.
2. This review is not intended to be exhaustive. It is intended to help the reader to develop an adequate awareness of the different types of findings obtained from important studies on the topic.
3. The TRI has been used mainly by the U.S. government and special interest groups to determine environmental discharges of manufacturing facilities. The TRI is based on self-reported information regarding environmental discharges to landfills, air and water, and disposal of hazardous waste. One of the advantages of the TRI database is that information is available for a single industry (Griffin & Mahon, 1997).
4. Further research is needed to better understand why the TRI may not be related to financial performance measures. One explanation offered by Griffin and Mahon (1997) for their study is that more stringent reporting requirements for TRI were released in 1992 and these may have negatively affected companies' overall social performance.
5. The ESG measures environment, social and corporate governance practices. It was developed by CRISIL, S&P, and KLD. It is sponsored by the International Finance Corporation (IFC).
6. Mitnick (2000) identifies three problems with the measurement of CSP that relate to the need to measure the metric of performance valuation (i.e., of what we value in CSP), the metric of performance measurement (i.e., of the achievement of CSP), and the metric of performance perception and belief in CSP.

REFERENCES

Andersen, M. L., & Dejoy, J. S. (2011). Corporate social and financial performance: The role of size, industry, risk, R&D, and advertising expenses as control variables. *Business and Society Review, 116*(2), 237–256.

Armstong, J. S., & Green, K. C. (2013). Effects of corporate social responsibility and irresponsibility policies. *Journal of Business Research, 66*(10), 1922–1927.

De Bakker, F. G., Groenewegen, P., & den Hond, F. (2005). A bibliometric analysis of 30 years of research and theory on corporate social responsibility and corporate social performance. *Business and Society, 44*(3), 283–317.

Baird, P. L, Geylani, P. C., & Roberts, J. A. (2012). Corporate social and financial performance re-examined: Industry effects in a linear mixed model analysis. *Journal of Business Ethics 109*, 367–388.

Barnett, M. L. (2007). Stakeholder influence capacity and the variability of financial returns to corporate social responsibility. *Academy of Management Review, 32*,(3), 794–816.

Barnett, M. L., & Salomon, R. M. (2006). Beyond dichotomy: The curvilinear relationship between social responsibility and financial performance. *Strategic Management Journal, 27*(11), 1101–1156.

Barnett, M. L., & Salomon, R. M. (2012). Does it pay to be *really* good? Addressing the shape of the relationship between social and financial performance. *Strategic Management Journal, 33*, 1304–1320.

Baron, D. P., Harjoto, M. A., & Jo, H. (2011). The economics and politics of corporate social performance. *Business and Politics, 13*(2), 1–46.

Boaventura, J. M. G., da Silva, R. S., & Bandeira-de-Mello, R. (2012). Corporate financial performance and corporate social performance: Methodological development and the theoretical contribution of empirical studies. *Revista Contabilidade & Finanças, 23*(60), 235–245.

Bowen, H. R. (1953). *Social responsibilities of the businessman.* New York, NY: Harper & Row.

Brammer, S., Brooks, C., & Pavelin, S. (2006). Corporate social performance and stock returns: UK evidence from disaggregate measures. *Financial Management, 35*(3), 97–116.

Brammer, S., & Millington, A. (2008). Does it pay to be different? An analysis of the relationship between corporate social and financial performance. *Strategic Management Journal, 29*(12), 1325–1343.

Beurden, P., & Gössling, T. (2008). The worth of values—A literature review on the relation between corporate social and financial performance. *Journal of Business Ethics, 82*, 407–424.

Callan, S. J., & Thomas, J. M. (2009). Corporate financial performance and corporate social performance: An update and reinvestigation. *Corporate Social Responsibility and Environmental Management, 16*, 61–78.

Campbell, J. (2007). Why would corporations behave in socially responsible ways? An institutional theory of corporate social responsibility. *Academy of Management Review, 32*(3), 946–967.

Carroll, A. B. (1977). *Managing corporate social responsibility.* Boston, MA: Little, Brown.

Carroll, A. B. (1979). A three-dimensional conceptual model of corporate social performance. *Academy of Management Review, 4,* 497–505.

Carroll, A. B. (1999). Corporate social responsibility: Evolution of a definitional construct. *Business and Society, 38*(3), 268–295.

Carroll, A. B. (2000). A commentary and an overview of key questions on corporate social performance. *Business and Society, 39*(4), 466–478.

Carroll, A. B., & Shabana, K. M. (2010). The business case for corporate social responsibility: A review of concepts, research and practice. *International Journal of Management Reviews, 12*(1), 85–105.

Chand, M. (2006). The relationship between corporate social performance and corporate financial performance: Industry type as a boundary condition. *The Business Review, 5*(1), 240–245.

Choi, J.-S., Kwak, Y.-M., & Choe, C. (2010). Corporate social responsibility and corporate financial performance: Evidence from Korea. *Australian Journal of Management, 35*(3), 291–311.

Christensen, L. J., Mackey, A., & Whetten, D. (2014). Taking responsibility for corporate social responsibility: The role of leaders in creating, implementing, sustaining, or avoiding socially responsible firm behaviors. *The Academy of Management Perspectives, 28*(2), 164–178.

Clarkson, M. B. E. (1991). Defining, evaluating, and managing corporate social performance: The stakeholder management model. *Research in Corporate Social Performance and Policy, 12,* 331–358.

Clarkson, M. B. E. (1995). A stakeholder framework for analyzing and evaluating corporate social performance. *Academy of Management Review, 20*(1), 92–117.

Coffey, B. S., & Fryxell, G. E. (1991). Institutional ownership of stock and dimensions of corporate social performance: An empirical examination. *Journal of Business Ethics, 10*(6), 437–444.

Cox, P., Brammer, S., & Millington, A. (2004). An empirical examination of institutional investor preferences for corporate social performance. *Journal of Business Ethics, 51*(1), 27–43.

Davenport, K. (2000). Corporate citizenship: A stakeholder approach for defining corporate social performance and identifying measures for assessing it. *Business and Society, 39*(2), 210–219.

Davis, K. (1973). The case for and against business assumption of social responsibilities. *Academy of Management Journal, 16*(2), 312–322.

Eells, R., & Walton, C. (1974). *Conceptual foundations of business* (3rd ed.). Burr Ridge, IL: Irwin.

Fauzi, H. (2009). Corporate social and financial performance: Empirical evidence from American companies. *Globsyn Management Journal, 3*(1), 25–34.

Fey, C. F., & Denison, D. R. (2003). Organizational culture and effectiveness: Can American theory be applied in Russia? *Organization Science, 14*(6), 686–706.

Frederick, W .C. (1960). The growing concern over business responsibility. *California Management Review, 2,* 54–61.

Frederick, W. C. (1994). From CSR1 to CSR2. *Business & Society, 33,* 150–164.

Freeman, R. E. (1984). *Strategic management: A stakeholder approach.* Boston, MA: Pitman.

Graves, S. B., & Waddock, S. A. (1994). Institutional owners and corporate social performance. *Academy of Management Journal, 37*(4), 1034–1046.

Griffin, J. J., & Mahon, J. F. (1997). The corporate social performance and corporate financial performance debate: Twenty-five years of incomparable research. *Business and Society, 36*(1), 5–31.

Husted, B. W. (2000). A contingency theory of corporate social performance. *Business and Society, 39*(1), 24–48.

Jensen, M. C. (2002). Value maximization, stakeholder theory, and the corporate objective function. *Business Ethics Quarterly, 12*(2), 235.

Johnson, H. L. (1971). *Business in contemporary society: Framework and issues.* Belmont, CA: Wadsworth.

Johnson, R. A., & Greening, D. W. (1999). The effects of corporate governance and institutional ownership types on corporate social performance. *Academy of Management Journal, 42*(5), 564–576.

Kapoor, S., & Shandhu, H. S. (2010). Does it pay to be socially responsible? An empirical examination of impact of corporate social responsibility on financial performance. *Global Business Review, 11*(2), 185–208.

Kotchen, M., & Moon, J.J. (2012). Corporate social responsibility for irresponsibility. *The B.E. Journal of Economic Analysis & Policy, 13*(1).

Lee, D. D., Faff, R. W., & Langfield-Smith, K. (2009). Revisiting the vexing question: Does superior corporate social performance lead to improved financial performance? *Australian Journal of Management, 34*(1), 21–49.

Lin-Hi, N., & Müller, K. (2013). The CSR bottom line: Preventing corporate social irresponsibility, *66*(10), 1928–1936.

Maignan, I., Ferrell, O. C., & Hult, G. T. (1999). Corporate citizenship: Cultural antecedents and business benefits. *Academy of Marketing Science, 27*(4), 455–469.

Margolis, J. D., Elfenbein, H. A., & Walsh, J. P. (2009). Does it pay to be good … and does it matter? A meta-analysis of the relationship between corporate social and financial performance. *SSRN Working Paper Series.* Retrieved from http://papers.ssrn.com/sol3/papers.cfm?abstract_id=1866371

Margolis, J. D., & Walsh, J. P. (2003). Misery loves companies: Rethinking social initiatives by business. *Administrative Science Quarterly, 48*, 268–305.

Marom, I. Y. (2006). Toward a unified theory of the CSP-CFP link. *Journal of Business Ethics, 67*, 191–200.

McWilliams, A., & Siegel, D. (2000). Corporate social responsibility and financial performance: Correlation or misspecification. *Strategic Management Journal, 21*(5), 603–609.

Melo, T. (2012). Determinants of corporate social performance: The influence of organizational culture, management tenure and financial performance. *Social Responsibility Journal, 8*(1), 33–47.

Michael, A. (2012). Pursuing organizational integrity to create humanistic organizations. In W. Amann & A. Stachowicz (Eds.), *Integrity in organizations—Building the foundations for humanistic management* (pp. 19–39). (Humanism in Business Series). London, England: Palgrave Macmillan.

Michael. A. (2014). Capitalism at a crossroad: Unfulfilled expectations and future challenges. In H. H. Kazeroony & A. Stachowicz (Eds.), *Capitalism and the social relationship: An organizational perspective* (pp. 303–319). London, England: Palgrave Macmillan.

Miller, C. C., Washburn, N. T., & Glick, W. H. (2013). The myth of firm performance. *Organization Science, 24*(3), 948–964.

Mitnick, B. (1993, March 19–21). *Organizing research in corporate social performance: The CSP system as core paradigm.* Paper presented as a showcase session at the Annual Meeting of the International Association for Business and Society (IABS), San Diego, CA.

Mitnick, B. M. (2000). Commitment, revelation, and the testament of belief: The metrics of measurement of corporate social performance. *Business and Society, 39*(4), 419–465.

Moore, G. (2001). Corporate social and financial performance: An investigation in the U.K. supermarket industry. *Journal of Business Ethics, 34*, 299–315.

Oikonomou, I., Brooks, C., & Pavelin, S. (2011). The effects of corporate social performance on the cost of corporate debt and credit ratings. *ICMA Centre Discussion Papers in Finance DP2011-19*, Henley Business School, University of Reading.

Orlitzky, M., Schmidt, F. L., Rynes, S. L. (2003). Corporate social and financial performance: A meta-analysis. *Organization Studies, 24*(3), 403–441.

Ormiston, M. E., & Wong, E. M. (2013). License to ill: The effects of corporate social responsibility and CEO moral identity on corporate social irresponsibility. *Personnel Psychology, 66*(4), 861–893.

Peloza, J. (2009). The challenges of measuring financial impacts from investments in corporate social performance. *Journal of Management, 35*(6), 1518–1541.

Perrini, F., Russo, A., Tencati, A., & Vurro, C. (2011). Deconstructing the relationship between corporate social and financial performance. *Journal of Business Ethics, 102*, 59–76.

Porter, M. E., & Kramer, M. R. (2006). Strategy and society: The link between competitive advantage and corporate social responsibility. *Harvard Business Review, 85*(12), 78–92.

Porter, M. E., & Kramer, M. R. (2011). Creating shared value. How to reinvent capitalism—and unleash a wave of innovation and growth. *Harvard Business Review, 89*(1), 62–77.

Preston, L. E., & Post, J. E. (1975). *Private management and public policy: The principle of public responsibility.* Englewood Cliffs, NJ: Prentice-Hall.

Roman, R. M., Hayibor, S., & Agle, B. R. (1999). The relationship between social and financial performance: Repainting a Portrait. *Business and Society, 38*(1), 109–125.

Rowley, T., & Berman, S. (2000). A brand new brand of corporate social performance. *Business and Society, 39*(4), 397–418.

Ruf, B. M., Muralidhar, K., Brown, R. M., Janney, J. J., & Paul, K. (2001). An empirical investigation of the relationship between change in corporate social performance and financial performance: A stakeholder theory perspective. *Journal of Business Ethics, 32*(2), 143–156.

Sethi, S. P. (1975). Dimensions of corporate social performance: An analytical framework. *California Management Review, 17*, 58–64.

Simerly, R. L. (1999). Measuring corporate social performance: An assessment of techniques. *International Journal of Management, 16*(2), 253–257.

Soana, M.-G. (2011). The relationship between corporate social performance and corporate financial performance in the banking sector. *Journal of Business Ethics, 104,* 133–148.

Stanwick, P. A., & Stanwick S. D. (1998a). The determinants of corporate social performance: An empirical examination. *American Business Review, 16*(1), 86–93.

Stanwick, P. A., & Stanwick, S. D. (1998b). The relationship between corporate social performance, and organizational size, financial performance, and environmental performance: An empirical examination. *Journal of Business Ethics, 17*(2), 195–204.

Suchman, M. C. (1995). Managing legitimacy: Strategic and institutional approaches. *Academy of Management Review, 20*(3), 571–610.

Surroca, J., Tribo, J. A., & Waddock, S. (2010). Corporate responsibility and financial performance: The role of intangible resources. *Strategic Management Journal, 31,* 463–490.

Swanson, D. L. (1995). Addressing a theoretical problem by reorienting the corporate social performance model. *Academy of Management Review, 20*(1), 43–64.

Swanson, D. L. (1999). Toward an integrative theory of business and society: A research strategy for corporate social performance. *Academy of Management Review, 24*(3), 506–521.

Tyagi, R., & Sharma, A.K. (2013). Corporate social performance and corporate financial performance: A link for the Indian firms. *Issues in Social and Environmental Accounting, 7*(1), 4–29.

Ullman, A. A. (1985). Data in search of a theory: Critical examination of the relationships among social performance, social disclosure, and economic performance of U.S. firms. *Academy of Management Review, 10*(3), 540–557.

Van der Laan, G., Van Ees, H., & Van Witteloostuijn, A. (2007). Corporate social and financial performance: An extended stakeholder theory, and empirical test with accounting measures. *Journal of Business Ethics, 79,* 299–310.

Varenova, D., Martin, S., & Combs, A. (2013). Corporate social responsibility and profitability: trade-off or synergy: Perceptions of executives of FTSE All-Share companies. *Sustainability Accounting, Management and Policy Journal, 4*(2), 190-215.

Waddock, S. A., & Graves, S. B. (1997). The corporate social performance-financial performance link. *Strategic Management Journal, 18*(4), 303–319.

Wang, H., & Choi, J. (2013). A new look at the corporate social-financial performance relationship: The moderating roles of temporal and interdomain consistency in corporate social performance. *Journal of Management, 39*(2), 416–441.

Wartick, S. L., & Cochran, P. L. (1985). The evolution of the corporate social performance model. *Academy of Management Review, 10*(4), 758–769.

Wartick, S. L., & Mahon, J. F. (1994). Toward a substantive definition of the corporate issue construct: A review and synthesis of the literature. *Business & Society, 33,* 293–311.

Windsor, D. (2001). The future of corporate social responsibility. *The International Journal of Organizational Analysis, 9*(3), 225–256.

Wood, D.J. (1991a). Corporate social performance revisited. *Academy of Management Review, 16*(4), 691–718.

Wood, D. J. (1991b). Social issues in management: Theory and research in corporate social performance. *Journal of Management, 1*(2), 383–406.

Wood, D. J. (2010). Measuring corporate social performance: A review. *International Journal of Management Review, 12*(1), 50–84.

Wood, D. J., & Jones, R. E. (1995). Stakeholder mismatching: A theoretical problem in empirical research on corporate social performance. *International Journal of Organisational Analysis, 3*, 229–267.

Wokutch, R. E., & Spencer, B. A. (1987). Corporate saints and sinners: The effects of philanthropic and illegal activity on organizational performance. *California Management Review, 29*(2), 62–77.

Wu, M.-L. (2006). Corporate social performance, corporate financial performance, and firm size: A meta-analysis. *Journal of American Academy of Business, 8*(1), 163–1671.

Zahra, S. A., Priem, R. L., & Rasheed, A. A. (2005). The antecedents and consequences of top management fraud. *Journal of Management, 31*(6), 803–828.

CHAPTER 9

CORPORATE SOCIAL RESPONSIBILITY (CSR) AS A DERIVATIVE OF CAPITALISTIC ANXIETIES

Adela J. McMurray, Susan Mravlek, and Claire A. Simmers

INTRODUCTION

This chapter examines the complex relationship between corporate social responsibility (CSR) as a social phenomenon and the key concepts that influence its effect on systemic managerial behavior responding to societal and organizational forces. Paradoxically, there is a denial that capitalism is fundamentally driven by what are considered "bad virtues" (Long, 2008). Greed, power, and corruption, commonplace in the business world, are too frequently denied (Hoggett, 2010; Long & Sievers, 2013). Collusive relationships (Chapman, 2003) often conflict with CSR moral reasoning and values where corporations frequently deny the existence of this undiscussable "dark side" of organizational life. It should be noted at the outset that we acknowledge the benefits, and note the worthiness, of studies addressing the positive virtues and pursuits of CSR. Instead our provocation and challenge for further research, is to examine CSR from a perspective (the darker side) that is frequently ignored and denied.

Since its inception in the 1950s (Carroll, 1999), the concept of CSR generated extensive theoretical and conceptual developments much of which is still underdeveloped and fragmented. A systematic review and analysis of the CSR quantitative and qualitative literature shows frameworks and models of either CSR performance or examples of organizational commitments to CSR. However, the emotional issues surrounding CSR are seldom examined and this represents a significant oversight in the literature. The "science" around quantifiable measures may appear somewhat more palatable and acceptable. Yet, there is avoidance in dealing with the painful reality that the social phenomenon surrounding CSR adoption may be window dressing—a façade concealing the management of ethical and moral tensions arising from balancing capitalistic expectations and CSR.

Globalization and the insurgence of social media redefined public expectations of management behaviors (Dobers & Halme, 2009). The advent of social media initiated a ground swell of activists and "socially conscious" consumers (Fyke & Buzzanell, 2013), but the power relations between corporations and the external environment are still characterized by hegemonic struggles. Recent studies addressing CSR globalization and commitment elucidate that corporations, more often than not, suffer from a paucity of will (Driver, 2006; Rose, 2006). Thus, while the prevailing argument is that the increase in public advocacy has greatly influenced organizational adoption of CSR frameworks, we argue that, in practice, the realities of CSR are often based on collusions and illusions.

Significant pressures are placed on corporations to "do good" (Folger & Skarlicki, 2008), in terms of their contributions to the well-being of society. This logic is arguably altruistic and better fits socialistic ideals, than linkage to capitalistic archetypes. We contend that using a certain lens, we can consider that CSR has become an oxymoron. The ideology underpinning the various CSR models and frameworks, we suggest, is frequently an illusionary instrument for inauthentic performance. CSR commitments enable corporations to superficially enact, while capitalistic logic is the reality. The altruistic demands of stakeholders such as consumers, governments and other nongovernmental organizations appear to be met. However, corporations present a "false self" (Costas & Fleming, 2009; Winnicott, 1960) in the adoption and development of CSR policies, in which the disclosure of intent is a disengagement from operational reality. The authentic performance or "true self" is commonly, a nondisclosure or denial of practices that are exploitive and opportunistic for the sake of profit and power (Pearce & Manz, 2011).[1] This is evident in such practices such as the crafting of "shell companies," "secrecy jurisdictions" and "opaque corporate ownership" structures that enable corporations to launder ill-gained profits on the one hand, while also proclaiming commitment to CSR on the other hand (Transparency International, 2014).

The premise of our supposition is not to disregard or discredit the virtuous principles that CSR practices embody or that many corporations practice, but to question how aspects of CSR may be used both consciously and unconsciously, at a broader societal level by stakeholders to contain anxieties around malevolent virtues of capitalism (Hoggett, 2010; Long, 2008). We consider CSR through an alternative lens, one that is rarely discussed, that is to acknowledge society's inability to effectively deal with the anxieties associated with greed, power and corruption. We consider how these collective emotions may be contained for the purposes of satisfying consumer demand and business function. We illuminate this through our neoteric CSR model (CSR as a derivative of capitalistic anxieties model), which consolidates the literature and identifies the paradigm deficiencies and commonalities, including the measurement of the CSR concept.

SYSTEMATIC REVIEW PROCESS

A systematic three stage review and analysis process (see Figure 9.1) informed the development of the CSR as a derivative of capitalistic anxieties model.

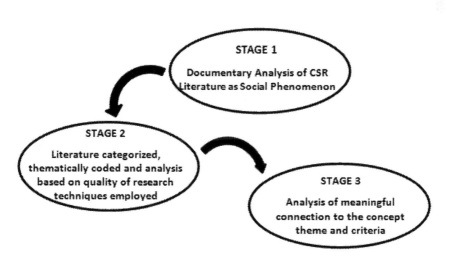

Figure 9.1.   Review and analysis processes.

In the first stage, qualitative and quantitative studies addressing CSR as a social phenomenon were documented and analyzed for their suitability to progress to the second stage. Their inclusion was based on links of CSR concepts to illusion and/or collusion criteria. The intent was to conduct a comparative analysis and to identify congruencies, if any, in the findings.

Stage 1

In Stage 1 search we reviewed the management, social science and ethical literatures. The focus was on the concepts of perversion, corruption, corporate governance, disclosure/nondisclosure, values, morality and ethics, which informed more specific searches (for particular concepts, issues and cases that related to illusions of CSR and/or collusive relationships). Stage one was comprised of a review of over 150 qualitative and 50 quantitative studies. Based on the selection for inclusion criteria, these were culled to 35 qualitative and 12 quantitative studies respectively for stage two. In addition, websites and documents from eight nongovernmental organizations (NGOs) were examined. NGOs are neither a part of a government nor for-profit organizations and may be funded by individuals, governments, foundations, or businesses. They are engaged in a wide range of activities, focusing their energies on influencing governments and inter-governmental processes. However, aided by advances in information and communications technology, they increasingly center attention on the social and environmental externalities of corporate activities (International Institute for Sustainable Development, 2013).

Stage 2

In Stage 2 we utilized a hermeneutic methodology to select and analyze the qualitative studies and the NGO information. Familiarization of the data involved reading through the 35 documents and clicking through the eight web sites and downloading and reading a sampling of documents to gain a general understanding of their nature and content. Thematic coding was developed inductively and categorized by subject and content. We used a criteria based methodology to select and analyze the quantitative studies, recording the research question, the sample, the data collection method, the data analysis technique, the independent variables and the dependent variables. Thematic coding was developed inductively and the studies categorized by independent and dependent variables thus giving us an understanding of the constructs and relationships empirically examined. Overall, we analyzed the qualitative and quantitative studies according to the quality of research techniques employed and in the case of the NGO information, we evaluated the web site quality and quantity of information and reports. This facilitated assessing links and patterns in terms of reference and conceptual development. Appendix A provides additional details.

Stage 3

In Stage 3 we analyzed the "diverse range of case studies together under a common framework so that findings would be cumulative ... to identify what it is we already 'know,' what it is we do not know and what it is we suspect" (Lucas, 1974, p. 1). In Stage 3 we focused on how the CSR concepts of illusion and collusion were represented in each document and how each was supported by research evidence (Appleton & Cowley, 1997). We organized the quantitative studies using a common set of criteria and inferences based on the results reported in each study. For example, we connected Rose's (2007) results which suggested that additional ethics education may have limited influence on many director's decisions to the concept of illusion.

ANALYSIS

Documents were critiqued and examined "as if they were research instruments in their own right" (Appleton & Cowley, 1997, p. 1010). What became increasingly evident in analyzing the plethora of qualitative documents was a lack of standardized format in the various research designs (Guba & Lincoln, 1981). This presented difficulty in identifying clear comparisons between the documents and methodological stances. However, using content analysis (Labuschagne, 2003), we reviewed the documents identifying major themes and categories and identified paradoxical stances on CSR. Embedded within the literature were key discourses and suppositions denoting the possibility that CSR was a tool for deflecting negative aspects of capitalism. We grouped the data into two key themes of 'illusion and collusion' enabling interpretation from a theoretical and conceptual context (Long & Harding, 2013). What surfaced from our analysis was a pattern of corporate social defensive behavior in relation to CSR.

Our findings from the qualitative and quantitative studies and the NGO information signified an interplay between publicly espoused values or concerns, public and legislative pressure for organizations to conform to their committed actions to CSR (Weber & Marley, 2012) and deceptive or collusive relations to ensure business ventures progressed unobstructed (Dela Rama, 2012). We used analytical induction (Lincoln & Guba, 1985) to facilitate the accommodation of the notions of illusion and collusion from a socioanalytical perspective to CSR. Next we discuss the evidence found to support our conclusions including a summary table of selected exemplary quotes found on each theme.

Illusion

Illusion is not a pathological phenomenon (Rycroft, 1995); however it does denote a false perception or defensive state. Based on a "grandiose fantasy" instead of reality, it is considered defensive. The intent is to avoid the reality of feeling depressed by a reinforcing a grandiose state of mind (Masterson, 1988). Winnicott (1965) refers to this state as the "False Self," in which the critical function is to conceal the "True Self" in being complicit with the demands from others. Organizational theorists such as Sievers (2003a, p. 21) hypothesize that organizations regressively use trust functions as an attempt to reinstate "order and organization" as means of coping with "disorder and disorganization." He contends that organizations engineering of trust is a surrogate for the subject of trust (p. 21). We extended this notion suggesting that CSR facilitates this function, in being an illusionary container (Armstrong, 2005) or instrument in which the appearance of "order and organization" is manufactured to cope with "disorder and disorganization," emanating from the reality of consumerism. The aspect of illusion can be considered as the shadow side or pathological form of every organization (Armstrong, 2005). We contend that CSR has a pathological version of itself. We believe that CSR serves as a "psychic retreat" (Steiner, 2011), where painful and shameful internal and external realities of capitalism threaten an organization's capacity function. We contend that by keeping up appearances, an organization's implementation of a CSR framework, together with society's influence on CSR policies, offers order and norm to group function within and across social structures.

CSR provides stakeholders (both internal and external) an ideal to preserve hope and restore trust. It is in effect a defense mechanism triggered by management anxieties, in their attempt to deal with chaos perpetuated by turbulent both internal and external environments (Sievers, 2003a). The literature in our sample reflected these concepts and tended to depict CSR as a phenomenon used to propagate and enhance organizational actualities (Sievers, 2003b). There appeared an apparent denial of the social impacts of corporate behavior. Divergent in views, we found CSR concepts and frameworks to be widely contested. Based on our sampling, we found a compelling picture around the theme of illusion, used to deny a consumerist and economic reality.

As Freud (1927) purported, "we live in a condition in which the terrors of nature, death and the privations of civilization make us feel helpless" (p. 18). These fears have not dissipated over time, especially when we consider the last global financial crises. In fact, one could plausibly argue that the terrors have significantly increased given the complexity of the world in which we currently live. Table 9.1 shows a sample of exemplar quotes we offer in support of our conclusions.

Table 9.1.   Illusion Exemplar Quotes

Key Theme	Exemplar Quotes
Illusion	*"To create an illusion of being 'changed,' a more socially responsible company; to regain political and public credibility"* (Weishaar, H., Collin, J., Smith, K., Grüning, T., Mandal, S., & Gilmore, A., 2012, p. 3).
	"The problem of integrating CSR principles with actual practice stems not from lack of resources or capacity per se, but paucity of will and political action" (Lim & Tsutsui, 2012, p. 89).
	"Corporate social responsibility and sustainability as ideological movements … are intended to legitimize and consolidate the power of large corporations" (Banerjee, 2008, p. 52).
	"Information that was incompatible with the idealized portrayal of the company was thus concealed or disregarded" (Duarte, 2010, p. 5)
	"sometimes companies are not willing to deal with possible stakeholder skepticism, so they utilize online media as if it were a traditional means of communication, a window to present themselves to the world" (Della Peruta, 2014, p. 98).
	"That is, directors were willing to make non-profit-maximizing decisions, avoid harming society, and cooperate with the spirit of law when they did not face a duty to maximize shareholder value" (Rose, 2007, p. 329).
	"Those hoping to see corruption swept up and addressed by a wave of traditional CSR activity are likely to be disappointed" (Carr & Outhwaite, 2010, p. 33).

These samples of exemplar quotes provide evidence of organizational attempts to elevate and/or deflect attention on CSR. Portraying the illusion of corporate social responsibility thus enables corporations, at both micro- and macrolevels, to present themselves as responsible corporate citizens.

Turning to collusion, our analysis of the documents suggested that corporations often manipulated their commitments to CSR and CSR performance measurements. In doing so, they demonstrated, on a superficial level, a willingness to participate in CSR initiatives. We provide further discussion and exemplars in the next section.

Collusion

Collusion, as defined by White (2011), is a surreptitious covenant between factions and/or participants with the aim to deceive. From a psychoanalytical perspective, it is the resistance among group members/ stakeholders, in which they are "interlocked in a tacit agreement to avoid a mutually fantasized catastrophe" (Karlsson, 2004, p. 567). Modern day theorists, such as Hirschhorn (1990), contend that unconscious collusion occurs as a defense against anxiety and presents in different forms in varying degrees of visibility and endurance (Steiner, 2011). Lawrence (1998, p. 54) described collusion as "rationale madness" that pervades the social realities that are collectively constructed by humans. Yet, institutions and the "larger containing society" tend to preserve a sense of stability by psychically retreating to models of hierarchical authority (p. 54). These anxieties may be of several different kinds, for example, sexual, ethical or metaphysical (Hoggett, 2010).

Table 9.2 shows a list of exemplar quotes which provide evidence to support our findings on this theme.

As indicated above, the exemplar quotes highlighted collusive relationships and the interdependence between internal and external stakeholders. The analyzed documents indicated that CSR initiatives facilitate the image of corporations as legitimate and plausible entities.

MODEL DEVELOPMENT

Using socioanalysis framework we integrated specific theories, such as open systems, group relations, sociosemiotics, social defences, stakeholders, and institutionalism (Bain, 1999; Fraher, 2004; Gould, Stapley, & Stein, 2001; Long, 2013; Long & Sievers, 2013) to develop our model. Our data analyses led us to this interdisciplinary approach "embedded in a social, cultural and global environment" (Long & Sievers, 2013, p. 4) as the best way to illustrate

Table 9.2.   Key Theme Collusion

Key Theme	Exemplar Quotes
Illusion	"*CSR should not be viewed as a zero-sum game but needs to take account of the interrelationships between business and society*" (Murphy & Schlegelmilch, 2013, p. 1809).
	"*The prevailing approach to CSR is fundamentally flawed in that it pits corporate interests against societal interests when they are clearly interdependent*" (Murphy & Schlegelmilch, 2013, p. 1808).
	"*A pattern of organized hypocrisy among developed countries is imposing CSR norms on developing countries while shielding their own economies from these norms*" (Lim & Tsutsui, 2012, p. 88).
	"*Corporations are being increasingly deemed as political subjects with their own personality for whom social wealth should be a priority ... the public often treats corporations as if they were people with their own objectives, preferences, styles, and personalities*" (Della Peruta, 2014, p. 100)
	"*The pervasive influence of business groups is often associated with an ethical ambivalence that can undermine the development of more rigorous, objective ethical standards, and the independent institutions that will uphold and enforce these ethical standards*" (Dela Rama, 2012, p. 518).
	"*a give-and-take relationship.... Consumers perceive CSR as interdependence, between a company and its stakeholders and an exchange of resources*" (Öberseder, Schlegelmilch, & Murphy, 2013, p. 1848)
	"*In a typical emerging market, politics, corruption, and CSR are interlocked because government agencies are one key stakeholder in an MNE's CSR framework and one major origin of widespread corruption*" (Luo, 2006, p. 762).
	"*organizations operate as sites of struggle where different groups compete to shape the social reality of organizations in ways that serve their own interests*" (Fyke & Buzzanell, 2013, p. 1624, as cited in Mumby & Clair, 1997, p. 182)

CSR as a derivative of capitalistic anxieties. Adopting key principles from each of the theories, this approach provided a useful structure to examine group relations that occur within and between a corporation and the various systems it interacts with in the external environment (Long, 2013). This allowed inclusion of a variety of standpoints including task, stakeholder, authority, boundary, social defences, and organizational dynamics (James & Huffington, 2004). In crafting our model, we utilized these academic theories a socioanalytic perspective as the foundation. The socioanalytic model, informed by multiple theories, offered a multilens way of thinking about organizations. This model considered collective psychological behavior experienced, felt or acted by an individual and group members, at either a conscious or unconscious level (Humphreys, 2010). It "provides a way of thinking about energizing or motivating forces resulting from the interconnection between various groups and sub-units of a social system" (Neumann, 1999, p. 57). We discuss these theories in the next section.

THEORETICAL UNDERPINNINGS

Organizations are not merely rational, dispassionate entities, but contain unconscious motivations, emotions and fantasies, linking subjective experience with wider political and societal forces

(Fischer, 2012, p. 1156)

Open Systems Theory

Open systems thinking traces its origins to Von Bertalanffy (1950) who extended a theoretical framework from mathematics to social sciences. Open systems theory enables researchers to understand the relationships between individuals, groups and the organization as a whole (Alderfer, 1980; Emery, 2000; Miller & Rice, 1967; Trist, 1980). It facilitates consideration of "the differentiation and integration of roles, tasks and resources consciously structured to accomplish substantive work within a changing environment" (Newton & Goodman, 2009, p. 293). Further, turbulent by nature, systems form relations and interdependencies with each other within a situated environment (p. 293). Organizational inner life interacts with societal contexts (Fischer, 2012). Considered a casual texture to the environment (Emery & Trist, 1965), systems are a complicated network of exchanges (Young & Goricanec, 2001). We believe open systems theory helps explain the dynamic interflow between internal and external environments.

Group Relations Theory

Group relations theory was initially developed during the Second World War from the War Office Officer Training Board in Britain (Morgan, 2009) and advanced by the Tavistock Institute (Fraher, 2004). A central assumption is that the life and dynamics of a group are primarily structured by task and the role relations of the members and affected by how a system exists in the mind of each member (Bion, 1961; Fraher, 2004; Gould et al., 2001; Wells, 1985). Group relations theory (Hinshelwood, 2009) can be considered as a creative collaboration between psychoanalysis and social science in the study of conscious and unconscious dynamics that exist within and between groups and organizations, in a holistic social system (Fraher, 2004). Located within these social systems are collective defences against anxiety, feelings of depression, guilt and a multitude of other emotions that organizations unconsciously structure (Long, 2008). This theory helps to show how internal groups might use collusion with external groups on CSR to reduce corporate anxieties.

Social Defence Theory

Freud was pivotal in popularizing the notion of psychological defence (Baumeister, Bratslavsky, Muraven, & Tice, 1998). However, it was Jaques (1955) and Menzies-Lyth (1960) who pioneered the studies of social defences in organizations. Menzies-Lyth (1960) was particularly pivotal in demonstrating how systems unconsciously develop and how structures reflect social interactions coalescing patterns of behavior into a "social system of defence" (Hoggett, 2010; Huffington, Armstrong, Halton, Hoyle, & Pooley, 2004). Considered a form of coping mechanism (Gould et al., 2001; Jaques, 1955; James & Huffington, 2004; Lawrence, 1998; Menzie-Lyth, 1960; Obholzer, 1999) social defences work in the service of the task or against it (Menzies-Lyth, 1960) and are often used by groups to defend against anxiety and uncomfortable emotions. Such anxieties may be inherent within a system and may arise out of environmental turbulence and uncertainty. Individuals defend against the fear of not making sense of reality, fear of loss and annihilation and for the fear of disorder and chaos, (Lawrence, 1998; Long, 2006; Menzies-Lyth, 1960). Social defence theory in its current iteration has extended from microlevel system exploration (groups and organizations) to incorporate macrosystems at a societal level (Chapman, 2003; Hinshelwood & Chiesa, 2002; Long, 2006). It supports the model development aspects of CSR as illusionary and being a self-defense mechanism.

Sociosemiotics Theory

Social semiotics is focused on investigating what emerges out of the collaborative interaction between humans, when rules are created, utilized and re-contracted using signs and symbols. The aim of each rule, which may vary in motivation, goal, and stance, is to produce communicative artifacts (Vannini, 2007). These artifacts then are interpreted in specific social situations and practices. Sociosemiotics is focused on context rather than what they symbolise and it is about making sense of power relationships (Vannini, 2007). As purported by Mitussis and Elliott (1999, p. 313), "language becomes a more complex dynamic socially constructed system which competitors may seek to influence in order to change or entrench individual consumers' constructions of social (market) structure" (p. 313). This is critical in understanding how the language of CSR (words, images and thoughts) is used by corporations to define responses to consumerism and activists. This mental model frames the social representations and explains the interaction between the cultures and dynamics of corporations and those espousing CSR.

Stakeholder Theory

Stakeholder theory addresses morals and values in managing an organization originating in the work of Freeman (1984). Stakeholder theory adds a sociopolitical level to organizational decision making and argues that the interests of many other parties are involved, including employees, customers, suppliers, financiers, communities, governmental bodies, political groups, trade associations, and trade unions (Donaldson & Preston, 1995; Laplume, Sonpar, & Litz, 2008). This theory is in direct contrast to the shareholder view of the organization, where creating and increasing shareholder value is the only purpose of the corporation, thus prioritizing self-interest (Friedman, 1970). This theory provides the broader context for our model with the dynamics of stakeholder interests as the catalyst for tensions and anxieties which need acknowledgement and resolution.

Institutional Theory

Powell and DiMaggio (1991) posit the rejection of the rational-actor models of classical economics and propose cognitive and cultural explanations for social and organizational phenomena. Scott (1995) indicates that, in order to survive, organizations must conform to the rules and belief systems prevailing in the environment thus earning the organization legitimacy (Dacin, 1997; Deephouse, 1996). For instance, multinational corporations (MNCs) operating in different countries with varying institutional environments will face pressures to conform to the local norms and rules. Other institutions exerting convergence pressures are (1) NGOs through reporting and certifications, and (2) educational institutions through common educational curricula in such areas of study as business. Our model builds upon this theory by suggesting that CSR can be a response to institutional pressures to conform.

Reconciling the data collected with the theories discussed above (Bansal & Roth, 2000), resulted in the crafting of the CSR as a derivative of capitalistic anxieties model depicted in Figure 9.2.

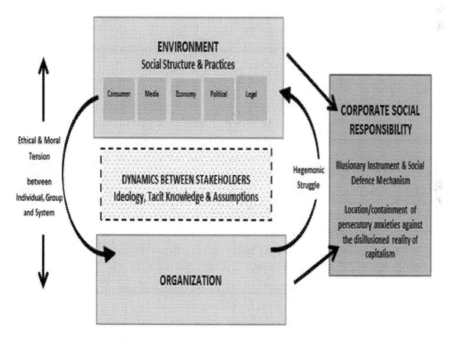

Figure 9.2.   CSR as a derivative of capitalistic anxieties model.

The elements that contribute to the development of the above model are drawn from the seminal notions of Emery (1980) and Miller and Rice (1967) and then extended in the work by Mitussis and Elliott (1999) and Morgan (2006). This conceptual model illustrates the role of CSR within an open system (De Board 1978; Miller & Rice, 1967; Morgan, 2006) and as an adaptive response (Emery, Emery, Caldwell, & Crombie, 1977) in the interplays among social representations, the external environment and the organization.

These social representations as purported by Mitussis and Elliott (1999, p. 313) and in citing Moscovici (1984) are "shared images that enable stakeholders to give objects, persons and events a definite form, locate them in a given category and gradually establish them as a model of a certain type, distinct and shared by a group of people" (p. 7). These inputs in turn, "influence and provide the system with a sense of order and social structure" (p. 7). In socioanalytical terms, these social representations are held by a culture that can be conceived as a "pool of thoughts" that are co-created symbols and meanings between individuals (Long, 2013). At a systemic level, this is referred to as the "associative unconscious ... covers all those associations available and potential within and among interacting social systems ... it is a rich vein of golden insight into the underlying dynamics of the system" (Long, 2013, p. xxiii).

In the context of CSR, the model serves to facilitate the link between the organization and the external environment, in which relations are "interrelated and interdependent" (Nossal, 2007, p. 60). This social phenomenon is the "collective psychological behaviour ... (it) provides a way of thinking about energizing or motivating forces resulting from the interconnection between various groups and sub-units of a social system" (Neumann, 1999, p. 57). The model enables us to consider the manifestation of CSR as ideology, the emergence of a "desired system state" and its effect on these social constructs. This ideology is presented as a logic and set of governing principles arisen from a set of shared symbolic circumstances (Fairclough, 1992). Deviations from norms are self-regulated by the system, to avoid the system becoming an oxidant state (Morgan, 2006). However, a paradox exists in having to manage the ethical and moral tensions associated with consumerism (Eisingerich, Rubera, Seifert, & Bhardwaj, 2011). As contended by Stohl and Cheney (2001), tensions are "the clash of ideas or principles or actions and to the discomfort that may arise as a result" (p. 354).

From a socioanalytical perspective, CSR acts as a receptacle; to unconsciously contain intolerable anxieties invoked from the negative social representations of capitalism (i.e., greed, envy, narcissism, corruption). This defense mechanism is used by "individuals, groups and organizations as a whole in order to relieve the painful aspects of their experiences, or preserve that which is cherished and loved" (De Gooijer, 2009, p. 215). In the context of capitalism, it is the preservation of market domination.

Collusive in nature, relations across the system and the environment become 'a hegemonic struggle' for market power (Mitussis & Elliott, 1999). Tensions are relieved by locating them in CSR and making the bad aspects of market driven consumerism palatable. CSR in turn, emerges as a formalized ideology, a set of doctrines, in which these tensions are re-imaged to form an illusionary quality of 'goodness' and as an authority structure of regulation (Rose, 2007).

CONCLUSION

Our consolidation of the CSR literature and theory illustrates an interdependence in managing the tensions of managerial logic and the ethical demands for CSR. This finding supports our hypothesis that at both a conscious and unconscious level, CSR can be a social defense mechanism in which to contain a society's anxieties and ethical/moral tensions associated with this paradox. The "sugar coating" of CSR (repression of emotional truth) facilitates the denial of the 'wickedness' of consumerism—the reality too painful to accept.

In many instances, CSR is an illusionary instrument; an opiate for the masses (Armstrong, 2005; Sungwon & Tai-Hing, 2013). A hallucinogenic that safely anaesthetizes our consciousness from the many societal iniquities (Arendt, 1963) that consumerism represents and of which we see many examples in the daily headlines (Delmas & Vanessa 2011). The headiness of consumerism is an addiction, endemic on a globalized scale. Facilitating collusive relationships, we propose that the ideology and doctrines of CSR give society the illusion of hope for the future—that is society can "right corporation wrongs," that we can control corporations and that capitalism is egalitarian.

We argue that society unconsciously uses CSR to relieve itself of the guilt and shame in being seduced by greed and a willingness to be deceived. Why must CSR most often be considered in the context of hopefulness or goodness? Why the timidity in exploring the darker aspects that may lie beneath the premise of CSR? What are the fears and anxieties of what might be "uncovered?" Is the resistance to do so, a validation of our contention?

We believe our corporate social responsibility (CSR) as a derivative of capitalistic anxieties model may offer researchers an opportunity, to consider further empirical investigation in how stakeholders overcome moral tensions associated with perverse system dynamics. The model could enable researchers to reconcile theory and provide a lens in which to frame a new realm across micro- and macroenvironmental domains.

Additionally, this model provides an opportunity for researchers to consider new approaches to the study of CSR. It may facilitate and advance CSR research in connection to morality and governance, particularly in gaining a deeper understanding of the complex interplay between the dynamics of power, control, and authenticity between consumers, organizations, communities, markets, economies, and government bodies.

NOTE

1. The reference to False Self/True Self is typically portrayed based on the original notions of D. W. Winnicott. However, the authors' contribution herein is a creative extension of this notion and to be considered from the perspective as a reverse of the original interpretation.

REFERENCES

Alderfer, C. P. (1980). Consulting to underbounded systems. In C. P. Alderfer & C. L. Cooper (Eds.), *Advances in experimental social processes* (pp. 267–295). New York, NY: John Wiley & Sons.

Appleton, J. V., & Cowley, S. (1997). Analyzing clinical practice guidelines. A method of documentary analysis. *Journal of Advanced Nursing, 25*(5), 1008–1017.

Armstrong, D. (2005). *Organization in the mind: Psychoanalysis, group relations and organizational consultancy. occasional papers 1989–2003.* R. French (Ed.). London, England: Karnac Books.

Arendt, H. (1963). *Eichmann in Jerusalem: A report on the banality of evil.* New York, NY: Viking Press.

Bain, A. (1999), On socio-analysis. *Socio-Analysis 1*(1), 1–17.

Banerjee, S. B. (2008). Corporate social responsibility: The good, the bad and the ugly. *Critical Sociology, 34*(1), 51–79.

Bansal, P., & Roth, K. (2000). Why companies go green: A model of ecological responsiveness. *Academy of Management Journal, 43*(4), 717–736.

Baumeister, R. E., Bratslavsky, E., Muraven, M., & Tice, D. M. (1998). Ego depletion: Is the active self a limited resource? *Journal of Personality and Social Psychology, 74*(5), 1252–1265.

Bion, W. R. (1961). *Experiences in groups.* London, England: Tavistock.

Carr, I. M., & Outhwaite, O. (2010). *Corruption, corporate social responsibility and corporate governance* (Working Paper). doi:http://dx.doi.org/10.2139/ssrn.1639610

Carroll, A. B. (1999). Corporate social responsibility evolution of a definitional construct. *Business & Society, 38*(3), 268–295.

Chapman, J. (2003). Hatred and corruption of task. *Organisational and Social Dynamics: An International Journal of Psychoanalytic, Systemic and Group Relations Perspectives, 3*(1), 40–60.

Costas, J., & Fleming, P. (2009). Beyond dis-identification: A discursive approach to self-alienation in contemporary organizations. *Human Relations, 62*(3), 353–378.

Dacin, M. T. (1997). Isomorphism in context: The power and prescription of institutional norms. *Academy of Management Journal, 40*(1), 46–81.

De Board, R. (1978). *The psychoanalysis of organizations: A psychoanalytic approach to behaviour in groups and organizations.* New York, NY: Routledge.

De Gooijer, J. (2009). *The murder in merger: A systems psychodynamic exploration of a corporate merger.* London, England: Karnac Books.

Deephouse, D. L. (1996). Does isomorphism legitimate? *Academy of Management Journal, 39*(4), 1024–1039.

Dela Rama, M. (2012). Corporate governance and corruption: Ethical dilemmas of Asian business groups. *Journal of Business Ethics, 109*(4), 501–519.

Della Peruta, M. R. (2014). Emerging markets, social network, and the question of legitimacy. In M. Del Giudice, M. R. Della Peruta, & E. G. Carayannis (Eds.), *Social media and emerging economies: Technological, cultural and economic implications* (pp. 89–107). New York, NY: Springer.

Delmas, M. A., & Vanessa, C. B. (2011). The drivers of greenwashing. *California Management Review, 54*(1), 64–87.

Dobers, P., & Halme, M. (2009). Corporate social responsibility and developing countries. *Corporate Social Responsibility and Environmental Management*, *16*(5), 237–249.

Donaldson, T., & Preston, L. E. (1995). The stakeholder theory of the corporation: concepts, evidence, and implications. *Academy of Management Review 20*(1): 65–91.

Driver, M. (2006). Beyond the stalemate of economics versus ethics: Corporate social responsibility and the discourse of the organizational self. *Journal of Business Ethics*, *66*(4), 337–356.

Duarte, F. (2010). Corporate social responsibility in a Brazilian mining company: "Official" and divergent narratives. *Social Responsibility Journal*, *6*(1), 4–17.

Eisingerich, A. B., Rubera, G., Seifert, M., & Bhardwaj, G. (2011). Doing good and doing better despite negative information: The role of corporate social responsibility in consumer resistance to negative information. *Journal of Service Research*, *14*(1), 60–75.

Emery, F. E. (1980). *Educational paradigms*. Melbourne, Australia: Education Department.

Emery, M. (2000). The current version of Emery's open systems theory. *Systemic Practice and Action Research*, *13*(5), 623–643.

Emery, F. E., & Trist, E. (1965). The causal texture of organizational environments. *Human Relations*, *18*, 12–32.

Emery, F. E., Emery, M., Caldwell, G., & Crombie, A. (1977). *Futures we are in*. Leiden, South Holland: Martinus Nijhoff.

Fairclough, N. (1992). Discourse and text: Linguistic and intertextual analysis within discourse analysis. *Discourse & Society*, *3*(2), 193–217.

Fischer, M. D. (2012). Organizational turbulence, trouble and trauma: Theorizing the collapse of a mental health setting. *Organization Studies*, *33*(9), 1153–1173.

Folger R., & Skarlicki, D. P. (2008). The evolutionary bases of deontic justice. In S. W. Gilliland, D. D. Steiner, & D. P. Skarlicki (Eds.), *Justice, morality, and social responsibility* (pp. 29–62). Charlotte, NC: Information Age Publishing.

Fraher, A. L. (2004). *A history of group study and psychodynamic organizations*. London, England: Free Association Books.

Freeman, R. E. (1984). *Strategic Management: A stakeholder approach*. Boston, MA: Pitman.

Freud, S. (1927). The future of an illusion. In *The standard edition of the complete psychological works of Sigmund Freud, volume XXI (1927-1931): The future of an illusion, civilization and its discontents, and other works* (pp. 1–56). London, England: Hogarth Press and Institute of Psychoanalysis.

Friedman, M. (1970). The social responsibility of business is to increase its profits. *New York Times Magazine*, *13*, 32–33.

Fyke, J. P., & Buzzanell, P. M. (2013). The ethics of conscious capitalism: Wicked problems in leading change and changing leaders. *Human Relations*, *66*(12), 1619–1643.

Gould, L. J., Stapley, L. F., & Stein, M. (2001). *The systems psychodynamics of organizations*. New York, NY: Karnac Books.

Guba, E. G., & Lincoln, Y. S. (1981). *Effective evaluation: Improving the usefulness of evaluation results through responsive and naturalistic approaches.* San Francisco, CA: Jossey-Bass.

Hinshelwood, R. D. (2009). Ideology and identity: A psychoanalytic investigation of a social phenomenon. *Psychoanalysis, Culture & Society, 14*(2), 131–148.

Hinshelwood, R., & Chiesa, M. (2001). *Organisations, anxieties and defences: Towards a psychoanalytic social psychology.* New York, NY: Brunner/Routledge.

Hirschhorn, L. (1990). *The workplace within: Psychodynamics of organizational life.* Cambridge, MA: MIT press.

Hoggett, P. (2010). Government and the perverse social defence. *The British Journal of Psychotherapy, 26*(2), 202–212.

Huffington, C., Armstrong, D., Halton, W., Hoyle, L., & Pooley, J. (2004). *Working below the surface: the emotional life of contemporary organizations.* London, England: Karnac.

Humphreys, J. (2010). Engaging stakeholders to create effective change. Retrieved from RMIT University website: http://researchbank. rmit. edu. au/eserv/rmit, 10375

International Institute for Sustainable Development. (2013). *The rise and role of NGOs in sustainable development.* Retrieved March 3, 2014, from http://www.iisd.org/business/ngo/roles.aspx

James, K., & Huffington, C. (2004). Containment of anxiety in organizational change: A case example of changing organizational boundaries. *Organizational and Social Dynamics 4,* 212–233.

Jaques, E. (1955). Social systems as a defence against persecutory and depressive anxiety. In M. Klein, P. Hiemann, & R. E. Money-Kyrle (Eds.), *New directions in psychoanalysis* (pp. 478–498). London, England: Tavistock.

Karlsson, R. (2004). Collusions as interactive resistances and possible stepping-stones out of impasses. *Psychoanalytic Psychology, 21*(4), 567–579.

Labuschagne, A. (2003). Qualitative research-airy fairy or fundamental. *The Qualitative Report, 8*(1), 100–103.

Laplume, A., Sonpar, K., & Litz, R. (2008). Stakeholder theory: Reviewing a theory that moves us. *Journal of Management, 34*(6), 1152–1189.

Lawrence, W. G. (1998). Unconscious social pressures on leaders. In E. B. Klein, F. Gabelnick, & P. Herr (Eds.), *The psychodynamics of leadership* (pp. 53–75). Madison, CT: Psychosocial Press.

Lim, A., & Tsutsui, K. (2012). Globalization and commitment in corporate social responsibility cross-national analyses of institutional and political-economy effects. *American Sociological Review, 77*(1), 69–98.

Lincoln, Y. S., & Guba, E. G. (1985). *Naturalistic inquiry.* London, England: Sage.

Long, S. (1999). The tyranny of the customer and the cost of consumerism: An analysis using systems and psychoanalytic approaches to groups and society. *Human Relations, 52*(6), 723–743.

Long, S. (2006). Organizational defences against anxiety: What has happened since the 1955 Jaques paper? *International Journal of Applied Psychoanalytic Studies, 3*(4), 279–295.

Long, S. (2008). *The perverse organization and its deadly sins.* London, England: Karnac Books.

Long, S. (Ed.). (2013). *Socioanalytic methods: Discovering the hidden in organizations and social systems*. London, England: Karnac Books.

Long, S., & Harding, W. (2013). Socioanalytic interviewing. In S. Long (Ed.). *Socioanalytic methods: Discovering the hidden in organisations and social systems* (pp. 91–106). London, England: Karnac Books.

Long, S., & Sievers, B. (Eds.). (2013). *Towards a socioanalysis of money, finance and capitalism: Beneath the surface of the financial industry* (Vol. 67). New York, NY: Routledge.

Lucas, W. A. (1974). *The case survey method: Aggregating case experience* (No. 1515). Santa Monica, CA: Rand.

Luo, Y. (2006). Political behavior, social responsibility, and perceived corruption: A structuration perspective. *Journal of International Business Studies*, *37*(6), 747–766.

Masterson, J. F. (1988). *Search for the real self: Unmasking the personality disorders of our age*. New York, NY: Free Press.

Menzies-Lyth, I. (1960). Social systems as a defense against anxiety: An empirical study of the nursing service of a general hospital. *Human Relations*, *13*, 95–121.

Miller, E. J., & Rice, A. K. (1967). *Systems of organisation: The control of task and sentiment boundaries*. London, England: Tavistock.

Mitussis, D., & Elliott, R. (1999). Representations, text; and practice: A discourse-analytic model of the consumer. *Advances in Consumer Research*, *26*, 312–319.

Morgan, G. (2006). *Images of organization* (2nd ed.). Beverley Hills, CA: Sage.

Morgan, J. (2009). Working with what is there: A systems psychodynamic framework for inter-agency collaboration. Retrieved from http://researchbank.rmit.edu.au

Moscovici, S. (1984). The phenomenon of social representations. In R. M. Farr & S. Moscovici (Eds.), *Social representations* (pp. 3–69). Cambridge, England: Cambridge University Press,

Mumby, D. K., & Clair, R. 1997. Organizational discourse. In T. A. van Dijk (Ed.), *Discourse as structure and process* (Vol. 2., pp. 181–205). London, England: Sage.

Murphy, P. E., & Schlegelmilch, B. B. (2013). Corporate social responsibility and corporate social irresponsibility: Introduction to a special topic section. *Journal of Business Research*, *66*(10), 1807–1813

Neumann J. E. (1999). Systems psychodynamics in the service of political organizational change. In R. French & R. Vince (Eds.), *Group relations, management and organization* (pp. 54-69). Oxford, England: Oxford University Press.

Newton, J. F., & Goodman, H. (2009). Only to connect: systems psychodynamics and communicative space. *Action Research*, *7*, 291–312.

Nossal, B. (2007). *Systems psychodynamics and consulting to organisations in Australia. A thesis presented for the degree of doctor of philosophy*. Retrieved from http://researchbank.rmit.edu.au

Öberseder, M., Schlegelmilch, B. B., & Murphy, P.E. (2013). CSR practices and consumer perceptions. *Journal of Business Research*, *66*(10), 1839–1851.

Obholzer, A. (1999). Managing the unconscious at work. *In R. French & R. Vince (Eds), Group relations, management and organization* (pp. 112-126). Oxford, England: Oxford University Press.

Pearce, C. L., & Manz, C. C. (2011). Leadership centrality and corporate social irresponsibility (CSIR): The potential ameliorating effects of self and shared leadership on CSIR. *Journal of Business Ethics, 102*(4), 563–579.

Powell, W. W., & DiMaggio, P. J., (1991). *The new institutionalism in organizational analysis*. Chicago, IL: University of Chicago Press.

Rose, J. (2007). Corporate directors and social responsibility: Ethics versus shareholder value. Journal of Business Ethics, *73*(3), 319–331.

Rycroft, C. (1995). *A critical dictionary of psychoanalysis* (2nd ed.). London, England: Puffin.

Scott, W. R. (1995). *Institutions and organizations*. Thousand Oaks, CA: Sage.

Sievers, B. (2003a). Against all reason: Trusting in trust. *Organisational and Social Dynamics: An International Journal of Psychoanalytic, Systemic and Group Relations Perspectives, 3*(1), 19–39.

Sievers, B. (2003b). Your money or your life? Psychotic implications of the pension fund system: Towards a socio-analysis of the financial services revolution. *Human Relations, 56*(2), 187–210.

Steiner, J. (2011). *Seeing and being seen: Emerging from a psychic retreat*. London, England: Routledge.

Stohl, C., & Cheney, G. (2001). Participatory processes/paradoxical practices: Communication and the dilemmas of organizational democracy. *Management Communication Quarterly, 14*(3), 349–407.

Sungwon, Y., & Tai-Hing, L. (2013). The illusion of righteousness: Corporate social responsibility practices of the alcohol industry. *BMC Public Health, 13*(1), 1–11

Transparency International. (2014, June 19). *Unmask the corrupt: Who says secret companies are bad? We do!* Retrieved March 3, 2014, from http://www.transparency. org/news/feature/unmask the corrupt

Trist, E. (1980). The environment and system-response capability. *Futures 12*(2), 113–127.

Weber, J., & Marley, K. A. (2012). In search of stakeholder salience: Exploring corporate social and sustainability reports. *Business and Society, 51*(4), 626–649.

Weishaar, H., Collin, J., Smith, K., Grüning, T., Mandal, S., & Gilmore, A. (2012). Global health governance and the commercial sector: A documentary analysis of tobacco company strategies to influence the WHO framework convention on tobacco control. *PLoS Med 9*(6), e1001249. doi:10.1371/journal. pmed.1001249.

Wells, L., Jr. (1985). The group-as-whole perspective and its theoretical roots. In A. D. Colman & M. H. Geller (Eds.), *Group relations reader 2* (pp. 109–126). Portland, OR: A. K. Rice Institute.

White, R. S. (2011). The nonverbal unconscious: collision and collusion of metaphor. *Psychoanalytic Inquiry: A Topical Journal for Mental Health Professionals 31*(2), 147-158.

Winnicott, D. W. (1965). Ego distortion in terms of true and false self. In M. M. R. Kahn (Ed.), *The maturational processes and the facilitating environment* (pp. 140–152). London, England: The Hogarth Press and the Institute of Psychoanalysis.

Vannini, P. (2007). Social semiotics and fieldwork method and analytics. *Qualitative Inquiry, 13*(1), 113–140.

Von Bertalanffy, L. (1950). The theory of open systems in physics and biology. *Science, 111*(2872), 23–29.

Young, D., & Goricanec, J. L. (2001). From resignation to active adaptation: Confronting the managerialist pathology in universities. *Public University Journal 1*, 5–15.

CHAPTER 10

CORPORATE SOCIAL RESPONSIBILITY AND CORPORATE SOCIAL PERFORMANCE

Neither Binary nor Righteous

Robert L. Heath and Damion Waymer

INTRODUCTION

Discussion of corporate social responsibility (CSR) originated in the business ethics literature. It centered on the argument of whether corporate businesses had any responsibility to society other than to produce profits and pay as little as possible in wages and taxes. Even though that debate is at least 50 years old, corporations of all kinds and sizes continue to plan and operate on what can be called a minimalistic commitment to the communities where they operate and to the potential mutuality of benefits with some key stakeholders (Sen & Cowley, 2013, benchmark the start of the CSR discussion in the early 1930s with the crash of the U.S. stock market.)

Corporate Social Performance:
Paradoxes, Pitfalls, and Pathways to the Better World, pp. 201–222
Copyright © 2015 by Information Age Publishing

Spending on anything else, so the argument goes, is inefficient and irrational economics and therefore ultimately unfair to stock shareholders.

That argument was famously made by economist Milton Friedman (1962, 1970) when he chided businessmen whom he viewed as incorrectly committed to "defending free enterprise when they declaim that business is not concerned 'merely' with profit but also with promoting desirable 'social ends.'" He criticized those who argued "that business has a 'social conscience' and takes seriously its responsibilities for providing employment, eliminating discrimination, avoiding pollution and whatever else may be the catchwords of the contemporary crop of reformers" (p. 32).

Friedman (1962, 1970) argued that executives are not beholding to society but to boards of directors and shareholders who want profits to be as high as possible. Updated, that theme presaged a political argument offered in 2013 to support the free market system and oppose any argument that could conservatively be interpreted to weaken individual self-responsibility. Taking this theme to its logical end, the Friedman view of CSR was that businesses were empowered to do all they could to adjust society to support the interests of each company. That model continues today and underscores the importance of discussing an efficient and rational market dedicated to profit maximization, shareholder value, and executive compensation under the conditions of elite stakeholder expectations.

Apropos to that discussion, a contrary view was advocated 30 years ago by Peter F. Drucker, one of the icons of U.S. management theory. Drucker (1984) reasoned that "The proper 'social responsibility' of business is to tame the dragon, that is, to turn a social problem into economic opportunity and economic benefit, into productive capacity, into human competence, into well-paid jobs, and into wealth" (p. 62). This logic, recently, has also been extended successfully to the nonprofit arena; yet rigid regulation deems it "not socially responsible" for nonprofits to use the power of the free market enterprise to address societal ills (Pallotta, 2008). Whether for profit (Drucker) or not for profit (Pallotta), the view is the same; it champions the perspective that organizations earn the right to operate and to reward once, or as, they bend themselves to serve society. Exploring that theme as it relates to the U.S. chemical industry, for instance, Sun and Stuebs (2013) reported "that CSR can lead to higher productivity in the chemical industry" (p. 251). That normative approach to strategic, reflective management and effective public relations supplies a rationale that justifies organizations' right to reward and to operate.

The turbulent last half of the 20th century in the United States saw these sorts of arguments contested by management advocates who called for higher standards of business ethics as a way of reducing the incentives to impose regulatory constraints on the free market. Critics were punishing corporations with legislation and regulation for failures to achieve societally constructed CSR standards; thus, the argument was that for a business to be legitimate, it needs to reduce the gap between what it is doing and how those actions compare to and satisfy criteria stakeholders use to judge corporate performance. Activists, often empowered through NGOs, have sought to raise the cost of violation of CSR standards as a carrot and rod incentive to effect a more responsive and reflective approach to management. Thus, CSR was born as a debate over whether the "will" and "spirit" of public policy would emerge from business or be imposed on it through regulation, legislation, and litigation. Such discussions led to advice on how businesses needed to think from outside themselves in to the executive suite.

Since those compelling arguments were made in the 1960s and 1970s, the discussion has dug deeply into the complexity of CSR. Some of that discussion suggested that strategic management changes had to be harnessed to make the organization more legitimate. Carried one step more, advocates largely with a marketing incentive, argued that companies could do well by doing good and that such actions could be measured as corporate social performance (CSP) and communicated to targeted stakeholders to gain marketplace advantage. CSP was also proposed to appeal to stakeholders who believed that such incentive, rather than regulation, could make organizations more responsive to the communities where they operate. Thus, these two perspectives have become variations of the Friedman-Drucker themes: (1) Serve society by knowing and meeting standards of operation that earn support rather than opposition, and (2) justify social responsibility by creating and implementing multidimensional programs that help the organization do well by doing good.

Since the 1960s, studies of business ethics morphed into a very robust discourse on the paradoxes and social constructions of CSR. Hundreds of papers, books, reports, studies, corporate management programs, and studies by CSR officers have explored the nooks and crannies of this topic. By the end of the 1980s, some of these explorations had affirmed contextual, multidimensional approaches and central themes. This work led to various taxonomies, such as these:

Topics relevant to the qualitative assessments of political economy such as economic, social, and political constructions and enactments (Wartick & Cochran, 1985).

- Topics relevant to reflective management concerns, such as ethical, technical, functional, conceptual, and operational (Hosmer, 1991).
- Topics relevant to stakeholders' evaluations and motivations for change, such as security, fairness, equality, and environmental quality/quality of life (Buchholz, Evans, & Wagley, 1985; Heath, 1988).

- Topics relevant to the intersection of functional dimensions and principles of corporate responsibility, such as economic, legal, ethical, and philanthropic (Carroll, 1991).

Such taxonomies suggest themes relevant to the discussion, understanding and application of CSR-CSP, and they also support the conclusion that the discipline is multidimensional, multilayered, and multitextual.

Based on an extensive literature review and analysis, this paper argues that CSR is not a binary concept but one that has levels of performative judgement by which organizations demonstrate ethics and earn the right to operate and right to reward. Into this battle is injected the argument that CSR and CSP can be a sham, a way that organizations can seem to be legitimate by doing and/or claiming some good, being marginally responsible by arguing for easy standards which they can demonstrate that they meet. Thus, the organization seeks to privilege its management policies by stating or implying the conditions for CSR and proclaiming how they are met. That line of reasoning short circuits the theme that organizations should not (and cannot unilaterally) set the standards, but that "society" does. Thus, the righteousness of the CSR-CSP standards is invariably the discursive product of social constructions relevant to each political economy.

This chapter will argue that CSR, and consequently CSP, are not binary concepts although they are treated as such all too often. Also, both concepts are often associated with claims of self-interested righteousness that can suggest that organizations are more ethical than is actually the case. CSR, and the measures of CSP, are multidimensional, multilayered, and multitextual, and if CSP is not well integrated with CSR, it is not a fully functioning concept.

FOUNDATIONAL CSR TAXONOMY AS CONTESTED GROUND

By 2000, CSR had become a key to unlocking the rationale for reflective management and to marketing/reputation planning and implementation. The assumption was that demonstrations of corporate social responsibility could give organizations, especially businesses, a competitive advantage through demonstration of performance on CSP measures. This strategy led to the philosophy that organizations could do well by doing good. The problem, however, is that point of view could ignore, be indifferent to, or even co-opt the battle over CSR that had transpired for the previous 40 years.

CSR as it is grounded in management, economics, and communication is anchored by the fundamental societal rationale that justifies the existence of organizations, especially businesses—the logic of the social contract. Humans by virtue of birth are natural citizens (however that is defined by each state, culture, and political economy). Organizations are creatures of the state; it is the community that gives them authority and legitimacy, however much that is the case. Even the legitimacy of government (as enacted through governmental agencies) (which authorizes businesses and nonprofits) is authorized by the "will" of the people.

Textually, monarchies, oligarchies, tightly managed sociopolitical economies, and autocracies are not exceptions but variations of that principle. Thus, one can find monarchies based on the divine right of God, serving the people. And, we have "people's" republics. In democratic/representative governments, court cases are brought in the name of the people: Commonwealth of X versus Organization (or person) Doe. Authority arises from the people, from the community; thus, an alleged crime has offended "the people."

Therein lies the textual rationale for legitimacy. Legitimacy is "defined" by the people, but we know that organizations through an infinite variety of communication tools work to define and use the rationale of society to justify themselves. Thus, for instance, a coal company defends its environmental impact by pointing to jobs created by mining, to the satisfaction of energy needs of customers relevant to their lifestyles, and to the economic benefits coal brings to a community, including taxes that translate into roads and schools.

A mass marketing retailer might prosper as it destroys the small business community town by town, buys products abroad to save labor costs, pays many employees—even if full time—wages below the poverty level and without benefits; but such companies tout their cost efficiency as the rational authority of their legitimacy. That return of investment (ROI) equation, however, tends to misjudge or ignore the total impact of the company on the community which is defined and constrained by standards of corporate social responsibility, but is not necessarily translated into favorable or unfavorable CSP assessments.

If social responsibility is a key to organizational success, then those who would enact that strategy need to understand its foundations. As noted in the introduction, the era of CSR and then CSP started with a careful examination of the multidimensional ethical conditions and standards that organizations, especially businesses, must understand and demonstrate as the willingness and ability to achieve legitimacy. The key to such analysis is that although the organizations under consideration help establish and define the CSR standards, such standards are ultimately and necessarily a complex product of discourse resources that transpire among them and their stakeholders. These players seek to maximize their self-interests as they help craft the standards.

The fundamental textual question is what are the legitimacy expectations by which the organization operates and deserves reward. The extent to which a difference exists between an organization and its stakeholders, that difference constitutes a legitimacy gap of varying degrees (Heath & Palenchar, 2009, 2011; Sethi, 1977). Gaps challenge the authority of the organization to operate as it prefers, not in total more often than not, but in specific ways. Such legitimacy might feature standards as daunting as size of carbon footprint or networked sustainability, but can be as specific as the quality of customer service and community engagement. And, whereas community engagement is a key to corporate CSP it is the essential legitimizing authority of NGOs and governmental agencies.

If a legitimacy gap exists between how key stakeholders expect organizations, especially businesses, to operate and how they actually or are perceived to perform, then what was considered a CSR gap becomes the subject of hundreds of studies that addressed broadly the harmony between business, ethics, and society (see Buchholz, 1982a, 1982b, 1985, 1988; Post, 1978, 1979, 1985; Post & Kelley, 1988; Post, Murray, Dickie, & Mahon, 1983). Critics have questioned whether companies could operate as they prefer or whether they must be guided by and bend in deference to stakeholder expectations. That question, rooted in concerns over legitimacy, was the rationale for the development of an extensive body of literature on corporate social responsibility including discussions of legitimacy.

CSR is a contested concept (Ihlen, Bartlett, & May, 2011). So too, by extension, are the standards that are relevant to each organization's right to operate and right to reward. These social constructions take on a narrative form and content that allow enactment but also imply the thematic and performative standards by which enactments are judged to be (il)legitimate. As such, legitimacy and CSR imply the textuality of socially constructed norms that define the conditions of stakeholder contests regarding ROI.

In that sense, investment is both tangible and intangible, as it is real and compelling whether defined as investment capital or employees' right to reward (security of their individual investment of work) for their time, talent, and skills. Broadly, that sense of ROI is inseparable from the dynamics of risk, reward, and enactment within socially constructed conditions. As noted above, the parameters of legitimacy arise from the discursive intersection between political economy, reflective management, organizational and society functionality, and the conditions of social and moral capital.

Since CSR is contested ground, the various taxonomies mentioned above offer a framework by which it can be defined, understood, and enacted—and translated into CSP measures. At the macrolevel, this analysis begins with an umbrella discussion of topics relevant to the qualitative assessments of each political economy such as economic, social, and political constructions and enactments (Wartick & Cochran, 1985). Each political economy (and this becomes really problematic in the discussion of global CSR since there is no authorized body to focus the analysis) offers a cultural narrative that defines the enactable conditions and sanctions: Economic, social and political. Thus, in the U.S. genetically modified organisms are variously more "legitimate" than is true in EU countries, New Zealand, Australia, and Asia. These are often touted as beneficial, especially to the poorest and neediest countries. But developers of GMO (including contests over evidence of safety) and product placement tend to oppose labeling. Such management strategies, rather than maximizing informed consumption worry that "biased" interpretations could hurt marketing. But, then, how do companies benefit (CSP measures) if they commit to and announce on their packaging that they are NON GMO Project Verified (see nongmoproject. org. Also see Uncle Sam cereal and other products distributed by Attunefoods [www.attudefoods.com] and General Mills' Cheerios.) The movie, "The Constant Gardner," uses popular culture to examine the potential/ alleged corruption that "might" exist if/as pharmaceutical companies use poor African populations as unwitting "test animals" in clinical trials. And, the rationale for the introduction of pharmaceuticals (in unregulated circumstances) can be masked as CSR philanthropy, the testing of life saving drugs at affordable prices.

Similarly, the Kyoto Protocol was created by international agreement, through the United Nations, to set and implement standards for binding emission reduction targets. Developing nations, and those whose economies were seemingly threatened by such nations, refused to meet that set of CSR expectations. Similarly some countries aggressively fight low income poverty by creating conditions that strengthen the economy from the grassroots. Other countries rely on supply side and trickle down economics which pit workers in industrial nations against the low paid workers in the global marketplace. The CSR standards of environmental impact, therefore, reflect the socially constructed political economy of various countries, international businesses, and the hierarchies of macrolevels of state.

A second component of the taxonomy of CSR consists of topics relevant to reflective management concerns, such as those conceptualized as ethical, technical, functional, conceptual, and operational (Hosmer, 1991). Reflective management is largely a European construct. As framed by Holmstrom (2010), for instance, reflective management features not only the difference between reflection and reflexivity, but also the tensions (as a Venn diagram) of self-understanding, sensitivity, and self-presentation. Each of those variables has implications for ethical, technical, functional, conceptual, and operational reflection.

The core CSR question is how well the organization understands itself as if seen and judged (because it is) from the outside. CSR standards/expectations provide the lens through which each organization is seen and judged against CSP measures. Thus, reflective management presumes the ability to apply self-aware decision making. Such discussion broadly affects the ability of each management to effect each organization's agency in context. By this logic, for instance, the National Security Administration in the United States has been criticized for a level of agentic functionality that exceeds the standards held by some stakeholders (inside the United States and outside). Given the necessity to achieve national security, when do technical capability, function conceptualizations, and operations exceed ethical standards? This CSR problem focuses on the clash between the agency of an organization and the agency of a community.

A third taxonomy outlined above features topics relevant to stakeholders' evaluations and motivations for change (generically within the outcomes of support and opposition), such as security, fairness, equality, and environmental quality/quality of life (Buchholz, Evans, & Wagley, 1985; Heath, 1988). If reflective management presumes internal assessment of the organization from an external perspective, this level features the motivations stakeholders have to judge and seek to correct the organization. If stakeholders believe, for instance, that employees are treated unfairly, the stakeholders become motivated to correct the organization, make it more reflective. Such CSP measures can predict the consumption preferences of some customers as well as laws and regulations proposed as well as the litigation undertaken to constrain the organization's plans and operations.

Ihlen (2007) suggested that the sociological (societal norms and values) dimension of public relations necessarily addresses conditions of symbolic and material resource capital. Using the work of Pierre Bourdieu, Ihlen featured three dimensions of capital. (1) *Habitus*: "A habitus is a structuring mechanism that generates strategies for actors in the social world and through which actors relate to the social world" (p. 270). This is a resource based view of capital (symbolic and tangible) that yields to the degree to which members of society believe themselves to enjoy security, be treated fairly and equally, and live an acceptable quality of life, including the quality of their physical and symbolic environment. The latter, for instance, could include conditions socially constructed relevant to race and gender (even age) which has a "return on investment" underpinning: Fair treatment, equality, security, and quality of life. Enacted, the question would be how race or gender are socially constructed and enacted in ways that are fair, equal, secure, and qualitatively approved.

Ihlen's (2007) list continues with (2) *field*: "A field has a dialectical relationship with habitus and is understood as a social space or network of relationships between positions occupied by actors" (p. 270). Such relationships are socially constructed standards of CSR. Finally, (3) *capital* is a key to the quality of field and habitus. Power is a key to the distribution of capital which is economic, cultural, and social. Rather than a linear relationship among these motivations and standards, it is best to see them as tautological, ironic, and paradoxical.

These three aspects of sociology, Ihlen (2007) extrapolated, can further be parsed as the conditions for institutionalization, economic capital, and knowledge capital. Thus, for instance, the management of an organization can argue for its institutionalization by bending economic and knowledge capital to the service of the organization's self-interest. Or it can achieve an institutionalization that is bent to the economic and knowledge capital of the community. It can even pit members of communities against one another. Thus, a company that manufactures high capacity clips for semi-automatic weapons might leave one of the states of the US and move to one more favorable to such products. The company "blames" its change on the critics of gun and firearm equipment ownership. The move can translate into loss of jobs and tax revenue for one state. In the making of such decisions, the company makes no apology for the change which it rationalizes by invoking the criticism of the opposition. Don't blame us for moving our operations; blame the "unfriendly" legislators who imposed unsound constraints on our product.

Such judgments are inherently "moral." Exploring the moral psychology of community association and identification, Haidt (2013) defined moral systems as "interlocking sets of values, virtues, norms, practices, identities, institutions, technologies, and evolved psychological mechanisms that work together to suppress or regulate self-interest and make cooperative societies possible" (p. 314). The moral narrative conditions of social capital are constituted by "the social ties among individuals and the norms of reciprocity and trustworthiness that arise from those ties" (pp. 338–339). Such ties, what can be framed as CSR enacted trust, provide the rationale for the narrative enactment of mind/ideation, self/identity, and society/relationships through self-interest as the rationale for individual, organizational, and societal return on investment (see Heath, Motion, & Leitch, 2010; Motion & Leitch, 2007).

Such reasoning is consolidated, Haidt (2013) concluded, as moral capital, *"the resources that sustain a moral community"* (p. 341, italics in original). Such resources arise from the evolved need for a dialectical and collaborative enactment of self-interest. As focused on the conditions of the third level taxonomy, the moral assessment of a society's social capital features the entrusted self-interests that seek fairness, equality, security, and environmental quality. Such enlightened self-interest focuses, for each individual and organization, on the tensions between the costs of supporting others' self-interests as judged against rewards to one's own self-interest.

Fundamentally, and simply (but overly simplified), the summative CSR question asked is what do I get for what I give?

That question focuses on the multidimensionality of trust. That sense of trust invokes the conditions of risk/uncertainty and the attendant presence of vulnerability which are inherent to CSR discussions. These themes interconnect with the contested, collaborative, and discursive themes that connect ROI and self-interest. Standard productivity measures presume that a favorable ratio between input and output demonstrates productivity. If input decreases with output remaining steady, productivity improves, for instance (Davis, 1955).

By extrapolation, that management/financial productivity measure can be seen as hostile to CSR. If CSR compliance, for instance, increases input (cost) and static output, it erodes an organization's productivity. That is one reason why, for instance, trade associations work to keep all competitors in an industry focused on the same CSR compliance standards so that a bad apple cannot spoil the barrel. That logic also motivates industries to achieve higher standards of CSR because it does not intrinsically give advantage to one organization, but to all insofar as each can be more efficient/productive in its meeting of CSR standards.

By another extrapolation, the formula for organizational productivity can be applied in a way that focuses on community productivity. One of the battlegrounds over CSR is whether organizations favor their self-interests at the expense of that of the communities where they operate. They can raise the input to output ratios for a community by shifting risk to the public while benefitting from lower operating standards. A company engaged in mixing agricultural fertilizer (West, Texas, United States) can, for instance, operate at standards that put the welfare of a community of risk. The company operates at low safety standards as well as shifts the cost of recovery to the adjacent property owners (or their insurance companies or government agencies) when it lacks the capital to pay for their recovery.

Similarly, Freedom Industries in West Virginia United States raised many CSR questions with its chemical release in January 2014. That release lowered the community productivity ratio and shifted risk from the company to the community. It also strained trust for the company by exposing how vulnerable the community was to the operating standards of the company. Such cases point to one of the paradoxes of CSR/CSP discussions. Is it possible that organizations, some but not all, actually do not emphasize either a commitment to CSR or care about CSP as the rationale for their management and communication? Sen and Cowley (2013) pointed to the unique relevance of that issue regarding small to medium sized businesses for which CSP may be either irrelevant or merely a function of the organizations' role in the community where they operate.

This discussion sets the foundation for the final taxonomy posed above: (4) Topics relevant to the intersection of functional dimensions, principles, and narratives of corporate responsibility, such as economic, legal, ethical, and philanthropic (Carroll, 1991). Each of these points of enactment is given rationale and guidance by the operating standards of CSR that frame self-interest. Self-interest as an enacted CSR becomes understood as strategic economic, legal, ethical, and philanthropic risk management. For instance, if the organization is known for its philanthropy will other aspects of its management be forgiven, even during crisis?

Such analysis presumes that the fundamental human condition is the collective management of risk, with attendant challenges of crisis and issues management (Heath & O'Hair, 2009; Heath & Palenchar, 2011; Palenchar, Hocke, & Heath, 2011). The relationship between actors by this logic parses them contextually into identifiable categories: Risk generators/creators, risk arbiters, risk bearers' advocates, risk researchers, risk informers (Palmlund, 1992). Such collective risk management is enacted as dramaturgical (Palmlund, 2009) and narrative CSR expectations (Wehmeier & Schultz, 2011).

Given this attention to co-managed self-interests as risk management, the focus of CSR necessarily takes a societal more than organizational focus. The grounding for this point of view is dramaturgical and narrative. It also presumes that businesses, for instance, like to shift the costs of risk management to others while trying to maximize the benefits of risk taking for themselves. By implications, the dramaturgical "characters" noted by Palmlund, share a public arena and enactment space that can only be effective if it leads to coordination however contentious and adversarial that relationship is. Wehmeier and Schultz (2011) emphasized the value of a narrativist sense making and sense giving approach to CSR. The advantage is both a normative and evaluative view of organizational performance, insofar as:

> It allows the explanation of corporate communication and change more appropriately by taking into account the normative and less argumentative reality constructions as developed within CSR communications, their negotiation within society, as well as their implications and consequences within the dimensions of time and space. (p. 468)

They reasoned that a narrativist approach overcomes an organization-centric perspective. And, "this approach helps uncover the complex challenges of CSR communication: corporations face a multiplicity of stakeholder interests such as profitability, public interests and ecology, which are often conflicting or incompatible" (p. 468). As a dialogic process, CSR communication addresses a social reality that "can be regarded as being mainly negotiated and organized through the interplay of different actors' stories, which communicatively construct norms and morality through 'sensegiving' and 'sensemaking' processes and in which they mainly build on such social narratives" (p. 468).

In this way, stakeholder theory and social capital theory combine to support CSR theory. Harkening back to the pioneering work of R. Edward Freeman (1984), stakeholder theory has been treated as a topic that focused on the interconnections of relationships and ethics. Sen and Cowley (2013) conceptualized stakeholder theory as a means for viewing "management choice as a function of stakeholder influences," "such organizations address a set of stakeholder expectations, economic objectives being the most important, by participating in social activities" (p. 414). Coupled to that view of the role of stakeholders, social capital can be conceptualized as a resource "embedded within the networks of mutual acquaintance and recognition" (p. 414). Such social capital can be either/both internal and external. Externally, it is a characteristic of "a network tying an individual, firm, or community to other external actors" (Pastoriza & Arino, 2013, p. 2). Such tying occurs as three narrative dimensions: structural, cognitive, and relational.

Such narratives reflect thematically the intersection of ethics and legitimacy, especially if legitimacy is broadly defined in terms of the rationale for and evaluation of relationships and ROI adjustments among self-interests. By implication, such legitimacy can feature self-oriented morality or other-oriented morality. By those communicative social constructions "organizational practices are considered socially and environmentally responsible according to a form of aspirational role for organizations in society at any point in time" (Bartlett & Devin, 2011, p. 50). Such social constructions, as viewed in this fourth CSR dimension are the enactment of economic, legal, ethical, and philanthropic narratives.

For these reasons, CSR be viewed as multidimensional, multilevel, and multitextual. Expanding that point, Bartlett and Devin (2011) stressed how CSR standards and their accompanying legitimacy enactments change over time and differ by political economies which also vary by sectors and specific firms. Therefore, CSR is not universally or temporally static. It is an ongoing process (p. 51) and inherently linked.

In conclusion, this section has recalled the origins and challenges of CSR with the intent to emphasize its dynamic, normative, narrative, and enactable character (individual, organizational, and societal). It is a collision and collaboration of self-interests that are shaped and enacted within multiple dimensions, levels, and texts. As a legitimacy move, such a perspective of CSR allows organizations of all kinds to participate in the erection and implementation of CSR standards by which self-interests are evaluated and enacted on the premise of what entities get as ROI enactments. Are the rewards for collective actions appropriate to the risks and inputs so that harmonious enactment leads to collective management of risks? How well should organizations be judged and rewarded for their CSR compliance, especially as CSP measures?

That theme is applied to a definition and the operating standards of corporate social performance (CSP) by which the entities of society achieve agency individually, collectively, and legitimately.

THE POWER OF ASSESSMENT? A CRITICAL EXAMINATION OF CORPORATE SOCIAL PERFORMANCE

Corporate audiences, including customers, potential employees, publics, investors, and other stakeholders, routinely rely on the information provided by firms, information provided through the media about those firms, and those firms' reputations when making investment decisions, career decisions, and product choices (Fombrun & Shanley, 1990). As such, businesses increasingly devote time and resources to socially responsible efforts and activities because advocates of CSR see such efforts as means of benefiting society as well as the organization: that is, engaging in CSR activities brings with it the potential to secure long-term profit by building and augmenting reputation and reducing cost by avoiding conflict among other benefits (Carroll, 1999).

Following the logic that engaging in CSR activities can contribute to corporate reputation (Carroll, 1999), and strong reputations may provide firms the ability to charge premium prices, attract better applicants, retain employees, enhance their access to capital markets, and attract investors (Fombrun & Shanley, 1990), researchers developed measures to evaluate how well organizations were meeting their corporate responsibilities. CSP is the result of those efforts and in short is the measure of a corporation's social responsibility and socially responsible actions (Albinger & Freeman, 2000; Luce, Barber, & Hillman, 2001; Turban & Greening, 1997; Waddock & Graves, 1997).

Kinder, Lydenberg, Domini & Co. (KLD) Company Profiles, founded in 1989, specializes in measuring companies' CSP. KLD collects information regarding firms based on nine criteria—five of which are primary corporate social performance dimensions that relate to most business regardless of industry: community relations, employee relations, diversity issues, product safety, and environment issues (the other four are military contracting, nuclear power, excessive compensation of executives, and quality programs). In addition, Sharfman (1996) tested the KLD rating scheme for construct validity and found it to be one of the best measures of corporate social performance available, but noted that it is more likely to identify "saints" rather than "sinners." That distinction is important, as will become apparent later in this chapter, because it is often only partially successful in judging legitimacy in its CSR complexity.

Despite this instrument's construct validity, the larger task of constructing a truly representative measure of CSP has proven rather difficult due to: "a) the multidimensionality of the theoretical construct itself and b) because it is believed that measurements of a single aspect of CSP (e.g., philanthropy) provide a limited perspective of the firm's performance in the broader social and environmental sense" (Ioannou & Serafeim, 2010, p. 19). As argued throughout this chapter, CSR is not only multidimensional, but also is multilevel and multiple textual. Texts especially are relevant to the logics of stakeholder self-interests which cannot be defined as binary or righteous.

While researchers push to advance the construct of CSP, it is important to reflect, analyze, and critique established constructs and methods of inquiry. For example, at the same time businesses worldwide were designing and implementing various CSR strategies, independent agencies, such as (KLD) and ASSET4 emerged to rank and rate companies on their dimensions. However, measurement and ranking is not a neutral exercise; in fact, scholars have found that "independent company rating and ranking schemes (e.g., Consumer Reports, Moody's) can significantly influence the behavior of consumers, sell-side analysts, and investors as well as the organizations being rated" (Ioannou & Serafeim, 2010, p. 2).

So what does it mean to be rated favorably by outside organizations? In terms of meeting the diversity dimension of CSP, organizations are taking these rankings seriously (Waymer & VanSlette, 2013). For example, at the time of their study, Waymer and VanSlette (2013) found that Coca-Cola ranked 12th on the 2011 Diversity Inc. list, and had its ranking along with all of its diversity related awards featured prominently on its "Our Progress" tab on its website. Such promotion masks other aspects of CSP that Coca-Cola may be challenged on by key stakeholders. Coca-Cola has been linked to the death of a mother of eight that consumed her products in large quantity (One News, 2013), and has been found to have large quantities of pesticides—enough to cause cancer, damage nervous and reproductive systems, as well as cause birth defects and severe disruptions of immune systems—in its products in India as early as 2003. Such findings prompted Coca-Cola (and Pepsi) to launch aggressive campaigns, including lawsuits, to discredit the Center for Science and Environment's findings as well as arguments set forth by the Joint Parliamentary Committee's first ever health and safety of Indians report (Dinkar, Center for Science and Environment, 2013). One insightful responder on the website noticed the inconsistency between what Coca-Cola espoused as its corporate socially responsible behaviors and what the company was actually doing in India:

It is sarcastic that Coca-Cola has a strong CSR (corporate social responsibility) program around its HQ and India. The decade-old issue of farmers
withering away in Kerala denied water for farming when it was diverted for
coke production seems to be a nonissue today. The modern age is such that
market forces' domination seems to win eventually.

Thus, while measures, rankings, and ratings such as CSP are important,
and scores of scholars are finding ways to see if CSP affects corporate financial responsibility (Rowley & Berman, 2000; Margolis, Elfenbein, & Walsh,
2007; Margolis & Walsh, 2001), this underscores the notion that scholars
and organizations alike are highly interested in using CSR to serve the ends
of the organization (through financial prosperity) as opposed to using CSR
as a means of bending the organization to reflect the will of society.

In these ways and others, the task of crafting a logic for and means to
measure CSP is daunting but valuable, if applied cautiously. That task necessarily arises from and cannot obscure the multidimensionality, multiple
levels, and textuality of CSR. It needs to apply concepts that are neither
limited to nor grounded in organizations' reputation management. Reputation management must, instead, be grounded in CSR-CSP. This analysis
must address the question regarding the performance and social capital
outcomes that arise from an organization's activities as well as the attributed
and communicated motives associated with it. If it is merely a reputational
tool with marketing implications, it can fail to achieve its promise. Smoke
and mirrors are even a violation of the CSR tradition.

The next section suggests some projections and trajectories based on the
analysis provided so far on this topic in this chapter.

Projections and Trajectories

Discursively approached, CSR provides standards and critical points
in the judgement of an organization's legitimacy. For that reason, Palazzo
and Scherer (2006; see also, Gamper & Turcanu, 2007, who championed
a multicriteria analysis of socially responsible planning sensitive to future
impacts) called for a shift to moral legitimacy from a commitment to a
model limited to efficiency standards of input/output and power ratios.
Such a shift moves from an approach that privileges powerful organizations
to one that presumes a deliberative approach to problem solving rather
than one driven by self-defining and justificatory preferences of elites.
However much organizations have an incentive toward diversity of CSR
expectations in all forms and fashions, social media provides additional
motive because so many voices create a dialogic arena that presumes that
no force can predetermine the CSR-CSP standards and outcomes. Given

that dynamic diversity, it becomes problematic when organizations of any kind can and do use their influence infrastructurally to deny the potential legitimacy of the discourse arena.

Such standards, Heath and Ni (2010) argued, can be framed by various levels in community relations: Nice organization, good organization, and reflective/responsible organization. The first two levels, in particular, can be more cosmetic than serious CSR assessment. They can even mask the lack of reflective responsible management. The first two levels are often ones featured in marketing CSP. For instance, a toothpaste manufacturer may subsidize dental care for poor children as a way of doing well by doing good. Such CSR efforts can sell more toothpaste by gaining market share, but does not assure society that the company meets fundamental CSR expectations.

The paradox is that CSR is not a binary concept. Doing something good does not make an organization "completely good" or good in crucial ways. In fact, doing good, being nice or good, can mask treating employees badly or being irresponsible to the environment. Toothpaste companies, for instance, waste paper products by using nice packaging that looks good when stacked on the shelf but adds no value to the product. Such packaging shifts the cost of resource risk to communities where it operates. Such a company also can utilize ingredients that arguably are harmful to health and packaging/tubes that is not biodegradable. Thus, to gain advantage as being reflective/responsible, some toothpaste companies argue that their aluminum tubes are recyclable whereas plastic tubes are not or may not be. Do the plastic tubes contain potentially harmful levels of chemicals such as bisphenol-a (BPA)?

Complying with regulatory guidelines can be another form of appearance legitimacy. Even if or when companies and NGOs battle over regulatory standards and legislative requirements, the standards, even though detested by the company, can serve as a societal and legal self defense. Food companies claim they meet standards for disclosing ingredients; therefore they are a "good" company. They may, for instance, list ingredients by "serving sizes" even though they market an amount of their product, such as a can of soft drink, which in actual use is one serving. They say that warning labels on products fairly warn customers so that the company is not liable for health or safety consequences associated with use or consumption of a product. Financial companies spend millions fighting regulation and then use the regulations to frame messages to consumers that defend the business against charges of unfair business practices. Such paradoxes also illuminate the differences between operations and policies that are "legal" but of questionable ethics.

That paradox presumes that as hard as organizations (individually and collectively, as through trade associations and marketing alliances) engage in communicating their self interests as power-knowledge, so do other entities of society. The literature is replete with the arguments as to what constitutes CSR standards, but also the concern expressed by Reich (2007, 2008) that CSR masks rather than meets CSR standards. On this paradox, he concluded: "The soothing promise of responsibility can deflect public attention from the need for stricter laws and regulations or convince the public that there's no real problem to begin with" (Reich, 2008, p. 5).

As a counterbalance to this cautionary, even deceitful approach to CSR, Kramer (2007) claimed that

> Whether one looks at changing consumer tastes, regulatory policy, or litiga-
> tion, the social consequences of corporate activities are a steadily increasing
> factor in financial success. The companies that get out ahead of these trends
> not only save money, they gain a competitive advantage over their sleeper
> competitors. Rather than being a detriment in today's global competition,
> factoring social considerations into corporate strategy is a necessity. (n.p.)

Is this an argument for the theme that legitimacy is not a matter of achieving a level of tolerance between organizations and stakeholders' expectations, but rather an aspirational standard for CSR that goes beyond merely achieving support and avoiding opposition. The "beyond" is perhaps the essence of the claim by Drucker (1984), cited earlier in this paper, that "The proper 'social responsibility' of business is to tame the dragon, that is, to turn a social problem into economic opportunity and economic benefit, into productive capacity, into human competence, into well-paid jogs, and into wealth" (p. 62). Such an aspirational sense of CSR as legitimacy ampli- fies the challenge to serve society's interest through the manifestation of organizational self-interest.

As much as that is lofty, it must be cautioned, it is exactly the problematic of an organization getting to set the measures of the bar by which it seeks to demonstrate that it can do well by doing good.

CONCLUSIONS, APPLICATIONS, AND QUANDARIES

Among the many realities and challenges to the CSR/CSP literature, several come to mind based on what has been discussed to this point.

1. CSP measures and attendant conclusions are no better than their CSR foundations and the rationale for the legitimate role of organi- zations in context driving the evaluation.
2. CSP assessments are confounded by the potential (and more than that) that organizations may presume a reactionary and defensive

approach to CSR rather than one that aspires to the rewards demonstrated or at least presumed by achieving higher standards.

3. The logic of self versus other is fundamental and daunting. For instance, some countries require that companies are transparent regarding ingredients and processes. Those countries often state that the burden of proving that an ingredient or process is safe rests on the shoulders of the company (organization) rather than society. Thus, rather than expecting society to defend its interests against organizations, the logic is that organizations must demonstrate their positive impact. This logic, therefore, would require that companies such as Freedom Industries know the hazard of exposure to the chemicals it uses, notifies emergency response personnel in a strategic and timely way of these chemicals and the appropriate emergency response to them. And, it would be capable of indemnifying the community of the harm that a release could incur. Taking a seemingly proactive view, the American Chemistry Council promotes this theme (as a principle of CSR): "Our nation's primary chemicals management law must be updated to keep pace with scientific advancements and to ensure that chemical products are safe for intended use—while also encouraging innovation and protecting American jobs" (http://www.americanchemistry.com/Policy/Chemical-Safety/TSCA).

4. CSP standards need to be developed, however collaboratively, in a manner that as applied serve society not merely or primarily the interest of organizations. As noted, one of the worries of CSR critics is the tendency and potentiality that organizations being evaluated not only craft/heavily influence the standards but use them not as motives but as legitimatizers.

5. Such efforts must emphasize the multidimensionality, multilevels, and textuality of CSR so that if an organization crafts and implements one CSR/CSP project that one does not become the defining CSR criteria by which the organization is measured. Nor should that project deflect attention from other and often more daunting CSR challenges and CSP evaluations.

6. Texts such as "that's just the way we (have to) operate," "create and save jobs," "save customers money by providing low price goods," "too big to fail," and "satisfying customer needs" must be viewed paradoxically and ironically.

7. CSP measures should be able to identify "saints," but more importantly, indict "sinners" but in a way that is not binary or righteous.

8. CSP measures can be viewed as serving the community, but they also always must be understood as crafted and implemented to serve organizations' self interests. Thus, for instance, as CSP mea-

sures are touted to sell products, drive up share value, and attract the best and brightest employees, those outcomes can suffer the criticism of bending to the community to the organization's interest. That cynicism must not blunt the CSR-CSP movement, but must center it by featuring the paradox and irony of the fundamental matter, the alignment of interests.

Analysis suggests that CSR concerns are more deeply textual and more multidimensional that are typically reflected in CSP measures. CSP measures may focus on the tip of the iceberg but not account for the biases created by reputation management and even indifference to such measures by many organizations. Despite these reservations, however, the challenges of boring deeply into this matter and seeking standards and measures that hold organizations accountable to the public interest are vital. These are only a few of the lessons learned by careful attention to the legitimacy of organizations as they are challenged to make societies more fully functioning.

REFERENCES

Albinger, H. S., & Freeman, S. J. (2000). Corporate social performance and attractiveness as an employer to different job seeking populations. *Journal of Business Ethics, 28*, 243–253.

Bartlett, J. L., & Devin, B. (2011). Management, communication, and social responsibility. In O. Ihlen, J. L. Bartlett, & S. May (Eds.), *The handbook of communication and corporate social responsibility* (pp. 47–66). Chichester, England: Wiley-Blackwell.

Buchholz, R. A. (1982a). *Business environment and public policy: Implications for management.* Englewood Cliffs, NJ: Prentice Hall.

Buchholz, R. A. (1982b). Education for public issues management: Key insights from a survey of top practitioners. *Public Affairs Review, 3*, 65–76.

Buchholz, R. A. (1985). *The essentials of public policy for management.* Englewood Cliffs, NJ: Prentice-Hall.

Buchholz, R. A. (1988). Adjusting corporations to the realities of public interests and policy. In R. L. Heath (Ed.), *Strategic issues management: How organizations influence and respond to public interests and policies* (pp. 50–72). San Francisco, CA: Jossey-Bass.

Buchholz, R. A., Evans, W. D., & Wagley, R. A. (1985). *Management response to public issues: Concepts and cases in strategy formulation.* Englewood Cliffs, NJ: Prentice Hall.

Carroll, A. B. (1991). The pyramid of corporate social responsibility: Evolution of a definitional construct. *Business Horizons, 34*(4), 39–48.

Carroll, A. B. (1999). Corporate social responsibility: Evolution of a definitional construct. *Business & Society, 38*, 268–295.

Davis, H. S. (1955). *Productivity accounting*. Philadelphia, PA: University of Pennsylvania Press.

Dinkar, Centre for Science and Environment. (2013). Pesticides in soft drinks. Retrieved January 9, 2014, from http://www.cseindia.org/node/527

Drucker, P. F. (1984). The new meaning of corporate social responsibility. *California Management Review, 26*(2), 53–63.

Fombrun, C., & Shanley, M. (1990). What's in a name? Reputation building and corporate strategy. *Academy of Management Journal, 33*, 233–258.

Freeman, R. E. (1984). *Strategic management: A stakeholder approach*. Marshfield, MA: Pitman.

Friedman, M. (1962). *Capitalism and freedom*. Chicago, IL: University of Chicago Press.

Friedman, M. (1970, September 13). The social responsibility of business is to increase its profits. *The New York Times Magazine*, pp. 32–33, 122–125.

Gamper, C. D., & Turcanu, C. (2007). On the governmental use of multi-criteria analysis. *Ecological Economics, 62*, 298–307.

Haidt, H. (2013). *The righteous mind: Why good people are divided by politics and religion*. New York, NY: Vintage Books.

Heath, R. L., (Ed.) (1988). *Strategic issues management*. San Francisco: Jossey-Bass.

Heath, R. L., Motion, J., & Leitch, S. (2010). Power and public relations. In R. L. Heath (Ed.) *SAGE handbook of public relations* (pp. 191–204). Thousand Oaks, CA: Sage.

Heath, R. L., & Ni, L. (2010). Community relations and corporate social responsibility. In R. L. Heath (Ed.), *SAGE handbook of public relations* (pp. 557–568). Thousand Oaks, CA: Sage.

Heath, R. L., & O'Hair, H. D. (Eds.) (2009). *Handbook of risk and crisis communication*. New York, NY: Routledge.

Heath, R. L., & Palenchar, M. J. (2009). *Strategic issues management; Organizations and public policy challenges* (2nd ed.). Thousand Oaks, CA: Sage.

Heath, R. L., & Palenchar, M. J. (2011). Corporate (social) responsibility and issues management: Motive and rationale for issue discourse and organizational change. In O. Ihlen, J. L. Bartlett, & S. May (Eds.), *The handbook of communication and corporate social responsibility* (pp. 316–337). Chichester, England: Wiley-Blackwell.

Holmstrom, S. (2010). Reflective management: Seeing the organization as if from outside. In R. L. Heath (Ed.), *SAGE handbook of public relations* (pp. 261–276). Thousand Oaks, CA: Sage.

Hosmer, L. T. (1991). Managerial responsibilities on the micro level. *Business Horizons, 34*(4), 49–55.

Ihlen, O. (2007). Building on Bourdieu: A sociological grasp of public relations. *Public Relations Review, 33*, 269–274.

Ihlen, O., Bartlett, J. L., & May, S. (2011). Corporate social responsibility and communication. In O. Ihlen, J. L. Bartlett, & S. May (Eds.) *The handbook of communication and corporate social responsibility* (pp. 3–22). Chicester, England; Wiley-Blackwell.

Ioannou, I., & Serafeim, G. (2010). What drives corporate social performance? International evidence from social, environmental and governance scores (Working Paper). Harvard Business School, Cambridge, MA.

Kramer, M. R. (2007, September 13). Why Robert Reich is wrong about corporate social responsibility. *HBR Blog Network*. Retrieved from hbr.org/2007/09/why-robert-reich-is-wrong-abou/

Luce, R. A., Barber, A. E., & Hillman, A. J. (2001). Good deeds and misdeeds: A mediated model of the effect of corporate social performance on organizational attractiveness. *Business and Society, 40,* 397–415.

Margolis, J. D., Elfenbein, H. A., & Walsh, J. P. (2007). *Does it pay to be good? A meta-analysis and redirection of research on the relationship between corporate social and financial performance* (Working paper). Harvard Business School, Cambridge MA.

Margolis, J. D., & Walsh, J. P. (2001). *People and profits: The search for a link between a company's social and financial performance.* Mahwah, NJ: Lawrence Erlbaum.

Motion, J., & Leitch, S. (2007). A toolbox of public relations: The *oeuvre* of Michel Foucault. *Public Relations Review, 33,* 263–268.

One News. (2013, February 12). Mum, 31, died after "excessive" Coca Cola intake —coroner. Retrieved January 9, 2014, from http://tvnz.co.nz/national-news/mum-31-died-after-excessive-coca-cola-intake-coroner-5339912

Palazzo, G., & Scherer, A. G. (2006). Corporate legitimacy as deliberation: A communicative framework. *Journal of Business Ethics, 66,* 71–88.

Palenchar, M. J. Hocke, T. M., & Heath, R. L. (2011). Risk communication and corporate social responsibility: The essence of sound management for risk bearers. In O. Ihlen, J. L. Bartlett, & S. May (Eds.), *The handbook of communication and corporate social responsibility* (pp. 188–207). Chichester, England: Wiley-Blackwell.

Pallotta, D. (2008). *Uncharitable: How restraints on nonprofits undermine their potential.* Vancouver, Canada: University of British Columbia Press.

Palmlund, I. (1992). Social drama and risk evaluation. In S. Krimsky & D. Golding (Eds.), *Social theories of risk* (pp. 197–212), Westport, CT: Praeger.

Palmlund, I. (2009). Risk and social dramaturgy. In Heath, R. L., & O'Hair, H. D. *Handbook of risk and crisis communication* (pp. 192–204). New York, NY: Routledge.

Pastoriza, D., & Arino, M. A. (2013). Does the ethical leadership of supervisors generate internal social capital? *Journal of Business Ethics, 118,* 1–12.

Post, J. E. (1978). *Corporate behavior and social change.* Reston, VA: Reston.

Post, J. E. (1979). Corporate response models and public affairs management. *Public Relations Quarterly, 24*(4), 27–32.

Post, J. E. (1985). Assessing the Nestle boycott: Corporate accountability and human rights. *California Management Review, 27,* 113–131.

Post, J. E., & Kelley, P. C. (1988). Lessons from the learning curve: The past, present, and future of issues management. In R. L. Heath (Ed.), *Strategic issues management: How organizations influence and respond to public interests and policies* (pp. 345–365). San Francisco, CA: Jossey-Bass.

Post, J. E., Murray, E. A., Jr., Dickie, R. B., & Mahon, J. F. (1983). Managing public affairs: The public affairs function. *California Management Review, 26,* 135–150.

Reich, R. B. (2007). *Supercapitalism: The transformation of business, democracy, and everyday life.* New York, NY: Vintage Books.

Reich, R. B. (2008, August 1). *The case against corporate social responsibility.* Berkeley, CA: Goldman School of Public Policy Working Paper No. GSPP08-003, University of California.

Rowley, T., & Berman, S. (2000). A brand new brand of corporate social performance. *Business & Society, 39,* 397–418.

Sen, S., & Cowley, J. (2013). The relevance of stakeholder theory and social capital theory in the context of CSR in SME's: An Australian perspective. *Journal of Business Ethics, 118,* 413–427.

Sethi, S. P. (1977). *Advocacy advertising and large corporations.* Lexington, MA; D. C. Heath.

Sharfman, M. (1996). The construct validity of the Kinder, Lydenberg, and Domini social performance ratings data. *Journal of Business Ethics, 15,* 287–296, 57–72.

Sun, L., & Stuebs, M. (2013). Corporate social responsibility and firm productivity: Evidence from the chemical industry in the United States. *Journal of Business Ethics, 118,* 251–263.

Turban, D. B., & Greening, D. W. (1997). Corporate social performance and organizational attractiveness to prospective employees. *Academy of Management Journal, 40,* 658–672.

Waddock, S. A., & Graves, S. B. (1997). The corporate social performance-financial performance link. *Strategic Management Journal, 18*(4), 303–319.

Wartick, S. L., & Cochran, P. L. (1985). The evolution of corporate social responsibility model. *Academy of Management Review, 10,* 759–769.

Waymer, D., & VanSlette, S. (2013). Corporate reputation management and issues of diversity. In C. Carroll (Ed.), *Handbook of communication and corporate reputation.* (pp. 471–483). Malden, MA: Wiley-Blackwell.

Wehmeier, S., & Schultz, F. (2011). Communication and corporate social responsibility: A storytelling perspective. In O. Ihlen, J. L. Bartlett, & S. May (Eds.), *The handbook of communication and corporate social responsibility* (pp. 467–488). Chichester, England: John Wiley & Sons.

CHAPTER 11

CSR AND EMPLOYER BRANDING IN WORK ORGANIZATIONS

Abubakr M. Suliman and Hadil T. Al-Khatib

INTRODUCTION TO EMPLOYER BRANDING

Employer branding is a long-term obligation that addresses existing talent and finds solutions and strategies to retain them and motivate them to perform better. It also works as a tool to attract new valuable talents that are available in the pool of new recruits (Herman & Gioia, 2001). Yaqub and Khan (2011) introduced the term in their study by stating that it is the science of branding and that "the core job of Employer Branding is to make the company attractive for the potential employees to get the maximum benefit of the market" (p. 58). It is also defined as the envisioned benefits that are gained as a result of working for an employer. According to Berthon, Ewing, and Hah (2005) "the more attractive an employer is perceived to be by potential employees, the stronger that particular organisation's Employer Brand equity" (p. 2309).

Corporate Social Performance:
Paradoxes, Pitfalls, and Pathways to the Better World, pp. 223–241
Copyright © 2015 by Information Age Publishing

Furthermore, employer attractiveness is a person's interest in following employment opportunities within an organization. Rosethorn (2009) clearly and effectively describes it in a wider frame by defining it as:

> The two-way deal between an organisation and its people. The reasons they choose to join and the reasons they choose ... and are permitted ... to stay. The art of Employer Branding is to articulate this deal in a way that is distinctive, compelling and relevant to the individual and to ensure that it is delivered throughout the lifecycle of the employee within that organisation. (p. 9)

The above definition is exceptionally important particularly because in today's world; organizations are no longer able to operate as autonomous units without considering the affect they have on society and the environment in which they operate. Globalization has resulted in companies operating internationally beyond their home grounds and in order for them to be successful, they must focus some effort towards public interest and the new environment in which they are seeking to establish themselves in. In turn, since governments are responsible for setting rules and regulations, it is only normal for the governments to associate themselves with companies that show due regard to all the key stakeholder interests including the environment and the public or as well as the society itself. Foster, Punjaisri, and Cheng (2010) also adds that:

> Because employees are central to corporate brand management, internal branding and Employer Branding have recently been introduced to the branding literature. While internal branding focuses largely on the adoption of the branding concept inside an organisation to ensure that employees deliver the brand promise to the external stakeholders, Employer Branding offers a way of ensuring that an organisation recruits the right people in the first instance. (p. 401)

Furthermore, Hatch and Schultz (2008, 2009) perceive branding slightly differently by defining it as a discipline of management that channels the brand's promise to all stakeholders both internally and externally by referring to it by the name "enterprise branding." Enterprise branding includes the complete interaction log of the organization in the community by means of more than just communication and marketing but via extensively engaging the core business with issues relating to the society and environment which are usually the concerns of the corporate social responsibility (CSR) segment so as to develop a common ground for both the enterprise and the community. This also allows stakeholders to engage positively by increasing the social performance of the firm, reducing environmental footprint and be more aware of the alignment between the firm's goals and the societal needs. The approach demonstrates CSR enterprise-wide.

In addition, other scholars such as Ambler and Barrow (1996) also define an Employer Brand as the functional, economic and psychological advantages that employees identify/perceive in their organization. Sullivan (2004) conceptualizes employer branding as "a targeted, long-term strategy to manage the awareness and perceptions of employees, potential employees, and related stakeholders with regards to a particular firm which puts forth an image showing the organisation as a good place to work" (p. 89). The Conference Board (2001) defined it as an important sense and being—an identity of the business which embraces the behaviors, procedures, and values of the company in pursuit of goals to attract, select, and retain the company's potential and future talent. The Conference Board, explains how businesses today are increasingly realizing the benefit of employer branding by assisting current employees in internalizing values relevant to their work and by assisting companies in retaining and attracting talent. Also, Ambler and Barrow found a positive relationship between employer branding and employment rate in a study conducted amongst 27 organizations to explore the benefits and relevance of it to the business and human resources management (HRM).

Based on what has been stated earlier on employer branding, it shows how in the past, Branding was originally understood to simply differentiate between tangible products. Now this definition has been extended to distinguish between individuals, businesses and even locations and more so in HRM. Employer branding today is mainly used to attract, retain recruits and ensure that current employees are motivated and engaged in the overall strategy and culture of the organization.

EMPLOYER BRANDING: THEORETICAL AND CONCEPTUAL FOUNDATION

An extensive review of the literature suggests that employer branding has achieved most of its consideration in the practitioner world but rarely in the academic one. Therefore, the fundamental theoretical groundwork is still immature and requires a lot of development and construction. Fortunately, Backhaus and Tikoo (2004) have proposed a theoretical foundation and a conceptual framework for its process that is explained below:

The resource-based view (RBV) supports the notion that employer branding practices bring value to an organization via human capital and skillful investment in capital by suggesting that the features of these resources may contribute to sustainable competitive advantage especially since such resources are difficult to imitate thus allowing the company to grow ahead of its rivals (Barney, 1991). For example, an IT company or technological firm can only create competitive advantage if it is backed with highly qualified and skilled IT software engineers who can effectively use the technologies the company offers. The authors further explain the external and internal marketing of the employer brand, which are two important aspects in this theoretical foundation. External marketing, works as an attraction feature which helps the firm get the best available workers from the talent pool. This distinctiveness in the brand provides distinctive human capital for the firm. Later on, once these people are recruited, the workers start developing in their minds their own promises, ideas and images of the business which allows them to melt into the big pot of the organization's culture and environment and engage in its values. On the other hand, the internal marketing is what disables other companies or competitors from imitating the brand developed by the firm which is incurred through exposing current employees to the value proposition of the employer brand that the company has set for their employees to act the way it wants and follow its values. Moreover, internal marketing also helps the company retain its staff by adopting the employer brand as a concept of "quality seeking, recruiting and retaining." This is likely to motivate employees to stay working for their employer to act as "good citizens."

This has also been explained by King and Grace (2008) who highlight that both internal and external marketing are required by employer branding and especially internal marketing which aids the company to attract the best talent and become an employer of choice in the marketplace. Internal marketing is a very important aspect of employer branding. The reason why it is important is simply because it holds the brand "promise" to the future recruits. It also helps develop the drive behind engaging employees in the values of the firms and its goals. An example is UPS in the United States where the company came up with a new brand campaign named "Brown" in the aim to link it to the brown uniforms of the firm's drivers. The name choice worked in promoting the high professionalism and dedication as well as flexibility of their delivery service. Furthermore, Jiang and Iles (2011) includes the concept of *organizational attractiveness* to the theoretical literature of the employer brand and how it acts as a powerful tool in attracting potential talent and helps current employees reflect on their self-image and become loyal to their employer. Foster et al. (2010) also added through the research conducted in their paper which agrees with Jiang and Iles that potential applicants compare their needs, personalities and values to the employer brand image, which is formulated based on the organization's intent statements to attract prospective employees. If an employer fails to deliver their employer brand promise to new staff and new recruits who look to validate their employment decision, "It is likely that the postentry performance of employees will be negatively affected and staff turnover will increase" (p. 403). Yaqub and Khan (2011) found a close relationship between the employer brand and talent management towards the organizational attractiveness. The authors emphasized on the role of talent management in the retention of current employees which emphasizes the role of HR towards organizational attractiveness. All of which is interlinked to the employer brand of the organization.

Two core assets evolved in conceptualizing employer branding, namely "employer brand loyalty" and "employer brand associations" (Backhaus & Tikoo, 2004). The later asset shapes the employer image which has a direct effect on the firm's impact on the appeal and attractiveness to others. Employer branding affects the culture and identity of the firm which leads to employer brand loyalty, which finally contributes to a higher productivity by the employee. A good example of this process is Railtrack, which is a railway service in the United Kingdom. The company has raised an employer branding movement to enhance and better its branding associations that its potential workers have or may have of their organization as future employer by stressing on opportunities and career flexibility. This has positively impacted Railtrack resulting in an increase of thirty percent in the applicants that applied to their professional vacant jobs (Hutton, 2001).

The employer brand plays an effective role in marketing the organization in the eyes of its potential applicants and it also adds value in improving the recruitment and retention strategies in the organization. In this respect, employer branding promotes the significance of individual career development in the firm as without career progression, employees can lose their "competitive edge," and so, in turn, would the firm (Rosenbaum, 1989). This has also been stated by Kelly (2008) who explains how in the current market, organizations have become extremely competitive in their selection of talent emphasizing how:

> it's vital for a company to have a strong brand with which to attract, engage and ultimately retain the highest calibre of employee. This is backed up by recent research carried out by the CIPD that shows approximately 75 percent of companies that use employees branding as a tool for requirement find it effective. (p. 2)

According to Suliman and Al Khatib (2014), in today's competing markets, more and more companies are seeing the benefit of linking their employer branding to CSR. Suliman and Al Khatib studied the role of CSR in predicting the employer branding in a public sector of one of the developing economies in the Middle East. Using both self-administered and online survey 13 state-owned organizations, in the United Arab Emirates (UAE), where approached in order to collect the primary data of the study. The findings uncover that CSR and employer branding are positively, significantly and strongly related at both global and factor levels. In other words, good management of CSR is likely to result in improved image/ brand of the organization, that is, being CSR-active, according Suliman and Al Khatib, results in the improvement of the brand of the organization. Mirvis and Hatch (2010) explain a four-aspect design step that makes it possible to create an effective synergy between the two notions—CSR and employer branding—if followed consistently by an organization:

1. Holistic thinking: Merging both CSR and branding means having a holistic viewpoint on the design of artefacts or pieces of work which in the commercial world takes into consideration the production, selling, usage and sourcing.
2. Multiple logics and criteria: Utility and functionality of designing the employer brand are two of the main creations looked into in the commercial world and the design thinking. Equally important, is imagination and creativity where employer brands look strongly into engaging stakeholders emotionally via multiple intelligences (IQ, EQ, including AQ and SQ) and to better assimilate the symbolic expressions and meaning of the brand, which enables organizations to consider future expectations and fresh ideas about CSR activities.
3. Participatory process: The key of this design process is participating and engaging all those involved and not involved whether voluntarily or involuntarily in establishing inventive brand strategies and CSR initiatives where both CSR and branding combines proactive and new ideas and initiatives from different perspectives.
4. Positive intention: Targets and goals are one of the most obvious and basic means of expressing how a firm wishes to approach their branding strategies based on it its commercial actions. If the main intention behind the act is a positive and pure intention towards the cause, then the CSR actions will blend in smoothly with the brand image which is well presented.

Aggerholm, Andersen, and Thomsen (2011a, 2011b) explain that introducing ethics into brands is critical for all employees. Employees own personal morals are tied to the choice between what is good and what is evil as they are expected to perform to the employers morals and wear that identity mask of the employer's face. Hence, establishments no longer are considered as rigid and isolated entities but are rather social co-constructions to be conferred by all organizational stakeholders. Moreover, communication is not only a tool to be used to channel certain issues but recognized as constitutive of the organization "in terms of dialogical processes, complex discursive formations and interpretation of meaning among the organisational stakeholders" (p. 2). In other words, the employer-employee relationship, in particular the employer brand, ought not be an isolated concept to communication but one that is within and channelled through communicative processes for it to become an integrated dimension of the CSR strategy in the organization.

CSR is an important and essential drive of corporate assets in today's businesses. The role of CSR in building brand identity is crucial at times when the public, customers and governmental regulatory firms are cynical about corporate actions in the areas of public health and safety, conservation of water and energy, environmental issues and many other numerous ethical and social matters. A number of businesses today have smartly chosen to implant their CSR initiatives into their employer branding to improve how they are presented as a socially-active and creative organization. It is true, that numerous firms outline formal CSR agenda and attend to societal matters in a responsible matter but rarely do they follow a strategy that links CSR and employer branding together. With this in mind, a business ought to focus its core practices and stated goals towards CSR and establish a strategy that aims to link between the two notions. Researchers have shown that more companies have started incorporating these matters as part of their corporate brands, which is a promising start (Mirvis & Hatch, 2010).

The four-step design process developed by Hatch and Mirvis (2010) suggest that since CSR stirs internal forces, whereas the brand makes it attractive externally and aids in creating social work in a socially meaningful and symbolic way which is beneficial to those within the organization and externally to its stakeholders and public. Hence, it is the brand that portrays the identity of the company as an image to the public and hence its selection of CSR projects will sure be understandable and familiar to anyone acquainted with that image or so called brand. Therefore, linking the brand to relevant CSR projects will similarly portrays a picture which is much more expressive to both external and internal stakeholders and which furthermore enhances the image and reputation of the company's brand to those who believe the organization is responsible to the community.

Attracting talent, motivating employees, improvements in employee selection, recruitment and retention and comforting the general public are few of the many benefits CSR can bring to the employer branding. Moreover, it also adds to CSR by making the gap between the company image and core business smaller, not only through providing standards and options for choice from an ever-lasting list of how to better the universe, but via presenting the choice options to best deliver them (Vassileva, 2009). It is inevitable to see that linking brand and CSR within a company will raise new creative ideas and innovative thoughts from the joint efforts and activities of the two notions. Moreover, it is also worth noting that in this area of talent management and recruitment, organizations driven to lead in CSR must employ an employer brand which embeds the CSR view into the employee value scheme. There are several ways in which a company can promote the numerous benefits of considering the employer-value scheme and value-based environment by employing the employer brand in CSR. A few have been stated by Strandberg (2009):

> Employee volunteer programs and community involvement are oft-cited company values expressed by employees, and found within employee value proposition and internal brand development efforts. Campus recruitment programs are ideal environments for CSR oriented recruitment. In such an environment, recruitment interviews include questions on ethics and CSR; the offer letter reinforces the corporate culture; and the early employee contact reinforces the CSR brand. (p. 14)

CSR holds an important place in the notion of brand expressiveness is as it exposes the corporate image in the eyes of the public. This thought is very important to be considered as environmental and social consciousness during the past decades have risen and Employers are more than ever conscious as their CSR actions are being monitored closely. Therefore, firms today are employing brand strategies to reflect and approach the external environment to which the business belongs.

There is a relatively low perception of the role on which CSR plays in developing corporate brands and branding. A number of literatures have been reviewed and analysed for the sake of gaining a wider understanding of the connection. One study of which was conducted by Vassileva (2009) discusses a number of questions which where looked into regarding the perceptions of members in and out of the organizations concerning CSR and the role it plays in developing employer branding. Interestingly, the author explained the queries through a conceptual model that combines the components of corporate brands and CSR and the brand developing approach as a "push-pull" cycle. This model addresses via the "stakeholders holistic view," the CSR impact on employer branding through a number of factors. By understanding these factors, leaders of CSR are aware of the impact that CSR has on branding strategies and the main managerial implications it holds. The recommended "pull" versus the "push" approach recommends that leaders and managers of CSR act proactively to the initial stage of concerns of their stakeholders rather than be "push"-ed to react to the authoritative regulation entities or external governmental pressure. At difficult times, the push strategy is not as smooth or efficient as it is. Companies, especially in the consumer markets are much more concerned with maintaining a good reputation and branding image as consumers are more aware of the CSR practices of the producers rather than just the product. One example of why at times the push reaction strategy is too late to apply is when the reputation is at risk and causes an epidemic such as boycotts (Vassileva, 2009). *The Economist* ("Boycotting Corporate America," 1990) stated "pressure groups are besieging American companies, politicizing business and often presenting executives with impossible choices. Consumer boycotts are becoming an epidemic for one simple reason: they work" (p. 69). Such reactions have a huge impact on both sales and the brand's reputation. There are several examples of companies that have suffered large losses and adverse publicities due to strikes or boycotts by its consumers because of the companies' involvement in unethical acts.

A good reflecting case was in year 1995 when the European boycotted Royal Dutch-Shell after it had decided to dump their oil residue in the sea and then on land: it was afterwards stopped by Greenpeace. Due to the boycott, the company endured a loss in sales up to 50% and negative world-wide publicity. This less socially responsible act mushroomed many criticisms by human right activists and environment-concerned agencies which taught a valuable lesson to all other organizations who do not take CSR seriously to live up to their social obligations and act accordingly (Smith, 2003). Nike—a market leader in apparel industry and footwear presents the most infamous story of our time. Nike's image has been heavily distorted and damaged due to allegations that it abuses its workers in harsh conditions at Asian suppliers. After the huge negative publicity and loss in sales along with pressures from NGOs and other authoritative parties, Nike has hired more than 90 employees in CSR roles and paid considerable attention to its supplier's third party independent audits (McCawley, 2000). This is an example of a company in the consumer market that in the past threw a blind eye to the importance of CSR activities outside its headquarters. On the contrary, the cosmetics company, the Body Shop (http://www.thebodyshop-usa.com/) holds values that promotes self-esteem, protects the planet, opposes testing on animals, supports community trade and human rights. Ben and Jerry's values quote

> we have a progressive, non-partisan social mission that seeks to meet human needs and eliminate injustices in our local, national and international communities by integrating these concerns into our day-to-day business activities. Our focus is on children and families, the environment and sustainable agriculture on family farms. (http://www.benjerry.com/values/issues-we-care-about)

The ice-cream company Ben and Jerry's have customers who are willing to pay extra money on their products only because of the company's active involvement in CSR (Smith, 2003).

SYNERGY BETWEEN CSR AND EMPLOYER BRANDING

The main hurdle to any kind of change in an organization is having uncoordinated actions that work in isolation instead of being strategically integrated. Companies with discrete CSR branding become weak as this isolation starts to take over and overall dysfunctions the employer brand of the company. Hence, unifying these two (CSR brand and employer brand) functions under the supervision of one division where all those involved across different levels of the organizations in public relations and marketing, communication, human resources and management can work hand-in-hand with the top management to foster the Employer Brand (Mirvis & Hatch, 2010). Several examples have been explained in detail by (Hatch & Mirvis, 2010) which are summarized in Table 11.1 below showing how CSR and branding are two powerful means that realign the corporation with the public and government interests and has the power to maintain a current mainstream of successful corporate practices. The companies studied by the authors (Hatch & Mirvis, 2010) were General Electric, IBM, Johnson and Johnson, and Unilever, which are real-life examples and that reflect upon how employer branding strategy and the processes of relationship linking come into play in these different yet common corporate contexts.

Table 11.1.   Linking Branding and CSR: Selected Examples

Company	New Brand Message	CSR Expression	Strengths	Weaknesses
General Electric	Ecoimagination greening	Business model with energy saving products	Central to growth strategy	Perceptions of greenwashing; tie to culture
IBM	Innovation that matters: social/ environmental	Portfolio of sociocommercial innovations	Builds on open sourcing and IBM's global integration	Not resonating with reputation
J&J	Committed to health and future	Nursing campaign	Signature program: win/ win	Limited relevance to product brands and businesses
Unilever	Vitality: healthy foods and personal care products	Product improvements and social campaigns	Repositions company in marketplace	Contradiction: Walk the talk?

Source: Hatch and Mirvis (2010, p. 51).

A study conducted by the Reputation Institute in the United States in 2013 found that CSR plays a significant role in employer branding. In the United States, 62% count CSR as a main driver in attracting employees to an organization. Surprisingly, other countries have shown even a higher percentage and a greater impact of CSR on the branding of the organization, such as 69% in India, 79% in China, 71% in Germany, and even higher in Argentina where the percentage reaches as high as 80.6 (Mirvis, DeJongh, Googins, Quinn, & Van Velsor, 2010). A further study also conveys that employees prefer to work for a socially responsible company rather than one that is not. This is the number one reason why tobacco companies have always faced challenges in recruiting and retaining high-calibre of talent (World Economic Forum, 2003).

GLOBAL STUDIES ON CSR AND EMPLOYER BRANDING

A number of studies conducted from around the world are displayed in the section below to understand the relationship and impact of CSR on Employer branding or "organization attractiveness" as referred to in some of the studies discussed below.

Aggerholm et al. (2011a, 2011b) Conceptualized employer branding in sustainable organizations in Denmark. Suggesting a framework to re-conceptualize employer branding as an integrated part of a CSR strategy, Aggerholm et al. found that:

> When organizations adapt strategies for sustainable development (including CSR), it affects how to approach stakeholder relations and organizational processes, including the employee-employer relationship and employer branding processes. However, current employer branding conceptualisations do not comply with such changed corporate conditions. (p. 105)

The findings of another study conducted by Turban and Greening (1997) supported the hypothesis that companies which measured higher in CSP were viewed as more attractive employers to work for. The findings also confirmed that the higher the organization's CSP, the more positive its reputation was and hence the more attractive they were perceived by potential talent compared to those organizations with lower CSP rating. Another study by Albinger and Freeman (2000) involving 2,100 MBA students found that the majority would favour working for a firm which provides a low salary but is socially responsible than be paid a high salary in an organization that is not involved in CSR. Additionally, a similar study was conducted by Stanford University which also found out that 94% of its students are willing to have a 14% reduction in salary (on average) to work for an organization that is environmentally friendly (Montgomery &

Ramus 2003). Furthermore, research conducted by Towers Perrin in year 2007 found that a company's reputation for CSR was listed as "one of the top 10 engagement drivers, along with senior management's interest in employee well-being, opportunities to improve skills and capabilities and input into decision-making" (European Alliance for CSR, 2008, p. 11).

Moreover, Altinbasak and Suher (2009) conducted a quantitative study at Yasar University in Turkey to understand the correlation between CSR orientation and employer attractiveness of business students. The findings were based on CSR Orientation ratings of graduate students who were exposed to the context of eight different companies to measure their attractiveness from CSR and ethics perspectives. The eight organizations categorized based on three essential variables which are high economic, high ethical, and high discretionary. They found that high discretionary organizations were rated as more attractive than low discretionary organizations and high ethical organizations were rated as more attractive than low ethical organizations. They also reported a positive link between concern for society orientation and ratings of employer attractiveness for firms with higher discretionary behavior. Altinbasak and Suher (2009) concluded that the most attractive organization of the eight companies fulfilled all economical, ethical and CSR criteria. The second most attractive company was rated highly in the two areas of economy and ethics yet failed at CSR and hence was put in the second ranking. It is therefore logical to say that an organization which fulfils economic power, ethical values and CSR to the community should be perceived as the most attractive and appealing to potential talent. However, the study also suggests that those which lack CSR but have good economic power and ethical values to the community can still be perceived to be attractive. Yet, economic power alone will not be perceived the same way, if either CSR and/or ethics are missing (Altinbasak & Suher, 2009). Rao (2014) argued that "socially responsible image of an organization also is one of those various factors which cannot be overlooked these days" (p. 188). He examined the link between the socially responsible image and its contribution to employer branding in large scale manufacturing organizations in India. The results uncover that CSR initiatives play significant role in shaping employee engagement and employer branding.

Besides the positive impact the CSR plays on an organization's Employer Brand, the above studies also prove that there is a high perception of CSR awareness across the general public which gives higher incentives for organizations to take cautious steps in their role towards the society and the environment. Also, organizations today should take into consideration that their CSR initiatives can act as a tool for their Employer Brand and a method to attract the highly-skilled calibre. As current and potential employees are looking into the CSR of their employers, it has been extremely difficult if not impossible for employers to ignore CSR in their Employer branding. Edward Jones, has been voted by *Fortune Magazine* as being the best organization to work for, the reason behind being the top on the rank is the high praises of its employees who rated the management's honesty to be high. Furthermore, CSR awareness of the organization's activities makes the employees think highly of it and praise it publicly (Smith, 2003). Similarly, Steve Jobs, the CEO of Apple, who has recently passed away, had offered a good example of putting his employees first. Employees at Apple work on the principle that their duty is to provide the best possible customer services to please Apple's customers and not Apple Inc. The top management took action by involving people within. Experienced workers were invited to advise Apple's management on the best customer service practices and how to retain their staff and customers rather than the other way around. Steve Jobs had created an empire from an environment that made employees feel valuable and worthy. In short, he amalgamated Apple not into the lives of the consumers but into the lives of the employees, who made it possible (Reeves-Ellington, 1998). This is a successful example of how leadership can consider employer branding to retain its current employees and also attract potential talent to want to be recruited by Apple, not for its success in business but because the attention it provides to its workers. This has also been affirmed by Jean Martin's managing director who quotes "some organisations are enjoying up to 20 percent higher levels of employee performance not because they pay more or provide better benefits but because they let each employee know how important they are to the success of the business" (Buchanan, 2004, p. 315). Whether CSR has a positive effect on Employer Branding and the corporate reputation or not, Smith (2003) argues that CSR at least helps to avoid and reduce the impact of poor corporate social performance criticism. It reduces low employee ethics and also reduces time spent on NGO's disparagements.

CSR AND EMPLOYER BRANDING: REAL EXAMPLES

This section will look into the synergy of CSR and employer branding presenting some real examples on managing CSR and employer branding from some global and national companies such as Nestle and the Emirates Airlines. These United Arab Emirates (UAE) based organizations are studied with the purpose of analyzing recent literature reviews regarding the concept of employer branding and the real practices/actions of MNC and local companies of various industries in the gulf region.

Nestle in the Middle East (NME)

One of the most recognizable names across the food industry brands, Nestle Middle East (NME) has thrived among the decades to portray a spotless corporate brand and leadership via its international corporate philosophy "Good Food, Good Life." This has been evident through a number of activities. Nestle has spent over 1½ half million dollars in staff development in the Middle East region alone, in order to develop staff's capacities to the full potential by also providing employees with opportunities to travel abroad and gain work experience by exposure to different assignments, a variety of cultures and nationalities, vocational training, team-building projects and much more (Sarabdeen, El-Rakhawy, & Khan, 2011). NME is also one of the leading and strategically-driven organizations which stands out by linking its CSR initiatives to its employer brand. This has been achieved by its quarterly and annually event organizing and participating in spreading awareness campaigns stressing on the vitality of a healthy lifestyle and eating habits while at the same time creating a feeling of belonging by involving and considering the social and realistic needs of its employees. Activities such as sports activities and marathons sports as well as "good eating habits" programs and many more are a few examples. Simultaneously, it acts responsibly back to the community via blood-donation and contributing constantly to local charities and special-aid organizations to assist in raising financial funds to those in need (Sarabdeen et al., 2011). The Dubai Cares campaign was one of NME's local contributions in the UAE through building two middle-sized schools for around one thousand students. NME's contributions also extend beyond UAE. The organization helped in restoring several historical sites and areas in Damascus, Syria in order to preserve its culture and promote the same as part of its CSR initiative to preserve cultural heritage worldwide (http://nestle-family.com/).

The Emirates Airlines (EA)

Emirates Airlines, part of the enormous Emirates Group umbrella, ranked amongst the top 20 profitable fleets in the world and awarded over 400 global prizes, is the second selected organization in this study conducted by Sarabdeen et al. (2011). Eight main features have been considered to learn more on how and why EA has been considered a leading success via its employer brand. *Employee recruitment*: EA human resources utilizes a number of recruitment tools and strategies to ensure the best talent and expertise of the highest calibre are found and selected as EA considers its employees the core value of its business. *Diversity of workforce:*

Over 150 nationalities from across the world are employed. A diverse work force at EA is considered a key strength as the basis of new thoughts, creative ideas and innovative strategies. *Development and training:* EA believes in constant development of all its employees and hence have established a Plateau Learning Management System for its training purposes and have adapted a learner-centric approach which allows each staff member to take accountability for his/her own career development and learning curve. *Employee reward and recognition:* Special supplementary benefits, annual increments, performance and retention bonuses do not involve any racism, discrimination or favoritism and are distributed and appointed to all staff in a fair and ethical manner. *Remuneration:* Both noncash and cash remuneration benefits are provided to EA's employees. They enjoy a competitive tax-free compensation package, annual accommodation and transportation allowances. Senior staff members are also provided with profit-sharing options and an exchange rate protection scheme for such cash remuneration benefits. Other noncash benefits such as holiday leave, airfares, children educational support allowance, pension, global, and local medical cover, all ensure that staff are highly comfortable, pleased and retained. *Website:* EA's communication team have illustrated a user-friendly and interactive website which provides its visitors with any relevant information they may need to learn about the organization regardless of the boundary lines or location. *Corporate social responsibility*: EA in this study has proven to be another real-case example of an organization that embeds its CSR initiatives to its employer brand. EA is an eco-friendly firm which takes huge steps to reduce its carbon footprint and resources by linking strategically its CSR initiatives to its departments and employer branding through a specialized team named "Strategy and Communications" (Emirates Airline, 2011). *Leadership:* Leadership support at EA is considered a main component of the employer branding concept. The president of group services and the Dubai National Air Travel agency (DNATA), Mr. Gary Capma, have explained in various media channels how the employees are the key reason for the overall success at EA and for this reason, he encourages extensive vocational training and development at a high and continuous level. The President of EA, Mr. Maurice Flanagan, adds that careful measures are considered in the recruitment of EA's talent—as they are the main reason behind why the company has been successful and established the way it is today.

Gulf Food Trading (GFT)

The third company presented in the study by Sarabdeen et al. (2011) is Gulf Food Trading (GFT) which is the main distributor of Mars GCC in the

UAE and was established in 2001 with a manpower force of 180 employees. The study stated that this company does not employ any CSR initiatives or standards to create its Employer Brand but rather undergoes several activities which prove its extensive involvement in CSR, employee engagement and well-being. GFT is engaged in a variety of lifestyle and health directives such as "fruits and vegetables" day once every week. Where freshly prepared sacks of vegetables and fruits are prepared and distributed to all GFT employees (www.gulfood.com). Also, employees participate in sports such as Yoga and championships of Cricket and Basketball where the company facilitates memberships at clubs and coordinates matches against teams of other companies. The firm also provides some financial-planning and well-being programs to encourage good health. In relation to the recruitment process, the human resources and interview panel have stressed the importance of job rotations, orientation programs and the "psychological contracts" where both GFT and the potential employees' expectations are aligned to reduce the gap to a more sensible, doable and realistic "promise" between the two parties of what is expected from each other at GFT.

Regulation and Supervision Bureau (RSB)

Finally, the fourth example is the RSB which has recently released a media campaign regarding a new billing system with new consumption bands images (Figure 11.1) as a way to address the consumption of water and electricity and influence long-term behavioral change of UAE residents, as the growing population and economic growth are putting more pressure on the world's resources. The consumption bands give an average range for water and electricity use, tools to manage consumption, depending on whether you live in an apartment or a villa (term used for all other premises).

 the ideal-average consumption

 the above ideal-average consumption

Whether in the "light gray" or in the "dark gray," you can adjust your electricity and water use to keep within the ideal range for your type of property.

Source: www.rsb.gov.ae (2012)

Figure 11.1.   Consumption bands of new bills – Abu Dhabi.

The media campaign that facilitated this CSR initiative was presented through street billboards, radio channels and physically as brochures in the water and electricity bills. Moreover, the HR manager also arranged to communicate it and announce it to all the public sectors of Abu Dhabi in an aim to improve the branding of the Bureau and spread awareness of this CSR initiative across the Emirates. These channels of communication of this positive CSR initiative towards Abu Dhabi's resources of water and energy have had a lot of positive feedback from sector organizations already. Customer-feedback is awaited in April 2012 as the new billing system goes live in March 2012. Moreover, the RSB has recently taken numerous initiatives to reduce the environmental impact of the high water and electricity consumption in Abu Dhabi. In November, 2011, it created two "Wise" offices in the sector to champion the water and electricity efficiency in the country. Waterwise office for example aims to build the evidence base for the effective management of water resources and promotes social benefits of water efficiency through consultation, education, and awareness campaigns. Similarly, the powerwise office addresses the same but for electricity and power (http://rsb.gov.ae/). These offices also presented the organization's CSR initiatives at the fifth World Future Energy Summit that took place in January 2012, where the bureau collaborated with Department of Municipal Affairs to achieve the "sustainable cities" theme at the summit (www.rsb.com, 2012). From a financial perspective, an organization's employer brand can be its most influential tool given that positive opinion can cause continued employee commitment and therefore positive profitable return. In 2010, a conference on the Arab Giving Forum in Abu Dhabi was steered towards making the civil society, entities in the private and public sectors conscious of the benefits that CSR can offer (http://www.mediame.com/en/taxonomy/term/52778).

The above examples have shown how several employers, international and national, operating in the UAE play a role in the importance of spreading CSR, promoting employee relations and engagement as well as overall well-being and show efforts in linking it with the help of its leaders and human resources to the employer brand. There is however a lot of work required in terms of employer brand modeling, strategic theories, and concrete practices that are absent and which are required for the maturity and development of this field.

REFERENCES

Aggerholm, H. K., Andersen, S. E., & Thomsen, C. (2011a). Conceptualising Employer Branding in sustainable organisations. *Corporate Communications, An International Journal*, 2(16), 105–123.

Aggerholm, H., Andersen, A. & Thomsen, C. (2011b). Conceptualising employer branding in sustainable organisations. *Corporate Communications: An International Journal*, 16(2), 105–123.

Albinger, H. S., & Freeman, S. J. (2000). Corporate social performance and attractiveness as an employer to different job seeking populations. *Journal of Business Ethics, 28*(3), 43–253.

Altinbasak, I., & Suher, I. K. (2009). Corporate social responsibility orientation and employer attractiveness. *Journal of Yasar University, 4*(15), 2303–2326.

Ambler, T., & Barrow, S. (1996). The employer brand. *Journal of Brand Management, 4*(1), 185–206.

Backhaus, K., & Tikoo, S., (2004). Conceptualizing and researching employer branding. *Career Development International, 9*(5), 501–517.

Barney, J. B. (1991). Firm resources and sustained competitive advantage. *Journal of Management, 17*(1), 99–120.

Berthon, P., Ewing, M., & Hah, L. (2005). Captivating company: Dimensions of attractiveness in employer branding. *International Journal of Advertising, 24*(2), 151–172.

Boycotting Corporate America. (1990, May 26). *The Economist*, p. 69.

Buchanan, L. (2004). The things they do for love. *Harvard Business Review, 82*(12), 19.

Conference Board. (2001). Engaging employees through your brand. New York, NY: Author.

Emirates Airline. (2011). Emirates Airline Online Booking & Planning. *Emirates Airline*. Retrieved March 26, 2012, from http://www.emirates.com/english/plan_book/plan_and_book.aspx

European Alliance for CSR. (2008). *Valuing Non-financial performance: A European frameworkfor company and investor dialogue*. Retrieved January 7, 2012: http://ec.europa.eu/enterprise/newsroom/cf/_getdocument.cfm?doc_id=5310

Foster, C., Punjaisri, K., & Cheng, R. (2010). Exploring the relationship between corporate internal and employer branding. *Journal of Product and Brand Management, 9*(6), 401–409

Hatch, M. J., & Schultz, M. (2008). *Taking brand initiative: How companies can align strategy, culture, and identity through corporate branding*. San Francisco, CA: Jossey-Bass.

Hatch, M. J., & Schultz, M. (2009). Of bricks and brands: From corporate to enterprise branding. *Organisational Dynamics, 38*(1), 117–130.

Herman, R. E., & Gioia, J. L. (2001). Helping your organisation become an employer of choice. *Employment Relations Today, 28*(2), 62–78.

Hutton, W. (2001, October 7). Blair's new world vision could see our disastrous railway system back on track. *Observer*, 1–17.

Jiang, T. T., & Iles, P. (2011). Employer-brand equity, organisational attractiveness and talent management in the Zhejiang private sector: China, *Journal of Technology Management, 6*(1), 97–110.

Kelly, D. (2008). Employer branding a vital tool for success. *Strategic Communication Management, 12*(1), 2.

King, C., & Grace, D. (2008). Exploring the employee's perspective. *Journal of Brand Management, 15*(5), 358–372.

McCawley, T. (2000). Racing to Improve its Reputation: Nike has Fought to Shed its Image as an Exploiter of Third-World Labour Yet it is Still a Target of Activists.

Mirvis, M. J., & Hatch, P. H. (2010). Designing a positive image: Corporate brand-ing and social responsibility, positive design and appreciative construction: From sustainable. *Advances in Appreciative Inquiry, 1*(3), 35–55.

Mirvis. P., DeJongh, D., Googins, B., Quinn, L., & Van Velsor, E. (2010). *Responsible leadership emerging.* 5–64. Retrieved from http://www.grli.org

Montgomery, D. B., & Ramus, C. A. (2003). *Corporate social responsibility reputation effects on MBA job choice. International Conference on Business Economics, Manage-ment, and Marketing.* Athens, Greece: DELTA.

Reeves-Ellington, R. H. (1998). Leadership and organisation. *Development Journal, 19*(2), 97–105

Rosenbaum, J. E. (1989). Employees' perceptions of an organization career system (Unpublished paper). Department of Sociology, Northwestern University.

Rosethorn, H. (2009). *The employer brand: Keeping faith with the deal.* Surrey, England: Gower.

Sarabdeen, J., El-Rakhawy, N., & Khan, H. N. (2011). Employer branding in selected companies in the United Arab Emirates. *Communication of the IBIMA. 2*(1), 1–9.

Smith, N. C. (2003). Corporate Social Responsibility: Not Whether, But How? Centre for Marketing, Working Paper No. 03-701, London Business School. Retrieved February 29 2012, ffom http://www.london.edu/marketing

Standberg, C. (2009). The role of human resource management in corporate social responsibility: Issue brief and roadmap. Retrieved February 19, 2012, from http://corostrandberg.com/wp-content/uploads/files/CSR_and_HR_Management1.pdf

Sullivan, J. (2004, February 23). *Eight elements of a successful employment brand. ER Daily.* Retrieved March 20 2012, from www.erexchange.com/articles/db/52 CB45FDADFAA4CD2BBC366659E26892A.asp

Suliman, A., & Al Khatib, A. (2014). Corporate social responsibility and employer branding: A study in the public sector. *Proceedings of 27th International Busi-ness Research Conference, 12–13 June 2014, Ryerson University, Toronto, Canada.* ISBN: 978-1-922069-53-5.

Rao, M. (2014). Role of CSR in employer branding: Emerging paradigm. *Review of HRM, 3,* 188–195.

Turban, D. B., & Greening, D. W. (1997). Corporate social performance and orga-nizational attractiveness to prospective employees. *Academy of Management Journal, 40*(1), 658–672.

Vassileva, B. (2009). *Corporate social responsibility–Corporate branding relationship: An empirical comparative study.* University of Economics-Varna, 13–28.

World Economic Forum. (2003). *Global corporate citizenship initiative in partnership with The Prince of Wales International Business Leaders Forum. Responding to the challenge: Findings of a CEO Survey on Global Corporate Citizenship, 2.* Retrieved March 19, 2012, from www.weforum.org/corporatecitizenship

Yaqub, B., & Khan, A. M. (2011). The role of employer branding and talent man-agement for organisational attractiveness. *Far East Journal of Psychology and Business, 5*(1), 57–65.

PART IV

PATHWAYS OF CORPORATE SOCIAL PERFORMANCE

CHAPTER 12

SUSTAINABLE MANAGEMENT OF RENEWABLE NATURAL RESOURCES

The Case of Fisheries Management Systems

Einar Svansson and Stefan Kalmansson

INTRODUCTION

The World Bank has estimated that waste of resource rent in world fisheries could be 50 billion USD a year (OECD, 2012). Illegal, unreported, and unregulated fishing in the world is worth between $10 and $23 billion each year (FAO, 2014a). The subject of this chapter is to theoretically review management systems for renewable resources. The focus is on fisheries systems based on transferable quotas, where the Icelandic system is used as a case. The analytical tool used is the sustainability triangle. The World Commission on Environment and Development was founded by the United Nations in the year 1983. In 1987 the commission issued the Brundtland

Corporate Social Performance:
Paradoxes, Pitfalls, and Pathways to the Better World, pp. 245–264
Copyright © 2015 by Information Age Publishing

report, *Our Common Future* (Brundtland, 1987) where sustainable development was first defined as:

> development that meets the needs of the present without compromising the ability of future generations to meet their own needs. (p. 43)

The report discusses the current and future outlook in environmental issues and warns that modern habits of living can create human suffering and environmental degradation. The concept has developed since its introduction into a three-way long-term perspective, where economic, social, and environmental dimensions need to be in balance. Triple Bottom Line is a popular version of the concept with its 3P as people, planet, and profit. A related version is the 3E with the dimensions of economics, environment, and equity. The core thinking in all these versions is that if one dimension is to survive then all three parts need to be balanced in a coherent way. Many organizations have taken this seriously and accepted their impact on society and the environment. The Triple Bottom Line has evolved into green audits of holistic impact of corporations where the environmental impact (and even social impact) has been measured (Elkington, 1998). This fits well to the three-way classification scheme from Charles (1992) about world fisheries debate perspectives: (a) Rational method for increased productivity (b) Conservation of the resource and (c) Social focus on welfare and equity.

The vision of sustainability is long-term use of natural resources for human consumption and welfare in an open society based on creativity and security, where all individuals take part and belong. In a sustainable society all stakeholders work together to build up and invest in the local environment in a sustainable manner (Rogers & Ryan, 2001; Taylor, Fletcher, & Peljo, 2006). The general public tends to understand sustainability as a mission for mankind to survive and avoid big environmental disasters. The practical and academic debate is sometimes more complex, but the focus is on a sustainable future welfare for mankind, where nature is only a tool to accomplish that mission (Jamieson, 1998).

The sustainability triangle based on the concept of sustainable development is an appropriate tool to analyze the sustainability of a fisheries resource system. It starts with the economic dimension, followed by the environmental and social factors.

ECONOMIC SUSTAINABILITY

Economics deal with the use of factors of production from the utility which lead to efficient production where the fundamental factor is the scarcity of resources. In Sloman (2006) scarcity was defined as "The excess of human wants over what can actually be produced to fulfil these wants" (p. 4). Based on this definition economics are set to undertake the use of limited resources in a sensible manner for current and future generations. Supply and demand based on market conditions contribute to achieving the most desirable economic results.

Property rights of natural resources are defined differently and traditions have often shaped the utility of them where the proprietary rights have been unclear. As demand increases, the distinctiveness of the property rights becomes an important factor regarding natural resources. The need for organization and management of the use of resources to prevent waste and depletion becomes constantly more pressing (Hannesson, 2004). An asset under a property right means that the owner has a clear interest to protect it with the aim for giving future returns. Common-property resources are managed in common rather than privately. When dealing with management of common-property resources, by official authorities, it is important for the same reason to build up an effective sustainable level of harvest (Gordon, 1954; Tietenberg, 2006).

Tietenberg (2006) takes the American bison as an example of the tragic consequences of open access to a natural resource. The inevitable consequence that follows under such circumstances is that the motivation to protect and preserve the hunting stock is missing. Each hunter is focused on increasing his catch from day to day but lacking the goal of long term sustainable yield of the stock. The economic welfare for the hunters in the long run will be dependent on maintaining a healthy and strong stock for them and coming generations.

A lot has been written about prerequisite of sustainable fisheries and the negative influence of open access to the ocean. Economic discussion on the importance of property rights in the fishing industry was first published by Gordon (1954). An important topic for economics would be to explicate how to control the access in as efficient a manner as possible. Fisheries management should have the aim to ensure sustainable fishing stocks and simultaneously maintain a profitable seafood industry for the countries that harvest the oceans.

When goals of fisheries management are put into action it is necessary to plan appropriate methods to achieve them. The OECD (2012) report "Rebuilding Fisheries: The Way Forward" points out those of most importance saying that "multiple management measures may include input and output controls as well as various technical measures" (p. 12). Input control refers to managing the fishing rights through legislation and regulation concerning such factors as gear, licenses, and technical restrictions. The output control means that management of the catch is based on decisions regarding total allowable catch (TAC) for specific species, areas, and time periods (OECD, 2012). The decision for TAC each year should be based on the best scientific results about each fish species' tolerance giving the maximum long-term sustainable yield. This means that specific rules are set for the TAC with allocation of fishing allowances to certain zones or vessels. Input and output controls are most often used together. Input controls alone are inefficient. Output controls based on TAC where the quota is allocated and transferable between participants is referred to as individual transferable quotas (ITQ's). Branch (2009) ascribes the origin of such management systems to Christy (1973) and Moloney and Pearse (1979). Those who have the exclusive right of the quota can use the quota for themselves, and either sell, or rent it, to other fishery companies. The important factor is that the quota has to be transferable based on market transactions. This provides options for different management improvements related to operational efficiency such as lower costs, more valuable catch, less overcapacity, and a better use of investments; all giving increased profitability for the industry (OECD, 2012). Such systems have given good results and helped to develop sustainable fisheries.

Different versions of fishery management systems have been used around the globe. The common economic foundation for such systems is to maximize the return for the industry by having as valuable catch with as little cost as possible, independent of how the benefits are divided between the industry and the owner of the natural resource. Field (2008) takes it as a given fact that unlimited open access will not be an option because of a high possibility of overcapitalization and overfishing. There are too many fishermen exploiting a fishery (Field, 2008). To avoid such situations the fishery management system has to include some kind of limitation on catch volume and some kind of allocation of fishing rights. Rights based fisheries management systems have led to economic benefits, but at the same time been criticized for concentration of the quotas and as such downgrading social justice.

Legislation has generally developed from a limited management of resources to a more comprehensive fisheries management system built on rights based fisheries management (Field, 2008). The first step of fisheries management is typically to limit access to fishing grounds and to restrict it to a number of fisheries in demarcated oceans or with territorial use rights. This happened sometimes when nations extended their fishing jurisdictions, giving the national authorities more control over the fishing grounds. Other kinds of restrictions can include command and control types with the aim of establishing increased control of the catch and thus protecting individual fish species. The restrictions can mean limiting the number of fishing days, closing of certain areas, and rules about allowable gear and types of vessels. The problem with such arrangements is that they can increase fishing costs. The motivation to get maximum value for the catch with minimum expenditure is lacking. Going along with such rules, often a fisherman's response is constantly trying to adapt to the new rules, or seeking new possibilities to avoid the rules, or by expanding into uncontrolled fishing grounds or new species (Field, 2008).

The third step in fisheries management would be to establish upper limits or TACs based on proposals from scientists where it is decided how much quantity to catch each year from individual fish stocks. If this is done without giving out quotas for each vessel or company the motivation for each fishery is still to get as much quantity as possible referred to as "derby fishery". A quota system to distribute the total quantity to individual vessels or companies means that a precise proportion of fishing rights are related to an individual fishery or quota. Having individual quota each participant can more easily plan the catch so that a maximum return is accomplished instead of focusing on getting as much as possible from the overall catch. An important development in this process is for the fisheries to be able to buy and sell the individual quotas, to establish individual transferable quotas. Such execution seems to encourage increased specialization and efficiency of individual fisheries and help to make the industry more sustainable economically (Field, 2008; Hentrich & Salomon, 2006). The inability of the EU Common Fishery Policies to protect the fish species and make the industry profitable have been explained partly by the lack of exclusive use rights so the fisheries do not have a long term motivation to rebuild and protect the fishing stocks from overexploitation. Hentrich and Salomon (2006) say: "First of all, these include fishing policies dominated by short term economic and political interest, an inadequate control regime and management that forces fisheries to race for their share instead of supporting sustainable fish stock management" (p. 713).

The main factors necessary for the authorities to build up effective fisheries management system based on individual transferable quotas are (Field, 2008, p. 254):

1. Establish economical and biological total allowable catch.
2. Divide and allocate the total allowable catch.
3. Allow individual quotas to be bought and sold, and keep track of them.
4. Control the catch quotas, so fisheries do not go over their quota holdings.
5. Monitor the quota market to manage economic, environmental, and social problems.

The conclusion is that fisheries management systems that are based on exclusive use rights seems to be able to reach the economic goal of long term efficiency in the industry and at the same time support the sustainability of the fish species. This means that the organization of the fisheries will be more efficient, the catch will be more focused on the demand of the markets, and increased profitability will be reached in the fishing industry (Hall, Kristófersson, Júlíusson, Agnarsson, & Knútsson, 2011). The economic benefits will increase and the natural resource will be able to give resource rent.

A resource rent can be created in industries which are based on licenses for use of natural resources. It is defined as the additional return which the use of the resource gives because of the limited access to it. With open access it is likely that rent will disappear because of too aggressive use of the resource (Guðmundsson et al., 2012). Guyader and Thébaud (2001) discuss the matter of opinion regarding how to divide the benefits from fishing grounds which are managed by allocation of quotas to private parties. How to evaluate the extra rent and how should it be split between the owner and the users of the resource? It can be argued that such questions are political and social subjects lying outside the field of economic analysis (OECD, 2012). However, it can hardly be avoided for economics to analyze the different arguments and how they are likely to give the best overall results. Guyader and Thébaud describe the controversial issue regarding the rent as twofold. One is that the management system should help to create equity and be based on fairness. The other is that those who have used the resource for ages have historical rights to continue to do so. These often are communities that have invested in fisheries and based their subsistence on what the ocean can give. These issues will be addressed later in this chapter but if taking notice of the economic viewpoint the argument will inevitably be that the natural resource should be managed and treated in a sustainable manner with the long term goal to maximize the value of the output. How to divide the return is not as obvious and will be an ongoing issue for dispute.

The Icelandic economy has to a large extent been built on fisheries for a long time. The resources of the ocean around the island are generous, a fact other nations were aware of and utilized for centuries. This resulted in overfishing and diminished stocks of many fish species in the years 1950–1980. The reaction of the Icelandic authorities was to extend the national fishing limits in steps to a 200 miles economic zone in 1975 after the third "cod war." At the same time the authorities realized that pushing out foreign vessels was not enough to rebuild the fishing stocks; some structure for management of the fisheries needed to be put in place. A fisheries management system was first founded in 1984, and further developed with legislation that came into effect from January 1, 1991. From then on the system has been based on TAC's and allocation of quotas originally based on fishing experience in the years prior to the implementation of the system. From 1991 a system of individual transferable quotas with a yearly allocation of allowable catch volume has been operational. The Icelandic Marine Research Institute gives proposals for total catch based on scientific research for each fish species. The final decision for the TACs is taken by the Minister of Fisheries valid from September 1 each year (Danielsson, 1997; Hannesson, 2004).

Fisheries management systems founded with such prerequisites have been successful and are well known in many countries. Iceland, New Zealand, and Canada have been among those countries that have implemented them in the last decades (Annala, 1996; Arnason, 1996; Symes & Crean, 1995). The main conclusion from several economists is that the experience of the Icelandic fisheries management system has been positive and better related to economic benefits than many other systems (Hall et al., 2011; Hannesson, 2004; Symes & Crean, 1995; Yagi, Clark, Anderson, Arnason, & Metzner, 2012). In a report from the Icelandic Institute of Economic Studies (Agnarsson, Haraldsson, Jóhannesdóttir, & Árnason, 2007) it was concluded that a turning point had been achieved in Icelandic fisheries because of rapid technology progress parallel with organizational enhancement in catch, treatment and processing of the fish. Utilization of assets and labor, increased coordination of catches, process, and marketing has improved considerably. This can be supported by looking at the numbers where the financial results of the fishery companies have shown almost constantly improved results (profits), and the industry has for many years been economically sustainable.

It has to be emphasized that as the fisheries management system is an important factor in rebuilding a healthy and sustainable fishing industry, it is more like a frame for successive progress in utilization of the marine resource. Many factors influence the success of the business, notably the wet fish auction markets, which increase the specialization and effectiveness of the industry. Research on the auction markets has given an indication of three important factors regarding their role in Iceland; specialization, stability in supply of the material, and efficient marketing. The larger companies who both run vessels and fish processing, use the auction markets to exchange fish species as the factories specialize in a limited number of species. The smaller fish processing units, which do not have their own vessels, buy raw material from the markets and also specialize to be able to compete. The most important issue seems to be to have a stable supply of fresh raw material (Knútsson, Klemensson, & Gestsson, 2010, 2012).

It is also noteworthy to see how fast the development has been for the last ten years in better utilization of the raw material. The so-called by-products from the catch have increased and become a significant factor in the seafood sector, which means that there has been a growing business in use of raw material that few years ago were discarded. The value chain has become broader and the value of the catch is based on more diverse products. It seems that the fisheries management system has encouraged the industry to increase specialization and integration of the value chain, which has changed from being mainly production oriented to being more market oriented (Knútsson et al., 2012). A fisheries management system where the total catch each year is decided based on the best scientific knowledge, and the fact that the seafood industry has the opportunity to maximize the benefits of the allowable catch based on individual transferable quotas seems to combine the goals of a sustainable fishing resource and an economically healthy business.

ENVIRONMENTAL SUSTAINABILITY

The environmental sustainability of world fisheries is a kind of paradox. It is even sometimes a struggle between conservation of the world fish stocks and the survival of small scale fisheries. It is estimated that fisheries and aquaculture are the sources of up to 50% of animal protein consumed in some Small Island Developing States (SIDS) and Asian countries (FAO, 2014b). The question is if the humans will be able to utilize and protect nature and its resources at the same time. The ocean seafood resources are good example of the difficulties in planning for logical use of natural resources. Experience has shown that open access to natural resources often leads to "the Tragedy of the Commons" and has driven many fish stocks and whale species to the brink of extinction (Hardin, 1968).

"Over the past 50 years, humans have changed the ecosystems more rapidly and extensively than in any comparable period of time in human history" (p. 1) was one of four main findings of the report from the Millennium Ecosystem Assessment (2005).

The exploitation of natural resources has given significant benefits for human well-being but concluded in a major sacrifice concerning many ecosystem services. The report concludes that 15 out of 24 of the ecosystem services analyzed during the assessment are being degraded or used unsustainably, including capture fisheries. The scale of fisheries worldwide is not sustainable and many fisheries have already collapsed, for example the Newfoundland cod stock in the last decade of the twentieth century. Such situations will take many decades to recover, if they ever will, even if harvesting is considerably reduced or eliminated (Millennium Ecosystem Assessment, 2005).

Robins (2005) states that there are already about 60 different methods and standards in use worldwide to measure sustainability and especially the environmental dimension. Environmental indicators are useful to track progress and as a means of creating measurable objectives for organizations and countries. The Millennium Ecosystem Assessment (2005), an initiative from the United Nations Secretary implemented between 2001 and 2005, was a valuable contribution in this direction, and for evaluating scenarios for the 21st century. Another interesting contribution to build and develop environmental indicators is the Biodiversity Indicator Partnership which has been supported by the Convention on Biological Diversity. The partnership brings together many organizations and aims at providing information and resources about the important metrics of biodiversity. The current strategy plan that the partnership follow, covers a comprehensive framework for managing and monitoring biodiversity for the period 2011–2020 (Biodiversity Indicator Partnership, n.d.).

FAO Committee on Fisheries (COFI), decided in its meeting in the summer of 2014 to take important steps to fight against illegal, unreported, and unregulated fishing with international voluntary guidelines (FAO, 2014a). The FAO code of practice for responsible fisheries from 1995 (Garcia & Staples, 2000) has influenced management of fisheries in many countries, including Iceland. These rules were originally put forward to fight against unsustainable fisheries worldwide. The Marine Stewardship Council (MSC), which is a member of the ISEAL (global membership association for sustainability standards), has tried to impose positive impact towards more responsible fisheries worldwide based on the FAO codes, concluding latest with the report Global Impacts Report 2013—monitoring and evaluation. The MSC's standard for sustainable fishing is based on three principles; health of the target fish stocks, impact of the fishery on the environment, and effective management of the fishery (Marine Stewardship Council, 2013). The statement on responsible fisheries in Iceland, released in 2007, is based on similar factors and the FAO's code of practice (Iceland Responsible Fisheries, 2007).

Sustainable management of fisheries has to be grounded in scientific methods to find what quantity is safe to catch each year based on measures of stock volume and their robustness in their natural habitat. Field (2008) claims that the right size of stock should be based on catches that brings sustained yields. It seems that the decision on the total catch of different species is not much related to the type of fisheries management system. The role of the management system is to lead to efficiency and productivity whatever the decision is each year on TAC (Hannesson, 2004). Branch (2009) has tried to map the environmental impact of transferable quotas on fisheries worldwide by analyzing 227 scientific papers (from social science and natural science journals) that touched partly, or in whole, on transferable quota systems. The result was that 58% of the papers evaluate environmental impact. Of the papers that discussed possible impact of transferable quota systems on the fisheries ecosystem about 50% are positive and around 30% negative. The scientific world seems rather to be positive toward such management systems. However, positive results are most often connected to sustainable TAC, and furthermore to a good inspection system that controls fisheries and catches. Negative results are often connected to illegal catches, unrecorded landings, and discarding of small fish and less valuable species. There are examples of collapse of stocks after implementation of transferable quota systems, but in these instances overfishing or inefficient control systems are the main cause. Branch points out that if inspection and control systems are not performing correctly, then transferable quota systems can hardly protect the resources in a sustainable way.

It seems that the impact and quality of different fisheries management systems has not been thoroughly analyzed in a comparative study (Branch, 2009), even though many nations have implemented transferable quotas to solve the environmental problems of fisheries (Matthíasson, 2003). There is limited research data on the impact of transferable quotas on the eco-system and habitat of individual species and it is considered a difficult task because of the complex ocean environment with so many variables. There is sometimes visible change of catching areas and development of fishing gear. The accuracy of measurement of stock metrics is most often improved by more participation of stakeholders. But although the impact is on the whole positive for fisheries that use transferable quotas as a part of their management system, scientists have pointed out some negative effects on other stocks that stand outside the system because they often are overfished if the catches are free from quota restriction.

Icelandic authorities have based their decision making on environmental foundation. The Icelandic legislation from 2006 states the objectives of fisheries management to be: "The mission of this legislation is preservation and efficient use of resources to lay the foundation for long-term employment and settlement in the country" (Law no. 116/2006, article 1). This text reflects objectives of efficient and sustainable fisheries and at the same time has a social dimension. A recent study compares Icelandic fisheries management to Japan and the United States, and the conclusion suggests that positive signs are visible in the Icelandic ocean ecosystem. Most stocks have either increased in volume or are currently at similar level as when the system was introduced (Yagi et al., 2012). For example the (summer) herring stock has significantly increased its size since the quota system was implemented (Jakobsson & Stefánsson, 1999). Another good example is the cod resource that has for a long time been the most important fish stock around Iceland. There was severe decrease in cod catches in the years 1986 to 1994, the period when the new quota management system was implemented (Danielsson, 1997). Based on scientific recommendations for a more sustainable level of catches the total quota was dramatically decreased. Following that decision total cod catches went down very fast from 392,000 metric tons in the year 1987 to 187,000 metric tons in the year 1995 (Christensen, Hegland, & Oddsson, 2009). Since the mid-nineties the cod TAC has been approximately 200,000 tons a year. Even if the downward spiral has been stopped, it has been criticized that the stocks have not recovered enough (Arnason, 1996). The explanation could be that Iceland saved its cod resources by implementing the quota system. The cod stock was overfished for at least a decade before the new management system was introduced, and catches were about 26% more than scientific recommendations in the years 1984 to 1996. At least half of this overfishing was because the TAC was allocated higher than the scientific recommendations (Danielsson, 1997). This can be explained by pointing to the first years of the new management system when politicians (ministry, government) only partly followed the TAC recommendations from the marine scientists. On the other hand small scale fisheries were partly outside the management system in the first years and caused some overfishing.

Discarding can possibly increase if the value difference between small and big fish of the same species is high (Branch, 2009). There is some indication from Icelandic cod fisheries that the right use of fishing gear that can choose bigger fish, can decrease discarding (Arnason, 1994). On the other hand Pálsson and Helgason, (1995) pointed out that high lease prices of quotas could influence fishermen and ship owners to discard more small fish. The discarding in Icelandic fisheries has been estimated to be from around 0,5% to 6% for haddock (Arnason, 1994; Branch, 2009; Sanchirico, Malvadkar, Hastings, & Wilen, 2006). It has to be highlighted that the Icelandic fisheries management system is not only built on transferable quotas, but based on responsible scientific research methods and sustainable yield rules and recommendations. The Icelandic system is supported by thorough inspection and control of catches and has a system of temporary closing of spawning areas (Christensen et al., 2009). All these methods combined build the structure of a coherent management fisheries system that seems to work in line with sustainable development.

SOCIAL SUSTAINABILITY

The social dimension of sustainability of transferable quota systems has been very controversial. The discussion in Europe is both positive and negative regarding transferable quota systems. Fisheries management could be improved in the European Union by decreasing investment in fleet and factories and upgrading productivity and sustainability of the ocean resources to an important degree (OECD, 2012). This would mean fewer ships and decreased employment in production, often in places where other job opportunities are scarce (Hannesson, 2004). This leads to increased criticism and demands some political response. The economic and environmental dimensions of transferable quota systems seem positive whereas the social side seems negative during the period of change.

Open access to fisheries is not feasible. Economists have highlighted the benefits of private allocation (ownership rights) to increase efficiency but such arrangements often face strong opposition. Transferable quotas drive weak and small players out of the industry. Fishing activities tend to concentrate in fewer bigger companies and access for new participants is heavily constrained by high barriers of investment cost. The big question is how these valuable resources that now are restricted to access should be divided to possible participants and the general public (Davis, 1996; Guyader & Thébaud, 2001). Thus while academics tend to be positive toward the economic result of such systems, they have questioned the social impact and fairness for stakeholders and future generations (Copes & Palsson, 2001; Orebech, 2005). It has also been pointed out that social ties can change and that transferable quota systems can entail negative social and cultural influences on small rural societies (Davis, 1996; Grafton, 1996a, 1996b; Salvanes & Squires, 1995). Field (2008) for example discusses social objectives that should be included in a public agenda for resource preservation. He talks about equity and fairness as a basic background for resource management. It is not enough to protect the fish stocks in an efficient way, there has to be in place a social agreement about the rules. The first allocation of quotas needs to be transparent and TAC of the main species based on solid scientific research. It is well known that stakeholders normally rather accept restrictions on fisheries by implementation of quota systems, if the allocation and fishing rights are based on the most recent yearly catches by the current group of fishermen (fishing companies). It is commonly thought to be reasonable to respect the previous system of fishing rights to make acceptance of the new system easier. In fact the worldwide experience is that current participants (companies, fishermen) commonly support methods of minimal system change and they do not take potential new or future participants into account. One of the main drawbacks of these systems is that they are inclined to freeze the past and can, in the worst case scenario, restrain innovation (Christensen et al., 2009). Experience has shown that if such systems develop private ownership of resources then it becomes very difficult to change the system and they become inflexible (Wilson, Nielsen, & Degnbol, 2003). Symes and Crean (1995) agree that system changes in fisheries management that include economic return are most often negative for social equity. If the resource is allocated to a restricted group of participants they should pay for the fishing rights to create a system of fairness to all stakeholders. When the quota system in Iceland was launched fishing rights were allocated based on catches in the years before but nothing was paid for the quotas. Discussion about the resource rent and its distribution has gained momentum recently and moved over to the political scene (Yagi et al., 2012).

SOCIAL IMPACT FROM ICELAND FISHERIES

The impact of the Icelandic fisheries management system is hard to evaluate because many factors influence social development in the last 30 years. There have been changes in rural settlement and mobility where seafood related activity in some towns has increased but in others gone down significantly. Technological changes have also played their part.

The big debate in Iceland has centered on the concentration of quota and marginal impact on villages that build their economies on the fisheries resource (Christensen et al., 2009). Transferable quotas often lead to fewer job opportunities even though medium income can increase and be more stable for those fishermen that survive the change (Crowley & Palsson, 1992). Fishing rights were fast consolidated by a few big seafood organizations after the implementation of the system in 1991 and the 20 biggest quota "owners" doubled their share from 25% up to more than 50% in the first decade. This development has had the worst consequences for small villages with less than 500 inhabitants and increased the acceleration of their degradation (Eythórsson, 2000). The number of employees in the seafood sector has decreased by 40% in the last 20 years down to around 9,000 in year 2012, while export value has grown in the same period. Fisheries are important for rural areas where 82% of those employed in the seafood sector work. About 12% of jobs in rural areas come from the seafood industry but only 1.5% of jobs in the capital area of Reykjavík (Íslandsbanki, 2013, p. 28).

It has been pointed out that the transferable quota system has been used as a scapegoat for the negative development of small rural seaside settlements, without considering that there is a general trend toward a society with bigger urban areas (Agnarsson et al., 2007; Hall, Jónsson, & Agnarsson, 2002). This can make it difficult to judge the impact of the quota system on marginal rural areas. It is possible to name examples of villages and towns that have lost most of their fishing industry, yet examples of towns that have increased their share in the last decades also abound. Nevertheless the question of fairness and equity for people living in seafood settlements where fishing rights are sold away cannot be dismissed (Helgason & Pálsson, 1998; Skaptadóttir, 2000). Lost jobs, changes in social structure, and concentration of wealth and power are not lightweight topics (McCay, 1995).

The original allocation of quotas was and still is debatable, however, most methods would have been questionable. The auction method, that is, bidding and paying for fishing rights upfront, could have created more equity and fairness among stakeholders, but would have given established participants more room to bid higher. When the quota system in Iceland was founded many seafood companies were weak financially and therefore it is understandable that auctioning was deemed unrealistic. Hannesson (2004) describes court cases in Iceland where the result is based on arguments about constitutional rights and freedom to work (go fishing), but this ruling does not answer what method would have protected the freedom to work better. The state mission to maximize resource value for the general public has had consequences, and maybe the more appropriate question is if and how to deal with the negative factors for those that see themselves as potential victims of the system. Iceland parliament has tried to impose "rural quotas" for those towns that have suffered the biggest decrease in catches but it is unclear what this method has achieved, though some places have profited from this arrangement (Christensen et al., 2009). Furthermore, opening the system for access to new players by implementing "coastal quotas" for small boats has been attempted. But the results are hard to judge because of limited research.

It has been claimed that the economic performance of the Icelandic fisheries management system is at the expense of social factors. Some scholars (Eythórsson, 1996) have even gone so far as to argue that this system is a big irreversible social experiment that has redistributed power and wealth in society. Many Icelanders find this system unfair because the rent from fisheries is not distributed fairly. The concentration of fishing rights to few companies can weaken and endanger the existence of such a system if the social problems are not considered seriously (Pálsson & Helgason, 1995). One of the most important criticisms waged against quota systems similar to the Icelandic one is the question who owns the fishing rights each time period, and how access for newcomers can be improved. Most academics admit that it is unavoidable to limit fisheries based on both environmental and economic grounds, but the question of how to ensure more open access is still unanswered (Hannesson, 2004). We need to consider that if maximization of social welfare is the main goal it will always call on some "trade-off" (Copes & Palsson, 2001). Goals for positive development in rural areas may be better achieved through specialized social projects than with solutions inside the fisheries management system (Hall et al., 2011).

CONCLUSIONS

It can easily be argued, even taken for granted, that unlimited open access to natural resources is not an option in the 21st century; too many fishermen with too much capacity would quickly deplete the stocks through overfishing. The Icelandic fishery system has been developed over the last three decades and is highlighted as a case in this chapter to analyze the sustainability status of the resource where the economic, environmental, and social dimensions are all considered important.

From the economic point of view we can first state that fisheries management systems have the goal to maximize the return for society and the fishery industry in the long run. To make that possible it is necessary to build sustainable fishing stocks. Different management systems have been applied but those that are based on private use rights of a quota from the total allowable catch seem to reach such aims better. The decision of the total catch of different species has to be based on scientific methods and will not be much related to the type of fisheries management systems. Its role is to gain long term profitability, and to this end it must support the environmental sustainability of the utilized fish species.

In Iceland the economy has been dependent on fisheries for a long time. From 1991 the fisheries management system has been based on annual decisions of total allowable catch for each species and a distribution of individual transferable quotas to the industry. The main conclusion of the economic part of the sustainability triangle is that the system has been beneficial for the industry and the society. This has been confirmed in many scientific articles and reports about the experience of the system and is supported by the financial results of the seafood sector. The management system has decreased uncertainty that has given the industry higher productivity levels and an increased focus on value creation. The outcome is, however, influenced by several other factors such as rapid technological progress, effective auction markets, and an increasingly efficient market driven industry.

The environmental part of the sustainability triangle deals with how to protect the fish stocks and support a sensible long term use of the resource. This seems to be in harmony with the economic part, even though the results are not unequivocal and could be sharper. When a fisheries management system is implemented its prime goal is normally to preserve the fish stocks and improve responsible fisheries. This is a fundamental element in the Icelandic legislation and in international agreements about good behavior in utilization of ocean resources. An important factor in achieving successful environmental results is establishing good inspection systems that control fisheries and catches. Failing this the fisheries management system will probably not protect the resources in a sustainable way. The Icelandic quota system has been supported with a robust monitor frame at the same time as the fisheries sector has supported reliable scientific decisions for the allowable catch. The conclusion is that a transferable quota system can encourage an industry to use the renewable resource in a responsible manner, and help to maintain a more sustainable ecosystem and simultaneously build an efficient and viable industry.

It can be concluded from the discussion that the social dimension of the sustainable triangle is suffering from the fisheries management systems that are based on individual transferable quotas. This leads to concentration of the quotas to the bigger companies, and access for new participants in the sector is constrained by high barriers of investment cost. Such a system can impose negative social and cultural influences on small rural societies. The changes in different areas and generations have in several cases been negative, and this has been criticized as unfair and brought about the need for political responses. The negative impact in the Icelandic case is difficult to evaluate because other variables affect the rural development toward a modern society. It seems fair to conclude that social justice has diminished as the economic element has become more sustainable. This has created strong political pressure on the fisheries industry to give back a larger part of the resource rent to society. How this will be done is still controversial, and remains unsolved by the political sector. There is still need for more comprehensive comparative research on how to deal with social issues in transferable quota systems. The big question is if, and how, the industry should be liable for social justice.

Overall the transferable quota systems can help to impose more sustainable fisheries. Hopefully other industries that are built on renewable resources can learn something from the experience of the fisheries management systems worldwide, both from the positive and negative factors.

REFERENCES

Agnarsson, S., Haraldsson, G., Jóhannesdóttir, K. B., & Árnason, R. (2007). Þjóðhagsleg áhrif aflareglu [Macroecenomic effects of harvest rule], C07–09. Reykjavík: Institute of Economic Studies, University of Iceland.

Annala, J. H. (1996). New Zealand's ITQ system: have the first eight years been a success or a failure? *Reviews in Fish Biology and Fisheries*, 6(1), 43–62. doi:10.1007/BF00058519

Arnason, R. (1994). On catch discarding in fisheries. *Marine Resource Economics*, 9(3), 189–207.

Arnason, R. (1996). On the ITQ fisheries management system in Iceland. *Reviews in Fish Biology and Fisheries*, 6(1), 63–90. doi:10.1007/BF00058520

Biodiversity Indicator Partnership (n.d.). *About the partnership*. Retrieved from http://www.bipindicators.net/about

Branch, T. A. (2009). How do individual transferable quotas affect marine ecosystems? *Fish and Fisheries*, 10(1), 39–57. doi:10.1111/j.1467-2979.2008.00294.x

Brundtland, G. H. (1987). *Our common future. World Commission on Environment and Development*. Oxford, England: Oxford University Press.

Charles, A. T. (1992). Fishery conflicts: A unified framework. *Marine Policy*, *16*(5), 379–393.

Christensen, A. S., Hegland, T. J., & Oddsson, G. (2009). The Icelandic ITQ System. In K. H. Hauge & D. C. Wilson (Eds.), *Comparative evaluations of innovative fisheries management* (pp. 97–118). The Netherlands: Springer.

Christy, F. T. J. (1973). Fisherman quotas: A tentative suggestion for domestic management. Retrieved February 12, 2014, from http://trid.trb.org/view.aspx?id=41540

Copes, P., & Palsson, G. (2001). Challenging ITQs: Legal and political action in Iceland, Canada and Latin America. International Institute of Fisheries Economics and Trade (IIFET) 10th Conference, July 10-14, 2000, Corvallis, Oregon, U.S.A. Retrieved February 12, 2014, from http://ir.library.oregonstate.edu/xmlui/handle/1957/30735

Crowley, R. W., & Palsson, H. (1992). Rights Based fisheries management in Canada. *Marine Resource Economics*, *7*(2), 1–21.

Danielsson, A. (1997). Fisheries management in Iceland. *Ocean & Coastal Management*, *35*(2–3), 121–135. doi:10.1016/S0964-5691(97)00029-X

Davis, A. (1996). Barbed wire and bandwagons: A comment on ITQ fisheries management. *Reviews in Fish Biology and Fisheries*, *6*, 97–107.

Elkington, J. (1998). Partnerships from cannibals with forks: The triple bottom line of 21st-century business. *Environmental Quality Management*, *8*(1), 37–51. doi:10.1002/tqem.3310080106

Eythórsson, E. (1996). Theory and practice of ITQs in Iceland. Privatization of common fishing rights. *Marine Policy*, *20*(3), 269–281. doi:10.1016/0308-597X(96)00009-7

Eythórsson, E. (2000). A decade of ITQ-management in Icelandic fisheries: consolidation without consensus. *Marine Policy*, *24*(6), 483–492. doi:10.1016/S0308-597X(00)00021-X

FAO. (2014a). *Countries crack down on illegal, unreported, and unregulated fishing*. Retrieved June 12 2014, from http://www.fao.org/news/story/en/item/233912/icode/

FAO. (2014b). *Fisheries: Urgent action needed on overfishing, pollution and climate change*. Retrieved June 12, 2014, from http://www.fao.org/news/story/en/item/234106/icode/

Field, B. C. (2008). *Natural resource economics: an introduction* (2nd ed.). Long Grove, IL: Waveland Press.

Garcia, S. M., & Staples, D. J. (2000). Sustainability reference systems and indicators for responsible marine capture fisheries: A review of concepts and elements for a set of guidelines. *Marine and Freshwater Research*, *51*(5), 385–426.

Gordon, H. S. (1954). The economic theory of a common-property resource: The Fishery. *Journal of Political Economy*, *62*(2), 124–142.

Grafton, R. Q. (1996a). Experiences with individual transferable quotas: An overview. *Canadian Journal of Economics*, *29*(s1), 135–38.

Grafton, R. Q. (1996b). Individual transferable quotas: Theory and practice. Reviews in *Fish Biology and Fisheries*, *6*(1), 5–20. doi:10.1007/BF00058517

Guðmundsson, A., Ingadóttir, Á., Tryggvason, G., Þorláksson, I. H., Arnalds, R. & Jónasdóttir, S. I. (2012). *Stefnumörkun í auðlindamálum - skýrsludrög. Auðlin-*

dastefnunefnd [Policy for natural resources - a report draft. Committee for policy-making of natural resources]. Retrieved March 7, 2014, from http://www.forsaetisraduneyti.is/media/Skyrslur/drog-skyrsla-audlindanefndar.pdf

Guyader, O., & Thébaud, O. (2001). Distributional issues in the operation of rights-based fisheries management systems. *Marine Policy, 25*(2), 103–112. doi:10.1016/S0308-597X(00)00041-5

Hall, A., Jónsson, A., & Agnarsson, S. (2002). *Byggðir og búseta* [Communities and settlement]. Reykjavík: Institute of Economic Studies, University of Iceland.

Hall, A., Kristófersson D. M., Júlíusson, G., Agnarsson, S., & Knútsson, Ö. (2011). *Greinargerð um hagræn áhrif af frumvarpi til nýrra laga um stjórn fiskveiða samkvæmt þingskjali 1475* [A report on economic impact of a parliamentary bill to new law about fisheries management see Icelandic Parliamentary paper 1475]. Sérfræðingahópur skipaður af sjávarútvegs- og landbúnaðarráðherra [Expert group appointed by the Minister of Fisheries and Agriculture]. Sjávarútvegs- og landbúnaðarráðuneytið [Ministery of Fisheries and Agriculture]. Retrieved March 7, 2014, from http://www.sjavarutvegsraduneyti.is/media/2011/grg_hagraen_ahrif.pdf

Hannesson, R. (2004). *the privatization of the oceans*. Cambridge, MA: MIT Press.

Hardin, G. (1968). The tragedy of the commons. *Science, 162*(3859), 1243–1248.

Helgason, A., & Pálsson, G. (1998). Cash for quotas: disputes over the legitimacy of an economic model of fishing in Iceland. In J.s G. Carrier & D. Miller (Eds.), *Virtualism: A new political economy* (pp. 117–135. Oxford, England: Berg.

Hentrich, S., & Salomon, M. (2006). Flexible management of fishing rights and a sustainable fisheries industry in Europe. *Marine Policy, 30*(6), 712–720. doi:10.1016/j.marpol.2005.11.003

Iceland Responsible Fisheries. (2007). Statement on responsible fisheries in Iceland. Retrieved February 18, 2013, from http://www.fisheries.is/management/government-policy/responsible-fisheries/

Íslandsbanki. (2013). *Íslenski sjávarútvegurinn* [Industry report]. Íslandsbanki. Retrieved March 17 2014 from http://www.islandsbanki.is/library/Skrar/Seafood-Reports/sjavarutvegsskyrsla-Lowres2.pdf

Jakobsson, J., & Stefánsson, G. (1999). Management of summer-spawning herring off Iceland. ICES *Journal of Marine Science*: Journal Du Conseil, *56*(6), 827–833. doi:10.1006/jmsc.1999.0542

Jamieson, D. (1998). Sustainability and beyond. *Ecological Economics, 24*(2–3), 183–192. doi:10.1016/S0921-8009(97)00142-0

Knútsson, Ö., Klemensson, Ó., & Gestsson, H. (2010). The role of fish-markets in the Icelandic value chain of cod. International Institute of Fisheries Economics and Trade (IIFET) 15th Conference, July 13–16, 2010, Montpellier, France. Retrieved March 17, 2014, from http://ir.library.oregonstate.edu/xmlui/handle/1957/39219

Knútsson, Ö., Kristófersson, D. M., & Gestsson, H. (2012). Áhrif fiskveiðistjórnunar á virðiskeðju íslensks bolfisks [The effects of fisheries management on the Icelandic demersal fish value chain]. *Tímarit Um Viðskipti Og Efnahagsmál [Journal of Business and Economics]*, *9*(2), 23.

Law no. 116/2006, article 1,116/2006, Pub. L. No. 116 (2006). Retrieved May 14th 2014 from http://www.althingi.is/lagas/140a/2006116.html

Marine Stewardship Council. (2013). *Global Impacts Report 2013: Monitoring and Evaluation*. London, England: MSC. Retrieved June 12, 2014, from http://www.msc.org/documents/environmental-benefits/global-impacts/msc-global-impacts-report-2013

Matthíasson, T. (2003). Closing the open sea: Development of fishery management in four Icelandic fisheries. *Natural Resources Forum, 27*(1), 1–18. doi:10.1111/1469-8219.00065-i1

McCay, B. J. (1995). Social and ecological implications of ITQs: An overview. *Ocean & Coastal Management, 28*(1–3), 3–22. doi:10.1016/0964-5691(96)00002-6

Millennium Ecosystem Assessment. (2005). *Ecosystems and human well-being: Synthesis*. Washington, DC: Island Press. Retrieved June 16, 2014, from http://www.unep.org/maweb/en/Synthesis.aspx

Moloney, D. G., & Pearse, P. H. (1979). Quantitative rights as an instrument for regulating commercial fisheries. *Journal of the Fisheries Research Board of Canada, 36*(7), 859–866. doi:10.1139/f79-124

OECD. (2012). *Rebuilding fisheries: The way forward*. Paris: OECD. Retrieved March 17, 2014, from http://dx.doi.org/10.1787/9789264176935-en

Orebech, P. (2005). What restoration schemes can do? Or, getting it right without fisheries transferable quotas. *Ocean Development & International Law, 36*(2), 159–178. doi:10.1080/00908320590944025

Pálsson, G., & Helgason, A. (1995). Figuring fish and measuring men: The individual transferable quota system in the Icelandic cod fishery. *Ocean & Coastal Management, 28*(1–3), 117–146. doi:10.1016/0964-5691(95)00041-0

Robins F. (2005). The future of corporate social responsibility. *Asian Business and Management, 4*, 95–115.

Rogers, M., & Ryan, R. (2001). The triple bottom line for sustainable community development. *Local Environment, 6*(3), 279–289. doi:10.1080/13549830120073275

Salvanes, K. G., & Squires, D. (1995). Transferable quotas, enforcement costs and typical firms: An empirical application to the Norwegian trawler fleet. *Environmental and Resource Economics, 6*(1), 1–21. doi:10.1007/BF00691408

Sanchirico, J. N., Malvadkar, U., Hastings, A., & Wilen, J. E. (2006). When are no-take zones an economically optimal fishery management strategy? *Ecological Applications, 16*(5), 1643–1659. doi:10.1890/1051-0761(2006)016[1643:WANZAE]2.0.CO;2

Skaptadóttir, U. D. (2000). Women coping with change in an Icelandic fishing community: A case study. *Women's Studies International Forum, 23*(3), 311–321. doi:10.1016/S0277-5395(00)00089-3

Sloman, J. (2006). *Economics* (6th ed.). London, England: Pearson Education Limited.

Symes, D., & Crean, K. (1995). Privatisation of the commons: the introduction of individual transferable quotas in developed fisheries. *Geoforum, 26*(2), 175–185. doi:10.1016/0016-7185(95)00024-F

Taylor, A. C., Fletcher, T. D., & Peljo, L. (2006). Triple-bottom-line assessment of stormwater quality projects: Sdvances in practicality, flexibility and rigour. *Urban Water Journal, 3*(2), 79–90. doi:10.1080/15730620600855969

Tietenberg, T. H. (2006). *Environmental and natural resource economics* (7th ed.). London, England: Pearson Education.

Wilson, D. C., Nielsen, J. R., & Degnbol, P. (2003). *The fisheries co-management experience: Accomplishments, challenges and prospects*. The Netherlands: Springer.

Yagi, N., Clark, M. L., Anderson, L. G., Arnason, R., & Metzner, R. (2012). Applicability of individual transferable quotas (ITQs) in Japanese fisheries: A comparison of rights-based fisheries management in Iceland, Japan, and United States. *Marine Policy*, *36*(1), 241–245. doi:10.1016/j.marpol.2011.05.011

CHAPTER 14

SUSTAINABILITY AND ITS PARADIGMS

Maurice Yolles and Gerhard Fink

INTRODUCTION

The concept of sustainability has been popular, having its first dictionary appearance in the late 1980s (Lutz Newton, & Freyfogle, 2005). The Online Oxford dictionary definition of the word relates it to some actor that is: *able to be maintained at a certain rate or level*, the word *maintaining* implying that it is process related. The term crosses a number of disciplines and "Given the large number of perspectives and contexts in which the term sustainability is used, its meaning varies widely across the literature" (Stepanyan, Littlejohn, & Margaryan, 2013, p. 94). The rise of the sustainability concept has drawn significant criticism (e.g., Beckerman, 2002; Harrison, 2000; Lutz Newton & Freyfogle, 2005; Swyngedouw, 2007) with comments that imply that it is an unsustainable concept due to its unconvincing, controversial or unclear nature and development. So what is the value of this confusion called sustainability? In this chapter we shall explore the development of the concept, and show that it actually arises from two distinct and competing paradigms as highlighted by Gladwin, Kennelly, and Krause (1995).

Corporate Social Performance:
Paradoxes, Pitfalls, and Pathways to the Better World, pp. 265–300
Copyright © 2015 by Information Age Publishing

Sustainability is a concept often bundled with that of viability, and this latter idea is also subject to variation in these paradigms. This relationship will also be briefly examined in this chapter.

It will also be shown that these two paradigms identified by Gladwin et al. (1995) are actually part of much broader perspectives that are often referred to as *individualism* and *collectivism* (Oyserman, Coon, & Kemmelmeier, 2002). Sustainability arises in corners of these paradigms. This will be illustrated using cultural agency theory (Yolles, Fink, & Dauber, 2011). In this theory, it will be shown that certain types of behavior can arise from different agency orientations. Once an agency can be associated with a given orientation, the propositions for behavior espoused by that agency can likely be anticipated.

BACKGROUND

Beer (2002) tells us that sustainability is directly connected with viability, where *viability is taken as the capacity for self-sustainability*. Here, a system is viable if it: can survive even under considerable perturbation because it can take avoiding action; can acclimatize, can accommodate; and it can adapt (Beer, 1989). So viability has attributes that include a capacity for sustainability and adaptability. This suggests that from viability comes sustainability. However, this connection may be more difficult to discern from other sources. Thus, Bossel (1999, as cited in Spangenberg, 2005) says that maintaining the viability of a system is *equivalent* to maintaining its sustainability, and viability is maintained if a system is able to react appropriately to changes in its system environment. This suggests that viability is dependent on sustainability.

This distinction appears to suggest a lack of common agreement among academics about the nature of viability and sustainability, and their relationship. Lack of clarity about one of these words will therefore likely be reflected in the other. According to Abeysuriya, Mitchell, and Willetts (2006, p. 3) sustainability has "intellectual turmoil" associated with it, which perhaps is due initially to an "ideological controversy" (Beckerman, 1994; Dowie, 1995; Gladwin, Kennelly, & Krause, 1995).

This turmoil and controversy are indicated by the family of competing sustainability paradigms that seem to be prevalent in the literature, creating problems in coherently identifying satisfactorily what sustainability is and what one needs to do to maintain it. As a result, a number of distinct and often opposing paradigms have developed, culminating in the transition to a new paradigm through revolution and "the usual developmental pattern of mature science" (Kuhn, 1970, p. 12, as cited in Abeysuriya, Mitchell, & Willetts, 2006).

Gladwin, Kennelly, and Krause (1995) have generalized two diametrically opposing paradigms of sustainability which have assigned epistemic keyword values that characterise them. Their classifications lead to two questions which we shall consider sequentially.

The first question is: *Do holders of one or the other of these paradigms always accept all of the values held by the given paradigm?*

A common sense[1] answer to this question should be negative since no two paradigm holders maintain the same values which, in any case, are likely to change over time through normal life cycle processes. However, it would be more convincing to have a more formal and explicit means than intuitive common sense by which this view could be verified. One way of doing this is to adopt theory that can be applied directly to the problematic situation. This was done for viability, for instance, by Stafford Beer (1979) in the development of his "Viable System Model" (VSM), thereby providing a theoretical framework to understanding something about its nature. He also gave criteria that: "addresses issues of diagnosing and designing the structures of an organization for viability and development" (Schwaninger, 2001, p. 139).

So, this chapter will provide a theoretical structure that can offer a more formal explicit systemic perspective on the nature of sustainability. It is a *social viable systems* approach that is generically able to describe the *principles* through which viable organizations can in principle operate sustainably. More specific modeling approaches are possible (though not discussed here) given more detailed "organizational specificities" that can result in detailed explanations, for instance, of how policy options for future development can be delivered that embrace issues of sustainability. To develop the generic approach a *cultural agency* (Yolles, Fink, & Dauber, 2011) will be defined that offers an ability through which intelligent organizations can be examined and their behavior can be anticipated, even under conditions of complexity. Unlike Beer's (1979) viable system model, it is not intended as a diagnostic theory, though could be coupled with VSM to provide access to the diagnostics of viability (Yolles & Fink, 2011). The cultural agency has not only a capacity for intelligence and adaptation, but is responsive to both internal and external environments.

This brings us to the second question: *Is there a way by which one can identify generically which values are acceptable and to which people?*

This is question is highly relevant if the answer to the first question is that holders of one or other of the two sustainability related paradigms do *not* always accept all of the values held by a given paradigm. If one is able to identify generically which values are acceptable to some general other, then under the condition that the general other can be assigned more specific identity and value characteristics, then some anticipation can be made about not only attitudes towards sustainability, but also the possibility of behaviors that reflect those attitudes.

In a development of cultural agency theory, traits will be assigned, some of which belong to a "normative personality," and this permits insights into plural agency mind-sets and anticipation of future agency patterns of behavior. From this, generic "mindset" types are identified which relate to cultural norms, and that represent control processes within an agency. Using a technique called semantic mapping, these will be related to the two opposing sustainability paradigms identified by Gladwin, Kennelly, and Krause (1995). The result will show that it the epistemic values of either paradigm are distributed across mindset types, and since different agencies are characterised by different types, agencies will not adopt all of the epistemic values of either of the sustainability paradigms. This suggests that unless agencies have a specific brief towards sustainability that results in strategy and hence policy and its implementation, it is unlikely that the issue of sustainability will have more than a peripheral impact.

UNDERSTANDING SUSTAINABILITY AND VIABILITY

In examining the meaning of sustainability it will be clear that its development has occurred with little coherence. The concept of sustainability came to popular notice after the 1987 Brundtland Report of the World Commission of Environment and Development, which defined *sustainable development* as: action that meets the needs of the present generation without compromising the ability of future generations to meet their own needs. Two years later, Robèrt Karl Henrik developed a consensus on requirements for a sustainable society which formulated a number of conditions to enable the maintenance of sustainability, this becoming a basis for conceptual developments in organizational sustainability (Ny, MacDonald, Broman, Yamamoto, & Robért, 2006).

Mensah and Castro (2004, p. 2) note that since it took on common use, the word sustainability has been vague and ambiguous in its definition and applicability. They argue that there are two main opposing schools of thought: the *pessimists* (made up generally by groups of ecologists and related others) who see that the earth cannot forever support the world's demand of renewable and non-renewable resources. In contrast the *optimists* (made up generally by groups of economists and related others) are equally convinced that market incentives, public policies, material substitution, recycling, and new technology can together satisfy the needs and improve the quality of human welfare for the future. The two schools may be thought of as competing paradigmatic approaches are in direct contrast to each other, and illustrative of a lack of coherence in organizational theory (Gladwin, Kennelly, & Krause, 1995; Sterling, 2003).

The optimistic paradigm holding group also has its divisions through the support of faction paradigms referred to as strong sustainability and weak sustainability. *Weak sustainability* is more optimistic that strong sustainability, and supports the view

> that what counts is the overall value of the bequest package. Natural and artificial capital are, in principle, substitutes. Therefore, the depreciation and degradation of natural capital is permissible under the idea of inter-generational justice if artificial capital is produced at the same rate. Note that "capital" is just shorthand for "means of production." The notion of natural capital is meant to emphasise the autopoietic nature of living nature. In contrast *strong sustainability* [is more pessimistic and] emphasises that the human sphere is embedded in a natural system ("biosphere") and assumes that natural limits ought to constrain our actions. Artificial capital can only sometimes substitute for natural capital. In general, both kinds of capital are complementary. Those who claim that a natural entity is substitutable bear the burden of proof. Strong sustainability argues in support of a constant natural-capital rule. It notes that natural capital has already grown scarce and will probably become the limiting factor for economic production. Therefore, strong sustainability suggests that developed societies should invest in natural capital. Which indicators we use to measure sustainability depends on the basic conceptual choice. (Ott, 2003, p. 62)

For Neumayer (1999) the *weak sustainability* paradigm (a sort of *substitutability* paradigm) requires that aggregate total net investment is maintained, and is equivalent to keeping the aggregate total value of man-made capital and natural capital at least constant. Natural capital and manmade capital can be seen as substitutes one for the other, both in relation to production and use. This allows for natural capital to be run down as long as enough human-made capital is built up in exchange. So, it is not important whether the current generation uses up non-renewable resources or dumps CO_2 in the atmosphere, so long as enough machines, roads and ports are built up in compensation. Neumayer takes it that *strong* sustainability (seemingly also referred to as the complementary paradigm) requires both the aggregate total value of man-made capital and natural capital and the total value of natural capital itself at least constant. Thus, both man-made and natural capital is complementary rather than being substitutable to each other. Strong sustainability also holds that rising consumption cannot compensate future generations for the declining natural stock of directly utility relevant renewable resources. These two perspectives have been more finely classified by Turner (1992), who further distinguishes between strong and very strong, and weak and very weak paradigms.

Bossel (2001) takes a pessimistic view of sustainability. In his approach holism is important, and centers on natural resource management under complexity. His interests lie in both sustainable development and viability. Sustainability is connected with performance, and viability is connected with the ability to survive and develop, where performance functions extend beyond "mere" viability requirements. The purpose of his study is to seek comprehensive indicator sets that assess viability and sustainability. His model of this complex system is presented in Figure 14.1.

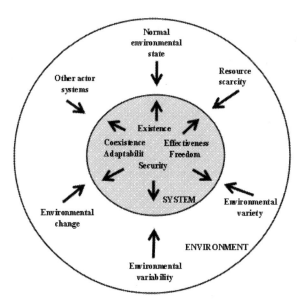

Figure 14.1.   Ecological perspective of the indicators of viability and sustainability (Bossel, 2001).

Another more pessimistic perspective comes from Ny et al. (2006). Seeing sustainability as future oriented, they take a systemic perspective that explores aspects of corporate life-cycles. The view is that normal life cycle approaches not only lack a sustainability perspective, but also do not connect with the difficult trade-offs between specificity and depth and comprehension and applicability. In their work they introduce what they call a "strategic life-cycle management" approach that is able to include sustainability in relation to future operative conduct, and involves the creation of strategic analysis that is holistic (i.e., having a tendency towards the pessimistic paradigm) in respect of sustainability and strategy imperatives that arrive at sustainability.

Not all the pessimists, however, are of one mind. One view, perhaps to be referred to as the want-to-be optimist's pessimism (since the paper is a negative critique of sustainability rather than formulating positive options), is that the concept of sustainability is bombing out more pragmatic perspectives of conservation. Thus, Lutz Newton and Freyfogle (2005) are concerned that sustainability is strategically unclear and undefined, and in particular is

> broadly conceived and considered in its many usages, sustainability has grave defects as a planning goal, particularly when used by conservationists: it confuses means and ends; it is vague about what is being sustained and who or what is doing the sustaining; ... it need not include a moral component; it is consistent with the view of humans as all-powerful manipulators of the planet; and, in general, it is such a malleable term that its popularity provides only a facade of consensus. When sustainability is defined broadly to include the full range of economic and social aspirations, it poses the particular risk that ecological and biodiversity concerns will be cast aside in favour of more pressing human wants. (p. 23)

Setting the discussion with the broader issue of conservation, they further note (Lutz Newton & Freyfogle, 2005) that

> Given the fragmentation within the conservation community, we cannot be sanguine about prospects for a unified goal. A useful start, though, would be to cast aside sustainability and begin talking about its replacement. What is conservation for? What kind of society does it envision, and what will the benefits be if we head in that direction? (p. 30)

Another critic of the common debates about sustainability is Swyngedouw (2007). His concern is with environmental politics and the global postideological politics (or postpolitics), that arose after the fall of Soviet ideology, of consensus condition. He discusses the nature of nature, and argues that the nature that enters political debate through issues of sustainability is radically conservative and reactionary. It sees nature as singular, ontologically stable and harmonious, which has been thrown out of synchronisation by human intervention. It denies that nature is plural, complex and unpredictable. Sustainability is used to code nature to enable a establish market based status quo solutions that miss debates concerning political questions referring to the kind of socioenvironmental futures that might be wanted. Further to this, he says (Swyngedouw, 2007: section 5) that that "The politics of sustainability and the environment, therefore, in their populist post-political guise are the antithesis of democracy, and contribute to a further hollowing out of ... the very horizon of democracy as a radically heterogeneous and conflicting one."

Consistent with this negative stance, Beckerman (2002, p. 5, as cited by Gordon, 2003), referring to economic welfare (referring to the level of prosperity and living standards of either an individual or a group of persons), says that the concept of sustainable development has nothing to add. It further reduces any objective to increase human welfare because the slogan of sustainable development seems to provide a blanket justification for almost any policy designed to promote human welfare, and this is irrespective of its cost and hence of the sacrifice of other ingredients of welfare.

As though in contrasting response, Atkisson (1999) considers that

> the definition of sustainability is neither vague nor abstract; it is very specific and is tied to measurable criteria describing how resources are used and distributed. Some of what currently gets called "unsustainable development" is no such thing, but that does not mean the concept should be dismissed, any more than the concept of democracy should be dismissed when it is misappropriated by a dictatorship. Sustainability, like democracy, is an ideal toward which we strive, a journey more than a destination. (p. 200)

Perhaps seeking a balance between the optimistic and pessimistic perspectives within a business context, *Financial Times Lexicon* (FTL, 2013) is interested in corporate business sustainable development. This, we are told, must address important issues at the macro level such as: economic efficiency (innovation, prosperity, and productivity), social equity (poverty, community, health and wellness, human rights) and environmental accountability (climate change, land use, biodiversity). FTL further elaborates on the idea that sustainability is strategic, saying that it draws on dynamic resiliency, a term that refers to an organizational ability to survive shocks due to an intimate connection to healthy economic, social and environmental systems that create economic value, and contributes to healthy ecosystems and strong communities.

Gladwin, Kennelly, and Krause (1995, p. 874) have gone further than FTL, explicitly seeking a synergy between the two opposing optimistic and pessimistic perspectives (Table 14.1). They refer to the optimistic paradigm as the *Technocentric* (through its faith in technology) and the pessimistic paradigm as *Ecocentric* (through its lack of faith in technology). They also propose an in-between position (referred to as the *Sustaincentrism* paradigm). Each of these paradigms is described through a set of epistemic values, which are collected under the three classifications of ontology/ethics, scientific/technological and economic/psychological beliefs/values (see Table 14.1).

In exploring sustainability, Gladwin, Kennelly, and Krause (1995) also recognise that it should be part of strategic management. This is consistent with Frechette (2010) who tells us that it drives long-term corporate growth, profitability, and corporate social responsibility. He also considers it to be future oriented, and often involves fundamental organizational change.

Table 14.1. Optimistic, Pessimistic, and In-Between Paradigms Related to Sustainability

Key Assumptions	Technocentrism	Ecocentrism	Sustaincentrism
Ontological & Ethical			
Metaphor of earth	Vast machine	Mother/ web of life	Life support system
Perception of earth	Dead/passive	Alive/sensitive	Home/managed
System composition	Atomistic/parts	Organic/wholes	Parts and wholes
System structure	Hierarchical	Heterarchical	Holarchical
Humans and nature	Disassociation	Indisassociation	Interdependence
Human role	Domination	Plain member	Stewardship
Value of nature	Anthropocentrism	Intrinsicalism	Inherentism
Ethical grounding	Narrow homocentric	Whole earth	Broad homocentric
Time/space scales	Short/near	Indefinite	Multiscale
Logic/reason	Egoist-rational	Holism/spiritualism	Vision/network
Scientific & Technological			
Resilience of nature	Tough/robust	Highly vulnerable	Varied/fragile
Carrying capacity limits	No limits	Already exceed	Approaching
Population size	No problem	Freeze/reduce	Stabilize soon
Growth pattern	Exponential	Hyperbolic	Logistic
Severity of problems	Trivial	Catastrophic	Consequential
Urgency of problem interventions	Little/wait	Extraordinary/now	Great/decades
Risk orientation	Risk taking	Risk aversion	Precaution
Faith in technology	Optimism	Pessimism	Skepticism
Technological pathways	Big/centralized	Small/decentralized	Benign/decoupled
Human vs. natural capital	Full substitutes	Complements	Partial substitutes
Economic & Psychological			
Primary objective	Efficient allocation	Ecological integrity	Quality of life
The good life	Materialism	Antimaterialism	Postmaterialism
Human nature	Homo economicus	Homo animalist	Homo sapient
Economic structure	Free market	Steady state	Green economy
Role of growth	Good/necessary	Bad/eliminate	Mixed/modify
Poverty alleviation	Growth trickle	Redistribution	Equal opportunity

(Table continues on next page)

Table 14.1.   (Continued)

Key Assumptions	Technocentrism	Ecocentrism	Sustaincentrism
	Economic & Psychological		
Natural capital	Exploit/convert	Enhance/expand	Conserve/ maintain
Discount rate	High/normal	Zero/inappropriate	Low/complement
Trade orientation	Global	Bioregional	National
Political structure	Centralized	Decentralized	Devolved

Source: Adapted from Gladwin, Kennelly, and, Krause (1995).

The ideological conflict and intellectual turbulence that occurs through a plurality of competing incommensurable paradigms leads to a lack of clarity not only in the definition of sustainability, but also in that of viability their relationship. This is illustrated by Baumgärtner and Quaas (2007) who take an optimistic economic perspective through their interest in strong sustainability—where different natural and economic capital stocks have to be maintained as physical quantities separately. However, they then bring in the concept of uncertainty, and argue that to deal with this they require a concept of viability that fits their own conceptual criteria. Their distinct definition of viability is that different components and functions of a dynamic stochastic system remain in a domain where the future existence of these components and functions is guaranteed with sufficiently high probability. This notion of viability takes a strategic commodity view which in essence relates to the continued existence of certain natural capital stocks, and to the continued existence of certain services flowing from capital stocks.

Espinosa (2004) sees viability as referring to a social body that regulates itself and adapts to its environment—even in turbulent times. It is more concerned with a long term survival, rather than sustainability which is more concerned with the dynamics of growth. The viable system needs to be able to cope with the environmental pressures and changes, and to maintain internal stability. Long-term survival happens as a result of effective interactions at other levels of recursion of the society we belong to (i.e., the eco-region, the nation, the planet). Analysis of sustainability, then, can be used to recognize and to monitor main issues concerning its own viability. In this view, weak sustainability would appear to be subsidiary to broad viability.

Schwaninger (2001), through his exploration of the intelligent organisation, recognises that ideas about the nature of viability may vary. As such he distinguishes between two senses of the word: (a) the narrow sense of word viability is understood as the ability to maintain a separate existence, thereby having a distinct configuration which makes a system identifiable as such, and can be assessed on the grounds of structural considerations which are not bound by the orientators of the strategic and operational levels; (b) the broad sense of the word viability is connected with evolving structures, in which an organization's identity may completely change. Such broader notions of viability are reflective of Argrys and Schön's (1980) double loop learning (inherent as opposed to just strategic or single loop learning) and triple loop learning (pragmatic interpretation), as explained by Sterling (2003) in his th*esis connecting sustainability to learning processes, especially with respect to broad viability.*

Schwaninger (2001) does not seem to be a supporter of narrow viability within the context of the intelligent organisation, since it: "has often led to the self-maintenance or self-production of systems which show a dysfunctional behaviour vis-a-vis the larger wholes into which they are embedded" (p. 143). The connection between viability and sustainability is also noted by him, his seeing sustainability as the capacity of an organisation to make positive net contributions to its own viability and the development of the larger supersystem in which it is embedded (p. 138).

AGENCY THEORY

Social cognitive theory provides a conceptual framework that explains how actors, taken as agencies, make choices and motivate and regulate their behavior on the basis of belief systems which is the foundation of agency (Bandura, 1997). An agency may be a singular entity (e.g. an individual) or a plural or collective entity (group decisions that still require each individual's effort and choice; Bandura, 2001).

Interest in plural agency concerns a collective of actors that act together under a common culture within which norms that guide its modes of being and behavior. The plural agency (related to the idea of the first person plural: Sellars, 1963) is here taken as a social "living" social viable system illustrated in Figure 14.2, defined to be "living" through it autopoietic nature which will be explained shortly.

An agency may be singular or plural. A plural agency operates through its collective norms, and its strategic component is referred to as its normative personality. These norms are due to its culture which influences its normative personality and that is responsible for attitudes, strategies, and the decision making imperatives. The nature of the normative personality can be represented through a set of three traits that determines the agency's mode of collective thinking and its behavioral orientation. We note that a cultural agency with a normative personality is an intelligent, self-organizing, proactive, self-regulating, and self-organizing plural body that is participative in creating its own behavior and contributes to its own life's circumstances (Yolles, Fink, & Dauber, 2011). These properties, however, may be susceptible to pathologies that can damage its social health.

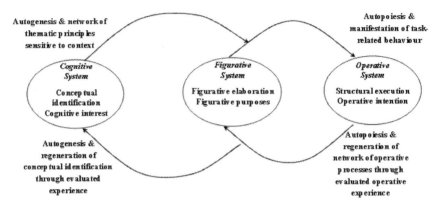

Figure 14.2.   Core concept of a cognitive living system.

Due to its properties, the agency may be considered to be a broadly viable system that develops strategies as part of its socially "living" processes that enables it to develop policies, the consequence of which include issues of sustainability.

The core representation of a living agency is shown in Figure 14.2 as an ontological supersystem composed of three interconnected systems. The supersystem can be identified as "living" if the interconnections satisfy the properties of autopoiesis[2] (Maturana & Varela, 1973/1980) and autogenesis[3] (Schwarz, 1997). The cognitive system offers an important directive for the living supersystem since it is here that identity constructs occur that act as a referent field of influence for the rest of the supersystem. Seeing these systems in terms of fields of influence, the cognitive system operates as a field attractor for the supersystem as a whole. Autopoiesis is constituted simply as a network of processes that enables cognitive system activity to become manifested operatively (Schwarz, 1997), and this is conditioned by autogenesis—a network of principles (that may be seen as second or higher order processes) that create a second order form of autopoiesis guiding autopoiesis. The conceptual system maintains conceptual entities that act as a formative reference for the figurative system in which conceptual entities are manifested through autogenesis as structured schematic entities, which create a strategic potential for the supersystem. The operative system operates through structured operative entities, manifested by autopoiesis from the figurative system, and from which together with stimuli from its operative environment it undertakes its operative functions. Feedback between each of the systems enables the supersystem as a whole to learn.

Autogenesis is a network of principles (second order processes) that facilitates an ability to create, organise, and prioritize according to some cognitive interest associated with self-identification that permeates the cognitive system for a given operative context. Autopoiesis occurs as a network of processes that are used to connect elaborated figurative schemas to a set of possible operative actions that conform to these schemas under the given context. Responses may be fed back to the figurative and cognitive system so as to amplify or supress particular figurative schemas or conceptual identifications. The *autogenetic conduit* is a generator of the strategic (or figurative schema) laws through which the agency operates, and an *autopoietic conduit* is a generator for operative laws and relationships (Schwarz, 1997).

While Figure 14.2 is a representation of the core concept of a living system, such an agency is represented in its simplest terms in Figure 14.3. Now, autogenesis is concept that is quite similar in nature to a concept originally introduced by Piaget (1963/2001, 1977) in the study of children learning and behavior, and is called operative intelligence (Yolles, Fink, & Dauber, 2011). Similarly, autogenesis is directly related to autopoiesis. It is feasible then to consider that an autopoietic network constitutes a conduit for operative intelligence, where strategic entities like goals can be manifested operatively. Similarly, autogenesis may be taken as a conduit for figurative intelligence, where conceptual entities like patterns of action related knowledge can inform strategy. Both operative and figurative feedback is also indicated in the figure. In the context of this generic model, the form of figurative intelligence taken is dependent on culture, and hence it is referred to as cultural (figurative) intelligence, while the operative intelligence is referred to as agency operative intelligence.

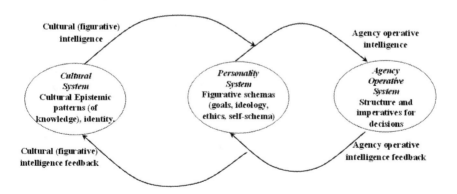

Figure 14.3.   Generic model for a living system agency.

For Piaget (as cited in Elkind, 1976, p.56), intelligence is something that creates an internal connective orientation within an agency (or its personality) towards its environment. This orientation is connected to the capacity of the agency to adapt (Piaget, 1963/2001, pp. 3–4, as cited in Plucker, 2012). The Piagetian (1977) intelligences include operative intelligence which frames how the world is understood and, where understanding is unsuccessful, operative intelligence changes.

Operative intelligence is concerned with the representation and manipulation of the transformational aspects of reality, and involves all actions that are undertaken so as to anticipate, follow or recover the operative transformations. It also refers to highly integrated and generalised sets of actions that are adaptive in nature (Schoenfeld, 1986). It can thus be thought of as the effective capacity to create a cycle of activity that manifests schemas operatively. There are two forms of operative intelligence illustrated in Figure 13.1: one is connected with the agency as a whole, and the other with its normative personality, and both have similar functions. Personality operative intelligence manifests strategic schemas from the figurative system to the operative system. Agency operative intelligence manifests agency schemas from the personality as a whole to the agency operative system. While both personality and agency operative intelligences are constituted as a network of self-producing processes, in the agency they involve bureaucracy—this being responsible for the implementation of policy that arises from the normative personality.

Figurative intelligence is a form of autogenesis (Schwarz, 1997; Yolles, Fink, & Dauber, 2011) that provides core relational explanations of reality as a reflection of epistemic patterns of knowledge or cognitive information. Connected with states of reality, it manifests epistemic patterns in the figurative system to enable strategic schema. These schema may be constituted as perception, drawing, mental imagery, language and imitation (Montangero & Maurice-Naville, 1997; Piaget, 1950; Piaget & Inhelder 1969).

Further development of Figure 14.3 is possible, noting that the nature of the core generic model in Figure 14.2 is that it is recursive (Yolles, 2006), and this permits one to seek a "living system" within the living system. Deeper recursions are also possible with the caveat that they make sense and are meaningful within the context that is defined for them. A full representation of an agency, involving culture, a normative personality, and an operative system in contact with an environment, is shown in Figure 14.4.

The normative personality is a strategic supersystem within the agency that has within it a cognitive, figurative, and operative system. The cognitive system is where cultural knowledge has been delivered as patterns of conceptual information that is directly relevant to contextual situations. It is here where context sensitive patterns of information reside that can

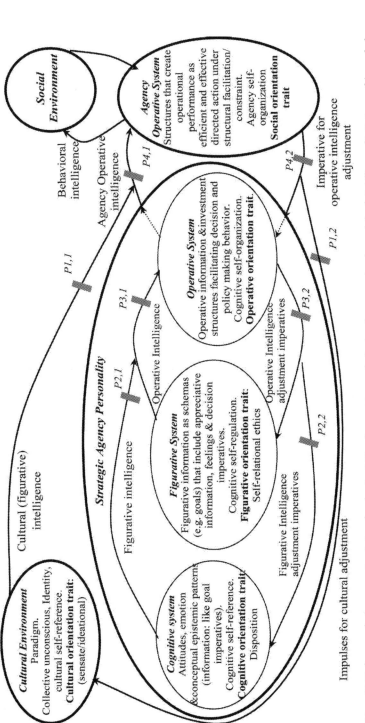

Cultural Environment
Paradigm.
Collective unconscious, Identity, cultural self-reference.
Cultural orientation trait: (sensate/ideational)

Social Environment

Agency Operative System
Structures that create operational performance as efficient and effective directed action under structural facilitation/constraint. Agency self-organization. **Social orientation trait**

Strategic Agency Personality

Cognitive system
Attitudes, emotion &conceptual epistemic patterns (information: like goal imperatives).
Cognitive self-reference.
Cognitive orientation trait: Disposition

Figurative System
Figurative information as schemas (e.g. goals) that include appreciative information, feelings & decision imperatives.
Cognitive self-regulation.
Figurative orientation trait: Self-relational ethics

Operative System
Operative information &investment structures facilitating decision and policy making behavior.
Cognitive self-organization.
Operative orientation trait.

Cultural (figurative) intelligence

Behavioral intelligence

Agency Operative intelligence

Figurative intelligence

Operative Intelligence

Operative Intelligence adjustment imperatives

Figurative Intelligence adjustment imperatives

Imperative for operative intelligence adjustment

Impulses for cultural adjustment

P1,1   P2,1   P3,1   P4,1   P4,2   P3,2   P2,2   P1,2

Note: P*i,j* (where pathology type *i = 1,4* and order *j= 1,2*) refers to type-pathologies that can arise through both *intelligence limitation* and *impeded efficacy.*

Figure 14.4.   A relational "living system" metamodel of an agency in interaction with its environments.

279

inform both strategic and operative needs. Where concepts of sustainability are important to the agency and there is knowledge about how this may occur, then patterns of sustainability information will be identifiable here. It is here that values about sustainability must be manifested from culture, or they simply reside in the background without strategic action.

The figurative system is where personality schemas reside as patterns of strategic information which include goals, ideology, ethics, and self-schema (this latter reflecting how an agency is expected to think, feel and behave in a particular situation in a way that is related to the perception of self: Crisp & Turner, 2010). It is here that through purpose schema are formulated that need to embed the principles of sustainability that are derived from the cognitive system, and which can be expressed through ideology and ethics, and specified through goals. Ideology and ethics interact here with other strategic schemas. While sustainability is a part of ideology it can inform strategic goals. If this does not happen, then either the sustainability concept is ideologically suppressed, or the interaction between then is pathological.

The operative system maintains patterns of structured information which enable decision to be formulated and executed. Here, decisions are made to enable strategic schemas to be manifested operatively, and according to strategic interests. Here these interests are related to sustainability, so decisions about a raft of specifications are made to enable operative sustainable operational processes to develop.

The intelligences couple these systems together. Both operative and figurative intelligence are networks of (first and second order) processes that are the result of collective actions that have occurred between components of the plural agency (e.g., cooperation among departments or project activities including communications). These intelligences are susceptible to pathologies, and may be due to poor communications, poor distribution of current knowledge, poor attitudes, or cultural incoherence due to a lack of normative definition.

The intelligences may be seen as a network of relational processes of transformation of a definable set of components of a given domain of the living system that: (1) through their interactions and transformations, continuously regenerate, realize and adapt the relations that produce them; and (2) constitute its sociocognitive nature as a concrete unity.

Here it may be seen that there are two forms of figurative intelligence in the agency: cultural (figurative) intelligence and personality figurative intelligence. Cultural (figurative) intelligence is used when knowledge is manifested from agency culture to the cognitive system in the personality as conceptual information. Through figurative intelligence within the personality, this information is then again manifested as a variety of strategic forms of schema like goals, ideology, ethics, and self-scripts the latter of which connect strategic expectations with operative structure and behavior.

An agency is interactive with an environment that may include other agencies, and this is also illustrated in Figure 14.4. It functions through behavioral intelligence, as represented through its *overt actions* (Ang et al., 2007, p.6). Behavioral intelligence is connected with how policy developed in the personality, is implemented. It occurs as a "structural coupling" (Maturana & Varela, 1987), meaning that there is an epistemic relationship between two "living system" coupled entities, which create an interactive connection between their past, present and future histories.

Operative intelligence may deliver information in a way that is efficacious, impacting on operative performance. In the plural agency, this is normally referred to as collective efficacy. Lindsley, Brass, and Thomas (1995) citing Guzzo, Yost, Campbell, and Shea (1993, p. 9) note that efficacy is a task specific potency that is meant to refer to a shared belief about general effectiveness across multiple tasks encountered by groups in complex environments. Efficacy is normally taken as the capability an agency has to organize and implement a series of actions to produce given attainments or performances (Bandura, 1997, 1986; Wood & Bandura, 1989). This capability is influenced by the capacity of operative intelligence to generate coherence, and (as noted by Bandura, 2005, p. 316) an agency's interactive, coordinative, and synergistic dynamics. Efficacy, through feedback to the figurative system, has also been seen to affect goal setting, choice of activity, amount of effort that will be expended, analytic strategies, and persistence of coping behavior (Bandura, 1997; Wood & Bandura, 1989, as cited in Lindsley, Brass, & Thomas (1995, p. 647).

Efficacy also influences figurative intelligence. It is concerned with the relationship between cognitive conceptualisation that are connected with cultural knowledge, and figurative schemas that include self-schemas, goals, ideology, and ethics. Efficacy is reduced with the development of pathologies $P_{i,j}$ in Figure 14.4, where (i,j) are such that they indicate type $i = 1,4$ and order $j = 1,2$. These pathologies can result in agency dysfunction.

AGENCY TRAITS AND MINDESTS

When referring to *normative personality* reference is being made to the norms in a collective that may together coalesce into a unitary cognitive structure such that a collective mind can be inferred, and from which an *emergent* normative personality arises. To explain this further, consider that a potentially durable collective develops a dominant culture within which shared beliefs arise in relation to its capacity to produce desired operative outcomes. Cultural anchors arise which enable the development of formal and informal norms to which patterns of behavior, modes of conduct and expression, forms of thought, attitudes, and values are more or less adhered to by those that compose the plural agency. When the norms refer to formal behaviors, then where the members of the collective contravene them, they are deemed to be engaging in illegitimate behavior which, if discovered, may result in formal retribution—the severity of which is determined from the agency's ideological and ethical positioning. This occurs with the rise of collective cognitive processes that start with information inputs and through communication and decision processes result in orientation towards action; and it does this with a sense of the collective mind and self. It is a short step to recognise that the collective mind has associated with it a normative personality. Where a normative personality is deemed to exist, it does not necessarily mean that individual members of the collective will all conform to all aspects of the normative processes: they may only do so "more or less." According to Yolles (2009), as long as a plural agency has a durable culture to which participants more or less conform through its norms, a "collective mind" is implied that operates through meaningful dialogue and agreement. As such the plural agency may appear to behave more or less like a singular cognitive agency. While the plural agency is ultimately composed of singular agencies, they are similar, can suffer from related pathologies that include: dysfunctions, neuroses, feelings of guilt, adopt and maintain collective psychological defences that reduce pain through denial and cover-up, and operate through processes of power that might be unproductive (Kets de Vries, 1991).

In the same way that singular agencies learn, so do plural agencies. The capacity of the normative personality for learning is represented through cognitive learning theory (e.g., Argote & Todorova, 2007; Argyris & Schön, 1978; Miller & Dollard, 1941; Miller, Galanter, & Pribram, 1960; Nobre, 2003; Piaget, 1950; Vygotsky, 1978), where "learning is seen in terms of the acquisition or reorganization of the cognitive structures through which agencies process and store information" (Good & Brophy, 1990, p. 187). Set within cognitive information process theory, the collective mind is seen as an information system that operates through a set of logical mental rules and strategies (e.g., Atkinson & Shiffrin, 1968; Bowlby, 1980; Novak, 1993; Wang, 2007).

The agency model has epistemic value properties that determine its characteristics, and hence enable anticipation for the patterns of behavior that are likely to develop. These characteristics determine its value system, its attitudes, its modus operandi, and its potential for behavior under given contexts. The traits that the agency has (Tables 14.2 and 14.4) take epistemic values, all of which arise from well researched, if disbursed, empirical studies (see Yolles & Fink, 2014; Yolles, Fink, & Dauber, 2011).

The nature of the normative personality can change. In the plural agency it is determined by its membership that defines its self-schema.

The characterisation of a normative personality can be determined by three traits, one for each of the personality systems, and each takes one of two polar opposite values (called enantiomers), or a balance between them (Table 14.2). Enantiomer key values are also indicated. These traits combine together to form mindset types that define the nature of a personality (Table 14.3). The nature of these types is that they fall into one of two broad classifications: Individualism and Collectivism (Yolles & Fink, 2013b).

It is possible to formulate *mindset types* against the polar enantiomers and their epistemic values as shown in Table 14.3. Though trait values may also occur as balances between the polar values, resulting in what we call congruences between mindset types. *It should be noted that the type numbers do not imply trait importance, but simply offer an accounting aid.* In Table 14.3 sets up the mindsets as types associated with polar traits, and a listing of key epistemic words that relate to these.

In Table 14.4 the mindset types have been formulated according to whether they broadly conform to individualism or collectivism (Yolles & Fink, 2013a). This arises because of the enantiomer driver of individualism (mastery) and that of collectivism (harmony). To put this into context it is appropriate to understand a little more the nature of individualism and collectivism. Following Oyserman, Coon, and Kemmelmeier (2002), individualism is the doctrine that all social phenomena (their structure and potential to change) are *in principle* explicable only in terms of individuals—for instance, their properties, goals, and beliefs. In contrast, collectivism *in principle and ideally* relates to people coming together in a collective to act unitarily through normative processes in order to satisfy some commonly agreed and understood purpose or interest. Agencies that strongly adopt either individualism or collectivism have realities that are differently framed, and hence maintain ontologically distinct boundaries constituting frames of reality, which could represent barriers for coherent meaningful mutual communications across these agencies. Individualism and collectivism are very broad concepts and can mean quite different things to different cultures, and this variation in their natures is reflected in the set of mindset types that can arise, and their congruent interconnections. Nevertheless Singelis, Triandis, Bhawuk, and Gelfand (1995) believed that an undifferentiated view of individualism and collectivism presented a satisfactory way of seeing them. However, Schwartz (1994) had found this unsatisfactory, and had replaced the broad notions of individualism and collectivism by his differentiated value universe devoid of reference to individualism and collectivism. It is also worth noting that Schwartz did not perceive individualism and collectivism as mutually exclusive opposites, but referred to values, for example, wisdom, that are related to both, which have a mutually supportive role to play.

Table 14.2.   Bipolar Traits Normative Personality Traits

Traits	Dimensions/Poles	Values/Items	Key Words
Cognitive	Intellectual Autonomy	Meaning is found in the uniqueness of the individual that is encouraged to express internal attributes (preferences, traits, feelings, motives). Intellectual autonomy takes it that individuals are encouraged to pursue their own ideas and intellectual directions independently (important values: curiosity, broadmindedness, creativity). Values are: exciting life, enjoying live, varied life, pleasure, and self-indulgence	Autonomy, creativity, expressivity, curiosity, broadmindedness.
	Embeddedness	Meaning in life can be found largely through social relationships, identifying with the group, participating in a shared way of life, and the adoption of shared goals. Values like social order, respect for tradition, security, and wisdom are important. There tends to be a conservative attitude in that support is provided for the status quo and restraining actions against inclinations towards the possible disruption of in-group solidarity or the traditional order.	Polite, obedient, forgiving, respect tradition, self-discipline, moderate, social order, family security, protect my public image, national security, honour elders, reciprocation of favors.
Figurative	Mastery & Affective Autonomy	Promotes the view that active self-assertion is needed in order to master, direct, and change the natural and social environment to attain group or personal goals (values: ambition, success, daring, competence). Tends to be dynamic, competitive, and oriented to achievement and success, and are likely to develop and use technology to manipulate and change the environment to achieve goals. Affective autonomy pursues positive affective experience. Values are: exciting life, enjoying live, varied life, pleasure, and self-indulgence.	Ambition, success, daring, competence, exciting life, enjoying live, varied life, pleasure, and self-indulgence. Acceptance of portion in life, world at peace, protect environment, unity with nature, world of beauty.

(Table continues on next page)

Table 14.2.   (Continued)

Traits	Dimensions/Poles	Values/Items	Key Words
	Harmony	The world should be accepted as it is, with attempts to understand and appreciate rather than to change, direct, or exploit. Emphasis on fitting harmoniously into the environment (values: unity with nature, protecting the environment, world at peace). There is an expectation that there will be a fit into the surrounding social and natural world. Leaders that adopt this type try to understand the social and environmental implications of organizational actions, and seek non-exploitative ways to work toward their goals.	Social power, authority, humility, wealth.
Operative	Hierarchy	Supports the ascription of roles for individuals to ensure responsible, productive behavior. Unequal distribution of power, roles, and resources are seen to be legitimate (values: social power, authority, humility, wealth). The hierarchical distribution of roles is taken for granted and to comply with the obligations and rules attached to their roles.	Quality, social justice, responsibility, honesty, loyal, equality, honesty, helpful, cooperation
	Egalitarianism	There is a recognition of others being moral equals who share basic interests. There is an internalisation of a commitment towards cooperation, and to feelings of concern for everyone's welfare. There is an expectation that people will act for the benefit of others as a matter of choice (values: equality, social justice, responsibility, honesty).	Loyal, equal-ity, responsible, honest, social justice, helpful

Table 14.3.   Mindset Types Identified With Their Enantiomer Values, and a Listing of Key Epistemic Words That Relate to Them

Mindset Type	Enantiomer	Epistemic Value
1: HI Hierarchical Individualism	Intellectual Autonomy	broad-mindedness, freedom, creativity, curious
	Mastery & Affective Autonomy	successful, ambitious, independent, influential, social recognition, choosing own goals, daring
		exciting life, varied life, pleasure, enjoying life, self-indulgent
	Hierarchy	authority, wealth, social power
2: EI Egalitarian Individualism *Maruyama: I (Independent Prince)*	Intellectual Autonomy	broad-mindedness, freedom, creativity, curious
	Mastery & Affective Autonomy	successful, ambitious, independent, influential, social recognition, choosing own goals, daring
		exciting life, varied life, pleasure, enjoying life, self-indulgent
	Egalitarianism	loyal, equality, responsible, honest, social justice, helpful
3: HS Hierarchical Synergism	Intellectual Autonomy	broad-mindedness, freedom, creativity, curious
	Harmony	accept my position in life, world at peace, protect environment, unity with nature, world of beauty
	Hierarchy	authority, wealth, social power
4: ES Egalitarian Synergism *Maruyama: G (Generative Revolutionary)*	Intellectual Autonomy	broad-mindedness, freedom, creativity, curious
	Harmony	accept my position in life, world at peace, protect environment, unity with nature, world of beauty
	Egalitarianism	loyal, equality, responsible, honest, social justice, helpful
5: HP Hierarchical Populism *Maruyama: H (Hierarchical Bureaucrat)*	Embeddedness	polite, obedient, forgiving, respect tradition, self-discipline, moderate, social order, family security, protect my public image, national security, honour elders, reciprocation of favours
	Mastery & Affective Autonomy	successful, ambitious, independent, influential, social recognition, choosing own goals, daring
		exciting life, varied life, pleasure, enjoying life, self-indulgent
	Hierarchy	authority, wealth, social power

(Table continues on next page)

Table 14.3.   (Continued)

Mindset Type	Enantiomer	Epistemic Value
6: *EP* Egalitarian Populism	Embeddedness	polite, obedient, forgiving, respect tradition, self-discipline, moderate, social order, family security, protect my public image, national security, honour elders, reciprocation of favours.
	Mastery & Affective Autonomy	successful, ambitious, independent, influential, social recognition, choosing own goals, daring exciting life, varied life, pleasure, enjoying life, self-indulgent
	Egalitarianism	loyal, equality, responsible, honest, social justice, helpful
7: *HC* Hierarchical Collectivism	Embeddedness	polite, obedient, forgiving, respect tradition, self-discipline, moderate, social order, family security, protect my public image, national security, honour elders, reciprocation of favours.
	Harmony	accept my position in life, world at peace, protect environment, unity with nature, world of beauty
	Hierarchy	authority, wealth, social power
8: *EC* Egalitarian Collectivism *Maruyama: S (Social Reformer)*	Embeddedness	polite, obedient, forgiving, respect tradition, self-discipline, moderate, social order, family security, protect my public image, national security, honour elders, reciprocation of favours.
	Harmony	accept my position in life, world at peace, protect environment, unity with nature, world of beauty
	Egalitarianism	loyal, equality, responsible, honest, social justice, helpful, cooperation

Different authors give different weight to specific aspects and illustrate their perceptions of individualism and collectivism with "two-word" constructs, like for instance in economics "methodological individualism" versus "'methodological institutionalism" (Davis, Marciano, & Runde, 2004), or more common to politics "transactional individualism" versus "relational collectivism" (Herrmann-Pillath, 2009; Glasman, Rutherford, Stears, & White, 2011; Tangen, 2009). However, we also find the use of the same term to describe different constructs, like "conservative individualism" as opposed to "socialist (or collective) individualism" or "transactional individualism" as opposed to "relational collectivism." The respective pairs strongly depend on the ideological position of those who adopt the terms as ideology is seated in the personality. Here, different weight may be given to the intellectual, spiritual, economic or social aspects of "individualism," or on the intellectual, spiritual, economic, or social aspects of "equality," or on the "'right to enjoy" individual achievements without boundaries or "responsibilities" to take care of other human beings and of natural resources.

Even so mindsets have powerful explanatory value for individualism/ collectivism when taken to operate as broad categories. Individualism frames the development goals of *autonomy and independence* while collectivism frames *relatedness and interdependence* (Schartz, Luychx, & Vignie, 2011 Tamis-LeMonda, Yoshikawa, Niwa, & Niwa, 2008). Individualism and collectivism both embrace distinct cultural identities (from which organizational structures are a reflection) that are manifested within individuals as self-identity that impacts on basic motives for action (Earley & Gibson, 1998). Viskovatoff (1999) also notes that individualism-collectivism represents a dualism, and recognizes attempts to overcome its effects by (a) adopting a poststructuralist approach; (b) recognizing that reality should be seen as chaotic (and hence subject to chaos), disorganized and fragmented (hence affecting the framing of development goals); and (c) viewing the social world in terms of the *decentred* subject (thus impacting on self-identity).

Collectivism and individualism each have their own value ranges, but the boundaries between their differentiations can become merged. Thus, the notions of Toennies (1957), Triandis (1995) and White and Nakurama (2004) connect through *transactional* and *relational* forms of collectivism (Yolles, 2009), so that for instance *transactional collectivism* is constituted as a boundary for individualism.

It is quite easy to identify the respective number of possible mindset types, if one well defines the possible states (two or more) of a bipolar trait and based on a consistent theory defines the number of traits. In addition to the extreme polar types in Table 14.4 (illustrated graphically in Figure 14.5) there are types that can arise from balanced traits. For 3 traits with 3 possible states (pole 1, balanced, pole 2) there are 27 possibilities in the system. This illustrates the capacity of mindset agency theory to engage with variation, which enables the modeling of the complexities of human personality beyond a simple classification scheme. These include 8 *biased* mindsets that are combination of the poles of the three traits—one in each of the 8 corners of the cube (the apexes), 1 *congruent* mindset composed of 3 balanced traits in the middle of the cube (Figure 14.5). There are 6 *strongly congruent* Mindsets with 2 traits in balance in the middle of the 6 sides of the cube. Finally, there are also 12 *weakly congruent* Mindsets with only 1 trait in balance in the middle of the 12 lateral edges of the cube (Figure 14.5).

However, the range of values (scores) that a personality trait may take between the two extreme polar enantiomers may be represented by a continuous variable This would result in the huge discrete set of possible Mindset types becoming a potentially continuous and hence infinite set that can represent any possible values or value balance of a personality. In practice, however, it will be useful that this range is limited to a discrete determinable set, where differences between types do matter.

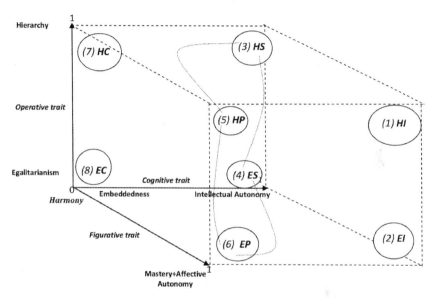

Figure 14.5. Mindset personality space showing eight mindset types, where congruencies may occur between them that derive from trait enantiomer balances.

We have indicated that personality mindset congruencies are in principle possible along each axis and on each plane of Figure 14.5. But, for them to exist there is a need for them to arise as stable combinations, something that depends on the current state of cultural values. We have said that these congruencies will be related to the values that the cultural trait of the agency takes. Sorokin (1937–1942/1962) noted that when the sensate and ideational enantiomers reach a common balance the *idealistic* state arises. In this case neither sensate nor ideational values dominate, but rather a synergy occurs between them so that both forms of value sets are regarded as valid in society. Thus, ideational people might find themselves in significant social roles just as people with sensate values, a situation not possible in a predominantly ideational or sensate culture. These roles will depend on the strengths of the individuals.

Since under normal conditions cultural trait values operate as an attractor for personality, the mindset values adopted are a reflection of the cultural trait, with either a tendency towards individualism or collectivism. The emergence of variations within individualism or collectivism in a given agency likely is a function of the "fine tuning" within a culture that may relate to desired goals and *outcomes*, that is, achievements and possible distortions through one-sided action.

We have indicated that the agency is not only composed of a normative personality, but also has a cultural and social system. These both have representative traits, each of which adopts epistemic enantiomer values. These traits and their enantiomers are shown in Table 14.5.

Table 14.5.   Cultural and Social Traits and Their Polar Enantiomer Values

Trait	Enantiomer	Nature	Key Words/ Values
Cultural	Sensate	Reality is sensory and material, pragmatism is normal, there is an interest in becoming rather than being, and happiness is paramount. People are externally oriented and tend to be instrumental and empiricism is important.	The senses, utilitarianism, materialism, becoming, process, change, flux, evolution, progress, transformation, pragmatism, temporal.
	Ideational	Reality is super-sensory, morality is unconditional, tradition is of importance, there is a tendency toward creation, and examination of self.	Super-sensory, spirituality, humanitarianism, self-deprivation, creativity of ideas, eternal.
Social	Dramatism	Individual relationships to others are important, constituted as sequences of interpersonal events. Communication is important, as are individuals and their proprietary belief systems, and individual social contracts. Goal formation should be for individual benefit. Ideocentric agencies are important, operating through social contracts between the rational wills of its individual members.	Sequenciality, communication, individualism, contractual, ideocentric.
	Patternism	Configurations are important in social and other forms of relationships. There is persistent curiosity. The social is influenced by relationships with individuals. Some importance is attached to symmetry, pattern, balance, and the dynamics of relationships. Goal seeking should be for collective benefit, and collective goal formation takes precedence over personal goal formation. Allocentric collectives are important, where the members operate subjectively.	Configurations, relationships, symmetry, pattern, balance, dynamics, collectivism, allocentric.

The cultural trait maintains an agency field that biases it towards either individualism or collectivism, depending on the value taken up by the cultural trait. Thus when the cultural trait takes an ideational value the normative personality takes an *individualist mindscape*, and when the cultural trait takes a sensate value normative personality takes a collectivistic value. Simlarly, an ideational value for the cultural trait results in a patternerning social trait value while a sensate value results in a dramatizing value, determining in the end whether an agency might be either say creative or instrumentalist, or whether they might operate together synergistically according to cultural conditions, this resulting in innovative material outputs typical of socioindustrial revolutions.

RELATING MINDSET TYPES TO SUSTAINABILITY PARADIGMS

Mensah and Castro (2004, p. 2) distinguished between the two broad groupings that support paradigms of sustainability, and suggested that the optimists tend to centre on economists and related others, while the pessimists on ecologists and related others. While for many economics is identified with individualism (Davis, Marciano, & Runde, 2004, p. 21). Following not all economists are individualists, and by this token, optimists. Nozick (1977, p. 359, as cited in Davis et al., 2004, p. 121) identifies two frames of reference in economics are methodological individualism and collectivistic methodological institutionalism. By the same token, it is likely that there will also be variation in the paradigms being supported by ecologists and related others.

This leads one back to the original interest in this paper, understanding the generic bases for the paradigms of sustainability. In Table 14.1 two opposing paradigms were identified, with an attempt at creating some in-between paradigm. Making an epistemic comparison between Table 14.1 and Tables 14.2 and 14.4 now provides a basis for a comparison between Mindsets and the optimistic/pessimistic paradigms of sustainability. To do this we shall use a technique called "epistemic mapping" which will make epistemic keyword comparisons between individualism/collectivism and pessimistic/optimistic sustainability in order to obtain their connection if any. To do this the epistemic values identified by Gladwin, Kennelly, and Krause (1995) for the paradigms of sustainability will be used as shown in Table 14.1, and the trait enantiomers for culture, social and normative personality orientations have been assembled and shown in Table 14.6.

The paradigms that Gladwin, Kennelly, and Krause (1995) have associated with pessimism (ecocentrism) and optimism (technocentrism) may therefore be considered to be catch-all entities. However, while they may be

**Table 14.6.   Broad Relationships Between Mindset Trait
Enantiomers and Susceptibility Paradigm Values**

Trait Enantiomer	Epistemic Values	Optimistic (Technocentrism) Values	Pessimistic (Ecocentric) Values
		Culture	
Sensate	The senses, utilitarianism, materialism, becoming, process, change, flux, evolution, progress, transformation, pragmatism, temporal	Materialism, Exploit/convert	
Ideational	Super-sensory, spirituality, humanitarianism, self-deprivation, creativity of ideas, eternal		Spiritualism, antimaterialism
		Normative Personality	
Intellectual Autonomy	Autonomy, creativity, expressivity, curiosity, broadmindedness.	No limits, Atomistic, disassociation	
Embeddedness	Polite, obedient, forgiving, respect tradition, self-discipline, moderate, social order, family security, protect my public image, national security, honour elders, reciprocation of favours.		Intrinsicalism
Mastery & Affective Autonomy	Ambition, success, daring, competence, exciting life, enjoying live, varied life, pleasure, and self-indulgence. **&** Acceptance of position in life, world at peace, protect environment, unity with nature, world of beauty.	Atomistic, disassociation, anthropocentrism	
Harmony	Social power, authority, humility, wealth.		Heterarchical, Ecological integrity, whole earth
Hierarchy	Quality, social justice, responsibility, honesty, loyal, equality, honesty, helpful, cooperation	Hierarchical, vast machine, domination, centralised	

(Table continues on next page)

Table 14.6.   (Continued)

Trait Enantiomer	Epistemic Values	Optimistic (Technocentrism) Values	Pessimistic (Ecocentric) Values
	Normative Personality		
Egalitarianism	Loyal, equality, responsible, honest, social justice, helpful		Ecological integrity, Redistribution, Indisassociation
	Social Trait		
Dramatism	Sequenciality, communication, individualism, contractual, ideocentric	Narrow homocentric, Egoist-rational, free market,	
Patternism	Configurations, relationships, symmetry, pattern, balance, dynamics, collectivism, allocentric		Whole earth, highly vulnerable, complements,

paradigms in the scientific sense of the word, they only constitute attributes of mindsets that agencies adopt and maintain. Specific agencies will adopt mindset types that do not capture all of these elements, or they may be balances between the polar enantiomers that result in compound mindset types.

Since these enantiomers are associated with different mindsets that broadly collect under individualism and collectivism, it is also clear that not all perspectives on sustainability are either in the extreme polar optimist or pessimist camps. These comparisons are indicative that there are some components of the pessimistic sustainability paradigm that are related to forms of individualism, as there are some components of the optimistic paradigm that are related to collectivism.

CONCLUSION

The significant public interest over the word sustainability (since its inception as a noun in 1987) in relation to environmental issues has also led to considerations about corporate sustainability, and accompanying this there has been confusion over its nature and its relationship with viability. More, the development of the concept of sustainability has been subject to ideological controversy and intellectual turmoil, and led to some public suggestions that the very concept of sustainability is unsustainable. In general, a result has been a common view that organisation theory has been unable to respond to the development of an adequate concept for sustainability, further contributing to uncertainty conflict and confusion in attempts explain sustainability.

There seems to be a solid recognition that ideas of sustainability are part of a process of intellectual turmoil and ideological controversy, this implying that it is not currently a sustainable concept. As a result some authors have attempted to explore the paradigmatic distinctions that have arisen. Mensah and Castro (2004) referred to two diametrically opposite paradigms that they referred to as *pessimistic* and *optimistic*. Gladwin, Kennelly, and Krause (1995) have sought to characterise these two paradigms, which they called *technocentrism* and *ecocentrism*, identifying for each a set of distinct epistemic values. They then showed that it was possible to have some in-between paradigm that they referred to as *sustaincentrism*, having epistemic values that were some balance between the two extreme paradigms.

This chapter has asked two questions. The first was: *do holders of one or the other of these paradigms always accept all of the values held by the given paradigm?* If it were found that the characterization of each paradigm a catch all for the opposing paradigm camps, then a second question becomes relevant: *is there a way by which one can identify generically which values are acceptable and to which people?*

In order to better respond to these questions a theoretical schema was adopted that could more clearly provide appropriate explanations. This schema is the cultural agency, which is broadly viable, and where sustainability is taken as a strategic process that derives from agency policy options. This agency is trait based, the traits operating as agency controllers. Coupling this with mindset theory enables modes of collective thought and related patterns of behavior to be identified and associated with epistemic types for any agency. Mindset types have been related to the sustainability paradigms, and it has been shown that the attributes of each of the opposing paradigms can be distinguished into Individualistic and collectivistic agency orientations. However, individualism and collectivism are very broad concepts, and distinct agency mindset types maintain broad associations with each of these orientations. As a result, a whole variety of views about sustainability are discernable across all of the possible mindset types, not only the three paradigms indicated by Gladwin, Kennelly, and Krause (1995). From mindset theory there are at least eight, and likely many more in the case that some mindset types meet as congruent mode of thought.

This outcome implicitly supports the argument of Lutz Newton, and Freyfogle (2005) suggesting that unless agencies have a specific determinable brief towards sustainability such that it develops into implementable strategic policy, then sustainability is not likely to become significant for the agency and will have no more than peripheral consequences.

NOTES

1. The problem with *common sense* is that "one person's common sense is another person's naïve platitude" (Rachels & Rachels, 1986)
2. Autopoiesis (Maturana & Varela, 1987; Schwarz, 1997) explains how a "living system" self-produces its core relational explanations of reality that influence behavior. This defines for the personality system it's own boundaries relative to its environment, develops its own unifying operational code, implements its own programmes, reproduces its own elements in a closed circuit, obeys its own laws of behavior, and potentially satisfies its own intentions (Jessop, 1990). It also self-produces the network of processes that enable it to produce its own personality components that exist in cognitive, figurative and operative bases.
3. Autogenesis is a second order form of autopoiesis (Schwarz, 1997) that has a higher level of processes—that is metaprocesses that may be represented for instance as guiding personality convictions, principle influences, or even spirit. It occurs when a selectable network of these meta-processes is able to project into the operative couple a set of espoused values as attitudes and mental schemas and operative personality patterns. In effect autogenesis defines the autonomous system through the creation of its own set of laws.

REFERENCES

Abeysuriya, K. R., Willetts, J. R. & Mitchell, C. A. (2006, December). Kuhn on sanitation: dignity, health and wealth for the children of the revolution. *In Proceedings of the Ninth Biennial Conference of the International Society for Ecological Economics: Ecological Sustainability and Human Well-being,* The International Societyfor Ecological Economics and The Indian Society for Ecological Economics, New Dehli, India, pp. 1–23.

Ang, S., Van Dyne, L., Koh, C. K. S., Ng, K. Y., Templer, K. J., Tay, C., & Chandrasekar, N. A., (2007). Cultural intelligence: Its measurement and effects on cultural judgment and decision making, cultural adaptation, and task performance. *Management and Organization Review, 3,* 335–371.

Argote L., & Todorova G. (2007). Organizational learning: Review and future directions. In G. P. Hodgkinson, & J. K. Ford (Eds.), *International Review of Industrial and Organizational Psychology* (pp. 193-234). New York, NY: Wiley.

Argyris, C., & Schön. D. (1978). *Organisational learning: A theory of action perspective.* Reading, MA: Addison-Wesley.

Atkisson, A. (1999). *Believing Cassandra: How to be an optimist in a pessimist's world* (2nd ed.). London, England: Earthscan.

Atkinson, R. C., & Shiffrin, R. M. (1968). Human memory: A proposed system and its control processes. In K. W. Spence & J. T. Spence (Eds.), *The psychology of learning and motivation: Advances in research and theory* (Vol. 2, pp. 90–196). New York, NY: Academic Press.

Bandura, A. (1997). *Self-efficacy. The exercise of control.* New York, NY: Freeman.

Bandura, A. (1986). *Social foundations of thought and action: A social cognitive theory.* Englewood Cliffs, NJ: Prentice-Hall

Bandura, A. (2001). Social cognitive theory: An agentic perspective. *Annual Review Psychology, 52,* 1–26.

Bandura, A. (2005), Guide for constructing self-efficacy scales. In F. Pajares & T. Urdan (Eds.), *Self-efficacy beliefs of adolescents* (pp. 1–43), Greenwich, CT: Information Age Publishing.

Baumgärtner, S., & Quaas, M.F. (2007). *Ecological-economic viability as a criterion of strong sustainability under uncertainty* (University of Lüneburg Working paper series in economics, No. 67). Retrieved June 2009, from http://hdl.handle.net/10419/28196

Beckerman, W. (1994). "Sustainable development": Is it a useful concept? *Environmental Values, 3*(3), 191–209.

Beckerman, W. (2002). *A poverty of reason: Sustainable development and economic growth.* Oakland, CA: The Independent Institute.

Beer, S. (1979). *The heart of enterprise.* Chichester, England: Wiley.

Beer, S. (1989). The viable system model: Its provenance, development, methodology and pathology. In E. Espejo & R. Harnden (Eds.), *Viable systems model: Interpretations and applications of Stafford Beer's VSM.* Chichester, England: Wiley. Retrieved November 2013, from http://quantumcybernetics.org/Uni-Work/Papers_of_Interest_files/Viable_System_Model-1989%20CwareIInst.pdf

Beer, S. (2002). What is cybernetics? *Kybernetes, 31*(2), 209–219.

Bossel, H. (1999). Indicators for sustainable development: Theory, method, applications; A report to the Balaton Group. International Institute for Sustainable Development, Winnipeg, Manitoba, Canada. Retrieved June 2009, from http://iisd.ca/about/prodcat/perfrep.htm#balaton.

Bowlby, J. (1980). *Attachment and loss: Sadness and depression.* New York, NY: Basic Books,

Crisp. R. J., & Turner, R. N. (2010). *Essential social psychology.* London, England: SAGE.

Davis, J., Marciano. A., & Runde, J. (2004). *The Elgar companion to economics and philosophy.* Cheltenham, England: Edward Elgar.

Dowie, M. (1995). *Losing ground: American environmentalism at the close of the twentieth century.* Cambridge, MA: The MIT Press.

Earley, P. C., & Gibson, C. B. (1998). Taking stock in our progress on individualism-collectivism: 100 years of solidarity and community. *Journal of Management, 8*(24), 265–304.

Elkind, D. (1976). *Child development and education: A Piagetian perspective.* New York, NY: Oxford University Press.

Espinosa, A. (2004, September 3rd). *Measurement systems in socio economic development programs from a cybernetic view.* Paper presented at the CybCon2004 Cybernetics and Public Administration conference, the Cybernetics Society, in St James Park, London England. Retrieved December 2014, from www.cybsoc.org/meassys-fin.doc

Financial Times Lexicon. (2013). Business sustainability. Retrieved December 2013, from http://lexicon.ft.com/Term?term=business-sustainability,

Frechette, H. (2010). Definition: sustainability. *Journal of Citizen Polity.* Retrieved November 2013, from http://citizenpolity.com/2010/07/26/defining-sustainability/

Singelis, T. M., Triandis, H. C., Bhawuk, D., & Gelfand, M. J. (1995). Horizontal and vertical dimensions of individualism and collectivism: A theoretical and measurement refinement. *Cross-Cultural Research, 29,* 240–275.

Gladwin, T. N., Kennelly, J. J., & Krause, T. S. (1995, Oct. 4). Shifting paradigms for sustainable development: Implications for management theory and research, *The Academy of Management Review, 20,* 874–907.

Glasman, M., Rutherford, J., Stears, M., & White, S. (2011). The Labour tradition and the politics of paradox, The Oxford London seminars 2010–11. Retrieved December 2013, from www.scribd.com/doc/55941677/Labour-Tradition-and-the-Politics-of-Paradox.

Good, T. L, & Brophy, J. E. (1990). *Educational psychology: A realistic approach* (4th ed.). White Plains, NY: Longman

Gordon, R.L. (2003, December). The unsustainability of sustainability. *Regulation, 26*(4). Retrieved Nov. 2013, http://object.cato.org/sites/cato.org/files/serials/files/regulation/2003/12/v26n4-review.pdf

Guzzo, R. A., Yost, P. R., Campbell, R. J., & Shea, G. P. 1993. Potency in groups: Articulating a construct. *British Journal of Social Psychology, 32,* 87–106.

Harrison, N. (2000). *Constructing sustainable development.* Albany, NY: State University of New York Press.

Herrmann-Pillath, C. (2009). *Social capital, Chinese style: Individualism, relational collectivism and the cultural embeddedness of the institutions-performance link* (Working Paper Series no 132). Frankfurt School of finance and Management, Retrieved December 2013, from http://d-nb.info/997649216/34

Jessop, B. (1990). *State theory.* Cambridge, England: Polity Press.

Kets de Vries, M. F. R. (1991). *Organisations on the couch: Clinical perspectives on organisational behaviour and change.* New Yor, NY: Jossey-Bass.

Kuhn, T. S. (1970). *The structure of scientific revolutions* (2nd ed.). Chicago, IL: University of Chicago Press.

Levin, C., & Coburn, T. (2011). Wall Street and the financial crisis: Anatomy of a financial collapse (Majority and Minority Staff Report), United States Senate Permanent Subcommittee on Investigations Committee on Homeland Security and Governmental Affairs, Retrieved from November 2012 http://www.ft.com/cms/fc7d55c8-661a-11e0-9d40-00144feab49a.pdf

Lindsley, D., Brass, D. J., & Thomas, J. B. (1995). Efficacy-performance spirals: A multilevel perspective. *Academy of Management Review, 20*(3), 645–678.

Lutz Newton, J., & Freyfogle, E. T. (2005). Sustainability: A dissent. *Conservation Biology, 19*(1), 23–32. Retrieved November 2013, from http://onlinelibrary.wiley.com/doi/10.1111/j.1523-1739.2005.538_1.x/full

Maturana, H., & Varela, F. (1980). *Autopoiesis and cognition: The realization of the Living.* In R. S. Cohen & M. W. Wartofsky (Eds.), *Boston studies in the philosophy of science.* Dordecht, England: D. Reidel. (Original work published 1973)

Maturana, H. R., & Varela, F. J. (1987). *The tree of knowledge.* London England: Shambhala.

Mensah, A. M., & Castro, L. C. (2004, November). Sustainable resource use & sustainable development: A contradiction?. *Center for Development Research, University of Bonn, Germany.* Retrieved November, 2013, from www.zef.de/fileadmin/downloads/forum/docprog/Termpapers/2004_3b_Mensah_Castro.pdf

Miller, N. E., & Dollard, J. (1941). *Social learning and imitation.* New Haven, CT: Yale University Press.

Miller, G. A., Galanter, E., & Pribram, K. H. (1960). Plans and the Structure of behavior. New York, NY: Holt, Rinehart & Winston.

Montangero, J., & Maurice-Naville, D. (1997). *Piaget, on the advance of knowledge: An overview and glossary.* Mahwah, NJ: Lawrence Erlbaum Associates.

Neumayer, E. (1999).*Global warming: Discounting is not the issue, but substitutability is. Energy Policy, 27*(1), 33–43.

Nobre, F.S. (2003, April). Perspectives on organisational systems: Towards a unified theory. Doctoral Consortium on Cognitive Science at the ICCM 2003, Bamberg, Germany.

Novak, J. G. (1993, March), How do we learn our lesson? *The Science Teacher, 60,* 50–55.

Nozick, R. (19770. On Austrian methodology. *Synthèse, 36,* 353–392.

Ny, H., MacDonald, J. P., Broman, G., Yamamoto, R., & Robért, K. H. (2006). Sustainability constraints as system boundaries: An approach to making life-cycle management strategic. *Journal of Industrial Ecology, 10*(1–2), 61–77.

Ott, K. (2003). The case for strong sustainability. *Greifswald's Environmental Ethics.* Greifswald, Germany: Steinbecker Verlag Ulrich Rose.

Oyserman, D., Coon, H .M., & Kemmelmeir, M., (2002). Rethinking individualism and collectivism: evaluation of theoretical assumptions and meta-analyses. *Psychological Bulletin, 128*(1), 3–72

Piaget, J. (1950). *The psychology of intelligence,* , New York, NY: Harcourt and Brace. (Reprinted in 1972 by Totowa, NJ: Littlefield Adams)

Piaget, J. (1977). *The development of thought: Equilibration of cognitive structure.* New York, NY: Viking.

Piaget, J. (2001). *The psychology of intelligence.* New York, NY: Routledge. (Original work published 1963)

Piaget, J., & Inhelder, B. (1969). *The psychology of the child* (H. Weaver, Trans.). New York, NY: Basic Books.

Piaget, J., & Inhelder, B. (1973). *Memory and intelligence.* London, England: Routledge and Kegan Paul.

Plucker, J. (2012). *Human intelligence.* Retrieved May, 2013, from www.indiana.edu/~intell/piaget.shtml

Russell, D. L. (2010). *Sustainability reconsidered: The technology link, American Institute of Chemical Engineers.* Retrieved from http://chenected.aiche.org/sustainability/sustainability-reconsidered-the-technology-link/

Rachels, J., & Rachels, S. (1986). *The elements of moral philosophy.* New York, NY: McGraw-Hill.

Schartz, S. J., Luychx, K., & Vignie, V. L. (2011). *Handbook of Identity theory and research: Structures and processes* (Vol. 1). New York, NY: Springer.

Sorokin, P. (1962). *Social and cultural dynamics* (4 volumes). New York, NY: Bedminster Press. (Originally work published in 1937–1942)

Schoenfeld, A. H. (Ed.). (1986). What's all the fuss about metacognition? In *Cognitive science and mathematical education*(pp. 189–215). Hillsdale, NJ: Lawrence Erlbaum Associates.

Schwaninger, M. (2001). Intelligent organizations: An integrative framework. *Systems Research and Behavioral Science, 18*, 137–158.

Schwartz, S. H. (1994). Beyond individualism/collectivism: New dimensions of values. In U. Kim, H. C. Triandis, C. Kagitcibasi, S. C. Choi, & G. Yoon, (Eds.), *Individualism and collectivism: Theory application and methods*. Newbury Park, CA: Sage

Schwarz, E. (1997). Towards a holistic cybernetics: From science through epistemology to being. *Cybernetics and Human Knowing, 4*(1), 17–50.

Sellars, W. (1963). Imperatives, intentions, and the logic of "ought". In H. N. Castañeda & G. Nakhnikian (Eds.), *Morality and the language of conduct*. Detroit, MI: Wayne State University Press.

Spangenberg, J. H. (2005). Economic sustainability of the economy: Concepts and Indicators. *Int. J. Sustainable Development, 8*(1/2), 47–64.

Stepanyan, K., Littlejohn, A., & Margaryan, A. (2013). Sustainable e-Learning: Toward a coherent body of knowledge. *Educational Technology & Society, 16*(2), 91–102. Retrieved November 2013, from www.ifets.info/others/download_pdf.php?j_id=59&a_id=1354

Sterling, S. (2003). *Whole systems thinking as a basis for paradigm change in education explorations in the context of sustainability* (PhD thesis). University of Bath, England. Retrieved Dec. 2013, from www.bath.ac.uk/cree/sterling/sterlingthesis.pdf.

Swyngedouw, E. (2007). Impossible sustainability and the post-political condition. In R. Krueger & D. Gibbs (Eds.), *The sustainable development paradox: Urban political economy in the United States and Europe* (pp. 13–40). London, England: Guildford Press.

Tamis-LeMonda, C. S., Yoshikawa, H., Niwa, K., & Niwa, E. Y. (2008). Parents' goals for children: The dynamic coexistence of individualism and collectivism in cultures and individuals. *Social Development, 17*(1), 183–209.

Tangen, K. I.. (2009). *Ecclesial identification beyond transactional individualism? A case study of life strategies in growing late modern churches* (PhD thesis). Oslo, Norway: MF Norwegian School of Theology.

Toennies, F. (1957). *Community and society* (Charles P. Loomis, Trans.). (Book I). East Lansing, MI: Michigan State University Press.

Triandis, H. C. (1995). *Individualism and collectivism*. Boulder, CO: Westview Press.

Vygotsky, L. S. (1978). *Mind in society: The development of higher psychological processes*. Cambridge, MA: Harvard University Press.

Viskovatoff, A. (1999). Foundations of Niklas Luhmann's theory of social systems. *Philosophy of the Social Sciences, 29*(4), 481–515.

Turner, K. (1992). Speculations on weak and strong sustainability: Global environmental change (Working Papers 1992-26). Retrieved from Centre for Social and Economic Research on the Global Environment (CSERGE): www.uea.ac.uldenvicserge/pub/wp/gec/gec_1992_26.htm

Wang, A. (2007). *The effects of varied instructional aids and field dependence-independence on learners' structural knowledge in a hypermedia environment*. Doctoral thesis presented to Department of Educational Studies, College of Education of Ohio University, Ohio, U.S., University of Ohio.

White, S., & Nakaruma, A. (2004, 10th July), Organisational and network collectivism, workshop of the journal of international business studies in association with academy of international business, University of South Carolina, Retrieved December 2004, from http://faculty.fuqua.duke.edu/ciber/programs/pdf/wnc.pdf.

Wood, R., & Bandura, A. (1989). Social cognitive theory of organizational management. *Academy of Management Review, 14*, 361–384.

Yolles, M. I. (2006). *Organizations as complex systems: An introduction to knowledge cybernetics*, Greenwich, CT: Information Age Publishing.

Yolles, M. I. (2009). A social psychological basis of corruption and sociopathology. *Journal of Organizational Change Management, 22*(6), 691–731.

Yolles, M. I., & Fink, G. (2011). Agencies, normative personalities, and the viable systems model. *Journal Organisational Transformation and Social Change, 8*(1), 83–116.

Yolles, M. I., & Fink, G. (2013a). An introduction to mindset theory (Working Paper of the Organisational Coherence and Trajectory (OCT) Project). Retrieved from www.octresearch.net

Yolles, M. I., & Fink, G. (2013b, January). *Exploring the common roots of culture, politics and economics*. Keynote address given by Yolles and the International Symposium, The Economic Crisis: Time For A Paradigm Shift—Towards a Systems Approach, Universitat de València, València, Spain.

Yolles, M., & Fink, G. (2014). Modelling mindsets of an agency. *Journal of Organisational Transformation and Social Change, 11*(1), 69–88.

Yolles, M., Fink, G., & Dauber, D. (2011). Organisations as emergent normative personalities: Part 1, the concepts. *Kybernetes,* (5/6), 635–669

CHAPTER 13

GLOBAL SUSTAINABILITY REPORTING INITIATIVES

Integrated Pathways for Economic, Environmental, Social, and Governance Organizational Performance

Marco Tavanti

INTRODUCTION

Most global corporations and international organizations welcome the principles and values associated with sustainability and social responsibility. This trend appears to be reinforced by a growing field of research in "corporate social responsibility" and "sustainable capitalism" suggesting how "doing well by doing good" is a profitable possibility and a growing global trend (Freemantle, 2008; Haynes, Murray, & Dillard, 2013; Tavanti, 2014). As always, the devil is in the details and the real challenges emerge in the measurement of their actual sustainability performances in relation to those values and principles. Fortunately, sustainability reporting has become a common 21st century business practice. Most corporations and

Corporate Social Performance:
Paradoxes, Pitfalls, and Pathways to the Better World, pp. 301–323
Copyright © 2015 by Information Age Publishing

organizations operating internationally now produce an annual public reporting of their impact in nonfinancial, economic, environmental, social, and governance performance. Where once only a few "green" and "community-oriented" organizations would disclose their social responsibility performance, today sustainability reporting is an expected practice for companies worldwide. Sustainability reporting is a generic term usually including other correlated types of organizational disclosures also known as "Corporate Social Responsibility Reports," "Global Citizenship Reports," "Corporate Citizenship," and "Environmental, Social, and Governance (ESG) Reporting."

Sustainability reporting deserves closer attention and critical studies should be done on the actual impact measurement of ESG organizational performance. The benefits of sustainability reporting go beyond financial risk, license to operate, or investment opportunities. Sustainability reporting benefit organizations by improving their reputation with investors, their relations with regulatory authorities, the loyalty of employee and consumers, along with their strategies, vision and values (EY & Boston College Center for Corporate Citizenship, 2013).

This chapter reviews the economic, environmental, social, and governance values of sustainability reporting. In the examination of the value integration and measurement standardization exemplified by the Global Reporting Initiative (GRI), correlated reporting and guidance frameworks, we discuss the opportunities and limits of complementary reporting. GRI is recognized as an authoritative sustainability-reporting framework helping organizations to increase transparency and accountability in nonfinancial reporting. Since its foundation in 1997 by a cooperative effort through the United Nations Environment Program (UNEP) and CERES, a nonprofit organization advocating for sustainability leadership, GRI has grown exponentially by continuously refining their reporting guidelines and providing a shared platform for disclosure standards across time, sectors, and nations.

THE GROWTH IN SUSTAINABILITY REPORTING

Corporate social responsibility, business ethics, stakeholder engagement, and sustainable value creation are becoming international norms in organizational leadership and management education (Avlonas & Nassos, 2014; Horrigan, 2010; Segerlund, 2010). Such trends explain the increased popularity of sustainability reporting, especially for organizations operating globally and constantly facing the urgency and complexity of social and environmental impact, value leadership, good governance, and multisector partnerships. Sustainability reporting is becoming a necessary tool for sharing performance and integrating management and leadership (governance) practices with economic, environmental and social performance, especially regarding human rights, labor rights, and human development (Lawrence & Beamish, 2013; Ruggie, 2013).

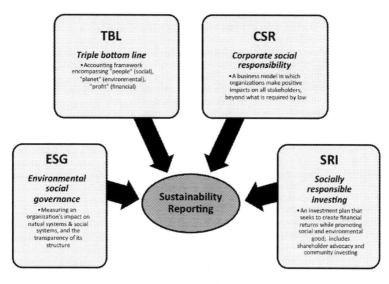

Elaborated by Marco Tavanti

Figure 13.1.   The socially responsible context of sustainability reporting.

Sustainability reporting provides valuable mechanisms for the promotion of a 'triple bottom line' corporate culture (Savitz & Weber, 2014). The reporting also implies prioritization processes that help organizations set goals, measure performance and manage change while also addressing the financial, economic, environmental, social, and governance values. In this process, sustainability reporting makes the "abstract" values "concrete" measurable and comparable outputs and outcomes that would make organizations and their operations more sustainable. Such integrated performances should generate organizational sustainability development aligned, centered and integrated with the organization's leadership, planning and strategies.

Effective standards integration in sustainability reporting, along with stakeholder transparency, grievance mechanisms and global accountability are necessary elements that are carefully measured in the Global Reporting Imitative (GRI) and its most recent G4 guidelines. Through carefully crafted guidelines, the GRI standards have been designed to harmonize with other prominent sustainability standards, including the OECD Guidelines for Multinational Organizations, ISO 26000 and the UN Global Compact among others. This is mindful that although one of the most prominent sustainability reporting standards, the GRI aims to be inclusive and complementary to other types of reporting. While acknowledging that voluntary disclosures and engagement in sustainable value creation are more important than imposed standards, GRI recognizes and promotes standardized sustainability reporting for improving ESG accountability, stakeholder transparency, and sector specific concerns.

The growth in sustainability reporting is documented in the GRI database since 1999 (Figure 13.2). In 2013, more than 3,100 organizations submitted sustainability reporting through the Global Reporting Initiative (GRI). More than 2,100 followed the specific GRI reporting guidelines provided in the so-called G1, G2, G3, G3.1 or the recently released G4. Many more have referenced the GRI or closely associated their sustainability reporting to these standards.

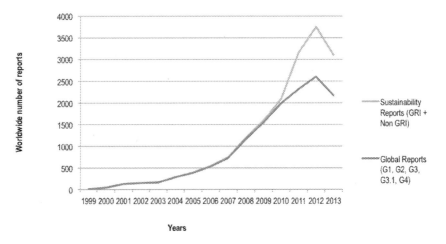

Source: Elaborated by Marco Tavanti with retrieved data from the GRI Database available at http://database.globalreporting.org/

Figure 13.2.   Growth of sustainability reporting.

Reporting on sustainability may not necessarily be an expression of value-based leadership or the mission of the organization. It may be simply motivated by industry standards, government requirements, or financial interests in socially responsible investing (SRI). The European Parliament recently passed a law requiring large EU corporations (those publicly traded and with more than 500 employees) to file a sustainability report along with their annual financial report. Companies will be encouraged to use standardized and recognized frameworks, such as the GRI Sustainability Reporting Guidelines and the U.N. Guiding Principles on Business and Human Rights—Protect, Respect and Remedy (Ruggie, 2013).

According to recent surveys, about 95% of the world's largest 250 corporations produce annual sustainability reports, including 86% of the largest U.S. companies (KPMG, 2011). With these growing trends and increasing regulations, the number of voluntary sustainability reports estimated around 2,500 companies will rise to nearly 7,000 by 2017 (http://www.sustainablebusiness.com/). Currently, there are more than 142 regulations in more than 30 countries that expect some level of organizational sustainability reporting either as a government or stock exchange requirement (GRI & KPMG, 2009). In addition, the approximately US$3.74 trillion in assets managed various SRI portfolios makes a compelling reason to file sustainability reports (James, Lisa, & Kenneth, 2014; Landier & Nair, 2009).

These are perhaps alternative interpretations or "motivations" behind sustainability reporting and corporate social responsibility. However, they are also part of a transformational trend to mainstream sustainability and to create internationally recognized standards in the governance and regulation of sustainability practices (Subhabrata, 2014). They are also a reflection of an evolution of the understanding and practices of CSR going from "defensive" and "charitable" perspectives to more engaged, transformative and systemic CSR practices (Visser, 2014).

THE PURPOSE AND PRINCIPLES IN SUSTAINABILITY REPORTING

Sustainability reporting is more than compiling categorized data on nonfinancial practices. The GRI and other ESG reporting are methods to internalize, streamline, and improve an organization's commitment to sustainability, social responsibility, human rights and multistakeholder engagement. In general, all types of sustainability reporting have the purpose of engaging organizations in "thinking beyond the bottom line" and for a more integrated approach to socially responsible management and sustainability leadership (Jones & Ratnatunga, 2012; Makower, 1994).

There are many reporting frameworks distinguishing themselves by the different core subjects and relevance for specific industries. Table 13.1 summarizes some of the main sustainability reporting starting from the most popular one, Global Reporting Initiative (GRI). Obviously the multiplicity of reporting should seek more harmonization avoiding fragmentation, industry isolation and monosectorial approaches.

Table 13.1.   Main Sustainability Reporting Frameworks

Sustainability Reporting Framework	Targeted Industries (Core Subjects)
Global Reporting Initiative (GRI) Sustainability Reporting Guidelines www.globalreporting.org	All public and private organizations (*Organizational governance, Human rights, Labor practices, The environment, Fair operating practices, Consumer issues, Community involvement and development*)
United Nations Global Compact (UNGC) Ten Principles www.unglobalcompact.org	Any company, business association, labor or civil society, government organization, NGO or academic institution. (*Labor practices, The environment, Consumer issues, Community involvement and development*)
OECD: Risk Awareness Tool for Multinational Enterprises in Weak Governance Zones www.oecd.org	Multinational enterprises, professional associations, trade unions, civil society organizations and international financial institutions. (*Organizational governance, Human rights, Labor practices, Fair operating practices, Community involvement and development*)
International Organization for Standardization ISO 26000 www.iso.org/iso	All types of organizations. (*Organizational governance, Human rights, Labor practices, The environment, Fair operating practices, Consumer issues, Community involvement and development*)
AccountAbility: The AA1000 Series of Standards www.accountability.org	Financial services, pharmaceuticals, energy and extractives, telecommunications, consumer goods, and food & beverages. (*Organizational governance, Human rights, Labor practices, The environment, Fair operating practices, Consumer issues, Community involvement and development*)
Carbon Disclosure Project (CDP) tool and framework www.cdproject.net	Firms from all types of industries report to CDP. (*The environment*)
International Integrated Reporting Council (IIRC) International Framework http://www.theiirc.org	All types of organizations. (*Organizational governance, Human rights, Labor practices, The environment, Fair operating practices, Consumer issues, Community involvement and development*)

(Table continues on next page)

Table 13.1.   (Continued)

Sustainability Reporting Framework	Targeted Industries (Core Subjects)
Sustainability Accounting Standards Board (SASB) www.sasb.org	89 industries in ten sectors: health care, financials, technology and communications, nonrenewables, transportation, services, resource transformation, consumption, renewables and alternative energy, and infrastructure. *(Organizational governance, Human rights, Labor practices, The environment, Fair operating practices, Consumer issues, Community involvement and development)*
WBCSD and World Resources Institute (WRI) The Greenhouse Gas (GHG) Protocol www.ghgprotocol.org	All types of organizations across industries. *(The environment)*

The complementarity of sustainability reporting frameworks is important for promoting sustainability practices and advancing our understanding of sustainable values. For example, the ISO 26000, although not precise in the prescription of the sustainable reporting as in the case of GRI-G4, it provides a precise structure for companies to organize their activities. In this regard, the ISO framework is instrumental for promoting internal quality development for not only responding to stakeholder concerns but to other relevant and significant issues to the organization.

Another important, but less well-known framework, is provided by the Earth Charter Initiative (http://www.earthcharterinaction.org/). An inspiring and visionary set of widely endorsed values and principles, the Earth Charter is a "declaration of fundamental ethical principles for building a just, sustainable and peaceful global society in the 21st century" (Bosselmann & Engel, 2010; Corcoran & Earth Charter International Secretariat, 2005). The Earth Charter, the United Nations Global Compact and the GRI share a common root in the 1987 Brundtland Commission report Our Common Future (World Commission on Environment and Development [WCED], 1987) and the document emerged from the 1992 United Nations Conference on Environment and Development (UNCED, 1993). Not surprisingly, all these three frameworks share five characteristics: sustainability-oriented, norms-based, globally relevant, partnership-based, and voluntary.

THE LIMITS OF SUSTAINABILITY REPORTING

Sustainability reporting is not without its critics. The term itself has been subjected to critique as some say "sustainability reporting" is not truly representative of the 'true' development-oriented conception of sustainability" (O'Dwyer & Owen, 2005, p. 207). The reasoning behind this goes back to the dispute about what sustainability really means and how it is defined. O'Dwyer and Owen (2005) argue that sustainability reports are too centered on the organization and its operations without giving proper concern to its economic activity relative to resource use.

Others argue that sustainability reporting is too "managerial," in that an organization's management personnel can have too much control over the production of its report and what information is disseminated; only providing information that can positively enhance the organization's image. This sacrifices the accountability of the organization and the transparency that is supposed to be present for its stakeholders. This type of managerial dominance can contribute to the further degradation of resources or sidelining of stakeholder groups who the report is supposed to serve. Related to this is the critique that reports can be incomplete, inaccurate or conducted improperly (O'Dwyer & Owen, 2005).

In order to mitigate these concerns, "assurance statements" are often included with "sustainability reports." The purpose of assurance statements is to provide verification from a third party to guarantee the accuracy, credibility, and completeness of the report to its stakeholders. They are often conducted by engineering, accountancy, or sustainability services firms (GRI-G4, 2013). Assurance is a good step towards increased transparency. However, as Adams and Evans (2004) have argued, it too can sideline stakeholders as it often lacks stakeholder involvement and it can be restricted to managerial scope. Additionally, assurors themselves can be indolent in verifying whether the report is complete which leads to the question of assurors' competence (as cited in O'Dwyer & Owen, 2005). All of these critiques are motivated by the concern that assurance practices are not doing what they are meant to do; to "enlighten, inform, and enable criticism and substantive change" (Power, 1997, p. 124, as cited in O'Dwyer & Owen, 2005). Rather, it further covers up the transparency which the sustainability reports are supposed to show; inhibiting further inquiry and serving as just a label to be uncontested (O'Dwyer & Owen, 2005).

THE ETHICAL EVOLUTION OF SUSTAINABILITY REPORTING

Sustainability reports represent a concrete step in the promotion, measurement and evolution in ethical performance. In spite of the diversity of frameworks, the limited harmonization, and the lack of universally accepted definitions, sustainability reporting shares the theme of "wholeness." For example, the World Business Council for Sustainable Development defines sustainability reporting as "public reports by companies to provide internal and external stakeholders with the picture of the corporate position and activities on economic, environmental, and social dimensions" (as cited in Roca & Searcy, 2012, p.105). Daub (2007) states

> a report can be considered a sustainability report in the strictest sense of the term if it is public … [and contains] qualitative and quantitative information on the extent to which the company as managed to improve its economic, environmental, and social effectiveness and efficiency in the reporting period and integrate these aspects in a sustainability management system. (p. 76)

Sustainability reporting, in the sense of the aforementioned definitions, can be seen as a successor of previous types of reports: annual reports, environmental, and social reports.

Environmental reports became popular among multinational companies toward the end of the 1980s. By 1998, of 250 Fortune Global 500 companies, 35% were publishing environmental reports and 32% were including the topic in their annual reports (Daub, 2007). Social reports, in which companies disclose the social components of their operations, are far less frequent and can be seen as being incorporated into company's environmental reports during the 1970s when there was a call for greater "social accounting." Social reports often come in the form of health and safety reports and signify a move towards sustainability reporting (Daub, 2007).

The purpose of sustainability reporting is so that an organization is aware of its performance from a sustainable development perspective. 'Sustainable development' started to earn its status as a buzzword in the international development field with the 1987 publication of *Our Common Future* (also known as the Brundtland Report) which defined it as "development that meets the needs of the present without compromising the ability of future generations to meet their own needs" (WCED, 1987). The emphasis on "sustainable development" integrates economic with social and environmental concerns. It should also dissipate narrow interpretations of environmental and social concerns. WCED member, Sonny Ramphal, reflects this view, stating that "environmentalists are 'more concerned about panda bears than human beings, and more concerned about increasing the number of bicycles in the Third World rather than that we should acquire trucks" (as cited in Langhelle, 1999, p. 131). This perception greatly contributed to the WCED's development and human-centered values.

Centindamar and Husoy (2007) have studied the motives that push organizations toward providing a voluntary sustainability reporting. They found that the "ethical" and "economic" motives often overlap. In their study researching why organizations participate in the UNGC they recognized this overlapping of economic and ethical values in the respondent's top four reasons. First: To be part of sustainable development efforts (ethical);

Second: To improve corporate image (economic); Third: To distinguish your firm (economic); and Fourth: To be a good citizen (ethical).

Hartman and Painter-Morland (2007) notice an ethical progress in GRI's changing of the terms it uses in its guidelines. An example is the incorporation of "ethics and integrity" that provides guidelines in what the best practices in ethics and compliance (GRI-G4, 2013). This section was previously absent, and reference to codes was only included in the "Governance, Commitments, and Engagement" section of the previous editions. Identifying basic ethics management is important to include in a sustainability report because it informs stakeholders of the organization's culture, and how their ESG initiatives are aligned with their internal ethics and principles. Overall, GRI and, sustainability reporting in general, is contributory to corporate and organizational culture, specifically its purpose and how it determines its success. These sustainability initiatives are making ESG principles and meaningful stakeholder engagement the norm in organizational operations.

THE GLOBAL REPORTING INITIATIVE (GRI)

Among the various frameworks for voluntary sustainability reporting, the guidelines provided by the Global Reporting Initiative (GRI) are favorably recognized standards. GRI's guidelines were created to enhance and complement pre-existing standards and codes such as the Global Sullivan Principles, Social Accountability 8000, United Nations Global Compact, OECD Guidelines for Multinational Enterprises, International Labor Organizations Conventions, AA1000 Assurance Standard, and the International Organization for Standardization 14000 Series.

In 2002, the GRI became an independent nongovernmental organization (NGO) with a global secretariat based in Amsterdam. GRI has the primary mission to promote a coherent and complex multistakeholder process for nonfinancial reporting. The multistakeholder GRI Network represents businesses, civil society organizations, labor and sector associations, and academics along with governmental and intergovernmental organizations. GRI produces a comprehensive Sustainability Reporting Framework (Framework) that includes the Sustainability Reporting Guidelines (Guidelines) regularly updated and enhanced. The Guidelines, currently in their G4 version, spell out a set of principles and standards for the organizational disclosures. These are widely used by numerous organizations around the world, voluntarily submitting their economic, environmental, and social performance and impacts. In addition to the general guidelines and the sector specific guidance, GRI provides a platform for international and multistakeholder accountability. This is based on the "due process" value with expert consultations and public comments period to guarantee that the framework is "consensus-based and reflects

the broadest possible stakeholder input" (http://www.globalreporting.org).
Beside the specific indicators included in the Guidelines, the GRI provides
a firm commitment for sustainability reporting based on transparency,
inclusiveness, auditability, clarity, completeness, comparability, relevance,
context, accuracy, and neutrality.

In general, the economic factors usually accounted in the sustainability
report may vary but in general relate to accountability / transparency, corporate governance, stakeholder value, economic performance, and financial
performance. The environmental factors may include energy, water, greenhouse gases, emissions, hazardous and non hazardous waste, recycling, and
packaging. The social factors may include the organizational performance
in community investment, working conditions, human rights and fair trade,
public policy, diversity, safety, and anticorruption. Figure 13.3 illustrates
the GRI-G4 measured components for economic, environmental, social
and its subcomponents for labor, human rights, community and products.

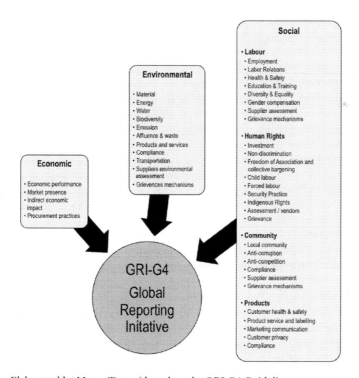

Source: Elaborated by Marco Tavanti based on the GRI-G4 Guidelines.

Figure 13.3.   Main components in the global reporting initiative—Guidelines 4
(GRI-G4).

The GRI's G4 is a successor of the G3 guidelines and 2002 Guide-lines. There have been instrumental changes between each that reflect the international community's commitment to sustainable development and stakeholder engagement. With each edition of the GRI Guidelines comes improvement on how organizations are to report their triple bottom line. These changes in the guidelines allow organizations to be more reflec-tive in what it needs to do to become more sustainable, and it provides a clearer picture for its stakeholders; allowing them to make better judgments regarding the quality of the information the organizations disseminate and their overall operations (Hartman & Painter-Morland, 2007).

The mainstreaming of sustainability reporting requires improvement and standardization of reporting frameworks. Most importantly, it requires general consensus on the principles guiding the reports and communication process for guaranteeing community transparency through multistake-holder accountability. The sustainability reporting is and should be seen as an organizational disclosure following the general standards associated ethics, integrity, corporate social responsibility, integrated reporting, stake-holder engagement, and good governance. Therefore, the sustainability reporting, in its historical and ongoing evolution, should be considered inclusive of other nonfinancial reporting including the environmental reporting, triple bottom line reporting, global citizenship reporting, and corporate social responsibility (CSR) reporting among others.

In line with the principles of "transparency," "traceability," and "com-pliance" the sustainability reporting system provided under the GRI-G4 guidelines attempts to avoid "green-washing," and promote 'accountability' (Baldarelli & Del, 2013). The upgraded guidelines for the compilation of the reports exemplified in the GRI-G4 clearly reflect these principles. Specifically, the GRI-G4 is based on important values and principles to evaluate the content and quality of the report. These include stakeholder inclusiveness, sustainability context, materiality and completeness. The "stakeholder inclusiveness" principle implies that "the organization should identify its stakeholders, and explain how it has responded to their reason-able expectations and interests" (Cohen, 2013). The sustainability context principle implies that "the report should present the organization's perfor-mance in the wider context of sustainability." The "materiality" principle implies that "the report should cover aspects that reflect the organization's significant economic, environmental and social impacts or substantively influence the assessments and decisions of stakeholders." The 'complete-ness' principle implies that "the report should include coverage of material aspects and their boundaries, sufficient to reflect significant economic, environmental and social impacts, and to enable stakeholders to assess the organization's performance in the reporting period (GRI-G4, 2013).

ENVIRONMENTAL, SOCIAL AND
GOVERNANCE (ESG) INTEGRATION

Sustainability reporting is primarily a nonfinancial set of measures at the environmental and social level. However, the integration of factors in relation to governance and financial performance remain key factors for the mainstreaming process of sustainability reporting. These dynamics are recognizable in the expansion of environmental, social and governance (ESG) performances in relation to socially responsible investing (SRI) (Hebb, 2012; Krosinsky & Robins, 2008). They are also visible in the trends toward integrated reporting for multiple bottom lines of economic, governance, social, ethical, and environmental (EGSEE) performance (Brockett & Rezaee, 2012).

Sustainability reporting is an essential part of integrating reporting combining financial and nonfinancial performance. Sustainability itself is an integrated concept aiming to assist organizations in setting goals and priorities, which combine long-term profitability with social and environmental responsibility. In an extended understanding of "sustainability" elements, the sustainability reporting provides a communication platform on the organization's economic, environmental, social, and governance performance—clearly reflecting positive and negative impacts. Integrated reporting also represents an important trend incorporating financial with nonfinancial impacts and the establishment of truly integrated bottom line reporting (Laszlo, 2003, 2010,).

ESG, in spite of its generic meaning, has become popular among market investors to evaluate corporate overall performance and financial future. Similar to other sustainability reporting, ESG reporting includes nofinancial performance indicators relative to sustainability, ethics, and corporate governance identifiable in specific issues such as the company's accountability systems and the management of its carbon footprint. The European Federation of Financial Analysts Societies (EFFAS) has defined a set of key performance indicators (KPIs) for reporting of ESG factors across sectors. These include energy efficiency, greenhouse gas (GHG) emissions, staff turnover, training & qualification, maturity of workforce, absenteeism rate, litigation risks, corruption, and revenues from new products (effas.net). The UN-backed Principles for Responsible Investment (UNPRI) provides a voluntary ESG framework for reporting. The six principles of PRI require the incorporation, promotion, and disclosure of ESG performance (http://www.unpri.org/).

A definitive list of ESG principles does not exist, however a report by the United Nations Environmental Program (UNEP) Finance Initiative determined that ESG issues consistently exhibit these characteristics: nonfinancial, nonmaterial; long-term horizon; qualitative objects that are readily quantifiable in monetary terms; externalities not adequately captured by market mechanisms; a changing regulatory or policy framework; patterns arising throughout a company's supply chain which allows them to be more susceptible to unknown risks; of concern to the public (WBCSD & UNEP FI, 2010).

ESG is often used interchangeably with the term socially responsible investing (SRI). Company investors recognize the value of predicting the financial future performance of an organization based on its financial and nonfinancial parameters. ESG, SRI, and their outcomes ethical investing, sustainable investing, and green investing, are all labels given to the practice of organizations creating sustainable value and the shareholders' acknowledgement of impact investing. This framework is not entirely new, the year 2007 saw major advance in ESG/SRI practices. In that year Belgium became the first country to pass a law prohibiting the investment in manufacturers of cluster munitions, a type of explosive weapon that releases smaller weapons called "submunitions" which are used in war but pose a great harm to civilians who become the unintended victims. In the same year the United States passed The Sudan Accountability and Divestment Act which permits state and local governments to cut ties with any companies doing business in Sudan. The purpose of this law was to put financial pressure on the Sudanese government to stop the genocide in Darfur. These types of proactive regulations were established at the macrolevel, by federal governments. Additional focus on ESG principles came about after the 2008 financial crisis. This global crisis resulted in higher demand for organizational transparency, particularly at the corporate level. Greater investment monitoring is now the trend in the business world, and investors are placing importance on inspecting investments for socially responsible issues (Stewart, Berard, & Fruscella, 2013).

Table 13.2 illustrates the complementarity and continuity of ESG principles laid out by the United Nations Global Compact (UNGC), the Organization for Economic Cooperation and Development (OECD), and the Global Reporting Initiative (GRI). These three frameworks provide guidelines and/or benchmarks for organizations wishing to act responsibly and provide transparency in order to promote the standards and principles for responsible organizational behavior, including social and human rights and economic and environmental issues. The environmental component of ESG is intended in reference to an organization's impacts on living and nonliving natural systems, including ecosystems, land, air, and water. The Social component is ESG is in relation to an organization's impact on the social systems in which it operates. The Governance component of ESG is in reference to an organization's transparency of its structure and composition to ensure the accountability of the relevant bodies and individuals.

Table 13.2.   Environmental, Social, and Governance Frameworks

	Environmental	*Social*	*Governance*
UNGC	*Businesses should* Support a precautionary approach to environment challenges. Undertake initiatives to promote greater environmental responsibility. Encourage the development and diffusion of environmentally friendly technologies.	*Businesses should* Support and respect the protection of internationally proclaimed human rights. Make sure they are not complicit in human rights abuses.	*Businesses should* work against corruption in all its forms, including extortion and bribery.
OECD	*Enterprises should* take due account of the need to protect the environment, public health and safety, generally to conduct their activities in a manner contributing to the wider goal of sustainable development.	*Enterprises should* Avoid infringing on the human rights of others and should address adverse human rights impacts with which they are involved. Have a policy commitment to respect human rights. Promote consultation and cooperation between employers and workers on matter of mutual concern. Observe favorable standards of employment.	*Enterprises should* Protect and facilitate the rights of stakeholders. Ensure the equitable treatment of all stakeholders. Ensure that timely and accurate disclosure is made on all material matters regarding the corporation, including the financial situation, performance, ownership, and governance of the company.

(Table continues on next page)

Table 13.2.   (Continued)

	Environmental	Social	Governance
G4	*Concerns the organization's* Inputs (i.e. energy, water) Outputs (i.e. emissions, effluents, waste) Biodiversity Transport Product/service related impacts Environmental compliance Expenditures	*Concerns the organization's* Labor/Management Relations | Occupational Health and Safety | Training and Education | Diversity and Equal Opportunity | Freedom of association | Collective bargaining | Child labor | Forced or compulsory labor | Security Practices | Supplier Assessment for Labor | Practices and Human Rights | Human Rights Grievance Mechanisms	*Concerns the organization's* highest governance body (HGB) and how it is established and structured in support of the organization's purpose, and economic, environmental and social (EES) dimensions. HGB's willingness and capability to understand, discuss, and effectively respond to EES impacts; and show if a process is in place, conducted internally or externally, to ensure continuing effectiveness HGB's involvement in developing and approving the organization's sustainability disclosures, and the degree by which it may be aligned with processes around financial reporting.

The ESG framework is helpful in the conversation of sustainability reporting values as it emphasizes the importance of governance. This is relevant for better integrating sustainability nonfinancial reports with leadership priorities and administration of the organization. It is also helpful for understanding the shared responsibility that corporations have in global governance, especially in postconflict, anticorruption, international development, and human rights (Davis, 2013; Ruggie, 2013; Wettstein, 2009; Wolf, Flohr, Rieth, & Schwindenhammer, 2010).

In addition to the governance aspect, ESG is also a valuable framework because its more recognized financial values in SRI. This "preexisting" value integration across financial and nonfinancial measures represents an opportunity for future integration on organizational reporting and business ethics performance (Carter, 2007).

SUSTAINABILITY REPORTING FOR PARTNERSHIPS AND LEADERSHIP

Our analysis of sustainability reporting and the values connected to ESG cannot be sufficiently discussed without properly acknowledging the importance of leadership in the implementation of those practices. Good ESG practices begin with a good leader who takes on the accountability of the organization, and his or her role as a global citizen whose actions have a ripple effect on society. Difficulties may arise when a leader attempts to incorporate the assortment of interests from stakeholders into the organization's long-term goals, especially while operating in an atmosphere that is ambiguous and evolving. D'Amato, Henderson, and Florence (2009) argue that leaders concerned with ESG principles are those that consider the needs, values, interests, and demands of all stakeholders including, but not limited to, employees, customers, suppliers, communities, shareholders, NGOs, the environment, and society at large. Sometimes it can be difficult for leaders to comprehend their role in the relationship between their organization and their range of stakeholders. Multiple perspectives can be used to manage how an organization can interact with its stakeholder as a means for organizational change long-term sustainable development. ESG reporting is a mechanism to further this goal as it is a means of communication and provides stakeholders with information that is currently being developed or has already been incorporated into the organization's operations. Often times, organizations will include stakeholders in all decision making processes, rendering them as not just stakeholders, but also as actors in sustainable development. Leaders who view their organization with the long-term horizon recognize the necessity of communicating with their stakeholders in the development of their ESG principles and actions. ESG performance relies on the leadership to fulfill these essential actions (D'Amato et al., 2009).

An organization that truly embodies sustainability values and practices requires "positive deviant" sustainability leaders (Parkin, 2010). Incorporation of ESG principle in an organization requires a leader who possesses a genuine sense of purpose, core values, and integrity that guides their actions toward sustainable development. Often, culture and political ideals can be the source of conflict when organizations implement an ESG framework. Leaders should be able to foster a culture that is educated, environmentally sound, socially inclusive, and economically sustainable;

these are the traits of an effective organization and leader in the current global society. Transparency and accountability is the manifestation of an organization that wishes to have a prolonged and effective association with its stakeholders. With sustainability quickly becoming the central focus of many organizations and companies across sectors, ESG performance expectations are subjected to more scrutiny and held to higher standards (D'Amato et al., 2009).

Organizations should be able to identify their role in the global society and as an actor of sustainable development. This is necessary as the roles and responsibilities of the public sector, private sector, and third/nonprofit sector have been merging and blurring the lines of what used to be clear boundaries. ESG practices require leaders, regardless of the sector, to assess the needs of their immediate stakeholders as well as national and international regulators, watchdogs, and activist groups (D'Amato et al., 2009).

As stated previously, sustainability and ESG reporting enhances an organization's ethics not just in principles but also in practices. This has been instrumental in the promotion of public-private partnerships (PPPs) and multistakeholder partnerships (MSPs) formed in the name of sustainable development. ESG reporting itself developed from environmental reporting. Companies responded to environmental groups about how their organizations impacted the ecological environment. This later developed into a standard practice promoted by international agencies and supported by governments and acts as a linkage between sectors engaging in sustainable activities. ESG initiatives bring together public and private actors to connect in forming a progressively positive and constructive *partnership*. The emphasis on partnership is important; it is the antithesis of the regulatory command-and-control that was once a feature of public-private engagement. PPPs encourage more involvement and contribution to sustainable development. The UNGC, OECD, and GRI exemplify partnerships, as they are voluntary initiatives that bring together multiple stakeholders across sectors to collectively construct solutions to ESG issues (Cetindamar & Husoy, 2007).

Collaborations between the public and private sectors brings together government with companies which have a role in the greater environment and social spheres and can possess the financial and technical capital needed to address sustainability issues. Partnerships between the government and third sector can materialize into joint training and educational initiatives and in a joint effort in the provision of services. Collaborations involving the private and third sector bring financial capital to environmental and social campaigns. These partnerships also make private entities, such as corporations, aware of the concerns of the greater public while creating a change in their operations to have less or no negative environmental or social impacts. However, it is imperative to remember that partnerships require time to yield the desired results. When using a multistakeholder approach there is a diversity of expectations coming from various actors. Consequently, substantial time is needed to solve problems arising throughout the relationship, particularly at the beginning (Cetindamar & Husoy, 2007).

CONCLUSION

This chapter has shown the growing importance and values of sustainability reporting for ESG practices, sustainable development and value leadership. In general, the analysis of GRI reaffirms the importance of integration across economic, environmental, social and governance elements and across financial and nonfinancial reporting. We also suggested that the integrated values of sustainability reporting go beyond the various frameworks and guidelines for reporting. The integration is really at the core of sustainability in general and sustainable development in particular.

As the number of companies and other organizations continue to increase their voluntary sustainability and ESG reporting, the need for integration, harmonization, accountability and transparency will become urgent and necessary. The multistakeholder network formula adopted by the GRI in its mandate for progressing the reporting systems will become the only solution for promoting true integrated sustainability practices across sectors and throughout the globe.

Within these trends in sustainability reporting and integrated ESG performances, it has become apparent that sustainable value creation and corporate sustainability performance are the basis of the world's sustainable future. The engagement and solutions offered by those organizations committed to contributing to our sustainable future come with important global sustainable responsibilities. Studies of integrated measurement models and standards for integrated economic, social, environmental, and governance performance are becoming a dominant feature in the literature and these measurement standards are becoming normative in organizational reporting. Indeed, standardized and integrated reporting has become an important factor for cultural change and organizational progression to sustainability values. Despite this, we continue to lack an understanding and sharing of effective practices that can be shared across sectors, fields, and comparable institutions.

Sustainability reporting has become a tool for increasing sustainable value performance beyond superficial solutions associated with "greenwashing" or "blue-washing" (in reference to corporate associations with the United Nation's mission). Treating sustainability activities as a simple checklist of performances may not be sufficient to move market-purposed actions into a value-centered, globally engaged, and socially responsible strategic plan.

The United Nations Global Compact (UNGC), the Organization for Economic Cooperation and Development (OECD), the Global Reporting Initiative (GRI), and other major frameworks for sustainability reporting, have become the world's most prevalent organizations for sustainable practice accountability. Their principles and platforms for reporting aim to promote and provide standards for the sustainable value performance of corporate businesses, public agencies, smaller enterprises, nongovernmental organizations, industry groups, and other organizations. Reporting these standards has become a routine activity in organizations, in addition to their financial and programming reporting. These trends are not reversible and the next few years will be crucial for developing both empirical studies and systemic studies for the promotion of integrated, competent and adequate model for sustainability reporting.

Engaged academia and civil society organizations have the responsibility to collaborative work with private organizations and public institutions for the developing due processes and appropriate mechanism for sustainable value across sectors and in an ever more complex global environment. Internationally agreed disclosures and metrics in sustainability reports need to be communicated clearly and with concrete examples in order to inform an organization's stakeholders. They also need to be developed and monitored through a publicly disclosed process where multiple stakeholders have voice and authority for a shared global social responsibility. The GRI, in its current G4 guidelines, is already a very good framework. However, as the complexity of regulations, diversity of sector-specific reporting, formulas for multisector partnerships (MSPs) will surely increase, the monitoring and reformulation or guidelines in sustainability reporting will also need to evolve. These trends represent a challenge but also an opportunity for multistakeholder governance, global citizenship engagement, global social responsibility.

REFERENCES

Adams, C. A., & Evans, R. (2004) Accountability, completeness, credibility and the audit expectations gap. *Journal of Corporate Citizenship, 14* (Summer), 97–115.

Avlonas, N., & Nassos, G. P. (2014). *Practical sustainability strategies: How to gain a competitive advantage.* New York, NY: Wiley.

Bosselmann, K., & Engel, J. R. (2010). *The Earth Charter: A framework for global governance.* Amsterdam, The Netherlands: KIT.

Brockett, A., & Rezaee, Z. (2012). *Corporate sustainability: Integrating performance and reporting.* Hoboken, NJ: Wiley.

Carter, C. (2007). *Business ethics as practice: Representation, reflexivity and performance*. Cheltenham, England: Edward Elgar.

Cetindamar, D., & Husoy K. (2007). Corporate social responsilbility practices and environmentally responsible behavior: The case of The United Nations Global Compact. *Journal of Business Ethics*, 76(2), 163–176.

Cohen, E. (2013). *Understanding G4: The concise guide to next generation sustainability reporting*. London, England: Sedition.

Corcoran, P. B., & Earth Charter International Secretariat. (2005). *The earth charter in action: Toward a sustainable world*. Amsterdam, The Netherlands: KIT.

D'Amato, A., Henderson, S., & Florence S. (2009). *Corporate social responsibility and sustainable business: A guide to leadership tasks and functions*. Greensboro, NC: CCL Press.

Daub, C. H. (2007). Assessing the quality of sustainability reporting: an alternative methodological approach. *Journal of Cleaner Production*, 15(1), 75–85.

Davis, P. (2013). *Corporations, global governance, and post-conflict reconstruction*. London, England: Routledge.

EY & Boston College Center for Corporate Citizenship. (2013). Value of sustainability reporting. Retrieved from http://www.ey.com/Publication/vwLUAssets/ EY_-_Value_of_sustainability_reporting/$FILE/EY-Value-of-Sustainability-Reporting.pdf

GRI-G4 (2013). *G4 sustainability reporting guidelines: Reporting principles and standards disclosure*. Retrieved fromhttps://www.globalreporting.org/resourcelibrary/ GRIG4-Part1-Reporting-Principles-and-Standard-Disclosures.pdf

GRI, U., & KPMG, U. (2009). *Carrots and sticks—Promoting transparency and sustainability: An update on trends in mandatory and voluntary sustainability reporting*. Nairobi: Global Reporting Initiative, United Nations Environment Programme, KPMG, Unit for Corporate Governance in Africa.

Hartman, L. P., & Painter-Morland, M. (2007). Exploring the Global Reporting Initiative (GRI) guidelines as a model for triple bottom-line reporting. *African Journal of Business Ethics*, 2(1), 45–57.

Hebb, T. (2012). *The next generation of responsible investing*. Dordrecht, The Netherlands: Springer.

Horrigan, B. (2010). *Corporate social responsibility in the 21st century: Debates, models and practices across government, law and business*. Cheltenham, England: Edward Elgar.

Jones, S., & Ratnatunga, J. (2012). *Contemporary issues in sustainability accounting, assurance and reporting*. Bingley, England: Emerald Group.

KPMG. (2011). International Corporate Responsibility Reporting Survey 2011. Retrieved from http://www.kpmg.com/global/en/issuesandinsights/articlespublications/corporate-responsibility/pages/2011-survey.aspx

Krosinsky, C., & Robins, N. (2008). *Sustainable investing: The art of long-term performance*. London: Earthscan.

Landier, A., & Nair, V. B. (2009). *Investing for change: Profit from responsible investment*. Oxford, England: Oxford University Press.

Langhelle, O. (1999). Sustainable development: Exploring the ethics of our common future. *International Political Science Review*, 20(2), 129–149.

Laszlo, C. (2003). *The sustainable company: How to create lasting value through social and environmental performance*. Washington, DC: Island Press.

Laszlo, C. (2010). *The business of sustainability*. Great Barrington, MA: Berkshire Publishing Group.

Lawrence, J. T., & Beamish, P. W. (2013). *Globally responsible leadership: Managing according to the UN Global Compact*. Thousand Oaks, CA: SAGE.

Makower, J., & Business for Social Responsibility. (1994). *Beyond the bottom line: Putting social responsibility to work for your business and the world*. New York, NY: Simon and Schuster.

O'Dwyer, B., & Owen, D. (2005). Assurance statement practice in environmental, social and sustainability reporting: a critical evaluation. *The British Accounting Review, 37*(2), 205–229.

Parkin, S. (2010). *The positive deviant: Sustainability leadership in a perverse world*. London, England: Routledge.

Roca, L. C., & Searcy C. (2012). An analysis of indicators disclosed in corporate sustainability reports. *Journal of Cleaner Production*, 103–118.

Ruggie, J. G. (2013). *Just business: Multinational corporations and human rights*. New York, NY: W. W. Norton.

Savitz, A. W., & Weber, K. (2014). *The triple bottom line: How today's best-run companies are achieving economic, social, and environmental success—and how you can too, revised and updated*. San Francisco, CA: Jossey-Bass.

Segerlund, L. (2010). *Making corporate social responsibility a global concern: Norm construction in a globalizing world*. Farnham, Surrey, England: Ashgate.

Stewart, G., Berard, S., & Fruscella. E. (2013). *Trends in environmental, social, and governance investing*. New York, NY: BNY Mellon.

United Nations Conference on Environment and Development, UNCED. (1993). *Agenda 21: Programme of action for sustainable development; Rio Declaration on Environment and Development ; Statement of forest principles*. New York, NY: United Nations.

WBCSD & UNEP FI. (2010). *Translating ESG into sustainable business value*. Retrieved fro http://www.unepfi.org/fileadmin/documents/translatingESG.pdf

Wettstein, F. (2009). *Multinational corporations and global justice: Human rights obligations of a quasi-governmental institution*. Stanford, CA: Stanford Business Books.

Wolf, K. D., Flohr, A., Rieth, L., & Schwindenhammer, S. (2010). *The role of business in global governance: Corporations as norm-entrepreneurs*. Basingstoke, England: Palgrave Macmillan.

World Commission on Environment and Development. (1987). *Our common future*. Oxford, England: Oxford University Press.

Tavanti, M. (2014). Sustainable development capitalism: Changing paradigms and practices for a more viable, equitable, bearable and just economic future for all. In H. H. Kazeroony & Agata Stachowicz-Stanusch (Eds.), *Capitalism and the social relationship: An organizational perspective* (pp. 163–182). New York, NY: Palgrave-MacMillan.

Haynes, K., Murray, A., & Dillard, J. F. (2013). *Corporate social responsibility: A research handbook*. London, England: Routledge.

Freemantle, A. (2008). *The sustainable business handbook: A comprehensive guide to responsible corporate behaviour and sustainable business practices across the triple-bottom-line*. Cape Town, South Africa: Trialogue.

Baldarelli, M.-G., & Del, B. M. (2013, April 1). The implementation of sustainability reporting in SGR Group: Some challenges of transition from "Greenwashing" to relational change. *International Journal of Social Ecology and Sustainable Development (ijsesd), 4*(2), 48–72.

James, W. C., Lisa, C. T., & Kenneth, W. G. (2014, January 1). Market-oriented sustainability: Moderating impact of stakeholder involvement. *Industrial Management & Data Systems, 114*(1), 21–36.

Subhabrata, B. B. (2014). A critical perspective on corporate social responsibility: Towards a global governance framework. *Critical Perspectives on International Business, 10*(1), 84–95.

Visser, W. (2014). *CSR 2.0: Transforming corporate sustainability and responsibility*. Heidelberg, Germany: Springer.

CHAPTER 15

IMPACT INVESTING

An Evolution of CSR or
a New Playground?

Veronica Vecchi, Niccolò Cusumano, and Manuela Brusoni

Impact investing is the new buzzword. The concept, proposed for the first time by the Rockefeller foundation back into 2007/2008, immediately attracted the interest of donors, financial institutions, and governments. Both the G8 and the World Economic Forum launched initiatives on this issue; the United Kingdom and the United States governments and the European Union (EU) have allocated resources to develop the nascent industry.

However, until now, impact investing lacks a clear definition and it is often mixed up with other related concepts: socially responsible investing, social investing, sustainable and responsible investing, blended value, values-based investing, triple-bottom line, mission-related/mission-driven investing, ethical investing, program related investing (Robeco, 2009).

Should we consider impact investing "just" a corporate social responsibility (CSR) practice undertaken by financial institutions, in order to polish their brand tarnished by the collapse of Lehman Brothers and junk bonds? Could it be regarded as a new financial product to be offered to

Corporate Social Performance:
Paradoxes, Pitfalls, and Pathways to the Better World, pp. 325–344
Copyright © 2015 by Information Age Publishing
325

environmental and social conscious investors—mainly institutional and high net worth individuals—frustrated by traditional approaches or to social enterprises, with very constrained access to capital (Bugg-Levine & Goldstein, 2009)? Are we instead dealing with a radically new paradigm that will provide not only a new investment approach or evaluation metrics, but also a new framework that recasts the relation between business, society and government in what has been called "the fourth sector" (Sabeti, 2009)?

The aim of this chapter is to shed light on the blurred concept of impact investing, trying to understand its background and evolution. As we discuss later in the "Doing Good Doing Well ..." section, its roots could be found in the CSR, stakeholder, and social enterprise theory and practice. We need to frame its peculiarities to understand the boundaries and the synergies with corporate strategies and with the CSR itself as well.

So far impact investing has been mainly perceived as a new investment approach, a way to attract and channel more resources into social ventures. However, in our opinion it might represent a way to reconsider the view of business as opposed to society and government. Indeed, this perspective has not been deeply analyzed and debated as yet. This chapter will attempt to do it!

Starting from an analysis of definitions of impact investing, the chapter traces back to the reason why it has emerged and looks at the relation with CSR and social enterprise theories. In the conclusions we discuss the real innovativeness of impact investing as a way to overcome a traditional approach to CSR and to stimulate businesses and investors to generate those innovations necessary to change the way in which they operate.

LOOKING FOR A COMMON DEFINITION

Back in 2007 the term "impact investing" was coined at Rockefeller Bellagio Center on the banks of Como lake in Italy (Rodin & Brandenburg, 2014). The goal of the American foundation was to build "a worldwide industry for investing for social and environmental impact" (Rockefeller Foundation, 2012). The idea is that social ventures lack a sufficient access to capital therefore not reaching the scale required to mitigate social and environmental challenges they are facing.

In 2009 the Monitor Institute, established by professor Michael Porter, provided the first definition of impact investing. Since then the term has attracted the interest of several other institutions and has in part evolved as shown in Table 15.1. Alongside Rockefeller Foundation, financial institutions, like J. P. Morgan and Credit Suisse have been the main promoters. In 2008, in the wake of the financial crisis, these organizations launched the Global Impact Investing Network, which in 2014 groups 199 members.[1]

Table 15.1.   Impact Investing Definitions

Author	Institution	Definition
Freireich & Fulton (2009)	The Monitor Institute with support of Rockefeller Foundation	*Actively placing capital in businesses and funds that generate social and/or environmental good and at least return nominal principal to the investor;*
Donohoe & Bugg-levine (2010)	J. P. Morgan	*Investments intended to create positive impact beyond financial return*
The Parthenon Group (2010)	Report commissioned by Bridges Venture & GIIN	*Actively placing capital in businesses and funds that generate social and/or environmental good and a range of returns, from principal to above market, to the investor*
Grabenwarter & Liechtenstein (2011)	IESE University	*Any profit-seeking investment activity that intentionally generates measurable benefits for society*
Brown & Swersky, (2012)	Boston Consulting Group for Big Society Capital	*The provision of finance to organisations with the explicit expectation of a social, as well as financial, return*
Credit Suisse (2012)	Credit Suisse	*Investments made with the primary intention of creating a measurable social impact, with the potential for some financial upside. The investment may face some risk of financial downside, but no deliberate aim of consuming capital as with a charitable donation*
Brest & Born (2013)	Stanford University and Hewlett Foundation	*Actively placing capital in enterprises that generate social or environmental goods, services, or ancillary benefits such as creating good jobs, with expected financial returns ranging from the highly concessionary to above market*
World Economic Forum (2013)	World Economic Forum	*An investment approach that intentionally seeks to create both financial return and positive social or environmental impact that is actively measured*
The Global Impact Investing Network (GIIN)	GIIN	*Investments made into companies, organizations, and funds with the intention to generate social and environmental impact alongside a financial return*
Rodin & Brandenburg, (2014)	Rockefeller Foundation	*A middle way between philanthropy and pure financial investment. A means of using capital to drive financial value and social environmental impact simultaneously.*

Discussions and research about impact investing in the professional and academic communities have been deployed mainly around the following issues:

a. **Nature**: the first issue has been to classify impact investing. Frei-reich and Fulton (2009) defined it as an *industry*; later Donohoe and Bugg-levine (2010) as an *asset class*; finally the World Economic Forum (2013) classified impact investing an *investment approach* or "a lens through which investment decisions are made."[2]

b. **Distinguishing features**: the second issue has been to define features that distinguish impact investing from philanthropy, venture philanthropy socially/environmentally responsible investing (SRI) and pure financial approaches. This issue is going to be analyzed in the "Impact Investing ..." section. In a nutshell, the main characteristics of impact investing are (Brest & Born, 2013; Rodin & Brandenburg, 2014):

- *Intentionality of social and/or environmental impacts,* that makes the difference from a pure financial investment;
- *Additionality,* that means the investment must increase the quantity or quality of the social or environmental outcome beyond what would otherwise have occurred in case of a traditional investment;
- *Generation of financial returns, that marks the* difference with a philanthropic approach.

c. **Outcomes**: generating financial returns alongside environmental and social impact raises the question of the existence of a trade-off between social and financial returns and the dichotomy between profit versus not for profit (Grabenwarter & Liechtenstein, 2011). This reflects the longstanding debate around the positive/negative contribution (or contribution at all) of CSR practices on companies performance (Barnett & Salomon, 2012; Carroll & Shabana, 2010; Cochran & Wood, 1984; Mcguire, Sundgren, & Schneeweis, 1988; Schreck, 2011; Soana, 2011; Tang, Hull, & Rothenberg, 2012). According to Koh, Karamchandani, & Katz (2012) and all the other authors cited in Table 15.1, impact investing seems able to attract consistent financial resources to be invested in companies able to generate that combination of value. The basket case is microfinance that from a pure philanthropic activity has become an 8 billion dollar global industry (MicroRate, 2013). Even if we take for granted the generation of financial returns by impact investments, it is still unresolved the issue about how social/environmental impact is defined, measured and correlated to financial performance (Reeder & Colantonio, 2013). However, according to Grabenwarter and Liechtenstein (2011), "a strategic approach to impact investing involves a strategic choice of sector; research-driven investment target selection with an organised deal funnel; strategic choices in asset allocation and portfolio strategy; and deliberate choices in impact and financial returns. The result is a clear definition of the target business models: how to produce social impact and financial return, and the excepted scope and scale per deal."

d. **Market dimension of impact investing**: the last matter of debate is the market dimension of impact investing. Freireich and Fulton (2009) of Monitor Institute estimate a potential demand in 2020 of $500 billion; Donohoe and Bugg-levine (2010) of J. P. Morgan foresee a potential demand at 2020 ranging from $400 billion to $1 trillion. Calvert Foundation (2012) in 2012 report a market potential of $650 billion. The World Economic Forum (2013) scales down these estimates and even though it does not provide a forecast, it points out that a market of $25 billion in 2012 will need to grow by 53% per year in order to reach previous estimates. It is worth noting that these numbers consider the capital that could be potentially invested and not the demand of capital (i.e., eligible projects/enterprises). As discussed in point c) we may wonder if cases like microfinance could be actually replicated. In fact, the authors quoted here have provided only anecdotal evidences so far. The deal flow of suitable investments is certainly an issue in the development of impact investing. As noted by McGoey (2014), Acumen Fund, a nonprofit group that funds market-based solutions to development challenges, analysed 5.000 potential companies over 10 years and it invested in just 65 of them. Brown and Swersky (2012) of Boston Consulting Group estimated that there could be a potential demand from the social sector of £1 billion by 2016, in the U.K. only. Most recent estimates of the market (J.P. Morgan, 2015) put at $60 billions the assets under management at the beginning of 2015 in impact investment funds

Based on the literature and the discussion till here, we can say that impact investing could be a new approach to:

1. Reconsider the way in which investors (i.e., individuals, foundations, investment funds, pension funds, sovereign wealth funds) allocate capital;
2. Generate a social/environmental impact intentionally, which should also be additional, measurable and correlated to the expected return on capital;

3. Generate a financial return intentionally, correlated to the expected impact and the risk embedded.

Impact investing may thus help to build innovative business models that can lead to the development of new enterprises in sectors where the government is retreating or cannot cope with the existent demand; or where traditional nonprofit organizations have not been able to generate a meaningful impact in a sustainable way because of the lack of capacities and resources, which have hampered the scalability of their initiatives.

Impact investing is therefore an approach that magnifies the concept of firm value creation for the primary benefit of shareholders that is enabled by "reverse strategies" or social innovation solutions.

Where to Position Impact Investing

As shown above, impact investing is different from concepts like socially responsible investments (SRI), venture philanthropy and traditional financial investments. In order to illustrate these differences in an effective way, we position the mentioned approaches along an investment continuum, which ideally shows the increasing investor propensity to include a social dimension in the asset allocation.

At one end we find socially neutral investments that aim only at maximizing financial returns. At the opposite we find concessionary investments also known as donations or mission related investments since these investments are motivated only by the mission pursued without considering the financial performance (B. P. Brest & Born, 2013). In between there are the so-called program-related investments that focus on the financial sustainability of the programs financed (such as venture philanthropy): they ask a repayment of the capital invested (the principal), but not a financial return. Whereas, impact investing does not aim only at the payback of the capital invested but also at a financial return.

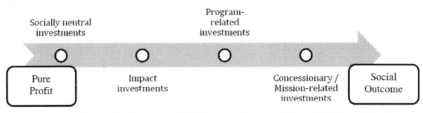

Source: Adapted from the framework laid down by Brest and Born (2013), and Pinsky (2011).

Figure 15.1. The investment continuum.

So, if we define the investment decision as a function of the equation:

$$E(\pi) + E(S) \geq r$$

Where:

$E(\pi)$:	Expected financial return
$E(S)$:	Expected social impact return
r:	Risk adjusted opportunity cost of the capital

B. P. Brest and Born (2013) and Freireich and Fulton (2009) define a pure profit driven and socially neutral investment when:

$$E(S) = 0$$

so that the investment function is:

$$E(\pi) \geq 0$$

In other words, a pure profit driven investment is made only if the return on investment is higher than opportunity cost of the capital.

In case of mission-related/concessionary investments the expected financial return $E(\pi)$ may tend to 0, since the main motivation of the investor is social. Therefore, the equation results as follow:

$$E(S) \geq r$$

It means that the donation occurs only if the expected social return is higher than the opportunity cost of the capital. The donor does not expect to get its money back; it expects its money to generate a social benefit. It considers the investment a failure only if that social benefit, as it has been defined, is not created (Brest & Born, 2013). Actually, in this second situation it would be more appropriate to apply a social (discount) rate (Layard, 1994): however, the debate on the suitable interest rate to be applied is well established in the economic literature and, with reference to philanthropic investments, it is still an open issue in the studies and applications of SROI (social return on investment) (Emerson & Cabaj, 2000).

Impact investments can be placed between the two opposites. Nonetheless, it may be useful also to understand the differences from other forms of hybrid investments such as program related investments,[3] where financial performance is still required but it is subordinated to the social/environmental outcome. In fact Impact Investing considers of the same importance the social outcome and the financial performance of an investment. Moreover Impact investing aims at explicitly correlating the two dimensions, thing that does not occur in the other approaches.

As clearly stated by Grabenwarter and Liechtenstein (2011):

> if one accepts the positive correlation between the impact to be achieved and the financial sustainability of the underlying business model as a prerequisite for impact investing, the trade-off between social impact and financial return can no longer be the decisive factor in investment selection. (p. 61)

IMPACT INVESTING, A SOLUTION TO OLD DILEMMAS?

Among the definitions of impact investing reported in this section, we want to now focus the attention on the one provided by the Rockefeller Foundation (2012), which describes it as a way to build "a worldwide industry for investing for social and environmental impact."

From a theoretical perspective, this goal stems at least from two schools of thought: social enterprise/social innovation and CSR/stakeholder theories.

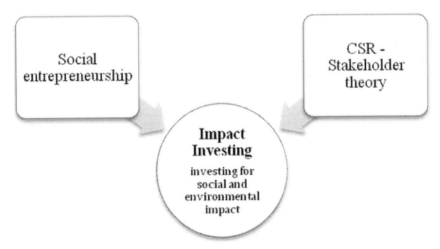

Figure 15.2. The contribution of social entrepreneurship and CSR-stakeholder theories to impact investing.

The left stem—social entrepreneurship—represents both the approach and the target of impact investing. For "approach" we intend the fact that impact investing aims at recombining financial returns and social/environmental impact, as social entrepreneurship does. Moreover social ventures constitute the target of impact investors. The right stem, CSR and stake-holder theories, provides on the one hand the reason why institutional investors (asset managers, pension funds, foundations, corporations) allocate resources into impact investing; on the other hand it gives a theoretical framework to address the multidimensionality of value creation.

Impact Investing, Social Enterprise, and Social Innovation

The combination of financial sustainability and social impact is often merged into social enterprises (Austin, Stevenson, & Wei-Skillern, 2006; Dees, 1998; Peredo & McLean, 2006; Wallace, 1999; Weerawardena & Mort, 2006) or can be made possible through social innovation (Kanter, 1999; Mulgan, Tucker, Ali, & Sanders, 2007). These two elements have become crucial in the last years, in theory and in practice, to address the more and more serious economic and societal challenges.

According to Dees (1998) a social enterprise is mission-related, and wealth creation is just a mean to reach the desired impact. The European Commission (2011) posited that the social enterprise is an operator in the social economy, whose main objective is to have a social impact rather than make a profit for their owners or stakeholders. These definitions do not exclude the possibility of profit generation, as ventures created by social entrepreneurs can certainly generate income, and they can be organized as either not-for-profits or for-profits (Martin & Osberg, 2007). Behind different definitions, the social enterprise's concept captures and describes organizations that adopt managerial models and tools to better answer societal needs. Therefore, it may be useful the suggestion (Nicholls, 2006) to approach social enterprises through the entrepreneurial and management lenses in order to overcome academic or judicial speculations, though it is important to understand the peculiar differences with traditional businesses.

With reference to social innovation, the literature has so far developed several definitions, which have been well analysed by Pol and Ville (2009), who propose a pragmatic definition of social innovation as: "(the) creation of new ideas able to generate a positive impact on the quantity and quality of life," overcoming the assumption that social innovation is generated by social organizations (Mulgan et al., 2007). Indeed, Kanter (1999), looking at the examples of IBM and Marriot Hotels, shows that social innovation is not necessarily generated by social enterprises or through a philanthropic approach; it can be produced instead also by private for profit companies, by looking at new targets that can create the stimulus to innovation.

The opportunity or the urgency to create a social impact has stimulated also the financial side, with the aim to identify the most appropriate financial strategies and instruments to fund social enterprises and scale social innovation. In this sense, impact investing is often perceived as a way to channel resources and fund social enterprises. Therefore, some social financial instruments have been associated to impact investing, such as: social lending; social impact bond; venture philanthropy (as equity investment).

However the capacity to attract capital relies on performance measurement (Leonard, Mcdonald, & Rangan, 2008) and the balance between financial and social return still remains an open dilemma for many.

The view of impact investing as a way to channel recourses into the social enterprise is clearly summarized by the Commission on Unclaimed Assets (The Commission on Unclaimed Asset, 2007), set up by the U.K. government, which led to the establishment of the first public impact investing fund in Britain. The following conclusions have been reached[4]:

- *If the third sector is to continue to grow and meet its goal of supporting marginalized communities in a way that neither the state nor the private sector can, it urgently needs greater investment and professional support. Suitable capital should be available for organizations at all stages of development, from charities without trading revenue all the way to social enterprises that reinvest some or all of their profits in their mission and commercial businesses with a social purpose.*
- *The most effective way of providing significant capital to the third sector is by facilitating access to private finance as well as to the broader capital markets.*

In Table 15.2, we traced the main steps undertaken by scholars and practitioners in the "social enterprise journey" towards the definition of the social business model and the measurement of social value as one of the core issue for the impact investing affirmation.

Impact Investing, CSR, and Stakeholder Theories

The notion that the firm has to be made accountable for the effects of its practices on the environment is certainly not new. The Pareto optimality calculation of a firm activity, according to welfare economics, should factor in also "indirect" aspects such as pollution, job destruction/creation that affect society and natural environment at large. Moreover investment decisions, as stated by social choice theories, are not only the result of the profit function maximization but also of the individual preferences aggregation.

Table 15.2.   The Long Journey of Social Enterprise Towards Impact Investing

1996	New social entrepreneurs: The success, challenge and lessons of nonprofit enterprise creation (Emerson & Twersky, 1996) : the paper provides a first definition of social enterprise as different from a traditional not for profit organization and a business enterprise
1997	Virtuous Capital: What Foundations Can Learn from Venture Capitalists, *Harvard Business Review* (Letts, Ryan, & Grossman, 1997): the authors propose a new approach to donation, borrowing from lessons learnt in the venture capital industry
1998	The Meaning of "Social Entrepreneurship" (Dees, 1998) : the article appeared in Harvard Business Review provide one of the most known definition of social entrepreneurship putting a strong emphasis on innovation and accountability
1999	Philanthropy's New Agenda: Creating Value (Porter & Kramer, 1999): the two authors call again a change of the approach of foundations and in general grant-making asking for more accountability on results achieved and a professional approach in grant-making
2000	Enterprising Communities: Wealth Beyond Welfare (Social Investment Task Force 2000) the report start to investigate the new role of private sector in providing public services
	Social return on investment: Exploring aspects of value creation (Emerson, Wachowicz, & Chun 2000): the paper calls for a more scientific approach in the way impact is measured
2003	The blended value proposition: Integrating social and financial returns (Emerson, 2003) the article and suggest that financial and social performances may be integrated
2004	Unleashing Entrepreneurship: Making Business Work For The Poor (UNDP 2004) also international institutions start to overcome a traditional approach to economic development based on donations, moving towards the use of market instruments
2009	Investing for Social and Environmental Impact (Freireich & Fulton, 2009): the first report providing a definition of impact investing as a nascent industry. The report underline how society/financial intermediaries failed to channel sufficient funds towards social ventures

Management studies translated these ideas into stakeholder and CSR theories. Stakeholder theory rejects profit maximization as a single over-arching objective of the firm and asserts that a company is accountable towards any group or individual who is affected by, or can affect directly or indirectly, the achievement of its objectives (Freeman, Harrison, Wicks, Parmar, & De Colle, 2010; Freeman, 1984; Jensen, 2010). This leads the way to CSR which assumes that the responsibility of a firm goes beyond its economic and legal duties (Carroll, 1979, 1991; Garriga & Melé, 2004) and according to some authors it outstretches to the administration of citizenship rights (Matten & Crane, 2005; Windsor, 2006).

However traditional approaches of both stakeholder and CSR theories fail to embed social/environmental considerations in the value creation process of a firm. The strategic approach to CSR (Baron, 2001; Bhattacharyya, 2010; McElhaney, 2009; Porter & Kramer, 2006), lately evolved into shared value (Porter & Kramer, 2006, 2011), attempts to solve some issues related to the social responsibility (Carroll & Shabana, 2010; Schreck, 2011) of a firm and to overcome the questions associated to value identification and measurement, as emerged in the classical stakeholder theory (Crane, Palazzo, Spence, & Matten, 2014).

Porter and Kramer (2006) argue that good citizenship, generic philanthropic contributions to local charities as well as mitigation of harms produced do not maximize the capacity of a company to generate value for society. On the contrary, a business should "identify the particular set of societal problems that it is best equipped to help resolve and from which it can gain the greatest competitive benefit." (p. 92).

Notably, by making social impact integral to the overall strategy, by using the words of Porter and Kramer (2006), businesses embed the social value into their profit generation objective, according to a new paradigm of capitalism, described by the authors as "profits that create societal benefits" (Porter & Kramer, 2011).

Their strategic approach to CSR, as opposed to a mere responsive approach, evolved into the famous concept of shared value, described as "policies and operating practices that enhance the competitiveness of a company while simultaneously advancing the economic and social conditions in the communities in which it operates" (Porter & Kramer, 2011). A company can therefore generate a shared value when it creates economic value by creating societal value. As the shared value approach combines the economic and the social value, overcoming the research of a trade-off, it could be considered a possible approach to impact investing, or better: companies that shape their strategies according to the shared value approach could be the target of impact investors.

However, if this new approach can be reached only through a "reverse strategy" or social innovation–as written before–it may require the creation of a new company as a spin off or the investment into promising start ups (following a corporate venturing approach). In fact, relevant or disruptive innovation is often impossible within the boundaries of established organizations.

DOING GOOD DOING WELL, MOVING BEYOND CSR, AND SOCIAL ENTERPRISE?

Impact investing may be the result of the drive to improve the performance of philanthropy (Porter & Kramer, 1999) and the ascent of the so called "philanthrocapitalism" (Bishop, 2013; McGoey, 2014; The Economist, 2006) that brings "hard-nosed" strategy, performance metrics, innovative financing models that aim to (1) make philanthropy more effective; and (2) make it a more lucrative industry in itself (McGoey, 2014). However at least three other trends are at stake.

The increasing marketization of the nonprofit sector (Eikenberry & Drapal Kluver, 2004) is blurring the line between "conventional" and "social" enterprises (Rodin & Brandenburg, 2014). It is therefore increasingly harder to distinguish between CSR practices and the pursuit of new business strategies. The decision made by GE Healthcare, back in 2009, to design and develop an ECG solution specifically for India reducing the cost of the appliance from $10,000 down to $500 without compromising the quality of diagnosis, may fit into a CSR decision to provide affordable healthcare as well as a way to tap on a huge underserved market, thus making CSR more strategic and generating shared value. Serving the poor is no more seen as a duty of government and charities, but also as an opportunity land for innovative entrepreneurs.

The increasing awareness on the effect of environmental and social issues on profits is pushing companies and investors to internalize externalities in their business model. During the last 10 years, companies like Coca Cola and Nestlé spent millions of dollars in water saving projects and pledged to cut respectively by 20%[5] and 33%[6] their water use because they were aware that the availability of water resource was critical for their operations. Nestlé is also helping its farmers to adopt sustainable water management practices. In 2013, Moody's, the rating agency, warned investors that water shortages may directly impact mining companies' profitability and credit risk profiles, and in turn the ratings the agency assign.[7] Investors like Calpers (California Public Employees' Retirement System) and Norwegian Oil Fund, with combined assets of over $1 trillion, require companies where they invest in to adopt water and environmental policies. In the meantime startups like WaterHealth International, which developed a low-cost modular system for processing healthy drinking water,[8] demonstrate that it is possible to build new businesses while solving social problems.

The last trend is represented by the emergence of the "gratis economy" (Anderson, 2009; Kelen, 2001). In its last book Rifkin (2014) advocates that the drive towards "extreme productivity" is bringing marginal costs to near zero and, since in a competitive market prices are equal to marginal costs, the prices are falling to zero as well. It is certainly true that the digital revolution is reshaping entire sectors of the economy driving down prices and creating dramatic opportunities of service's accessibility. However this does not mean that capital investment is nil. Who is going to provide the capital? How these investments are going to be evaluated in presence of zero/close to zero prices and possibly razor-thin margins?

In 2013 Amazon generated $20 billion of net revenues and posted $274 millions in profit, with a $162 billion market capitalization[9] its price-earnings ratio is about 560.[10] Clearly, in this case investors are not evaluating the company on the sole basis of profits. This example demonstrates that the problem of how to assess and measure value is not confined to impact investing, but is becoming central in many industries where the zero marginal cost theory applies.

These trends (marketization of nonprofit sector, internalization of externalities, zero marginal costs) show that impact investing, CSR, and social entrepreneurship are increasingly blending with standard business practice. Shall we argue that impact investing is no more than venture capital/private equity applied to social/environmental sector rather than a whole new investment approach?

CONCLUSION: A PROPOSED COMMON FRAMEWORK AND ISSUES AT STAKE

As discussed above, impact investing may have the potential to bring together and to evolve social enterprise and CSR theories. In a recent work, (Clark, Emerson, & Thornley, 2014), try to lay a common framework. They adopt a double perspective, the enterprise side and the investment side, and identify two main features of new investment model:

1. The explicit focus on outcomes (i.e., impact);
2. The internalization of environmental, social and governance (ESG) risks in the assessment of corporate and investment strategies as a matter of risk mitigation.

The following figure could be useful to draw a possible framework to understand how impact investing could represent an evolution of social enterprise and CSR consistent with the emerging need to fix capitalism (Porter & Kramer, 2011) but also to find new domains where to allocate financial resources, globally available. Based on Stiglitz and Wallsten (1999), the matrix places impact investing as an evolution from social enterprise and CSR/shared value-oriented business.

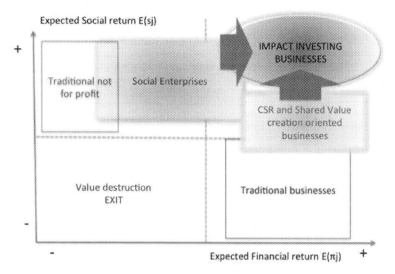

r = risk adjusted opportunity cost of the capital

Source: Author elaboration.

Figure 15.3. The stretch to impact investing.

In this imperfect graphical representation, we assume that impact investing could address financial return set at the coherent commercial or market value, considering the risk born by investors. In this way, impact investing may be seen as a new frontier and a possible evolution of social enterprise with the aim to attract in a stable and conventional way financial resources. If we look impact investing from the perspective of the shared value, it could represent a market niche in which new business models/social innovation could trigger the generation of new enterprises in sectors that could be critical for improving the quantity and quality of life. Or, alternatively, a frontier for businesses that decide to fully base their competitive advantage on shared value, which results also as an evolution of CSR.

However, this more conservative view may curtail the hybrids that spangle the discussion. Indeed, attracting the necessary resources to sustain the business lifecycle in a stable way may require certain level of financial return.

Actually, analyzing Impact Investing in comparison with CSR and social enterprise theory has shown the need for a breakthrough perspective by which to reframe the study of this phenomenon. It's time for encouraging all the actors to start applying a "reverse" approach: in other words there is nothing left to do, but in order to prompt it, the key would-be that the players (entrepreneurs, companies, investors, and even the government) would apply/experiment directly the main points underpinning impact investing into new businesses.

As to the role of scholars, we should observe, study and try to explain this phenomenon in evolution through an inductive—deductive approach focused on an extended perimeter of impact investing, to define its distinctive value—if any—and to trigger its takeoff.

NOTES

1. http://www.thegiin.org/cgi-bin/iowa/network/members/index.html
2. An asset class as defined by investopedia is "a group of securities that exhibit similar characteristics, behave similarly in the marketplace, and are subject to the same laws and regulations. The three main asset classes are equities (stocks), fixed-income (bonds) and cash equivalents (money market instruments)."
3. Concessionary investments are defined as investments whose primary purpose is to accomplish one or more of the foundation's exempt purposes and where production of income or appreciation is not a significant purpose. IRS, "Program Related Investments," http://www.irs.gov/Charities-&-Non-Profits/Private-Foundations/Program-Related- Investments (April 30, 2013). PRIs count toward a foundation's required minimum annual distribution, or pay-out.
4. Page 1 conclusions 1 and 5
5. Compared to 2004, source Coca Cola water stewardship report. The target has been reached in 2011.
6. Compared to 2005, source Nestlé in society—creating shared value and meeting our commitments 2013
7. Source: Moody's (2013), Special Comment: Global Mining Industry: Water Scarcity To Raise Capex And Operating Costs, Heighten Operational Risks
8. See also The Fast Company, The Case For For-Profit Solutions To The World's Water Problems
9. In July 2014
10. As Investopedia explains: the P/E is sometimes referred to as the "multiple", because it shows how much investors are willing to pay per dollar of earnings. If a company were currently trading at a multiple (P/E) of 20, the interpretation is that an investor is willing to pay $20 for $1 of current earnings. So it anticipates future earnings.

REFERENCES

Anderson, C. (2009). *Free: The future of a radical price.* New York, NY: Random House.

Austin, J., Stevenson, H., & Wei-Skillern. (2006). Social and commercial entrepreneurship: Same, different, or both? *Entrepreneurship Theory and Practice*, *30*(1), 1–22.

Barnett, M. L., & Salomon, R. M. (2012). Does it pay to be really good? Addressing the shape of the relationship between social and financial performance. *Strategic Management Journal*, *33*(11), 1304–1320.

Baron, D. P. (2001). Private politics, corporate social responsibility, and integrated strategy. *Journal of Economics & Management Strategy*, *10*(1), 7–45.

Bhattacharyya, S. S. (2010). Exploring the concept of strategic corporate social responsibility for an integrated perspective. *European Business Review*, *22*(1), 82–101.

Bishop, M. (2013). Philanthrocapitalism: Solving public problems through private means. *Social Research*, *80*(2), 473–490.

Brest, P., & Born, K. (2013). Unpacking the impact in impact investing. *Standford Social Innovation Review*, 1–14. Retrieved from http://www.ssireview.org/articles/entry/unpacking_the_impact_in_impact_investing

Brown, A., & Swersky, A. (2012). *The first billion a forecast of social investment*. London, England: Boston Consulting Group/Young Foundation.

Bugg-Levine, A., & Goldstein, J. (2009). Impact investing: Harnessing capital markets to solve problems at scale. *Community Development Investment Review*, *5*(2), 30–41.

Calvert Foundation. (2012). *Gateways to impact*. Retrieved from http://www.calvertfoundation.org/storage/documents/Gateways-to-Impact.pdf

Carroll, A. B. (1979). A three-dimensional conceptual model of corporate performance. *The Academy of Management Review*, *4*(4), 497. doi:10.2307/257850

Carroll, A. B. (1991). The pyramid of corporate social responsibility: Toward the moral management of organizational stakeholders. *Business Horizons*, 39–48.

Carroll, A. B., & Shabana, K. M. (2010). The business case for corporate social responsibility: A Review of concepts, research and practice. *International Journal of Management Reviews*, *12*(1), 85–105. doi:10.1111/j.1468-2370.2009.00275.x

Clark, C., Emerson, J., & Thornley, B. (2014). *Collaborative capitalism and the rise of impact investing*. Hoboken, NJ: John Wiley & Sons.

Cochran, P. L., & Wood, R. A. (1984). Corporate Social responsibility and financial performance. *Academy of Management Journal*, *27*(1), 42–56.

The Commission on Unclaimed Asset. (2007). *The social investment bank its organisation and role in driving development of the third sector*.

Crane, A., Palazzo, G., Spence, L. J., & Matten, D. (2014). Contesting the value of "creating shared value." *California Management Review*, *56*(2), 130–153. doi:10.1525/cmr.2014.56.2.130

Credit Suisse. (2012). Investing for Impact how social entrepreneurship is redefining the meaning of return. Retrieved from https://publications.credit-suisse.com/tasks/render/file/index.cfm?fileid=88E808B6-83E8-EB92-9D52FE6556283AAA

Dees, J. G. (1998). Enterprising non profits. *Harvard Business Review*, *76*(1), 54–67. Retrieved from http://www.ncbi.nlm.nih.gov/pubmed/10176919

Donohoe, N. O., & Bugg-levine, A. (2010). *Impact investments: An emerging asset class* (No. November 2010). Retrieved from http://www.jpmorganchase.com/corporate/socialfinance/document/impact_investments_nov2010.pdf

The Economist. (2006). The birth of philanthrocapitalism. *The Economist*, 1–6.

Eikenberry, A. M., & Drapal Kluver, J. (2004). The marketization of the nonprofit sector: Civil society at risk? *Public Administration Review*, *64*(2), 132–140.

Emerson, J. (2003). Where money meets mission. *Stanford Social Innovation Review*, *1*(2), 38–47.

Emerson, J., & Cabaj, M. (2000). Social return on investment. *Making Waves*, *11*(2), 10–14. Retrieved from http://hdl.handle.net/2149/1028

Emerson, J., Wachowicz, J., & Chun, S. (2000). Social return on investment: Exploring aspects of value creation in the nonprofit sector. *The Box Set: Social Purpose Enterprises and Venture Philanthropy in the New Millennium*, *2*, 130–173.

European Commission. (2011). *682 final social business initative* (2011). Brussels, Belgium: Author.

Freeman, R. E. (1984). *Strategic management: A stakeholder approach*. Boston, MA: Pitman.

Freeman, R. E., Harrison, J. S., Wicks, A. C., Parmar, B. L., & De Colle, S. (2010). *Stakeholder theory: The state of the art*. Cambridge, England: Cambridge University Press.

Freireich, J., & Fulton, K. (2009). *Investing for social & environmental impact*. Retrieved from http://monitorinstitute.com/downloads/what-we-think/impact-investing/Impact_Investing.pdf

Garriga, E., & Melé, D. (2004). Corporate social responsibility theories: Mapping the territory. *Journal of Business Ethics*, *53*, 51–71.

Grabenwarter, U., & Liechtenstein, H. (2011). In search of gamma: An unconventional perspective on impact investing. *SSRN Electronic Journal*. doi:10.2139/ssrn.2120040

J.P. Morgan. (2015). Eyes on the horizon: The impact investor survey. Retrieved from http://www.thegiin.org/cgi-bin/iowa/resources/research/662.html

Jensen, M. C. (2010). Value maximization, stakeholder theory, and the corporate objective function. *Journal of Applied Corporate Finance*, *22*(1), 32–42.

Kanter, R. M. (1999). From spare change to real change: The social sector as beta site for business innovation. *Harvard Business Review*, *77*, 122–133.

Kelen, A. (2001). *The gratis economy: privately provided public goods*. Budapest, Hungary: Central European University Press.

Koh, H., Karamchandani, A., & Katz, R. (2012). *From blueprint to scale*. Retrieved from http://www.mim.monitor.com/blueprinttoscale.html

Layard, P. R. G. (1994). Cost-benefit analysis (R. Layard & S. Glaister, Eds.). New York, NY: Cambridge University Press.

Leonard, H. B., Mcdonald, S., & Rangan, V. K. (2008). *The future of social enterprise* (No. 08-103). *Harvard Business School Working Paper*.

Martin, B. R. L., & Osberg, S. (2007). Social entrepreneurship: The case for definition. *Standford Social Innovation Review*. Retrieved from http://www.ssireview.org/articles/entry/social_entrepreneurship_the_case_for_definition

Matten, D., & Crane, A. (2005). Corporate citizenship: Toward an extended theoretical conceptualization. *Academy of Management Review*, *30*(1), 166–179.

McElhaney, K. (2009). A strategic approach to corporate social responsibility. *Leader to Leader*, *52*(1), 30–36.

McGoey, L. (2014). The philanthropic state: Market-state hybrids in the philanthrocapitalist turn. *Third World Quarterly*, *35*(1), 109–125. doi:10.1080/0143 6597.2014.868989

Mcguire, J. B., Sundgren, A., & Schneeweis, T. (1988). Corporate social responsibility and firm financial performance. *Academy of Management Journal*, *31*(4), 854–872.

MicroRate. (2013). *The State of Microfinance Investment 2013 Survey and Analysis of MIVs* (8th ed.). Retrieved from http://www.microrate.com/media/downloads/2013/11/MicroRate-The-State-of-Microfinance-Investment-2013.pdf

Mulgan, G., Tucker, S., Ali, R., & Sanders, B. (2007). *Social innovation: What it is, why it matters and how it can be accelerated*. Skoll Centre for Social Entrepreneurship. Retrieved from http://youngfoundation.org/publications/social-innovation-what-it-is-why-it-matters-how-it-can-be-accelerated/

Nicholls, A. (2006). *Social entrepreneurship: New models of sustainable social change* (2008th ed.). Oxford, England: Oxford University Press.

The Parthenon Group. (2010). Investing for Impact. Retrieved from http://www.parthenon.com/GetFile.aspx?u=%2FLists%2FThoughtLeadership%2FAttachments%2F15%2FInvesting%2520for%2520Impact.pdf

Peredo, A. M., & McLean, M. (2006). Social entrepreneurship: A critical review of the concept. *Journal of World Business*, *41*(1), 56–65. doi:10.1016/j.jwb.2005.10.007

Pinsky, M. (2011). "Impact Investing": Theory, meet practice. *Community Development Investment Review*, 7(2), 48–52. Retrieved from http://www.frbsf.org/community-development/files/IR-vol-7-num-2-Jan-5-for-Web.pdf

Pol, E., & Ville, S. (2009). Social innovation: Buzz word or enduring term? *The Journal of Socio-Economics*, *38*(6), 878–885.

Porter, M. E., & Kramer, M. R. (1999). Philanthropy's new agenda: Creating value. *Harvard Business Review*, 77, 121–131.

Porter, M. E., & Kramer, M. R. (2006). Strategy and society: The link between competitive advantage and corporate social responsibility. *Harvard Business Review*, (December), 78–93.

Porter, M. E., & Kramer, M. R. (2011). Creating shared value. *Harvard Business Review*, (February), 62–77.

Reeder, N., & Colantonio, A. (2013). *Measuring impact and non-financial returns in impact investing : A critical overview of concepts and practice* (EIBURS Working Paper 2013/01). Retrieved from http://files.lsecities.net/files/2013/10/Measuring_Impact-full-length-Oct-20131.pdf

Rifkin, J. (2014). *The zero marginal cost society: The Internet of things, the collaborative commons, and the eclipse of capitalism*. London, England: Macmillan.

Robeco, B. (2009). *Responsible investing: A paradigm shift. From Niche to mainstream.* Retrieved from http://www.strategyand.pwc.com/media/uploads/Responsible-Investing-Paradigm-Shift.pdf

Rockefeller Foundation. (2012). *Accelerating impact: Achievements challenges and what's next in building the impact investing industry*. New York, NY: Author.

Rodin, J., & Brandenburg, M. (2014). *The power of impact investing: Putting markets to work for profit and global good*. Wharton Digital Press.

Sabeti, H. (2009). *The emerging fourth sector*. Retrieved from http://www.cami-health. org/documents/4th-sector-paper-exec-summary.pdf

Schreck, P. (2011). Reviewing the business case for corporate social responsibility: New evidence and analysis. *Journal of Business Ethics*, *103*(2), 167–188. doi:10.1007/s10551-011-0867-0

Soana, M.-G. (2011). The relationship between corporate social performance and corporate financial performance in the banking sector. *Journal of Business Ethics*, *104*(1), 133–148.

Stiglitz, J. E., & Wallsten, S. J. (1999). Public-private technology partnerships promises and pitfalls. *American Behavioral Scientist*, *43*(1), 52–73.

Tang, Z., Hull, C. E., & Rothenberg, S. (2012). How corporate social responsibility engagement strategy moderates the CSR–financial performance relationship. *Journal of Management Studies*, *49*(7), 1274–1303.

Wallace, S. L. (1999). Social entrepreneurship: The role of social purpose enterprises in facilitating community economic development. *Journal of Developmental Entrepreneurship*, *4*(2), 153–174.

Weerawardena, J., & Mort, G. S. (2006). Investigating social entrepreneurship: A multidimensional model. *Journal of World Business*, *41*(1), 21–35. doi:10.1016/j. jwb.2005.09.001

Windsor, D. (2006). Corporate social responsibility: Three key approaches. *Journal of Management Studies*, *43*(1), 93–114.

World Economic Forum. (2013). *From the margins to the mainstream assessment of the impact investment sector and opportunities to engage mainstream investors*. Retrieved from http://www3.weforum.org/docs/WEF_II_FromMarginsMainstream_Report_2013.pdf

CHAPTER 16

MEDIA RESPONSIBILITY 2.0

A New Responsibility Model in the Media Sector

Lida Tsene and Betty Tsakarestou

SOCIAL FRAMEWORK AND RESEARCH QUESTIONS

We are living in an era, where we experience multiple challenges as a global community. Financial crisis and technological development shape new landscapes and results in new values. Moreover, social organizations, institutions and companies face an enormous credibility crisis.[1] In these turbulent times, the demand for responsible, sustainable behavior on behalf of the social, political and economical sector, as well as responsibility as a political act for every citizen seems a necessity (Giddens, 1999).

Media today are experiencing, more than ever, a legitimization, trustworthiness and accountability crisis (Cohen & Levy, 2008) that relates to the risks and challenges we are facing as a global community. Public opinion stands critical or overly opposite to media practices and demands quality and accountability in news production, both in terms of content production

Corporate Social Performance:
Paradoxes, Pitfalls, and Pathways to the Better World, pp. 345–372

and dissemination (by journalists), as well as corporate governance and business strategy by media owners.

Traditional media, for their part, are seeking ways to remain sustainable and powerful, while Web 2.0 is putting the monopolies under question and changing the balance of power. The influence of media is not singular anymore, but shared. Everybody can operate as a medium (Gillmor, 2004) and can participate in the process of curating and distributing information. In this context, how can we define the role and priorities of media companies? How do they keep balance between their social, environmental and economical aspects and impact? Do we need a change in media's operational and regulation model? Are we standing before a paradigm shift?

Many media companies, taking under consideration the social and marketing demands, are now turning towards corporate social responsibility (CSR) but they seem to blindly follow an agenda rather than understanding the responsibility concept as a value and as a sustainable business strategy. This is concluded partly from the surveys held regarding the responsible profile of the media sector[2] and partly from the fact that we, as media consumers or prosumers hesitate to even comment on the way traditional media operates. Why the so called corporate responsibility in most of media companies does not take the form of a CSR leadership vision applied into decision making processes, in their internal and external environment, but rather as a compliance driven, indicators box-ticking exercise?

On the other hand, social media platforms appear to include social responsibility in their core cultural and operational model. From blogs to businesses, from individuals to NGOs, sharing has been replacing exchanging, transparency has been taking the lead over secrecy, collaboration is transforming zero-sum competition into a co-competitive win-win game (Leadbeater, 2008). At the same time, industrial economy tends to be replaced by an emerging network economy, collective intelligence has replaced individual knowledge, products have given their place over to human capital investment, monolog over conversation, elites over creative minds (Tapscott & Williams, 2008).

We are attempting to sketch a new model for media, deriving from and combining social media's values and principles with more classical theories for media deontology and responsibility. Also, we are proposing a series of values describing media responsibility 2.0: stakeholders' engagement, collaboration, society in the heart of interest, accountability, transparency, quality, independence, public dialogue, innovation, freedom of expression, and creativity.

In this chapter we will examine the correlations between social media values, as they are embedded in evolving practices and CSR values with a focus on media companies. We are addressing the following questions: How has social media been changing the way media industries approach responsibility? Is our hypothesis that social media propose a new organizational, operational and cultural model for media business, with an orientation to accountable and socially responsible behavior valid and what would the limitations be?

METHODOLOGY

In this research and in order to support our research questions we applied a qualitative multi-method approach. We chose qualitative methodology, as we wanted to understand better and in depth current trends, behaviors, and perceptions, rather than gathering absolute numbers. In addition, when this research took place (in 2008), the fields of media responsibility and social media were under development in Greece, so we did not have enough samples to run a quantitative research.

More specifically, we applied in depth interviews with semi structured questionnaires with Greek journalists, bloggers, media executives, and communication professionals from Greece that constitute the key actors, influencers and stakeholders around the evolving media and social media landscape.

Interviews provided us with multi sided data and gave us the opportunity (a) to collect the data fast and (b) to get to the heart of the story. We used semi structured questionnaires with open ended questions divided in three main parts according to our research questions: (a) how do you describe the current media landscape, in terms of product, deontology, business model, journalist profile, relation with the audiences, (b) what is your opinion about social media and the changes they are bringing in society, politics, culture, economy, media, and communication, (c) how do you perceive the term social responsibility and media social responsibility.

We interviewed 32 people ranging in terms of age, working backgrounds (press, TV, radio journalists, editorial cartoonists, online media, bloggers, media executives and officers, communication and media consultants with an interest in CSR, media professors) and working status (more or less experienced, freelancers, working with permanent contracts, from public or private sector etc). Our sample consisted of:

a.   22 journalists, 13 of them were press journalists working at newspapers, four were working at TV channels, three at the radio, one at a web news site and one at an international media organization. Moreover, one of them was working both at TV and radio, two of them at press and TV, one at a corporate magazine and four at free press. Three of them were freelancers, two were working at the National Broadcasting and one of them at a municipal media business. In addition, one of them was journalist and publisher of his own magazine, while five of them were chief editors. Finally, one of them was member of the administrative council of the media organization he was working.

b. one editorial cartoonist
c. a general director of a media organization
d. a president of the board of directors
e. two journalists working at a press office
f. two communication consultants
g. a media professor with a focus on media law
h. three bloggers

We interviewed 7 women and 25 men aging from 25 to 55.

The time span of the interviews was June of 2008. We decided to conduct all 32 interviews during June 2008 to capitalize on the fertile ground of ongoing conferences and symposia focusing on media crisis, social media empowerment, and transparency potential as well as ferment of social media dialogues and encounters on the same premises.[3] Greece was, and still is, facing constant political and financial changes and we wanted to conduct the interviews during a period that appeared more stable. Although the interviews took place several years ago, it is rather interesting to see the development or lack of in the researched field over the last few years. The interviews were recorded and we applied the historical research approach in order to answer the following: What was the operational model for media organizations within the years? What does social responsibility mean for media industries? Where do we stand now?

We also employed the case study technique focusing on seven different cases from Greece and abroad in order to map the field better. We chose to study both traditional media and more digital ones, as well as new models from the media ecosystem. The cases were selected based on their relation with social media and social responsibility and/or with the new model we are proposing (incorporating social media and responsibility values from the beginning as a strategic part of their operational model).

Additionally, we included two cases-landmarks to the responsibility field at the time: BBC, an established news organization associated with a "strong sense of public service," also an international benchmark on impartial journalism that builds on this tradition and reputation in the digital and social media era and *Huffington Post,* the phenomenal digital-social media news platform, making its own rules, introducing search engine optimization techniques to outperform its competitors and was a master to use the power of social media.[4] Their operational model proved in a way our proposed model, so we used them as role-models to our research. The basic questions we wanted to address through the cases were formulated as such: (a) what is their operational and business model? (b) do they follow classical CSR practices? (c) do they use social media? (d) do they adopt values such as collaboration, transparency, sharing, civic engagement, and so forth?

Finally, in order to highlight more some findings we applied comparative analysis in the cases of the two public media (ERT and BBC). At the beginning of our research (2007), ERT was developing a CSR policy, a leader in responsible policies and culture that actively implemented CSR policies since 2006, was set as a benchmark in our comparative analysis with ERT This comparison could give us some useful insights about the implementation of our proposed model in Greek media organizations. Some might say, that this comparison was far fetched, as the BBC is a leading organization in media industries. That made our analysis even more interesting, as we had to go back to the reasons and political/social/technological/cultural factors that made the BBC a leader and add them to our study as research variables. Finally, it gave us the opportunity to be able to propose more practical solutions for Greek media in order to become more socially responsible.

In this chapter we will present only the case study of *Huffington Post* as a leading landmark in adopting social media values and social responsibility from the very beginning of its operation.

THE CURRENT MEDIA LANDSCAPE

Before going deeper into our research question, it would be useful to describe the current media landscape. How did we get to media crisis and what does media crisis mean? How has the journalistic profession been shaped throughout the years? How does social media and new technologies affect the media ecosystem? Are there new business and operational models for media organizations?

Crisis for media sector has a double meaning and multiple results. On one hand, there is financial crisis and on the other a crisis of trust and accountability (Iordanidou & Tsene, 2014).

Financial crisis affects journalists as well, as we witness major organizations cutting down on their expenses and personnel[5] and not being able to invest in more quality content production or to educate their stuff. Journalists are losing their jobs more often than in the past, and young journalists face difficulties in finding jobs. According to the Annual Survey of Journalism and Mass Communication Graduates held by University of Georgia,

just 55.5% of 2009 journalism and communication graduates with a bachelor degree were able to find full-time work within a year of leaving school.

That is down 4.9 percentage points from the year before and stands in stark contrast with the 70.2% of graduates who found work as recently as 2007. (Becker, Vlad, Simpson, & Kalpen, 2012)

This crisis might be cruel for media companies, but credibility crisis is crueler. Media organizations score really low in most of the related surveys[6] and the audience is no longer willing to pay for content that does not satisfy them. This crisis though, is not a characteristic of our era, but has its roots back in the very beginning of media industries. The strong relations with political and economical authorities[7] as well as the pursuit for more profit (without a sustainable business model) against quality puts journalism in the lead among the most unaccountable professions (Jeanneney, 2011). Citizens expected media to act as an intermediate between civic society and political society, but instead media were transferring contracted news. Their social responsibility towards citizens was disproved resulting in a loss of social acceptance. Media and journalists committed to deontology, but during these years we witnessed a plethora of unethical behaviors (Curran & Seaton, 2007).

Nowadays, audiences are standing cautious towards media and journalists, who are also trying to find their new role inside the current landscape. Digital tools and social platforms propose a different ecosystem both for media and audiences. Today, the audience seems to be more active and willing to engage in a continuous dialogue with journalists. As Jay Rosen (2006) states,

> The people, formerly known as the audience, wish to inform media people of their existence, and of a shift in power that goes with the platform shift you've all heard about. Think of passengers on your ship who have got a boat of their own. The writing readers. The viewers who picked up a camera. The formerly atomized listeners who with modest effort can connect with each other and gain the means to speak—to the world, as it were.

Also, they are digital savvy, owners and users of the new devices (PCs, tablets, smart phones) and mostly always online. The Digital Media Junkies generation often participate to the process of collecting and distributing information and they are for sure more demanding consumers.

We are all observing a revolution in the media sector, a process of transformation and transition from mass communication to a more democratized and open content creation in the digital and social media platforms (Gillmor, 2004). The balances change, media and journalists are no longer the "rulers" of information and the only gatekeepers. The wisdom of the crowds (Surowieki, 2004) highlights a collaborative production and exchange of knowledge between peers (Johnson, 2012). We experience evolution of journalism from lecture to an open dialogue (Gillmor, 2004), putting back at its heart citizens and public sphere. This evolution brings about a series of new values, skills and behaviors, a new quest for quality and responsibility. According to Jarvis (2008), "press stops to be self centered and it's been replaced by a sphere, where anyone from multiple sources is able, thanks to the links, to add a story and fulfill the need or the desire for news or information."

In addition, during the past few years we could claim that there is a rise in the so called startup culture and within media industries. Dan Gillmor (2010) argues that although media is facing a meltdown, we should be optimists about journalism's future, "because so many people are trying new things, mostly outside big enterprises but also inside the more progressive ones; because experimentation is so inexpensive and because we can already see the outlines of what's emerging."

Under this scope, journalists should develop new skills and media organizations should reinvent themselves in order to adapt to the needs of the digital economy and audiences. People demand quality in their information and a qualified curator (Jarvis, 2009) to guide them through the noise of multiple sources. Journalists need to become more aware of their responsibilities, as the journalistic game has become a multiplayer one (Tsene, 2014). Media organizations, on their behalf, should develop a more sustainable business model that will balance their social with their business aspect.

THEORETICAL FRAMEWORK

In the last 15 years there has been a strong discussion regarding the social, political, environmental and economic changes that affect us as a global community. But apart from the positive aspect those changes may have (such as the technological evolution or the progress in the field of medicine and biology) on how we live our everyday lives, we now face new risks, such as ecological disasters, terrorist attacks or major health challenges or crises. Living in such a risk society (Giddens, 1999) demands a more responsible profile on behalf of the public, private and business sector.

Taking into consideration the aforementioned, governments, NGOs, companies, and citizens ask for practices that empower the relationship between public, private and business sector aiming for the upgrade in the quality of everyday life. Within this context concepts such as corporate social responsibility and ethical consumption appear.

CSR has its roots in the idea of the parallel relation between economical and social growth supported by classical and modern academics such as M. Webber or A. Sen. This relation was first adopted by corporations into the practices of sponsorship, corporate philanthropy and as part of their business ethics agenda. Although all the aforementioned may be fractions of a social responsible strategy, CSR has a wider and more essential meaning. It consists of an ongoing open dialogue between each organization and the stakeholders (Freeman, Harrison, Wicks, Parmar, & de Colle, 2010) that examines its values, identity, organizational structure and function. It is also about cross-sector partnerships and collaborative schemes between business, public and private sector aiming at more sustainable business and social solutions promoting social cohesion and stability. CSR is a novel way of strategic thought and corporate policy implemented as a new set of practices, methodologies, and metrics that help organizations to manage their impact in society contributing to financial growth in terms of returns on their investments (ROI) while at the same time contributing to social prosperity. CSR oriented organizations and corporations also aspire to build a strong corporate reputation based on their CSR practices. (Bowen, 1953; Elkington, 1998; Freeman, 1984).

The concept of responsible organizations started to appear during the 80's as a reaction to the ecological issues and challenges of that period. Today, CSR is an international political and social term and its practices are being supported by the European Union and other institutions.[8]

At the same time the global expansion of multinational companies as well as of many international brands brought a change to the act of consuming. During the 90s social and economic studies portray the consumer not only as a person who buys products but as a citizen who acts in a more conscientious way in the marketplace taking into consideration wider economical, social and cultural concerns, whilst making consumer choices. The term ethical-responsible consuming (Harrison, Shaw, & Newholm, 2005) followed later by the term political consuming have been trying to conceptualize and describe this socially minded consumer cluster. A political consumer, according to H. R. Jensen (2001) is a hybrid between political and social activist, is a person that adopts social, political, and ethical criteria in his consuming actions.

Today, CSR moves toward the term social sustainability, giving a broader meaning and adopting a longterm approach, following the definition and arguing that "development is sustainable if companies' present needs can be met without compromising the ability of future generations to meet their own needs" (WCED, 1987).

New technologies and Web 2.0 have affected social responsibility both as a concept and as a corporate practice. In 2009, Elinor Ostrom was awarded a Nobel Prize for her work that was focused on economical and political actions, on a local and global level, under the scope of sharing and social innovation. Social media bring upon us changes on how we produce, consume, collaborate and innovate (Leadbeater, 2008). Those changes have become the subject of research by many scholars trying to define the new culture of social networks. The ability of co-creation of knowledge by peers (Johnson, 2012), the practice of sharing and collaboration (Botsman & Rodgers, 2010), the "power of organizing without organizations" (Shirky, 2009) and the rise of the quest for transparency, shape the new model for corporate social responsibility and sustainability 2.0. According to Wayne Visser (2011) CSR 2.0 is

> defined by global commons, innovative partnerships and stakeholder involvement. Its mechanisms include diverse stakeholder panels, real-time transparent reporting and new wave social entrepreneurship. In addition, recognizing a shift in power from centralized to decentralized; a change in scale from few and big to many and small; a change in application from single and exclusive to multiple and shared.

This concept might also be applied to startup culture. Although there has not yet been a wide research regarding the correlation of startups with social responsibility, we can draw some conclusions by researches focused on small businesses. According to Chrisman and Archer (1984), customer satisfaction seems to be the primary social responsibility for small businesses and startups, with product quality and employee responsibility to follow. Entrepreneurship, in the way it has been developed nowadays seems to incorporate the following values (Lefebre & Lefebre, 2012)

- Honesty: operating with transparency and integrity and being trustworthy.
- Fairness: treating employees and suppliers as they would like to be treated themselves, providing
- meaningful work and good workplace practices and conditions.
- Respect: dealing with people, without discrimination, as individuals, honoring their human rights and contributions.
- Responsibility: recognizing the need for sustainable development and acting upon it.
- Generosity: sharing success, both within the company and the community.

The above values are being enriched by a growing culture of sharing economy (Aigrin, 2012) where companies and citizens interact in more sustainable and collaborative ways.

In addition, according to Carol Sanford (2012), we can describe four archetypes of responsible entrepreneurs:

- the freedom entrepreneur
- the social entrepreneur

- the reciprocity entrepreneur
- the regenerative entrepreneur

Most of those new companies seem to embody social responsibility in their core operational model, even though they do not name it as such. Transparency, openness, peer to peer collaboration, innovation and creativity are fundamental to most startups as well us an in depth understanding and use of social media, promoting a more sustainable model for businesses.

Concluding, it is clear that we can witness correlations between CSR values (global commons, stakeholder involvement, transparency, decentralization, sharing) and social media values (collaboration, stakeholder involvement, transparency, sharing). Although, there are certain limitations that one should take into consideration when studying social media culture and its relation with social responsibility. For example, open data and access to them by big corporations in order to develop their strategies and products by profiling each one of us, without our direct agreement, might be one important issue in terms of privacy and human rights.

We referred to social responsibility and responsible consumers as an evolution and adjustment to the needs of our society. The critical question is how media organizations respond to the responsibility and CSR trend. Do media, journalists and also citizens, as consumers of media products, adopt a more responsible behavior? In order to articulate more clearly this question we are quoting R. Lambert (2004),

> McDonald's and Coca Cola are in the business of putting stuff inside people's bellies, so everyone—and especially the media—expects them to take responsibility for their nutritional effect. Shell and BP are in the business of taking stuff out of the ground and everyone—especially the media—expects them to take responsibility for their environmental impact. The media are in the business of putting stuff inside people's heads. But what responsibility do they take for their social and political impact?

Media organizations carry, due to their nature as sociopolitical institutions, responsibilities towards society and duties in order to defend public interest (McQuail, 2003). Apart from the responsibility for delivering accurate and reliable information, Media have historically and socially got the responsibility to protect public values, to insure the privileges deriving from the function of the public sphere, to enrich public dialogue, to defend human rights and to guard democracy (Kovach & Rosenstiel, 2001).

In order to establish and protect media's responsible public behavior, political authorities along with media organizations have enforced certain laws, codes and regulations. However, the role and structure of media is constantly changing and those regulations have to follow those changes.[9]

In addition, in the last twenty years media organizations have became powerful economic corporations. This, in conjunction with their social profile would lead to the conclusion that media should have been the pioneers in adopting social responsible practices as part of their organizational agenda.

However and despite the efforts for reassuring media's public function, according to surveys media are listed among the least trusted of responsible organizations and journalism among the least trusted of responsible professions.[10] Public opinion demands a reconsideration of the role and products of Media and citizens seem willing to participate more actively in the process of presenting and analyzing information.[11]

Media deontology, media ethics, or other existing codes and laws appear to need some reconsideration. Most of the time, the existing regulative frames apply only to journalists and not to the entire organization, resulting in the maintenance of an internal struggle between values and priorities and in addition operating as an excuse for irresponsible journalism (e.g., journalistic truth vs commercial truth, defending democracy and human rights vs personal career, journalist vs businessman, etc.). Adding to the aforementioned is the fact that media are now powerful companies functioning under market laws and that people demand transparency and responsibility and we conclude that the reexamination of the regulatory frame that conditions the operation of media deems to be a necessity.

We can examine the media social responsibility (MSR) agenda by categorizing the critical issues in the following categories, according MSR agenda by KPMG (2004):

- Common issues of CSR.
- Common issues of CSR that appear as special characteristics applied in media organizations.
- Unique issues of media CSR.

The first category consists of every action each organization should take in order to be responsible towards its stakeholders. Media having a double role, as a social institution and as powerful corporation and also having an important stakeholder role, should adjust their existing responsibilities towards society to the needs of the modern era.

The second category refers to:

a. issues concerning the information provided to public opinion, the quality of the product/ service media offer.
b. issues such as education, human rights, protection of personal data.

The first subcategory relates to the quality of the product/service media offer to citizens. Studying social reports produced by media organizations, such as the BBC, or BSkyB, we conclude that the most important element of their social responsibility strategy is to build trustful relationships with their audiences. People as unique citizens are in the heart of their corporate actions. Media organizations try to offer them programs and services that could upgrade social quality. media product is after all the first and most critical field where CSR must be applied, exactly as it occurs in other corporate products.

The second subcategory refers to the unique role media play in the protection of human rights. Human rights, being a complicated issue having ethical, political and legal aspects for all organizations, have been placed in the heart of CSR by international institutions and documents such as *European Commission's Green Book of Corporate Social Responsibility* (2001). More specifically, in media organizations the protection of human rights has an ambiguous role, both as responsibility and as ethical dilemma. Journalists are obliged to reveal the truth under any circumstances. At the same time they are obliged to pay respect to human dignity and the rest of human rights. Sometimes those two obligations oppose each other and the struggle becomes even more demanding if we add the strong commercial character of contemporary media. Journalists may face ethical dilemmas everyday when they approach stories where the respect to human rights opposes the revealing of truth or the service of public interest or even their own career. Their responsibility is to make the right choice.

Finally, the third category involves the values of freedom of press and freedom of expression. Nowadays media concentration provokes state intervention making it harder for media organizations to be a free market of ideas. Media are, by law, not obliged to give account for their actions because that opposes their right for freedom of expression. The need for reconsideration of the regulation model that will involve media accountability is strong in order for freedom of expression and media social responsibility to be restored.

In addition, according to Sustainability's (2004) "Through the Looking Glass: Corporate Social Responsibility in the Media and Entertainment Sector," "Media CSR consists of four correlated approaches: open and transparent business practices, responsible behavior, respect towards stakeholders, strong performance in economic, social and environmental issues." This Media Manifesto (Sustainability, 2004) suggests to media organizations, in order to reach social responsibility, innovation, impact management, adoption and sharing of ethical values, transparency in the relations with political authorities and the business sector, engagement with stakeholders and experimentation for more quality media products.

If we attempt to correlate both aforementioned approaches we could conclude that they describe media responsibility values in a similar way: the proposed transparency towards political and financial authorities by Sustainability's Media Manifesto equals creative independence and objective media products, stated by CSR Media Forum. Ethical behavior ranges from freedom of expression to quality, pluralism and citizen's participation. Respecting stakeholders demands collaboration, while financial, social, and environmental action relates with sustainability.

MEDIA RESPONSIBILITY 2.0

We claim that social media networks and platforms provide a hybrid model that interconnects the operational and cultural elements of organizational-corporate-media responsibility, capable to answer to the challenges of our era. If we wanted to briefly describe those elements, we could summarize them as such:

- stakeholders participation
- collaboration
- accountability
- transparency
- plurality/freedom of speech
- innovation
- creativity
- quality
- society and citizens at the heart of interest

All the above are also main characteristics described by the majority of social responsibility theories (Kotler & Lee, 2004). The definition and the agenda of social responsibility for media organizations does not differ much from the concept applied to other corporate sectors. It is also formed by the particular character and role of media, that is illustrated and codified in Table 16.1, where " we attempt to describe the correlations between media responsibility values as have been described mostly by deontological/ normative documents and codes, media responsibility as it has been applied today and social media values.

If we attempt to describe the correlations between media responsibility values as have been described mostly by deontological/ normative documents and codes, media responsibility as it has been applied today and social media values, as we presented them above, we could observe the following (Tsene, 2012).

Table 16.1.   From Media Responsibility to Media Responsibility 2.0

Media Responsibility Values	Media CSR	Media Responsibility 2.0
Transparency and appropriate management of working relations.	Organizational model: strict hierarchies, many "working rights" related issues are still open.	Organizational model: flexible, abolition of hierarchies, self-organization.
Economic transparency, viability and sustainability.	Business Model: advertising, no transparent economic policies.	Business Model: investment in quality content and direct financial support to it.
Journalism as conversation. Discussion of issues that really concern citizens.	Production and promotion of information, the agenda setting comes only from an elite (gatekeepers).	The production and promotion of information and the agenda setting comes from professionals in collaboration with citizens. Peer to peer production. Journalist as curator.
Quality and reliable content	No quality in the content. You don't have a choice but to consume specific media products in specific hours.	Form your own quality. Through link ethos and with the help of the journalist curator/authenticator you can check the reliability of information.
Transparency during the production of information. Objectivity.	Limitations on cross checking the sources.	Transparency during the production of information through links. "Transparency is the new objectivity" (Weinberger, 2009).
Independence, freedom of speech.	Independence often collides with political and economical expediencies.	Independence and plurality through collaboration and peer to peer contribution.
Accountability.	Lack of accountability and openness.	Open to direct criticism and feedback.
Participation of stakeholders, innovation, creativity.	CSR relies on stand alone environmental or social actions.	Participation of stakeholders, innovation, creativity.

As Clay Shirky (2008) argues,

What journalism needs now is not nostalgia but experimentation. It's time to get on with the essential task of trying everything we can think of to create effective new models of reporting, ones that take the existing capabilities of the Internet for granted.

Social media are not standing opposite traditional media. Social media are challenging traditional media to reconsider their model. We should not consider this challenge as a "who wins, who loses" calculus, but as a "win win" one.

RESEARCH ANALYSIS

At this point, we will present the key findings of our research and we will try to discuss them in the current media environment.

The majority of the participants in the interviews described the media landscape as suffering from a crisis both in a financial and moral level. "The trend reported by surveys regarding media credibility crisis is true. Media concentration, the interdependent relation between Media and financial schemes, economical crisis, low deontological and ethical standards are some of the reasons for this situation," one of the journalists claims. They also emphasize the lowering of quality of media content due to the monothematic orientation of media agenda (politics or finance) and the fact that "journalists today are not standing against the system criticizing it, but instead they are part of it," and they highlight the need for "fixing" the media ecosystem in terms of media production, regulation, business model, journalists' profile. and role.

They propose a balance between economic sustainability and social responsibility, but they also acknowledge this proposition as a challenging one. Media, according to their opinion, are "unhealthy companies" that need to reconsider their business model. "You must be able to balance sustainability and profits with quality product production," both bloggers and journalists argue and media owners as well as journalists have their own part to play in this balance.

All the above responses are in line with the global trends in the media industry. According to several surveys media organizations and journalists belong to those institutions and professions that receive negative commentary in terms of credibility, trust and transparency and they need to rethink their business and operational model in order to regain trust.

Accountability and regulation are described as crucial for journalists and media owners. And although there are lots of regulations and professional codes of conduct for media in Greece, the participants portray a rather chaotic landscape. More than half of the journalists participated to the interviews argue that many journalists ignore or disrespect the deontological code for journalistic profession and that often even the official audit authorities allow for irresponsible media behavior. "Codes and laws are sufficient and well documented. If they were applied, everything might be better," underlines the media professor and almost all stress the need for development of codes of conduct not only for journalists, but also for media organizations, that will emerge from social collaboration and dialogue. "It is really important to have the opportunity to gather and exchange opinions and experiences in order to give birth, in a collaborative way, to common values that can work as the basis for the development of codes of conduct," a blogger propose. Media organizations seem to fail to meet the accountability expectations of professional journalists and media audiences alike, supported by the relevant literature (Curran & Seaton, 2003) as well as an observation deriving from participating and engaging in the conversation in social media.

Regarding the concept of social responsibility, although some of the interviewees were not familiar with the terminology, they could still approximate a description for it. Independence, quality, transparency, accountability and stakeholders' engagement are the elements they highlight as media responsibility characteristics, the same elements stated that social responsibility theories refer as well. It is also interesting the fact that most of them argue that social responsibility should be at the core of a media corporate strategy and not something that comes as requirement and they add that most media seem not to be able to understand and adopt responsibility as an operational and cultural model.

> In Greece, CSR seems to be more like a trend and most media organizations do not understand what is it about. Most of the time, they adopt CSR practices only for PR reasons or because it is a EU regulation", underlines one of the communication consultants. They also highlight the fact that there is a need for more fundamental changes in the field of Greek Media in order to be able to even talk about CSR. "When Media are part of the political and financial ecosystem having a relationship of "exchanges" then accountability is out of the question."

This assumption is being verified by most researches about media responsibility[12] in traditional media companies.

As far as it is concerns social media and the new paradigm they propose, it is interesting to point out that most of the research participants say that journalists understand the need for using new media tools, but they cannot understand in depth the values and culture they bring along. In other words, they might learn how to use twitter or facebook, but it is not certain that they will realize the collaborative and open to transparency and open to accountability culture of those platforms. This assumption was highly supported by the bloggers and the younger journalists of our research, while the answers of the elder ones implied the same, though without acknowledging it. This is an argument also documented by international researches.[13] In Greece, in particular, even today it seems not to have changed according to a new, recent research that underlines this exactly.

(Iordanidou & Tsene, 2014). While the professionals interviewed described the advantages of social media as such: decentralization of information, pluralism, participation, collaboration, objectivity, transparency, the main thought is that there is still a long way to go in order for those values and practices to be adopted by traditional media. They believe that in order for social media platforms to be able to propose a new paradigm shift for media industry we need as a society to get rid off established pathogenesis such as political corruption.

If we attempted to summarize the conclusions of our interviews, we could conclude that Greek key media and communication stakeholders recognize the need for a change in media practices. They also recognize some of the most important characteristics of social responsibility and they correlate them with those of social media. However they feel that there is a need for more time for both society and media industry to adopt and finally implement those new values. Factors such as corrupted institutions (political, economical, social), lack of a strong and active public sphere, interconnections between media and politics,[14] problematic audit mechanisms for media operations,[15] bad understanding of the terms sustainability and business model[16] for media, resulted to the above perception. Although, most of them agree to the fact that social media and social responsibility could be a step towards a more transparent, qualitative and efficient journalism, we could highlight the fact that younger journalists and bloggers seem to strongly embrace this claim, while older and more traditional journalists stand more hesitant towards the implementation of social media values.

It is rather interesting to try and sketch out briefly, where we stand now in terms of all the aforementioned variables. Did Greek media organizations move to a more social responsible model? Are there any examples of new organizational models? Did Greek journalists embrace social media as a tool for responsible media content production? Collecting some data from more recent and ongoing surveys,[17] as well as by observing the media landscape over the years we can conclude the following: the perception of both media professionals and audiences towards social responsibility performance of media organizations in Greece has not changed a lot. Financial and credibility crisis seem to have been established. On the other hand, although we have witnessed a few more organized efforts on behalf of some media organizations towards CSR[18] the perception that they need to do more in order to incorporate responsibility as a strategic policy, remains.[19] Regarding social media, more and more journalists are using them as a tool in order to make their job easier and better, but few are the media organizations that are using them in order to enrich the stakeholder dialogue and the transparency of the produced media content. Although, there is a rise of civic engagement and Greek citizens are participating more in the process of collecting and sharing data. In this context, some new media models appeared, such as *Radiobubble*[20] or *The Press Project*,[21] taking into account social media and social responsibility values (collaboration, sharing, transparency, independence, creativity etc) or even the newly formed media startup *oikomedia*,[22] trying to foster collaboration between media professionals across the world.

And, if in Greece, things are moving pretty slow in the particular sector, globally we observe a big revolution in the ways media organizations—traditional or digital—move towards responsibility 2.0. John Hickox, Partner of KPMG U.S. states at the KPMG Survey of Corporate Responsibility Reporting 2013,

> social media is changing the way companies report. Many companies are using social media tools and technologies to communicate their CR activities and in particular their CR reporting content. Social media enables companies to communicate more frequently on their CR efforts, expand the reach of their sustainability message, receive feedback and enhance transparency with stakeholders.

The same survey reports a progress of CR reporting among media companies (75%), in comparison with the 2008 survey, where their CR reporting rates were among the lowest (47%). Additionally, more and more media startups make their appearance,[23] embracing social media and social responsibility values, in a mission to fix journalism.[24]

CASE STUDY: *HUFFINGTON POST*

Taking as case study *Huffington Post* we will try to observe if this new media model that is being proposed could stand as a starting point of how social media could challenge traditional media to rethink responsibility.

Huffington Post is a liberal Internet newspaper, founded by Arianna Huffington and Kenneth Lerer. "It's a very vital and dynamic blend of breaking news, aggregated news and real-time commentary, meaning that you can find out the information you want and immediately see what people have been saying about it," comments Roy Sekoff, *HuffPost's* Founding Editor.[25] *HuffPost* gathered more than 250 different people from different backgrounds to contribute to a group blog covering issues from politics and media, to sports and entertainment. From Madeleine Albright to Jamie Lee Curtis and from Arianna Huffington herself to Jeff Jarvis and Hillary Clinton, *Huffington Post* "seeks to be a community, not merely a collection of links, an Internet curator with a distinct attitude, mixing blog posts, original news and links to other sources."[26] Plus to the contribution of those people comes as added value the posts by the permanent stuff of *Huffington Post*—among them the former political reporter at *Washington Post* Thomas

D. Edsall or Betsy Morgan, former CBSNews.com's general manager—but as well as from citizens through, for example, the "Off the Bus" project.

In July 2007 the journey of the *HuffPost* Bus begun as an experimental though innovative method to cover the presidential elections of 2008. The project was based on collaboration since its very fresh beginning as it was a joint venture between Jay Rosen's newassignment.net site for "pro-am" reporting and the *Huffington Post*. "Participate in politics by covering the campaign" was the motto that invited eventually over 12,000 people to the bus of original grassroots journalism. Based on the wisdom of crowds theory (Surowieki, 2005) "Off the Bus" was an experiment with useful results on what we had already learned regarding Web 2.0 and citizen journalism and how this knowledge could be expanded and enriched. As Arianna Huffington stated

> According to Surowiecki smart is independence, decentralization and diversity. Our citizen journalists will be independent—focused on their puzzle, and what everyone around them thinks. They will be decentralized—spread across the country. And they will be as diverse as possible. The mosaic of their perspectives will add a varied portrait to the traditional coverage of the candidates and their campaigns.[27]

This varied portrait was pretty obvious in Mayhill Fowler's (2008) "Obama: No surprise that hard- pressed Pennsylvanians turn bitter."[28] The "Bittergate" caused a media storm as Barack Obama's comments on working-class voters were not—let us say—his best public speech. Mayill Fowler, an Obama supporter and fundraiser and a citizen journalist as well as a contributor to "Off the Bus" did not fear to say what she thought and to challenge the political and journalistic world to take upon their responsibilities towards citizens.

Collaboration and engagement, media as conversation and sharing is the key on how *Huffington Post* is mixing professional journalists and citizens in a networked gathering, distribution and commentary on everyday news. The result is more and diverse sources of information, more space for individual voices to emerge, an innovative and insightful ground-level reporting, and real news from real people. As J. D. Lasica (2003) argues "Instead of looking at blogging and traditional journalism as rivals for readers' eyeballs, we should recognize that we're entering an era in which they complement each other, intersect with each other, play off one another."

Apart from trying to bridge the best from traditional and new media, *Huffington Post* proposes innovative ways to shape a sustainable and competitive media model. Web 2.0 is not changing only media. It changes also society. It changes economy. Consumers now more than ever can become prosumers, open source projects and products are now developing and business should find new ways to, distribute, sell and open a dialogue about their services and products. Economy in the years to come will depend not in productivity but in knowledge, not only in the classical implementable and technological aspect of the "knowledge economy" as stated by Drucker (1969) but expanded as the power of creating links and networks in order to share growth.

This change in economy is more obvious to business focused on content, like media.

> Like other information goods, the production model of news is shifting from an industrial model—be it the monopoly city paper, IBM in its monopoly heyday, or Microsoft, or Britannica—to a networked model that integrates a wider range of practices into the production system: market and non-market, large scale and small, for profit and nonprofit, organized and individual.

Benkler (2009) argues.[29] People are not willing to pay anymore in order to have access to media they do not trust. And so ventures will not be willing to invest in businesses that do not sell. It is rather important that media companies should rethink and probably reshape their operational structure.

Huffington Post is working on a new model and recently made a huge step by proposing a fund for investigative journalism out of foundation and public donations. Can this fund save journalism or is *Huffington Post's* move a sign of surrender in the hunt for a sustainable business model for journalism as Jeff Jarvis questions?[30]

Before moving to the analysis of this strategic decision it would be necessary to point out some things regarding the economic model of *Huffington Post* and how it has evolved during the years (before the buying out by AOL). *HuffPost* began building a sustainable profitability by investing in human capital and interesting content. The more traffic it got the more it raised its revenues from advertisers first and then funders. As Roy Sekoff states "It has become a link-based economy. You are not being paid in dollars any more for your piece, but rather you are being paid in traffic"[31]

But how debatable is this model? Can monetization of social media kill their social mission? Free content and unpaid journalists threaten a sustainable media business model? *Huffington Post* has been criticized for not paying its bloggers. Arianna Huffington argues "*HuffPost* pays its editors and its reporters. We don't pay for opinion pieces but, then again bloggers have no deadlines or commitments. They contribute when they want and as often or as infrequently as they like."[39]

And they moved a step forward. On March 29, 2009 they announced a fund that starts with $ 1.75 million towards investigative journalism. Journalists will be paid to dig and cover stories about an important issue,the economy. And they will be encouraged to reproduce the content virally for maximum exposure and not only on *Huffington Post*. A joint venture as well between *HuffPost* and several donors seeking to give a new aspect on foundation and public support of the media and to inspire others to fund similar ventures. As Jeff Jarvis stated, "This is where foundation and public support will enter into the new ecosystem of journalism: not by taking over newspapers but by funding investigations and other slices of a new journalistic pie."[33] "In the two biggest stories of our recent time—the war in Iraq and our financial meltdown—investigative journalism did not fulfill its mission. We all have a real stake in not only preserving what investigative journalism is but in making it better." Huffington argued in an interview with Jeff Jarvis.[34]

In an era when traditional media is finding it hard to keep their audiences and where even the funding of public broadcasting has been under debate this investigative fund opens the discussion of how media will find an innovative and sustainable way of gaining profits. Investing on the content, on covering issues related to political, on economical transparency and responsibility and on news will become an added unique value. We do not argue that this model cannot raise criticism on how donors can affect the coverage. But we can argue that it is probably worthy of risk. As Jeff Jarvis put it

> This, I believe, is how journalism will get money directly from readers—not through subscriptions, micro-payments, and pay walls but from the generous contributions of the few who pay for efforts that benefit the many. That is the 1 percent rule behind Wikipedia: 1 percent of its readers write it. And that is how public broadcasting is supported today in the U.S. I can't imagine the public wanting to pay to buy the sinking Titanics of old-media failures; I don't want to contribute to failed newspapers anymore than I want my tax money going to failed banks and auto companies. But I can imagine readers contributing to assure that government is watched."[34]

Did *Huffington Post* appear as one of the messiahs that will save media? Definitely not. But it definitely has opened the road towards the use of Web 2.0 not as a technological instrument, but as a social catalyst in the change of organizational, operational and cultural behavior of media business.

Inside the operational model of *Huffington Post* we find elements of the new DNA of media responsibility, even though they never refer to it as such. Watching how *HuffPost* has been working, we are all the media and we are all social stakeholders participating in the decision making process. Open and transparent, following the link ethos and acting as an Internet curator, connecting the web's flooding of information *Huffington Post* inspires us and places us before several open issues. What does responsibility means for media? What does responsibility mean for each of us, now that we are all becoming media?

CONCLUSIONS

Taking under consideration all the aforementioned we conclude that the field of media and communication is entering a new era where media organizations and journalists should play a more responsible part in the process of networked journalism, that is evolving nowadays. As societal expectations for more corporate responsibility are getting more pressing, one should ask "Why should the media be different? The qualities which are associated with corporate governance for companies in general are precisely those we should want to be attached to our media: integrity, decency, ethical behavior, trust."[35] Media organizations need more active citizens and engaging consumers and citizens need more accountable and transparent media. Mutual stakeholder responsibility incorporates those two needs as a novel strategic management approach. Social media bring with them a new culture focusing on transparency, collaboration, dialogue, innovation, and creativity. Although most of traditional media seem not to be able to answer the demand for responsibility, social media and the values they organically propose, respond to that need. We should consider though, social responsibility as a way towards the transformation of today's journalists into sustainable entrepreneurs,[36] creative problem solvers that will make "journalism smarter."[37]

We have tried to test and validate our hypothesis that social media propose a new organizational, operational, and cultural model for media business, with an orientation to accountable and socially responsible behavior. Since 2008, that we have conducted our empirical qualitative research, we kept following the transformations within the media sector and media organizations, the evolution of social media, and the development of new digital platforms. We observed the emphasis on open data and entrepreneurial journalism and we are witnessing the emergence of not one new dominant journalism and new media model, but mostly we " highlight the ways new possibilities for journalism require new forms of organization."[38]

There is no doubt that we are witnessing a fascinating story developing in front of our own eyes. Social media along with traditional media organizations are shaping a new operational model for media industries based on accountability, transparency, stakeholder engagement. It will take time though for this model to be established, and as the field is evolving we have to remain sceptic and take into consideration possible pitfalls and limitations. Social media are not here to replace traditional, but to co-create a more responsible media ecosystem.

NOTES

1. According to Edelman Trust Barometer since 2009 government, business, media face are not trusted institutions any more, on behalf of citizens. For detailed information: http://www.edelman.com

2. According to the Oekom Research (2011), "Are they coming clean?" from the 25 media corporations that participated, very few scored high on their environmental or other social performance. The vast majority was rated with a C.

3. In June 2008 the first survey regarding media social responsibility was published by Institute of Communication (www.instofcom.gr/wp-content/uploads/2014/02/ioc_csrmedia08.pdf), while at the same time Hellenic Federation of Enterprises organized the first forum on media, deontology and accountability (http://www.anoiktoforum.gr/html/of-08-conclusions.htm)

4. Shapiro, M. (2012), Six degrees of aggregation. Columbia Journalism Review. Retrieved May 10, 2013, from http://www.cjr.org/cover_story/six_degrees_of_aggregation.php?page=all

5. In 2009, *Wall Street Journal* announced the cutting of 80 job places. By the end of 2009 80.000 journalists had lost their jobs. In 2012, Greek newspaper Eleuterotypia closed and 800 journalists lost their jobs.

6. We refer indicatively to GFK Custom Research Worldwide's survey (2003), where journalists came in second place, right after politicians, in terms of trustworthiness or going by Edelman's Trust Barometer where media was placed the last position in terms of trust. According to Media Standard Trusts research (A more accountable press) or Globe Scan's Research (on behalf of BBC, Reuters, and Media Center), journalists and media score really low regarding credibility.

7. In his book, *Une histoire des medias*, J. Jeanneny (2011) writes about the theatrical comedy, entitled The Staple of News, performed in London in 1626 where we witness an attack against journalists and their unaccountable behavior.

8. In 2001, European Commission published The Green Book of CSR and since then CSR has been at the heart of European Commission documents.

9. For example, over the past years there has been an intense conversation on the regulation of Internet and online media.

10. According to *Good News and Bad: The Media, Corporate Social Responsibility and Sustainable* Development published by Sustainability in 2002 "media are amongst the most powerful yet least trusted organizations."

11. The past years we are witnessing the rise of citizen journalism, blogging and other journalistic actions on behalf of citizens.

12. According to the Sixth Annual Edelman Trust Barometer (2005) held in Europe, U.S., Canada, Brazil, China, and Japan only 28% of American citizens and 32% of European citizens trust media to act responsibly. Additionally in the list of the 100 most trusted British companies (published in *Sunday Times* in April 2005) only six are media organizations and all of them are ranked below the 30th place. Finally the results of the collective volume *Good News and Bad: The Media, Corporate Social Responsibility and Sustainable Development* published by Sustainability in 2002 proves that "media are amongst the most powerful yet least trusted organizations."

13. Knight Foundation (2007). Investing in the Future of News: Training for Midcareer Journalists. Retrieved January 2, 2014, http://www.newsimproved.org/documents/Survey_KeyFindings.pdf

14. In Greece, often we witness formal journalists become members of parliament or to take active roles in political parties. For example former journalist T. Roussopoulos was appointed Minister of State.

15. In Greece it is common even if Greek National Council for Television and Radio applies a penalty to a media organization, this penalty can be overcome in several ways. For example, TV shows that were banned, returned after a short period of time, by just changing their name title (for example T. Anastasiadi's show "Ola" that has been running for almost 10 years, despite all penalties).

16. Most Greek media organizations are owned by well known business men. Their business model is not based on their product, but they operate rather like a spin off company of the owner's other businesses (from example, SKAI TV is owned by Mr Alafouzos, owner and president of shipping companies).

17. For example the survey on media responsibility, published by Institute of Communication in 2008. Retrieved from http://www.instofcom.gr/wp-content/uploads/2014/02/ioc_csrmedia08.pdf or the ongoing research *Developing Life Long Learning in a Field Undergoing a Paradigmatic Shift: The Role of Distance Learning Institutions and the Crisis of Journalism* (Iordanidou & Tsene, 2014)

18. In 2007 ERT published the first CSR report a Greek media organization has ever published. Since 2006 SKAI TV is running campaigns and organizing actions with environmental and social impact. In 2008, five private Greek TV channels become members of Hellenic Federation of Enterprises and sign the Charter of Obligations and Rights for Enterprises, featuring principles similar to those proposed by CSR.

19. Over the past years in Greece, many media scandals have been revealed. In February 2008, a sex scandal involving former Culture Ministry General Secretary Christos Zahopoulos surfaced. DVDs of the minister having sex with his female assistant was produced in the office of Prime Minister Costas Karamanlis. It was referred to as the 'sex lied and dvd' scandal by the media   (http://www.pfhub.com/top-7-political-scandals-in-greece/#sthash.hYeeLKIq.dpuf)

20. Radiobubble is one of the pioneer Greek web radios based on crowd sourcing information, citizen journalism and collaboration between professionals and citizens in order to produce better media content. For more information: radiobubble.gr

21. The Press Project is a Greek news and media content aggregator. For more information: thepressproject.gr

22. For more information visit: oikomedia.org

23. Schumpeter. (2014). Digital Media Startups: Hot or fraught? *The Economist*. Retrieved June 10, 2014, from http://www.economist.com/blogs/schumpeter/2014/01/digital-media-start-ups

24. Levy, N. (2014). Media startups take New York. Capital. Retrieved June 10, 2014 from http://www.capitalnewyork.com/article/media/2014/02/8540884/media-startups-take-new-york

25. Heald E. (2009) "Doing More with Less: Nailing the new media business model at the Huffington Post." *Editorsweblog*. February 20, 2009, from http://

www.editorsweblog.org/analysis/2009/01/doing_more_with_less_nailing_
the_new_med.php

26. Stelter B. (2008) "Citizen Huff." *The New York Times*. Retrieved April 29, 2009, from http://www.nytimes.com/2008/03/31/business/media/31huffington. html?_r=1

27. Huffington, A. (2007). "New HuffPost Project: The Wisdom of the Crowd hits the '08 Campaign Trail." *Huffington Post*. Retrieved April 5, 2008, from http://www.huffingtonpost.com/arianna-huffington/new-huffpost-project-the_b_44321.html

28. Fowler M. (2008) "Obama: No surprise that hard-pressed Pensylvannians turn bitter." *Huffington Post*. Retrieved April 20, 2008, from http://www.huffingtonpost.com/mayhill-fowler/obama-no-surprise-that-ha_b_96188.html

29. Benkler, Y. (2009). "Correspondence: A new era of corruption?" *The New Republic*. Retrieved March 20, 2009, from http://www.tnr.com/story_print.html?id=c84d2eda-0e95-42fe-99a2-5400e7dd8eab

30. Jarvis J. (2009). "Arianna Huffington Saves Journalism." *Buzzmachine*. Retrieved April 10, 2009, from http://www.buzzmachine.com/2009/04/06/arianna-huffington-saves-journalism/

31. Heald E. (2009). "Doing More with Less: Nailing the New Media Business Model at the Huffington Post." *Editorsweblog*. Retrieved February 20, 2009, from http://www.editorsweblog.org/analysis/2009/01/doing_more_with_less_nailing_the_new_med.php

32. Phillips P. (2009). "Arianna Huffington: HuffPost Won't Help Kill Newspapers." *I Want Media*. Retrieved January 20, 2009, from http://www.iwantmedia.com/people/people77.html

33. Jarvis J. (2009). "HuffPost's Investigative Fund: New Slice of a New News Pie." *Huffington Post*. Retrieved March 29, 2009, from http://www.huffington-post.com/jeff-jarvis/huffpos-investigative-fun_b_180487.html

34. Jarvis J. (2009) "Arianna Huffington Saves Journalism. *Buzzmachine*. Retrieved April 7, 2009, from http://www.buzzmachine.com/2009/04/06/arianna-huffington-saves-journalism/

35. Jarvis J. (2009) "Arianna Huffington Saves Journalism." *Buzzmachine*. April 7, 2009, from http://www.buzzmachine.com/2009/04/06/arianna-huffington-saves-journalism/

36. Quote from R. Lambert's lecture at Nottingham University Business School entitled "Socially Responsible Media," December 2004.

37. Dvorkin L. (2013, January 29), Inside Forbes: The Rise of the Entrepreneurial Journalist in a World Seeking Credible Voices. Retrieved January 10, 2014, from http://www.forbes.com/sites/lewisdvorkin/2013/01/29/inside-forbes-the-rise-of-the-entrepreneurial-journalist-in-a-world-seeking-credible-voices/

38. Anderson, C. W., Bell, E., & Shirky, C. (2012), Postindustrial Journalism: Adapting to the present. Retrieved June 10, 2014, from http://towcenter.org/wp-content/uploads/2012/11/TOWCenter-Post_Industrial_Journalism.pdf

REFERENCES

Aigrin, P. (2012). *Sharing: Culture and the Evonomy in the Internet Age*. Amsterdam: Amsterdam University Press.

Becker, L. B., Vlad T., Simpson H.,& Kalpen K. (2012), *Annual survey of journalism and mass communication graduates*. University of Georgia. Retrieved February 7, 2014, from http://www.grady.uga.edu/annualsurveys/Graduate_Survey/Graduate_2012/Grdrpt2012mergedv2.pdf,

Benkler, Y. (2006). *The wealth of networks: How social production transforms markets and freedom*. New Heaven, CT: Yale University Press.

Botsman, R., & Rodgers, R. (2010). *What's mine is yours: The rise of collaborative consumption*. New York, NY: Harper Business.

Bowen, H., (1953). *Social responsibilities of the businessman*. New York, NY: Harper

Chrisman, J. J., & Archer, R. W. (1984). Small business social responsibility: some perceptions and insights. *American Journal of Small Business, 9*(2), 46–58

Cohen, P., & Levy, E. (2008). *Notre Metier a mal tourne*. Paris, France: Mille et un Nuits.

Curran, J., & Seaton, J. (2007). *Power without responsibility. The press, broadcasting and new media in Britain*. London, England: Routledge.

Drucker, P. (1969). *The age of discontinuity: Guidelines to our changing society*. New York, NY: Harper and Row.

Elkington, J. (1998). Cannibals with forks: The triple bottom line of 21st century business. London, England: Sustainability.

European Commission. (2001). Green Paper: Promoting a European framework for Corporate Social Responsibility. Retrieved March 15, 2003, from http://eur-lex.europa.eu/legal-content/EN/TXT/PDF/?uri=CELEX:52001DC0366&from=EN

Freeman, E. R. (1984). *Strategic management: A stakeholder approach*. Pitman.

Freeman, E. R., Harrison, J. S., Wicks, A. C., Parmar, B. L., de Colle S. (2010). *Stakeholder theory: The state of the art*. Cambridge, England: Cambridge University Press.

Fowler, M. (2008). Obama: No surprise that hard-pressed Pensylvannians turn bitter. *Huffington Post*. Retrieved April 27, 2008, from http://www.huffingtonpost.com

Giddens, A. (1999). Risk and responsibility. *Modern Law Review, 62*(1), 1–10.

Gillmor, D. (2004). *We the media*. Sebastopol, CA: O'Reilly Media.

Gillmor, D., (2010), Mediactive. Retrieved December 5, 2010, from http://mediactive.com/wp-content/uploads/2010/12/mediactive_gillmor.pdf

Harrison, R., Shaw, D., & Newholm, T. (2005). *The ethical consumer*. London, England: SAGE.

Heald, E. (2009). Doing more with less: Nailing the new media business model at the Huffington Post. *Editorsweblog*. Retrieved February 2, 2009, from http://www.editorsweblog.org

Huffington, A. (2007). New HuffPost project: The wisdom of the crowd hits the '08 campaign trail. Retrieved April 2, 2008, from http://www.huffingtonpost.com/

International Press Institute. (2010). Navigating the New Media Landscape. Retrievd from http://www.comm.hkbu.edu.hk/poynter/doc/IPI_Poynter_ report.pdf

Iordanidou, S., & Tsene, L. (2014). The role of distance learning in journalism: Preliminary findings from journalists' perspectives. *Media Studies, 9*, 43–60. Retrieved from http://hrcak.srce.hr/index.php?show=clanak&id_clanak_ jezik=188577

Jarvis, J. (2008). *The press becomes the press-sphere.* Retrieved April 16, 2008, from http://www.buzzmachine.com

Jarvis, J. (2008). *Defining quality in journalism.* Retrieved May 5 2008, from www. buzzmachine.com

Jarvis, J. (2009). HuffPost's investigative fund: New slice of a new news pie. *Huffington Post.* Retrieved April 8 2009, from www.buzzmachine.com

Jarvis, J. (2009). Death of curator: Long live the curator. Retrieved May 5, 2009, from www.buzzmachine.com

Jarvis, J. (2009). Arianna Huffington saves journalism. *Buzzmachine.* Retrieved April 8, 2009, from www.buzzmachine.com

Jarvis, J. (2009). Journalists: where do you add value. Retrieved April 30, 2008, from www.buzzmachine.com

Jensen, H. R. (2001). Staging political consumption. *Asia Pacific Advances in Consumer Research, 4*, 276—280.

Jeanneney, J. N. (2011). *Une histoire des medias: Des origines a nos jours.* Paris: Points.

Johnson, S. (2012). *Future perfect: The case for progress in a networked age.* Riverhead.

Kotler, P., & Lee, N. (2004). *Corporate social responsibility: Doing the most good for your company and your cause.* New York, NY: Wiley.

Kovach, B., & Rosenstiel, T. (2001). *The elements of journalism. What newspapers should know and what the public should expect.* New York, NY: Three Rivers Press,

KPMG. (2004). KPMG and the Media CSR Forum. Retrieved May 10, 2014, from http://www.pioneersgroup.co.uk/uploads/stored/Media%20CSR%20 Forum%20Issues%20Feb04.pdf

KPMG (2013). The KPMG Survey of Corporate Responsibility Reporting 2013. Retrieved May 8, 2014, from http://www.kpmg.com/Global/en/IssuesAndInsights/ArticlesPublications/corporate-responsibility/Documents/ corporate-responsibility-reporting-survey-2013-v2.pdf

Lambert, R. (2004), *Socially responsible media.* Lecture at Nottingham University, Business School.

Lasica, J. D. (2003). Blogs and journalism need each other, Neiman reports. *Journalism and Black America: Then and Now, 57*(3), 70–74.

Lasica, J. D. (2003). What is participatory journalism? Retrieved September 16, 2009, from www.ojr.org/

Lasica, J. D. (2008). *Newspapers must innovate or die.* Retrieved March 15, 2008, http://www.pbs.org/idealab

Leadbeater, C. (2008). *We think. mass innovation, not mass production.* London, England: Profile Books.

Lefebre, V., & Lefebre, M. R. (2012). Integrating corporate social responsibility at the start-up level: Constraint or catalyst for opportunity identification? *International Business Research, 5*, 7.

McQuail D. (2003). *Media accountability and freedom of publication.* Oxford, England: Oxford University Press.

Rosen J. (2006, June 27), The people formerly known as the audience. Retrieved March 10, 2008, from   http://archive.pressthink.org/2006/06/27/ppl_frmr. html

Sanford, C., (2012). *The responsible entrepreneur.* Retrieved July 12, 2012, from http:// www.ssireview.org/blog/entry/the_responsible_entrepreneur

Shirky, C. (2008). What newspapers and journalism need now: Experimentation not Nostalgia. Retrieved April 15, 2008, from www.britannica.com/blogs

Shirky, C. (2009). *Here comes everybody. The power of organizing without organizations.* London, England: Allen Lane.

Surowieki, J. (2004). *The wisdom of crowds: Why the many are smarter than the few and how collective wisdom shapes business, economies, societies and nations.* New York, NY: Doubleday.

Sustainability. (2002). *Good news and bad: The media, corporate social responsibility and sustainable development.* London, England: Author.

Sustainability. (2005). *Through the looking glass: Corporate and social responsibility in the media and entertainment sector.* London, England: Author

Tapscott, D., & Williams, A. (2008). *Wikinomics: How mass collaboration changes everything.* New York, NY: Portfolio.

Tsakarestou, B. (2005). The experiment of market extension. In A. Habisch, J. Jonker, M. Wegner, & R. Schmidpeter (Eds.). *Corporate social responsibility across Europe.* Berlin, Germany: Springe

Tsene, L. (2012). *From media crisis to social media: A new responsibility model for media.* Athens, Greece: Aiora.

Tsene., L. (2014). *Journalism as a multiplayer game. Applying online multiplayer games theory to journalism.* (Working Paper).

Visser, W. (2011). *The age of responsibility: CSR 2.0 and the new DNA of business.* New York, NY: Wiley.

WCED. (1987). *Our common future.* Oxford, England: Oxford University Press.

Weinberger, D. (2009). Transparency is the new objectivity. Retrieved June 15, 2010, from http://www.hyperorg.com/blogger/2009/07/19/transparency-is-the-new-objectivity/

CHAPTER 17

RECONCEPTUALIZING CORPORATE SOCIAL RESPONSIBILITY (CSR) AS CORPORATE PUBLIC RESPONSIBILITY (CPR)

Soojin Kim, Laishan Tam, and Jeong-Nam Kim

On January 23, 2014, two companies became the winners of the 2014 *Public Eye Awards* for their environmental pollution and human rights violations: Gazprom and Gap. The *Public Eye Awards* are given to the most highly nominated companies for their irresponsible business practices (The Public Eye Awards, 2014). Every year, the worst companies are nominated by a jury and the public, and the results are released around the time of the annual meeting of World Economic Forum. This online campaign highlights the consequences of the behaviors of large corporations (Chaudhuri, 2012). The cases released by the *Public Eye Awards* make us question what makes corporations socially responsible and raise doubts about the effectiveness and efficacy of CSR activities when the same corporations are also accused of being socially irresponsible.

Corporate Social Performance:
Paradoxes, Pitfalls, and Pathways to the Better World, pp. 373–388
Copyright © 2015 by Information Age Publishing
All rights of reproduction in any form reserved.

Numerous researchers attempted to define and conceptualize corporate social responsibility using multiple approaches (e.g., Carroll, 1999; Dahlsrud, 2008; Marrewijk, 2003; Podnar, 2008). However, it is still unclear what types of corporate social responsibility (hereafter CSR) activities corporations should conduct not only to fulfill their social responsibilities but also to bring tangible outcomes to their organizations. Precisely, the purpose of organizations' involvement in CSR is to contribute to social betterment, but it may also bring good tangible outcomes such as improving reputation. Even though CSR is generally seen as serving the purpose of benefiting society at large and that corporations have often been advised to be engaged in CSR activities altruistically without seeking anything in return, organizations ought to invest their resources wisely and strategically.

There remain a number of unanswered questions in CSR research and practices, such as when CSR activities are considered to be benefiting society and legitimate in the public eye, what kinds of CSR activities bring organizational effectiveness to corporations, and how to define the broad concept of society as the beneficiary of CSR activities. These unanswered questions often leave many corporations confused and make it difficult for them to devise and implement strategic CSR programs. In addition, being engaged in a variety of CSR activities which do not have any connections with their core business activities and stakeholders always lead to the criticism on the purpose of CSR activities.

A major challenge for corporations is that they have multiple stakeholders to whom they have different responsibilities. On the one hand, they have to maximize profits for their shareholders. On the other hand, they have to find a balance between profit maximization and social responsibilities. Because corporations are constrained by limited resources, they are obligated to make strategic choices about the CSR activities they are engaged in. When the BP oil spill took place, the news media criticized their CSR campaign, *Beyond Petroleum*, for failing to reveal their primary interest in profit maximization (Freeland, 2010). Its campaign has been criticized as BP's attempt to greenwash its image (Landman, 2010) although there are also positive comments about its commitment to renewable energies (David, 2013).

Another challenge for corporations is that investing a lot of money in CSR does not necessarily make them socially responsible. The authors postulate that this is because (a) the scope of CSR is often too broad to make a tangible link to the bottom line; (b) the meaning of CSR does not always mean the same thing to everyone; and (c) some organizations conduct CSR programs to create a positive image in order to cover up their misdeeds on their key publics and stakeholders. Promoting CSR activities is not necessarily unethical. However, when a corporation fails to address the needs of its key publics and fails to manage the negative consequences of its behaviors on them, CSR is considered to be serving the purpose of influencing public perceptions of organizational behaviors only.

The purpose of this book chapter is to show how corporations are criticized for being socially irresponsible despite their active involvement in CSR activities. Based on two case examples, the authors suggest a reconceptualization of CSR as *corporate public responsibility* (CPR). We propose that corporations should strategically invest their limited resources to prioritize their responsibilities to their immediate publics before they extend their CSR activities to society at large. With the new proposed concept of CSR, this book chapter seeks to address the limitation proposed in existing CSR literature that CSR is not strategic and practical.

LITERATURE REVIEW

While many scholars attempted to define CSR (e.g., Carroll, 1991; Moir, 2001; Marrewijk, 2003; Matten & Crane, 2005), not everyone understands and uses CSR in the same way (Campbell, 2007; Votaw, 1972). There are also similar terms to CSR such as corporate citizenship (Matten & Crane, 2005), corporate philanthropy, and strategic philanthropy. Although CSR has been studied and practiced for decades, there has been no consensus on what CSR is (McWilliams, Siegel, & Wright, 2006) and how organizations should conduct CSR. In other words, we are not certain about what a desirable and practical form of CSR is for both organizations and society. No organizations would ever argue that they are not obligated to fulfill their social responsibilities. CSR has become one of the most important activities for business survival (Esrock & Leichty, 1998; Sen & Bahattachrya, 2001; as cited in Kim, 2011). However, the unlimited scope of social responsibilities often makes organizations question how far their CSR activities should go (Kim, Kim, & Tam, 2015) considering their limited resources and how they can make their CSR activities more relevant to their businesses.

Among the different ways of categorizing CSR approaches, one way to view CSR as a concept is to put it on the continuum between two disciplines: ethics and economics (Windsor, 2006). One end of the continuum represents the societal approach which focuses on an organization's responsibility to society at large (e.g., Marrewijk, 2003), while the other end represents the shareholder approach which emphasizes profit maximization for shareholders and owners (Friedman, 2007). While the shareholder approach is viewed as a narrow approach because it does not consider other important stakeholders, the societal approach is seen as a broad approach because it requires organizations to take society as a whole into consideration for their CSR programs. Stewardship theory (Donaldson & Davis, 1991) can be seen as part of the societal approach which emphasizes the moral imperative, whereby organizations are expected to do the right thing regardless of its consequences on the financial performance (McWilliams, Siegel, & Wright, 2006).

The stakeholder approach (Carroll, 1999; Clarkson, 1995; Donaldson & Preston, 1995; Freeman, 1984; Garriga & Melé, 2004) became popular among many scholars when it emerged as a response to the shareholder approach. It has been considered a good compromise between the shareholder approach and the societal approach. Although it is widely accepted that the interests of stakeholders should be integrated into an organization's decision-making process, it is a challenge for organizations to decide which stakeholders should be prioritized. Carroll (1991) suggested the use of stakeholders' legitimacy and stakeholders' power as two criteria to determine the importance of stakeholders. However, Kakabadse, Rozuel, and Lee-Davies (2005) point out that the stakeholder approach is still vague for managers when it comes to dealing with the multiple and diverse interests of stakeholders.

We believe that the stakeholder approach is still a broad and impractical concept for CSR because not all stakeholders are relevant to organizations across time. Also, it does not help organizations discover a clear connection between their CSR efforts and consequences. Scholars who advocate the stakeholder approach need to propose a more delicate strategy and conceptual procedure to help organizations decide the importance or legitimacy of stakeholders. Although it is encouraging to witness the increasing number of organizations' contributing to resolving social issues, the societal approach is not feasible either, especially for organizations with limited resources. Another problem with the societal approach is that even if organizations conduct CSR activities to address broad social issues, there are many instances when they are still considered irresponsible. Even if CSR activities are conducted 'beyond' the scope of the interests of the firm (McWilliams & Siegel, 2001; McWilliams, Siegel, & Wright, 2006), they are not able to justify the misdeeds of the organization. Finally, because the fundamental responsibility of organizations is to survive, the concept and practice of CSR should be relevant and practical enough for organizations to meet their organizational goals and missions as well as to serve their stakeholders.

We also need to consider the current criticisms and problems regarding CSR practices. In many cases, the concept of CSR in corporate communication or public relations has been misunderstood and misused. For instance, CSR has been used under the instrumental or the functionalist approach to influence how stakeholders or the general population perceive the behaviors of organizations (e.g., Pomering & Johnson, 2009a, 2009b) or to cover up their wrongdoings, so CSR is sometimes considered "an invention of PR" (Frankental, 2001, p. 20). In other words, in these cases, organizations attempt to buy good images by conducting CSR activities. L'Etang (1994) was one of scholars who criticized this unethical aspect of CSR. In addition, Du, Bhattacharya, and Sen (2010) pointed out that one of the key challenges for CSR communication is the skepticism among stakeholders and publics. They argue that this skepticism is caused by problems in CSR communication, such as message content. However, promoting CSR programs is not necessarily unethical as long as it recognizes and addresses the needs of stakeholders and portrays truthful information. Problems arise when organizations focus only on improving their images by implementing CSR activities while neglecting their actual responsibilities. Stakeholders' skepticism for CSR is mainly caused by the broad scope of CSR activities which is irrelevant to stakeholders, or by organizations' irresponsible actions that do not match their words.

In addition, although there are other CSR theories which attempted to propose a more practical approach to CSR, we believe that those are not helpful for organizations in gaining legitimacy for their CSR activities. For organizations seeking to engage in CSR more strategically while maximizing profits at the same time, Wernerfelt (1984) originally proposed the resource-based-view-of-the-firm (RBV), which was later refined by Barney (1991) and then by McWilliams and Siegel's (2001) theory of the firm perspective. According to the RBV theory, CSR is used as a corporate strategy for gaining competitive advantage or for differentiating themselves from their competitors by adding social attributes to their products (McWilliams, Siegel, & Wright, 2006). For example, Hart (1995) suggested that environmental social responsibility could help organizations gain competitive advantage. From the perspective of return on investment, the RBV theory is very appealing to corporations. However, this approach fails to address the issue of whether CSR activities based on this organization-centric approach can be considered legitimate to publics even though they are relevant to business goals and generate returns on investments.

Thus, it is necessary to reconsider the practicality of the CSR concepts in current CSR-related literature and practices, and to suggest a normative, better-aimed form of CSR that addresses the needs of an organization and its stakeholders and that gives more actionable direction for organizations that seek relevance between CSR and their businesses. Based on the above discussion, the following research questions are proposed:

RQ1: How can the scope of CSR be redefined for corporations to gain practicality and relevance from their CSR activities?

RQ2: How can organizations make their CSR activities legitimate?

RECONCEPTUALIZING CSR AS
CORPORATE PUBLIC RESPONSIBILITY

This study proposes the reconceptualization of CSR as corporate public responsibility (CPR). Corporate public responsibility (hereafter CPR) is conceptually based on Grunig and Hunt's (1984) concept of public responsibility. Grung and Hunt suggest that organizations need to pay attention to the consequences of their behaviors or decisions on their immediate *publics* first before moving on to addressing general social problems. Although the term *public responsibility* was first used by Preston and Post (1975), they focused on influencing regulations that affected organizational activities rather than on publics who are affected by organizational activities (Garriga & Melé, 2004).

To explain why publics should be the focus of CSR, *publics* should be distinguished from *stakeholders* and *society*. Where CSR is discussed, it is often said that a "license to operate" is given to organizations from society at large and that their fulfillment of social responsibilities is required to serve the needs of society. Society is a broad term; it can mean either a local community or a global community (Garriga & Melé, 2004). While many scholars use the terms, *stakeholders* and *publics*, interchangeably, it should be noted that these two terms are conceptually different. According to Phillips (2003) stakeholders are people "who can assist or hinder the achievement of the organization's objectives" (p. 16). Freeman (1984, 1994, 2001) sees stakeholders as any individuals or groups affected by the organization's actions, policies, and decisions.

Publics are subgroups that arise from a stakeholder group (Grunig & Repper, 1992). According to Grunig and Repper's (1992) model for the strategic management of public relations, there are three stages: the stakeholder stage, the public stage, and the issue stage. In the stakeholder stage, both the organization and its stakeholders have behavioral consequences on each other. However, not all stakeholders become publics who perform communicative actions about the problems or issues that affect them. Publics arise when stakeholders recognize problems that they are motivated to resolve (Blumer, 1966; Dewey, 1927; Grunig, 1997, 2003). Their actions can be explained by their problem recognition, involvement recognition, constraint recognition and referent criterion (Kim & Grunig, 2011). In the issue stage, publics organize and make issues out of problems that they want to resolve as their problem solving efforts (Grunig & Repper, 1992; Kim & Grunig, 2011).

We propose CPR as an alternative CSR concept that organizations can adopt for guiding their CSR activities, so that they can find relevance of their CSR activities to their businesses and fulfill their social responsibilities at the same time. By replacing "social" with "public" in the concept of corporate social responsibility, we emphasize the responsibilities that organizations often ignore for their key publics when they expand their CSR activities to society at large (RQ1). Specifically, Grunig and Hunt (1984) define *publics* as a group of individuals who are affected by organizational decisions, recognize the problems, and decide to do something about them. Thus, organizations are advised to strategically invest resources to build relationships with them and incorporate their interests into their organizational decision processes to minimize the negative impact of organizational behaviors on them.

To explain, we suggest that good corporate social responsibility starts with good public relations by which organizations build and maintain positive relationships with their key publics by addressing the needs or issues that affect their key publics. Under the CPR approach, an organization's behaviors should match their words when dealing with its strategic publics. When it comes to prioritizing resources for fulfilling social responsibilities, the focus of CSR should be on publics instead of stakeholders. In addition, the CPR approach requires organizations to bring their 'substantive actions' not to harm their key publics and if they cause harm, they need to rectify their problematic actions (Campbell, 2007; Grunig & Kim, 2011; Kim, Hung-Baeseke, Yang, & Grunig, 2013).

If we apply the concept of CPR to the conceptual evolution of the CSR concept proposed by Verčič and Grunig (2000), CPR falls under the category of CSR 4 (corporate social reason). Corporate social responsibility (CSR1) requires corporations to be socially responsible for the general population and is often considered undesirable and impossible. Corporate social responsiveness (CSR2) is considered a practical approach with more emphasis on the management of relationships with society (Frederick, 1994a, 1994b, as cited in Verčič & Grunig, 2000) and issue management, whereas corporate social rectitude (CSR 3) is the value-added and ethical concept of corporate social responsiveness (CSR 2) that is the same as two-way symmetrical public relations. Corporate social rectitude (CSR 3) involves the proactive and interactive efforts made by public relations departments to make the organization socially responsible whereas corporate social reason (CSR 4) makes these efforts more strategic.

Hence, the CPR approach is built on the premise that organizations should fulfill their immediate responsibilities to their key publics before addressing broad social issues. For instance, if a corporation is heavily engaged in community activities but fails to meet the expectations of its employees, it is still seen as being socially irresponsible. Corporations should always strive to prioritize their publics, build relationships with them to negotiate mutual expectations, and fulfill their responsibilities to them accordingly. By prioritizing key publics and key issues concerning them, corporations are more likely to build good relationships with their strategic constituencies, the quality of which can be a good indicator of the success of CSR, and thus, their success in fulfilling their responsibilities to key publics. If these efforts are made through systematic, formalized public relations activities or as a strategic management function, then corporate public responsibility and corporate social reason (CSR4) are being practiced. When they can fulfill their corporate public responsibilities, their activities can be considered legitimate in the public eye (RQ2). In this regard, Smith, Palazzo, and Bhattacharya (2010) and Golob, Johansen, and Nielsen (2013) pointed out that consumers and suppliers are often excluded in organizations' CSR activities and that these organizations are unwilling to revise their behaviors that cause problems upon their customers and suppliers who are actually the backbones of their businesses.

Under the CPR approach, organizations are required to adjust or revise their behaviors and decisions to address the issues or needs of their publics. Without fulfilling their responsibilities for their key publics, their CSR programs for society at large are not considered socially responsible behaviors (Kim, Kim, & Tam, 2015). CPR is a proactive form of CSR whereby organizations try to reduce their problematic behaviors or revise their decisions so that they can narrow the gap of the differences between the positions of the management and its publics. Because it seeks to build good organization-public relationships and promote joint problem solving, it is a more effective way of reducing potential risks, issues and conflicts between an organization and its publics, compared to managing corporate images by conducting CSR activities which are not actually solving problems that affect key publics. In essence, CPR is about managing organizational or corporate behaviors and consequences more proactively so that it helps organizations and corporations reconcile what strategic publics expect with organizational interests. As such, organizations can become more prosocial and responsible to social actors who are potentially affected by their organizational behaviors (i.e., behavioral, strategic management paradigm of public relations, Grunig & Kim, 2011). CSR should not be employed as an instrumental activity to buy off positive images/reputation/legitimacy to influence stakeholders' perceptions of the behaviors of the organization when its behaviors are not legitimate.

METHOD

To explain a conceptualization of CPR, two case studies were selected. One of the cases involves one of the top three conglomerates in South Korea and the other one is a leading cosmetics company in South Korea. We collected information about their CSR activities and their corporate misconduct from newspaper articles, online media, and websites from August 2010 to January 2013. The authors then revisited the sources online in March 2014 for updating the cases. For the first case, Naver.com, one of the most popular portal websites in Korea, was used with specified search conditions. The keywords used included a corporate name, corporate name+ CSR, anti- + corporate name for the case search. Keyword search was applied in the title and the content. For the second case, the press releases from the corporate website, the news articles published about its misconduct collected from the Factiva database during and after the crisis, and the messages posted by publics on its Facebook page during and after the crisis, were used. Upon collection of these data, descriptions of the cases were written as shown below.

CASE EXAMPLES

Case 1. Temporary Employees From Outsourcing Companies

Company A is a global automobile manufacturer. As a leading global automaker, it has a wide range of social responsibility programs throughout the world. It claims that its sustainability activities cover India, China, Malaysia, Singapore, Australia, New Zealand, Turkey, Greece, Germany, Poland, Czech Republic, Azerbaijan, Bosnia, Ukraine, Croatia, the United States, Chile, Peru, South Africa, Morocco, Oman, and Nigeria. These activities include clean production, recycle programs, reduction of gas emissions, and development of alternative fuels. Its sustainability reports claim that as a responsible corporate citizen, it is open to communication with interested stakeholders regarding their sustainability activities. In the report, the firm acknowledges that its practices and performance may affect its stakeholders, and states that it seeks stakeholders' involvement in and relations with the firm.

However, some media reported on the low quality production of this automaker, arguing that this low quality originated from the company's illegal outsourcing system that provided poor working conditions for its temporary workers. The percentage of temporary employees among the total employee population of the company is reported to be 24%. To secure treatment equal to full-time workers, the temporary workers filed a lawsuit against the firm. In July 2010, the Supreme Court handed down its decision that the firm should hire the temporary workers as full-time workers. However, the firm did not follow the court decision; as a result, the temporary workers went on strike beginning in November 2010. Production was halted by the strike; the firm claimed that they incurred a financial loss of 200 million dollars, and that the strike was illegal. The conflict between the labor union for temporary employees and the firm became violent. With the help of armed police, the firm attacked the temporary workers who were working in the plant; the workers were beaten by police and other employees. When it looked like the strike would continue, one temporary worker tried to burn himself to death. Fortunately, his life was saved, but this act called public attention to the seriousness of this situation.

This face-off between the firm and its temporary employees will not be resolved any time soon; in 2014, the company has filed a series of lawsuit against its labor union for its activists' causing financial damages to the company since the strike in 2010. This case raises doubts about whether the company has been socially responsible to its stakeholders. What could the company have done before the conflict started? Although the strike could be considered illegal, is filing a lawsuit the only way to solve the problem? Does it really "seek stakeholder's involvement and relations with the firm" as it claims on its website? Can their social responsibility activities throughout the world legitimize their misdeeds in Korea? In their sustainability report, Korea is not included in the list of countries where the firm seeks to fulfill its social responsibilities, thus it can be argued that this firm is acting responsibly globally but not locally.

Case 2. Customer Discrimination

In January 2013, Company B, a Korean skincare and cosmetics company, was accused of discriminatorily classifying their customers into Hong Kong customers and mainland Chinese customers. A customer posted a message on Facebook, accusing the skincare company of only selling its special gift sets to mainland Chinese tourists but not local Hong Kong customers. The message immediately provoked public disapproval as hundreds of Facebook users posted the complaint on the company's Facebook page. On the following day, the issue became widely reported in the Hong Kong press; it even became the front-page story for some local newspapers.

As a result, the skincare company's Hong Kong branch published an apologetic press release on its Facebook page, its website, and various newspapers. In the apology, it pledged to start selling the gift sets to Hong Kong customers again and to take a series of measures to improve its customer service. At the end of the press release, it mentioned its CSR activities, including allowing its staff to be involved in voluntarily activities during their work hours, setting up scholarships for local universities, and making contributions to Hong Kong society.

In spite of the apology, the cosmetics company received negative comments about its policy. Gary Fan, a legislative councilor, criticized the company for trying to legitimize its reasons for the discriminatory sale policy, whereas another Legislative Councilor, Yiu Si-Wing, urged the company to be fair to all customers in its policies. Several op-ed columns related the issue to the social phenomenon of Hong Kong customers' becoming increasingly relegated as "secondary citizens" in Hong Kong. Chairman of the Hong Kong Corporate Governance Forum Prof. Simon Ho, suggested that the company's reputation had already been damaged even though the public might have accepted the apology.

In reaction to the issue, a number of customers criticized the company on its Facebook page. Some coined the apology as a fake apology, whereas others expressed discontent with the company's classification of customers which discriminated against local Hong Kong customers. Regardless of CSR activities which were mentioned in the apology, customers disregarded the activities. One Facebook user urged the company to close all their stores and get out of Hong Kong because of its irresponsible behaviors. One user re-interpreted the CSR activities mentioned in the press release as benefitting their preferred mainland Chinese customers only. Over 800 posts were found on the page within a week, most of which were criticisms, urging customers to boycott the company.

This case reflected an issue embedded in the policies of the skincare company, and that regardless of whether a corporation is actively engaged in CSR activities, its CSR activities could be reinterpreted as unethical activities when a crisis emerged. Without treating all its customers in a fair manner and building good relationships with them, a company can end up in a crisis causing them to be seen as an unethical entity in spite of their CSR involvement.

FINDINGS FROM CASES

Two case examples showed that engaging in CSR activities cannot legitimize corporate misbehaviors, and that being active in CSR activities does not necessarily make organizations socially responsible. Organizations need to watch out for the consequences of their irresponsible acts upon their immediate publics and stakeholders. In the given cases, those two corporations conducted CSR activities actively but what they do does not match how they want to be seen by the general population. In the first case, the company's involvement in CSR programs all over the world could not prevent it from being criticized for mistreating its employees, who are considered the most immediate public for an organization. In the second case, the company's references to its involvement in CSR activities could not prevent it from being accused of discriminating its customers, who are also an important strategic constituency. If they were engaged in a boycott against the organization as they suggested in their Facebook posts, they could affect the company's survival. Thus, when corporate behaviors were considered irresponsible, their CSR efforts can be considered as serving the purpose of greenwashing (Laufer, 2003) or buying a publicly responsible image. Organizations should rectify their problems that affect their key publics, such as employees or customers, before they address broad social issues such as helping underdeveloped countries or offering academic scholarships.

From the point of view of returns on investment, investing money in CSR while ignoring direct strategic publics who are the foundation of business operations is not a strategic investment. Prioritizing resources to first address the most immediate concerns of their key publics is a more strategic decision compared to helping less relevant publics or non-publics. Organizations should rethink the efficacy of their CSR activities and review their decisions or policies that may be problematic to their key publics. Organizations should realize that good public relations as organization-public relationship management is actually a foundational, yet very challenging task for fulfilling their social responsibilities.

DISCUSSION AND IMPLICATIONS

Even though CSR has almost become a mandate for every business, it is unclear what good CSR means when there are abundant cases of corporate irresponsibility conducted by the self-proclaimed socially responsible companies. We found that current CSR concepts and approaches are still vague and impractical and provide no clear direction for action. We suggested that the concept and scope of CSR be redefined as corporate public responsibility to help organizations prioritize their responsibilities to their key publics and fulfill their social responsibilities more effectively.

This study has several implications for CSR research and practices. First, this study suggests corporate public responsibility as a new CSR approach by focusing on an organization's responsibility to its key publics. Although the stakeholder approach has been considered a compromise between the shareholder approach and the societal approach, this study urges organizations to narrow down the scope of their CSR activities even further from *stakeholders* to *publics*. We believe that the CPR approach helps organizations utilize their limited sources more wisely to address issues that affect their key publics as well as their business while fulfilling their social responsibilities.

We believe that the CPR approach is a more practical and feasible way to make organizations sustainable and authentic in the public eye than other existing CSR approaches. Going beyond the scope of an organization's self-interests has been often considered moral CSR activities. However, a reconceptualization of CSR as CPR and the two case examples clearly show that going beyond the scope can still be considered immoral or irresponsible when an organization does not first fulfill its responsibilities to its key publics. Under this approach, public relations managers play a crucial role in identifying potential issues that affect publics and its management and inform the management of viable action plans to address those issues so that the organization can minimize conflicts between the organization and its key publics and improve its relationships with the publics. By fulfilling corporate public responsibility, the organization can gain competitive advantage and sustainability in the turbulent environment by winning public support.

In addition, this study attempted to clarify the current misunderstanding about CSR in public relations. Promoting CSR activities is not necessarily unethical. However, when it is employed only to create a publicly responsible image that does not match an organization's actual behaviors, it becomes problematic. When public relations is properly practiced in CSR, organizations can realize that their CSR activities start with good understanding of their key publics and issues. Their CSR activities cannot evolve into broader activities without CPR. Addressing broad social issues while ignoring key publics is not considered a legitimate social responsibility. As Grunig and Hunt (1984) said, "Publics decide whether organizations have been responsible" (p. 52). By rectifying problematic behaviors that may cause troubles on its key publics, an organization and its publics can narrow the gaps in their stances on the problems that affect both the management and the publics. Good CSR is conducted based on the strategic management of public relations. This conceptual study used case examples that contrasted active CSR efforts and socially irresponsible behaviors of corporations. Because this study did not utilize interviews with or obtain comments from the representatives of those two organizations, the findings in this study could be considered limited. Further study should be conducted to explain why the CPR approach is more effective approach than other approaches in improving business performance and organization-public relationships. Empirical research could also be done to examine whether CPR practices could potentially protect an organization from crises.

REFERENCES

Barney, J. (1991). Firm resources and sustained competitive advantage. *Journal of Management, 17*, 99–120.

Blumer, H. (1966). The mass, the public, and public opinion. In B. Berelson & M. Janowitz (Eds.), *Reader in public opinion and communication* (pp. 43–50). New York, NY: Free Press.

Campbell, J. L. (2007). Why would corporations behave in socially responsible ways? An institutional theory of corporate social responsibility. *Academy of Management, 32*(3), 946–967.

Carroll, A. B. (1991). The pyramid of corporate social responsibility: Toward the moral management of organizational stakeholders. *Business Horizons, 34,* 39–48.

Carroll, A. B. (1999). Corporate social responsibility—evolution of a definitional construction. *Business and Society, 38*(3), 268–295.

Chaudhuri, S. (2012). Public Eye award singles out mining company Vale, Barclays. *The Guardian.* Retrieved from http://www.theguardian.com/environment/2012/jan/27/public-eye-awards-vale-barclays

Clarkson, M. B. E. (1995). A stakeholder framework for analyzing and evaluating corporate social performance. *Academy of Management Journal, 27,* 42–56.

Dahlsrud, A. (2008), How corporate social responsibility is defined: An analysis of 37 definitions. *Corporate Social Responsibility and Environmental Management, 15,* 1–13.

David, J. E. (2013). "Beyond Petroleum" no more? BP goes back to basic. *CNBC.* Retrieved from http://www.cnbc.com/id/100647034

Dewey, J. (1927). *The public and its problems.* Athens, NY: Henry Holt and Company.

Donaldson, L., & Davis, J. H. (1991). Stewardship theory or agency theory: CEO governance and shareholder returns. *Australian Journal of Management, 16,* 49–64.

Donaldson, T., & Preston, L. E. (1995). The stakeholder theory of the corporation: Concepts, evidence, and implications. *Academy of Management Review, 20*(1), 65–91.

Du, S., Bhattacharya, C. B., & Sen, S. (2010). Maximizing business returns to corporate social responsibility (CSR): The role of CSR communication. *International Journal of Management Reviews.* doi:10.1111/j.1468-2370.2009.00276.x

Esrock, S. L., & Leichty, G. B. (1998). Social responsibility and corporate web pages: Self-presentation or agenda setting? *Public Relations Review, 24,* 305–319.

Frankental, P. (2001). Corporate social responsibility—a PR invention? *Corporate Communications: An International Journal, 6*(1), 18–23.

Frederick W. C. (1994a). Coda: 1994. *Business and Society, 33*(2), 165–166.

Frederick W. C. (1994b). From CSR1 to CSR2: The maturing of business-and-society thought. *Business and Society. 33*(2), 150–164.

Freeland, C. (2010, July 18). What's BP's social responsibility? *The Washington Post.* Retrieved from http://www.washingtonpost.com/wp-dyn/content/article/2010/07/16/AR2010071604070.html

Freeman, R. E. (1984). *Strategic management: A stakeholder approach.* Boston, MA: Pitman.

Freeman, R. E. (1994). The politics of stakeholder theory: Some future directions. *Business Ethics Quarterly, 4*(4), 409–421.

Freeman, R. E. (2001). Stakeholder theory of the modern corporation. In W. M. Hoffman, R. E. Frederick, & M. S. Schwartz (Eds.), *Business ethics: Readings and cases in corporate morality* (pp. 79–85). Boston, MA: McGraw-Hill.

Friedman, M. (2007). The social responsibility of business is to increase its profits. corporate ethics and corporate governance. In W. C. Zimmerli, K.

Richter, & M. Holzinger (Eds.), *Corporate ethics and corporate governance* (pp. 173–178). Berlin Heidelberg: Springer.

Garriga, E., & Mele, D. (2004). Corporate social responsibility theories: Mapping the territory. *Journal of Business Ethics, 53*, 51–71.

Golob, U., Johansen, T. S., & Nielsen, A. E. (2013, July). Corporate social responsibility as a messy problem: Linking systems and sensemaking perspectives. *Systematic Practices and Action Research,* 1–14, doi:10.1007/s11213-013-9287-7

Grunig, J. E. (1997). A situational theory of publics: Conceptual history, recent challenges and new research. In D. Moss, T. MacManus, & D. Vercic (Eds.), *Public relations research: An international perspective* (pp. 3–48). London, England: International Thomson Business Press.

Grunig, J. E. (2003). Constructing public relations theory and practice. In B. Dervin, S. Chaffee, & L. Foreman-Wernet (Eds.), *Communication, another kind of horse race: Essays honoring Richard F. Carter* (pp. 85–115). Cresskill, NJ: Hampton Press.

Grunig, J. E., & Hunt, T. (1984). *Managing public relations.* New York, NY: Holt, Rinehart and Winston.

Grunig, J. E., & Kim, J.-N. (2011). Actions speak louder than words: How a strategic management approach to public relations can shape a company's brand and reputation through relationship. *Insight Train, 1*, 36–51.

Grunig, J. E., & Repper, F. C. (1992). Strategic management, publics and issues. In J. E. Grunig (Ed.), *Excellence in public relations and communication management* (pp. 31–64). Hillsdale, NJ; Lawrence Erlbaum.

Hart, S. (1995). A natural resource-based view of the firm. *Academy of Management Review, 20*, 986–1014.

Kakabadse, N. K., Rozuel, C., & Lee-Davies, L. (2005). Corporate social responsibility and stakeholder approach: A conceptual view. *International Journal of Business Governance and Ethics, 1*(4), 277–302.

Kim, J.-N., Hung-Baesecke, C.-J., Yang, S-U., & Grunig, J. E. (2013). A strategic management approach to reputation, relationships, and publics: The research heritage of the excellence theory. In C. Carroll (Ed.), *Handbook of communication and corporate reputation* (pp. 197–212). New York, NY: Wiley Blackwell.

Kim, S. (2011). Transferring effects of CSR strategy on consumer response: The synergistic model of corporate communication strategy. *Journal of Public Relations Research, 23*(2), 218–241.

Kim, J. N., & Grunig, J. E. (2011). Problem solving and communicative action: A situational theory of problem solving. *Journal of Communication, 61*, 120–149.

Kim, S., Kim, J.-N., & Tam, L. (2015). Think socially but act publicly: Refocusing CSR as corporate public responsibility. *Journal of Public Affairs.* doi:10.1002/pa.1560

Landman, A. (2010). BP's "Beyond Petroleum" campaign losing its sheen. *PR Watch.* Retrieved from http://www.prwatch.org/news/2010/05/9038/bps-beyond-petroleum-campaign-losing-its-sheen

Laufer, W. S. (2003). Social accountability and corporate greenwashing. *Journal of Business Ethics, 43*(3), 253–261.

L'Etang, J. (1995). Ethical corporate social responsibility: A framework for managers. *Journal of Business Ethics, 14*(2), 125–132.

Marrewijk, M. (2003). Concepts and definitions of CSR and corporate sustainability: Between agency and communion. *Journal of Business Ethics, 44*, 95–105.

Matten, D., & Crane, A. (2005). Corporate citizenship: Toward an extended theoretical conceptualization. *The Academy of Management Review, 30*(1), 166–179.

McWilliams, A., & Siegel, D. (2001). Corporate social responsibility: A theory of the firm perspective. *Academy of Management Review, 26*, 117–127.

McWilliams, A., Siegel, D., & Wright, P. M. (2006). Guest editors' introduction. Corporate Social Responsibility: Strategic implications. *Journal of Management Studies, 43*(1), 1–18.

Moir, L. (2001). What do we mean by corporate social responsibility? *Corporate Governance, 1* (2), 16–22.

Phillips, R. (2003). *Stakeholder theory and organizational ethics*. San Francisco, CA: Berrett-Koehler.

Podnar, K. (2008). Guest editorial: Communicating corporate social responsibility. *Journal of Marketing Communications, 14*(2), 75–81.

Pomering, A., & Johnson, L. W. (2009a). Advertising corporate social responsibility initiatives to communicate corporate image: Inhibiting skepticism to enhance persuasion. *Corporate Communications: An International Journal, 14*(4), 420–439.

Pomering, A., & Johnson, L. W. (2009b). Constructing a corporate social responsibility reputation using corporate image advertising. *Austrian Marketing Journal, 17*(2), 106–114.

Preston, L. E., & Post, J. E. (1975). *Private management and public policy: The principle of public responsibility*. Englewood-Cliffs, NJ: Prentice-Hall.

Sen, S., & Bhattacharay, C. B. (2001). Does doing good always lead to doing better? Consumer reactions to corporate social responsibility. *Journal of Marketing Research*, 38, 225–243.

Smith, N. C., Palazzo, G., & Bhattacharya, C. B. (2010). Marketing's consequences: Stakeholder meeting and supply chain corporate social responsibilities. *Business Ethics Quarterly, 20*(4), 617–614.

The Public Eyes Award. (2014). The Public Eyes Award. Retrieved from http://publiceye.ch/

Verčič, D., & Grunig, J. E. (2000). The origins of public relations theory in economics and strategic management. In D. Moss, D. Verčič, & G. Warnaby (Eds.), *Perspectives on public relations research* (pp. 7–58), London, England: Routledge.

Votaw, D. (1972). Genius became rare: A comment on the doctrine of social responsibility. *California Management Review, 15*(2), 25–31.

Wernerfelt, B. (1984). A resource based view of the firm. *Strategic Management Journal, 5*, 171–180.

Windsor, D. (2006). Corporate social responsibility: Three key approaches. *Journal of Management Studies, 43*(1), 93–114.

CHAPTER 18

ORGANIZATIONAL MINDFULNESS IN CORPORATE SOCIAL RESPONSIBILITY

Yi-Hui Ho and Chieh-Yu Lin

INTRODUCTION

The growing global concerns on social responsibility issues have moved an increasing number of firms to include corporate social responsibility (CSR) in their business operations. Many firms regard commitment to CSR as an important variable within the current competitive scenarios. CSR issues have also received sustained research interest over time due to the multitude of factors that can affect CSR efforts. Firms can achieve considerable corporate social performance by successfully implementing CSR practices in their business systems. However, they may fail to achieve deep usage beyond initial adoption because engaging in CSR often calls for significant investment of organizational resources. CSR may start with top management awareness of the need for corporate responses to social responsibility issues, leads to policy commitment, and ideally, ends with implementation at the operational level. Successful implementation of

Corporate Social Performance:
Paradoxes, Pitfalls, and Pathways to the Better World, pp. 389–408
Copyright © 2015 by Information Age Publishing
389

CSR requires significant involvement in developing operational responses to social responsibility issues.

While implementing CSR activities, corporates are faced with the task of analyzing the ramifications of the CSR concepts or practices on their firms (Aguinis & Glavas, 2012). Under such circumstances, deciding on whether a particular CSR concept or practice is a good thing for the firm, whether the timing of the implementation is appropriate, and how the implementation is best carried out requires firms to be mindful of engaging in CSR with reasoning grounded in their own facts and specifics (Sarre, Doig, & Fiedler, 2001). In organizational decision making, mindfulness is a state of being alert and aware. It is a characteristic that is believed to aid in making contextually differentiated interpretations of situations and information scenarios (Hoy, 2003; Ndubisi, 2012b; Weick & Sutcliffe, 2006).

The mindfulness approach recognizes the value of managerial flexibility in structuring and timing investment decisions on the face of uncertain conditions, varying levels of risks at different stages of an investment project (Fiol & O'Connor, 2003; Ndubisi, 2012b). Organizational mindfulness is the connection and sharing of the mindfulness of individuals to help both individuals and organization achieve greater congruence between their intentions and outcomes (Malhotra, Lee, & Uslay, 2012; Weick & Sutcliffe, 2006). Accordingly, mindfulness theory is deemed suitable for application to investigating a firm's CSR implementation. Firms need to keep mindfulness thinking when engaging in CSR (Sarre et al., 2001; Waddock, 2001). As a result, it is necessary to understand the issues about mindfulness in implementing CSR within firms.

Although mindfulness has been considered by researchers across different disciplines and subjects (e.g., Bjurström, 2012; Dane, 2011; Ndubisi, 2012a, 2012c; Ray, Baker, & Plowman, 2011), the concept of mindfulness has not yet been employed in research on CSR in the literature. To fill the research gap, the main purpose of this chapter is to attempt to explore the application of the mindfulness concept to CSR and build a conceptual framework describing antecedents and consequences of organizational mindfulness in CSR.

The recognition of the key role of organizational mindfulness in firms' CSR implementation would be valuable for both managerial and research purposes. Understanding antecedents and consequences of mindfulness in CSR is essential for practitioners to best implement CSR activities as well as for researchers to best understand the issues that need to be addressed. A better understanding of the mechanisms supporting mindfulness in CSR advances selection and development efforts aimed at improving corporate social performance.

The followings demonstrate a review of literature on mindfulness concept in organizational behavior, illustrate an explanation for the association between mindfulness concept and corporate social responsibility, and address a discussion on the potential antecedents and consequences of organizational mindfulness in CSR. Also, a summary of the conceptual model is concluded.

MINDFULNESS CONCEPT IN ORGANIZATIONAL BEHAVIOR

Mindfulness, at its roots, is a psychological notion that reflects upon an individual's cognitive qualities (Langer, 1989; Langer & Moldoveanu, 2000). It is a state of alertness and lively awareness that characterizes active information processing, creation and refinement of different categories, and awareness of multiple perspectives. At the individual level, mindfulness can be conceptualized as a cognitive ability that is reflected by openness to novelty, alertness to distinction, sensitivity to different contexts, awareness of multiple perspectives, and orientation in the present (Langer, 1997; Sternberg, 2000). Openness to novelty includes the ability to reason about new kinds of stimuli. Alertness to distinction includes the ability to compare, contrast, and make judgments about the similarities and differences. Sensitivity to different contexts includes the awareness of the characteristics of particular situations and the changes in such situations. Awareness of multiple perspectives includes the ability to see things from different points of view. Orientation in the present includes the ability to pay attention to the immediate situation (Sternberg, 2000).

Individual mindfulness focuses on the ability to continuously create and use new categories in perception and interpretation of the world (Langer, 1997). Mindfulness captures a quality of consciousness characterized by clarity and vividness of current experience and functioning. In contrast, mindlessness is characterized by less conscious states, where people tend to function habitually and automatically (Brown & Ryan, 2003). Individuals who are mindfully engaged in a task are both motivated and able to explore a wider variety of perspectives, make more relevant and precise distinctions about phenomena in their environments, enabling them to adapt to shifts in those environments (Butler & Gray, 2006; Fiol & O'Connor, 2003).

Originally defined as an individual level characteristic, the notion of mindfulness was subsequently extended to the organizational level (Weick, 1995). But a mindful organization is more than the sum of mindful individuals (Hoy, 2003). At the organizational level, mindfulness is defined as an organizational property or capability that allows firms to operate under conditions that are characterized by high risk of functional and technological complexity and with little scope to learn from trial and error. Firms make mindful decisions based on reasoning grounded in their own organizational facts and specifics (Swanson & Ramiller, 2004). In recent years, the mindfulness concept has been introduced into organizational studies via the examination of individual and collective mindfulness within an organization.

In a study of high reliability organizations (such as air traffic control systems, nuclear power generating plants, emergency departments in hospitals, etc.), Weick and his colleagues (Weick & Sutcliffe, 2001; Weick, Sutcliffe, & Obstfeld, 1999) identify five dimensions that underlie organizational mindfulness including preoccupation with failure, reluctance to simplify interpretations, sensitivity to operations, commitment to resilience, and deference to expertise. They found that, following the five dimensions, high reliability organizations can successfully operate under risky and complicated conditions and avoid failures and accidents. Accordingly, these five characteristics have been identified as the indicators of mindfulness of organizations in managing their day to day operations (Fichman, 2004; Weick & Sutcliffe, 2001). Together these five dimensions contribute organizational mindfulness.

Preoccupation with failure refers to a perspective that assumes that errors, problems and unusual events, no matter how small, are potentially important indicators of potential problems with the health of the organization and potentially unexpected aspects of the situation. This implies that each event should be attended to understand its causes and implications. Mindful organizations are constantly looking for failures, regardless of size and seriousness, as symptoms to a larger problem. They treat any irregularity, or slight disruption, as a symptom that something is wrong, possibly resulting in severe consequences. Mindful organizations treat any unplanned changes as if something has gone wrong and could become catastrophic. They are suspicious of potential liabilities related to ongoing success, and are especially concerned with complacency, temptations to reduce margins of safety, and automatic processing. Mindful organizations support and reward individuals who identify errors, then analyze them to make improvements and prevent future occurrences (Weick & Sutcliffe, 2001).

Reluctance to simplify interpretations involves taking clear steps to avoid making things easier or over simplifying the daily operations. Members in mindful organizations share the concept that the world around them is complex and unpredictable. Expectations are not taken for granted but rather questioned. Assumptions are identified and challenged at every point. Mindful organizations situate themselves to see as much as possible, even though the world is a complex, unstable, and unpredictable place. They push the boundaries for acquiring knowledge without destroying the nuances that diverse people identify. Mindful organizations do not want to restrict or limit their opinion or view. They promote employees with diverse backgrounds and encourage them to have skepticism and criticism.

All employees must pay close attention to business operations, with the expectation of avoiding over simplification (Weick & Sutcliffe, 2001).

Sensitivity to operations denotes to have a precise understanding of all aspects of the business, both operationally and strategically. Mindful organizations are cognizant of all operations and have a well-developed situational awareness, enabling them to continuously make adjustments to prevent errors. They closely analyze routine tests to reveal any potential or real failures, which might result in an unexpected disaster. Mindful organizations regard near misses as evidence of successes, and build an environment in which imperfections and error reporting is encouraged. They are constantly looking for ambiguity or problems which may result in a failure within their workflows and processes. Employees are rewarded for questioning and testing assumptions, to find mistakes and errors (Weick & Sutcliffe, 2001).

Commitment to resilience is to be mindful of errors and correct them before they get worse. Resilience is the ability to quickly recover when disasters strike. Mindful organizations have developed the capacity to extemporize and can bounce back from organizational setbacks. They anticipate problems and come up with resolutions before problems occur. Mindful organizations resist the temptation to fret indefinitely about what has happened and instead act. They are willing to act quickly—to quickly study a situation, engage in real-time learning, and then act (Weick & Sutcliffe, 2001).

Deference to expertise implies finding the most qualified individual to make a decision or complete a job. Mindful organizations have the hierarchal structure that not only recognizes when decisions need to be made by the most qualified individual, but also has the capacity to appropriately escalate emergency situations. They recognize that expertise is not necessarily matched with hierarchical position, and thus push decisions down to the lowest levels possible (Weick & Sutcliffe, 2001).

In summary, mindfulness denotes that the ability of individuals and organizations to achieve reliable performance in a changing environment depends on how individuals and organizations think, gather information and perceive the world around them, and on whether they are able to change their perspective to reflect the situation. Mindfulness requires a desire to update situational awareness on a continuing basis, to cast doubt, and to probe further to resolve doubtfulness. Although normal business operations are carried out by firms under significantly less stringent conditions than high reliability organizations, inculcating the above five characteristics in their organizational operations can reduce chances of failure by avoiding errors in the first place (Weick & Sutcliffe 2001). Thus, mindfulness can be thought of as a desirable property or state that all firms, irrespective of their line of operation should strive to achieve, since it will make them more adept in managing unexpected circumstances (Ndubisi, 2012b; Ray et al., 2011).

As a result, since Weick and his colleagues' studies in high reliability organizations (Weick, 1995; Weick & Roberts, 1993; Weick & Sutcliffe, 2001; Weick et al., 1999), the notion of mindfulness has been receiving heightened interests in the context of different aspects of organizational behavior such as organizational learning and attention (Levinthal & Rerup 2006; McIntyre, Harvey, & Moeller, 2012; Veil, 2011; Weick & Sutcliffe, 2006), organizational information technology innovation (Butler & Gray, 2006; Carlo, Lyytinen, & Boland, 2012; Fichman, 2004; Fiol & O'Connor, 2003; Swanson & Ramiller, 2004; Valorinta, 2009; Wolf, Beck, & Pahlke, 2012; Wong & Lai, 2008; Wong, Lai, & Teo, 2009), organizational accident management (Goh, Love, Brown, & Spickett, 2012), organizational implementation of complex health improvement programs (Hales, Kroes, Chen, & Kang, 2012; Issel & Narasimha, 2007), quality management (Bjurström, 2012; Owusu-Frimpong & Nwankwo, 2012), school management (Capel, 2012; Hoy, 2003; Hoy, Gage, & Tarter, 2006; Ray et al., 2011; Vogus & Sutcliffe, 2012), human resource management (Vogus & Welbourne, 2003), marketing strategy implementation (Malhotra et al., 2012; Ndubisi, 2012c), product failure management (Itabashi-Campbell, Gluesing & Perelli, 2012), and RFID implementation (Goethals, Tütüncü, & Lin, 2010; Teo, Srivastava, Ranganathan, & Loo, 2011). Literature review revealed that the amount of organizational mindfulness studies has risen over the past few years. While mindfulness is generally considered to be a favorable property or characteristic to possess for a firm, there is still lack of research applying the mindfulness concept to CSR.

MINDFULNESS CONCEPT AND CSR

We argue that the mindfulness concept is also suitable for CSR. According to above discussions on the mindfulness concept, we hold that mindfulness in CSR, here denoted as *CSR mindfulness*, is a way of working during CSR implementation marked by a focus on the present, attention to operational detail, willingness to consider alternative perspectives and an interest in investigating and understanding failures (Langer, 1989; Weick & Sutcliffe, 2001). Firms need to keep mindfulness thinking when engaging in CSR.

Within the CSR literature, there are a variety of definitions of CSR. CSR along with the related notions of corporate social performance, corporate social responsiveness, and corporate social responses have been the subject of many conceptualizations originating mainly from the management literature over the past decades. Defining socially responsible corporate behavior is not an easy work. It involves comparing corporate behavior with some standard, such as those posed by the law or international organizations. It involves specifying the type of corporate behavior with which we are concerned. There are many possibilities, such as how a firm treats the environment, its employees, its customers, and so on. No single conceptualization of CSR has dominated past research (Montiel, 2008). Davis (1973) defines CSR as "the firm's consideration of, and response to, issues beyond the narrow economic, technical, and legal requirements of the firm." The most often cited definition is Carroll's (1979) statement that "the social responsibility of business encompasses the economic, legal, ethical, and discretionary expectations that society has of organizations at a given point in time" (Montiel, 2008). CSR refers to the notion of responsibility for the impact of corporate activities on the society. It is beyond obeying the law. CSR focuses on furthering some social good, beyond the interests of the firm and that which is required by law (McWilliams & Siegel, 2001).

CSR activities that companies carry out include monitoring and assessing environmental conditions (e.g., environmentally friendly manufacturing processes), attending to stakeholder demands (e.g., donations to charities), and designing plans and policies aimed at enhancing the firm's positive impacts (e.g., human rights programs, and corporate governance). Carroll (1991) proposes a four-level hierarchy of CSR activities: (1) economic responsibilities which aim to translate business and provide needed products and services in a market economy; (2) legal responsibilities which aim to obey laws which represent a form of codified ethics; (3) ethical responsibilities which aim to transact business in a manner expected and viewed by society as being fair and reasonable, even though not legally required; and (4) voluntary/discretionary responsibilities which aim to conduct activities which are more guided by business's discretion than actual responsibility or expectation.

Companies themselves increasingly recognize that their future profitability depends on their willingness to assume responsibility for the social and environmental consequences of their business operations. From the perspective of an investor, the goal of most companies is to pursue maximum return. However, intangible costs of the society are also being consumed at the same time when companies seek for profits. While such costs are not reflected on the financial statements, companies should keep in mind the need to put social responsibilities into practice. Otherwise, the companies may face rejection of their products by the consumers and create a negative image if they fail to fulfill their social responsibilities. CSR is no longer a heavy cost to the operations of companies. The realization and fulfillment of social responsibilities as a core operational strategy is already a topic that calls for serious consideration for companies seeking sustainable development and profits.

Companies are social systems where the collective creation of shared meanings socializes employees as they strive to make sense of their environment. To improve corporate social performance, many firms engage in CSR activities reactively or proactively. Many researchers have used a variety of theories to analyze various CSR issues (Aguinis & Glavas, 2012; Taneja, Taneja, & Gupta, 2011). Among an amount of CSR studies, however, little attention has been paid on analyzing mindful behaviors associated with CSR implementation within organizations. The implementation of a CSR concept or practice does not guarantee that there is a widespread usage of the CSR concept or practice within the firm to fulfill the CSR benefits (Dobele, Westberg, Steel, & Flowers, 2014). No matter undertaking CSR reactively or proactively, a CSR concept or practice may be introduced with a great enthusiasm; nevertheless it may fail to be thoroughly deployed among many firms.

CSR can be viewed as a form of investment (McWilliams & Siegel, 2001). CSR usually starts with top management awareness of the need for corporate responses to social issues, leads to policy commitment, and ideally, ends with implementation at the operational level. There are fundamental difficulties associated with selecting appropriate CSR concepts and practices from many possibilities. As part of this, CSR practices may be presented in ways that overemphasize benefits, downplay challenges, exaggerate the scope of applicability, and seek to create urgency by claiming that widespread industry-level adoption is inevitable and that organizational implementation is absolutely critical for the continued success and survival of the firm. In this environment, social pressures or bandwagon effects may significantly impact a firm's decisions regarding CSR (Vallaster, Lindgreen, & Maon, 2012). "Me-too" motivations can lead firms to engage in CSR activities in ways that are only partially grounded in the organizational facts and specifics.

Engaging in CSR sometimes calls for significant investment of organizational resources. Managers are faced with the task of analyzing the ramifications of CSR on their firms. Under such circumstances, deciding on whether a particular CSR concept or practice is a good thing for the firm, whether the timing of the implementation is appropriate, and how the implementation is best carried out, requires firms to be mindful of CSR with reasoning grounded in their own facts and specifics. As a result, firms require mindfulness thinking in CSR. In organizational decision-making, mindfulness is a characteristic that is believed to aid in making contextually differentiated interpretations of situations and information scenarios (Hoy, 2003; Ndubisi, 2012b; Weick & Sutcliffe, 2006). Mindfulness in the context of CSR refers to not only being knowledgeable about the CSR concept or practice and its implications, but also being able to contextualize this understanding regarding the concept or practice based on the specific circumstances prevailing in the firm and their implications on the implementation.

In a study of high reliability organizations, Weick and Sutcliffe (2001) addressed that the mindfulness approach reflects the fact that many disasters are caused not by the presence of a large, catastrophic error but rather by the unfortunate combination of small ones. Likewise successful CSR is often the result of not a single large project or decision, but the outgrowth of a fortuitous combination of many small ones (Blackman, Kennedy, & Quazi, 2013). Small disruptions, errors, and opportunities are most likely to be noticed first on the front lines of the firm where individuals involved with a firm's day-to-day operations reside. If these unexpected situations are dealt with swiftly, there is an opportunity to avoid their escalation into larger problems or to leverage them to facilitate change. Mindful firms encourage people to report all errors, near misses, and improvement opportunities and to treat them as systemic issues rather than individual events. With regard to CSR, mindful firms who are preoccupied with failure, sensitivity to operations, and deference to expertise will pay more attention to the potential pitfalls associated with implementing new CSR concepts or practices as they appear. Mindful firms are more likely to empower knowledgeable team members allowing them to deal with an incipient problem and act on emerging opportunities. Also, they will be more likely to recognize problems not as isolated events that must be dealt with simply to maintain current operations, but rather as indicative of system issues that provide opportunities for further CSR implementation. Taking together these aspects of organizational mindfulness prepare a firm to be better able to manage both the initial introduction and subsequent implementation of CSR.

For firms seeking to maximize their ability to undertake CSR, reluctance to simplify interpretations is important because some CSR activities, such as environmental management, may be prone to surprises, complexity, and the unexpected. Identification and evaluation of some CSR concepts or practices requires firms to engage in a hype-saturated, noisy information environment. Potential CSR concepts or practices must be evaluated based on second-hand information about their impact on other firms or in other contexts (Aguinis & Glavas, 2012; Kleine & Hauff, 2009). In this situation, there is the temptation to apply bandwagon logic and assume that other firms' success with CSR is a strong indicator of what a firm can expect when they implement CSR activities (Balmer, 2013; Sarre et al., 2001). Reluctance to simplify interpretations and commitment to resilience help to protect firms against this, keeping them focused on the need to understand specifically how a concept or practice is likely to fit with the unique characteristics and particular needs of their organizations (Fiol & O'Connor, 2003). Likewise, mindful firms with both reluctance to simplify interpretations and commitment to resilience are more likely to identify latent opportunities for CSR implementation because they are less likely to assume that the current processes and structures are necessarily the most appropriate. Mindful firms are likely to be better able to navigate the challenges of CSR implementation because they are less likely to become fixated on initial claims, plans, and even first round deployment objectives.

Levinthal and Rerup (2006) address that sustained mindfulness in a firm requires both the attentiveness to one's context as well as the capacity to respond to unanticipated cues or signals from one's context. This duality of mindfulness encompasses both cognitive and behavioral dimensions, and provides a helpful perspective for studying mindfulness in organizations. The cognitive aspect of mindfulness refers to gathering relevant information on the internal and external environment and being able to understand what this information means. It connotes an enhanced awareness of multiple perspectives of the current experience and present reality (Brown & Ryan, 2003; Langer, 1997). The behavioral dimension implies the enactment on the processed information, like motivation that causes the arousal to act (Miller & Chen, 1994; Mitchell, 1982), and routines that provide repertoires of action (Levinthal & Rerup, 2006). Therefore, mindfulness is a state of being alert and aware. It is a desirable organizational property that is primarily in the context of managing day-to-day operations of organizations (Weick, 1995). It considers not only how an organization creates value by integrating its competencies but also how it acts to attain business performance, that is, monitors its internal and external needs (Wong et al., 2009). Accordingly, firms also require mindfulness in implementing CSR activities. Mindfulness approach, characterized by an ability to detect changes in the environment and to contextually interpret their importance for the firm, is argued to be important for CSR. Firms need to keep organizational mindfulness when engaging in CSR.

CSR can be regarded as a firm being accountable for its business operations that affect people, the society, and the environment. This implies that any harm to people, society and environment should be acknowledged and corrected if at all possible while implementing CSR practices. Drawing on the literature of mindfulness, we define CSR mindfulness as a way of working during CSR implementation marked by a focus on the present, attention to operational detail, willingness to consider alternative perspectives and an interest in investigating and understanding failures. CSR implementation requires cultivation of organizational CSR mindfulness, a vigilant and constant awareness of the possibility of wrong-doing. CSR mindfulness can be conceptualized as an ability that is reflected by preoccupation with failure, reluctance to simplify interpretations, sensitivity to operations, commitment to resilience, and deference to expertise.

ANTECEDENTS OF CSR MINDFULNESS

In addition to investigating the nature of mindfulness in organizations, prior research on mindfulness in organizational behavior has focused on demonstrating its contributions to organizational decision making and performance. Less attention has been given to understanding potential antecedents of mindfulness (Vogus & Sutcliffe, 2012). Here, we propose some potential organizational-level predictors that may motivate CSR mindfulness within a firm.

Firms provide important organizational contexts for influencing individuals' behaviors (Hackman, 1992). The organizational context implies the processes and attributes that constrain or facilitate CSR mindfulness. Regarding CSR, several studies have discussed the influences of a variety of organizational characteristics such as quality of human resources, organizational culture, organizational size, top management's leadership, organizational support, and many others on CSR strategy (Aguinis & Glavas, 2012; Taneja et al., 2011). However, less attention has been given to understanding potential antecedents of mindfulness (Vogus & Sutcliffe, 2012). Based on a review of related literature, we propose some organizational antecedents in the present study.

External Stakeholder Focus

Stakeholders are individuals or groups who affect a firm's activities and are also affected by the firm's activities. Stakeholder pressure has been regarded as one of the most prominent factors influencing a firm's CSR strategy (Aguinis & Glavas, 2012; Dobele et al., 2014; Taneja et al., 2011; Wood, 1991). According to the stakeholder theory, firms carry out activities to satisfy their main stakeholders. CSR consciousness of a firm implies harmonizing firm performance with stakeholders' expectations. Under the circumstance of high stakeholder pressure, firms are apt to be reluctance to simplify interpretations of stakeholders' varied CSR requirements, and to keep commitment to resilience. Furthermore, reflecting firm members' collective perceptions about the relevance and value of CSR as a critical firm function, external focus has been identified as important for firms that are highly interdependent with external constituents (Choi, 2002). Firms that collectively value CSR practices should be more likely to incorporate them into their firm strategy, monitor these practices accordingly, and actively encourage CSR mindfulness throughout the firm's operations. Therefore, we propose the following proposition:

P1: A firm's focuses on external stakeholders will have a positive effect on organizational CSR mindfulness.

Organizational Learning Capability

Mindfulness calls for an awareness of sensitivity to operations and reluctance to simplify interpretations. In the context of CSR, this translates into consideration towards the different ramifications of the CSR practice on the firm's operational and strategic advantages. Qualified firm members with the ability to consider a variety of approaches to a problem simultaneously and elaborate on the details of an idea and carry it out will make a firm aware of the multiple perspectives of CSR. CSR is related to complex issues such as environmental management, human resource management, health and safety ar work, relations with local communities and relations with suppliers and consumers (Branco & Rodrignes, 2006). CSR practices sometimes incorporate both tacit and explicit knowledge. For example, the tacit knowledge regarding some environmental management activities may be inherent in identifying sources of pollution, reacting quickly to accidental spills, and proposing preventive solutions (Boiral, 2002; Gallego-Alvarez, Prado-Lorenzo, & Garcia-Sanchez, 2011). A concept or practice containing a lot of tacit knowledge requires laborious efforts to learn and diffuse. The difficulty in learning and sharing tacit knowledge makes it relatively difficult to implement a CSR concept or practice, and consequently the firm may be apt to be deference to expertise and reluctant to simplify interpretations. Furthermore, because some CSR practices are additions to firms' current business processes, implementing CSR practices is not a single event but can be described as a process of knowledge accumulation and integration. Managing the ambiguities and uncertainties surrounding societal expectations around CSR issues requires managers to explore new routines for making decisions, performing tasks, and deploying resource combinations. Organizational learning is central to implement CSR that requires firms to gain understanding of new ways of doing things (Blackman et al., 2013; Roome & Wijen, 2005). The firm members' CSR training, such as self-learning, professional education and job training, is to a certain extent a determinant factor of the level of development of the firm's CSR strategy. Enhanced firm members' awareness of CSR issues leads to improved organizational CSR mindfulness. Therefore, we propose the following proposition:

P2: A firm's organizational learning capabilities will have a positive effect on organizational CSR mindfulness.

Organizational Ethical Culture

Organizational culture is a broad term that essentially refers to a shared understanding of the reality by the members of the organization. Organizational culture governs the ways in which an organization deals with failure and mishaps, and how rewards systems are defined within the organization (Schein, 1985). Organizational culture is also associated with mindfulness behavior. Based on an analysis of high reliability organizations, Weick and Sutcliffe (2001) argue that informed organizational culture can foster mindfulness among organizations. Regarding CSR, a firm's CSR strategy is related to organizational ethical culture (Aguinis & Dlavas, 2012). The activities of CSR policymaking, auditing and strategy must be carried out in an ethical climate to create a moral corporate culture. Organizational ethical culture is a complex interplay of formal and informal systems that can support either ethical or unethical organizational behavior. Formal ethical systems embrace factors such as organizational policies, authority structures, and reward systems, while informal systems include factors such as peer behavior and perceived organizational norms and expectations (Trevino, 1990). Organizational ethical culture will influence employees' behavior. Employees' perceptions of the ethical culture in their firm influence the likelihood of dysfunctional or unethical behavior as well as affective outcomes such as organizational commitment and job satisfaction. The perceived ethical culture essentially defines what is considered legitimate or acceptable within the firm (Kaptein, 2011; Trevino, Butterfield, & McCabe, 1998). Implementing CSR can be regarded as ethical behavior (Aguinis & Glavas, 2012). Therefore, we propose the following proposition:

P3: A firm's organizational ethical culture will have a positive effect on organizational CSR mindfulness.

Business Strategic Proactivity

Business strategic proactivity implies an ability to develop entrepreneurial, engineering, and administrative skills and processes in order to actively seize and capitalize on new opportunities rather than merely react to change (Miles & Snow, 1978). This capability involves early identification of new opportunities for technological leadership, managing flexible technologies to facilitate speedy response, adopting organizational structures and processes that reduce uncertainty and facilitate innovation, and increasing innovation in managing strategic issues (Miles & Snow, 1978). A firm's business strategic attitude is relevant for the selection of CSR strategies. The capability of business strategic proactivity is positively associated with the development of proactive CSR strategy (McWilliams & Siegel, 2001; Sharma, Aragon-Correa, & Rueda-Manzanares, 2007). A firm engaging in CSR proactively would be willing to explore new CSR practices, provide more resources required for CSR implementation, and keep mindful thinking in CSR. Therefore, we propose the following proposition:

> **P4:** *A firm's business strategic proactivity will have a positive effect on organizational CSR mindfulness.*

Firm Size

Firm size is repeatedly taken as a relevant organizational factor influencing firms' CSR activities (Etzion, 2007; Udayasankar, 2008). In general, large firms have more resource availability to devote to CSR. They receive more pressure from their social and economic environment and are frequently the primary objective of local governments and nongovernmental organizations. The CSR efforts of large firms have a positive impact on a larger number of customers. Large firms tend to pay more efforts in implementing CSR than small ones. Therefore, we propose the following proposition:

> **P5:** *There is a positive association between firm size and organizational CSR mindfulness.*

CONSEQUENCES OF CSR MINDFULNESS

This chapter expects organizational CSR mindfulness to be positively related to firms' CSR and economic performance. Existing studies of organizational mindfulness and CSR support this assertion. It is believed that better CSR performance can be achieved when CSR aspects are systematically identified and managed. The main goal of implementing CSR practices is to improve CSR performance. Anecdotal information and many studies have provided a body of evidence for the positive CSR benefits from implementing CSR. Also, there are many studies supporting the hypothesis that implementing CSR is positively related to economic performance (Aguinis & Glavas, 2012; Gallego-Alvarez et al., 2011; Taneja et al., 2011). Furthermore, organizational mindfulness can help firms pay much attention to the utilization of management practices and concepts (Ndubisi, 2012b; Weick & Sutcliffe, 2001). Therefore, we propose the following propositions:

> **P6:** *Organizational CSR mindfulness will be positively related to a firm's CSR performance.*

P7: *Organizational CSR mindfulness will be positively related to a firm's economic performance.*

In addition, we suppose individual role overload that a firm member experiences is another consequence of CSR mindfulness. Despite the purported benefits of CSR mindfulness for firms, keeping CSR mindfulness is stressful and challenging, requiring considerable effort and time, and these characteristics likely contribute to role overload (Langer, 1997; Sternberg, 2000). Role overload, which exists when a firm member has too much work to do in the time available, is a type of person-role conflict in which the individual must decide on which activities to do and which to delay (Marrone, Tesluk, & Carson, 2007). These costs in terms of effort and time are largely attributable to the fact that those engaging in CSR mindfulness are responsible for actively managing a variety of internal and external contingencies either simultaneously or sequentially. Carrying out these externally directed behaviors which require the firm members to be connected both internally to their firms and externally to outsiders can contribute to role overload. Furthermore, because CSR mindfulness requires a balance with internally focused processes (Langer, 1997; Sternberg, 2000), firm members may find that they have significantly greater internal role demands as they engage in additional CSR activities. This can generate role overload by increasing the total number of role demands a firm member experiences.

Although firm members will experience greater role overload when they have high CSR mindfulness, there are also conceptual reasons for suggesting that individual role overload may be reduced when firms as a whole engage in organizational CSR mindfulness (Choi, 2002; Marrone et al., 2007). Firms engaging in higher organizational mindfulness may receive more support from firm top managers, perhaps in the form of resources that may help firm members manage their CSR responsibilities and obligations and help minimize firm members' role overload (Del Brio & Junquera, 2003; Weick & Sutcliffe, 2001). Organizational CSR mindfulness may reduce the degree to which individual firm members experience role overload. Therefore, we propose the following proposition:

P8: *Organizational CSR mindfulness will be negatively related to the amount of individual role overload that firm members experience.*

SUMMARY

While an increase in the number of CSR articles appears in the literature, there is still lack of research focusing on utilizing the mindfulness concept in CSR issues. According to above discussions, we define CSR mindfulness as a way of working during CSR implementation marked by a focus on the present, attention to operational detail, willingness to consider alternative perspectives and an interest in investigating and understanding failures. We also propose a conceptual framework about the antecedents and consequences of CSR mindfulness, as illustrated in Figure 18.1.

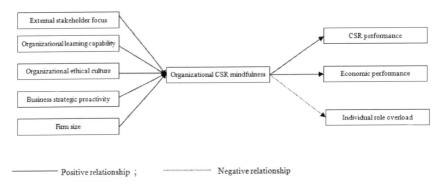

—————— Positive relationship ;   ···················· Negative relationship

Figure 18.1.   Conceptual framework.

Undertaking CSR is generally believed to impart strategic and competitive benefits to the firms. However, it also involves significant resource commitments on behalf of the firm. Chances of failing to successfully implement CSR or to appropriate business value from it are often quite high. Thus, firms are faced with a complex scenario of deciding to implement a CSR concept or practice that is relatively new and uncertain in terms of expected outcomes, but calls for large resource investments on the firm's behalf. CSR may be introduced with a great enthusiasm; nevertheless it may fail to be thoroughly deployed among many firms. Based on the literature review and theoretical considerations, we think it is time to add more understanding on mindfulness in CSR.

Although there is not an abundance of research on mindfulness in organizational behavior, those studies that deal with mindfulness provide some useful clues to the present study. While there is an increase in theoretical and case-based empirical works regarding the nature of mindfulness, understanding the antecedents and consequences of mindfulness remains a challenge. As a result, this chapter attempts to build a conceptual framework exploring the antecedents and consequences of CSR mindfulness. The present study can broaden the scope of research both on CSR issues and mindfulness theory. Based on the proposed CSR mindfulness concept, the future study can equip research on CSR mindfulness with some empirical evidence.

REFERENCES

Aguinis, H., & Glavas, A. (2012). What we know and don't know about corporate social responsibility: a review and research agenda. *Journal of Management, 38*(4), 932–968.

Balmer, J. M. T. (2013). Corporate brand orientation: What is it? What of it? *Journal of Brand Management*, 20(9), 723–741.

Bjurström, E. (2012). Minding the contexts of mindfulness in quality management. *International Journal of Quality & Reliability Management, 29*(6), 699–713.

Blackman, D., Kennedy, M., & Quaz, A. (2013). Corporate social responsibility and individual resistance: Learning as the missing link in implementation. *Management Learning*, 44(3), 237–252.

Boiral, O. (2002). Tacit knowledge and environmental management. *Long Range Planning*, 35(3), 291–317.

Branco, M., & Rodrigues, L. L. (2006). Corporate social responsibility and resource-based perspective. *Journal of Business Ethics*, 69(2), 111–132.

Brown, K. W., & Ryan, R. M. (2003). The benefits of being present: mindfulness and its role in psychological well-being. *Journal of Personality and Social Psychology, 84*(4), 822–848.

Butler, B., & Gray, P. H. (2006). Reliability, mindfulness, and information systems. *MIS Quarterly, 30*(2), 211–224.

Capel., C. M. (2012). Mindlessness/mindfulness, classroom practices and quality of early childhood education: An auto-ethnographic and intrinsic case research. *International Journal of Quality & Reliability Management, 29*(6), 666–680.

Carlo, J. L., Lyytinen, K., Boland Jr., R. J. (2012). Dialectics of collective minding: contradictory appropriations of information technology in a high-risk project. *MIS Quarterly, 36*(4), 1081–1108.

Carroll, A. B. (1979). A three-dimensional conceptual model of corporate social performance. *Academy of Management Review*, 4, 497–505.

Carroll, A. B. 1991. The pyramid of corporate social responsibility: Toward the moral management of organizational stakeholders. *Business Horizons*, 34, 39–48.

Choi, J. N. (2002). External activities and team effectiveness: review and theoretical development. *Small Group Research, 33*(1): 181–208.

Dane, E. (2011). Paying attention to mindfulness and its effects on task performance in the workplace. *Journal of Management*, 37(4), 997–1018.

Davis, K. (1973). The case for and against business assumption of social responsibilities. *Academy of Management Journal*, 16, 312–322.

Del Brio, J. A., & Junquera, B. (2003). A review of the literature on environmental innovation management in SMEs: implications for public policies. *Technovation, 23*(12), 939–948.

Dobele, A. R., Westberg, K., Steel, M., & Flowers, K. (2014). An examination of corporate social responsibility implementation and stakeholder engagement: A case study in the Australian mining industry. *Business Strategy & the Environment*, 23(3), 145–159.

Etzion, D. (2007). Research on organizations and the natural environment, 1992–present: A review. *Journal of Management*, 33(4), 637–664.

Fichman, R. G. (2004). Going beyond the dominant paradigm for information technology innovation research: Emerging concepts and methods. *Journal of the Association for Information Systems, 5*(8), 314–355.

Fiol, C. M. & O'Connor, E. J. (2003). Waking up! Mindfulness in the face of band-wagons. *Academy of Management Review, 28*(1), 54–70.

Gallego-Alvarez, I, Prado-Lorenzo, J. M., & Garcia-Sanchez, I.-M. (2011). Corporate social responsibility and innovation: a resource-based theory. *Management Decision, 49*(10), 1709–1727.

Goethals, F., Tütüncü, Y., & Lin, C. Y. (2010), Drivers for RFID implementations. *Lecture Notes in Business Information Processing, 52*, 67–79.

Goh, Y. M., Love, P. E. D., Brown, H., & Spickett, J. (2012). Organizational accidents: a systemic model of production versus protection. *Journal of Management Studies, 49*(1), 52–76.

Hackman, J. R. (1992). Group influences on individuals in organizations. In M. D. Dunnette & L. H. Hough (Eds.), *Handbook of industrial and organizational psychology:* 199–267. Palo Alto, CA: Consulting Psychologists Press.

Hales, D. N., Krobes, J., Chen, Y., & Kang, K. W. (2012). The cost of mindfulness: a case study. *Journal of Business Research, 65*(4), 570–578.

Hoy, W. K. (2003). An analysis of enabling and mindful school structures: Some theoretical, research and practical considerations. *Journal of Educational Administration, 41*(1), 87–108.

Hoy, W. K., Gage, C. Q., & Tarter, C. J. (2006). School mindfulness and faculty trust: necessary conditions for each other? *Educational Administration Quarterly, 42*(2), 236–255.

Issel, L. M., & Narasimha, K. M. (2007). Creating complex health improvement programs as mindful organizations: from theory to action. *Journal of Health Organization and Management, 21*(2), 166–183.

Itabashi-Campbell, R., Gluesing, J., & Perelli, S. (2012). Mindfulness and product failure management: an engineering epistemology. *International Journal of Quality & Reliability Management, 29***(6)**, 642–665.

Kaptein, M. (2011). Understanding unethical behavior by unraveling ethical culture. *Human Relations, 64*(6), 843–869.

Kleine, A., & Hauff, M. (2009). Sustainable-driven implementation of corporate social responsibility: Application of the integrative sustainability triangle. *Journal of Business Ethics, 85*(3), 517–533.

Langer, E. J. (1989). *Mindfulness.* Reading, MA: Addison Wesley.

Langer, E. J. (1997). *The power of mindful learning.* Reading, MA: Addison Wesley.

Langer, E. J., & Moldoveanu, M. (2000). The construct of mindfulness. *Journal of Social Issues, 56*(1), 1–9.

Levinthal, D., & Rerup, C. (2006). Crossing an apparent chasm: bridging mindful and less-mindful perspectives on organizational learning. *Organization Science, 17*(4), 502–513.

Malhotra, N. K., Lee, O. F., & Uslay, C. (2012). Mind the gap: the mediating role of mindful marketing between market and quality orientations, their interaction, and consequences. *International Journal of Quality & Reliability Management, 29*(6), 607–625.

Marrone, J. A., Tesluk, P. E., & Carson, J. B. (2007). A multilevel investigation of ancedents and consequences of team member boundary-spanning behavior. *Academy of Management Journal, 50*(6), 1423–1439.

McIntyre, N. H., Harvey, M., & Moeller, M. (2012). The role of managerial curiosity in organizational learning: a theoretical inquiry. *International Journal of Management, 29*(2), 659–676.

McWilliams, A., & Siegel, D. (2001). Corporate social responsibility: A theory of the firm perspective. *Academy of Management Review, 26*(1), 117–127.

Miles, R., & Snow, C. (1978). *Organizational strategy, structure and process,* New York: McGraw Hill.

Miller, D., & Chen, M. J. (1994). Sources and consequences of competitive inertia: a study of the U.S. airline industry. *Administrative Science Quarterly, 39*(1), 1–23.

Mitchell, T. R. (1982). Motivation: new directions for theory, research, and practice. *Academy of Management Review, 7*(1), 80–88.

Montiel, I. (2008). Corporate social responsibility and corporate sustainability separate pasts, common futures. *Organization & Environment,* 21, 245–269.

Ndubisi, N. O. (2012a). Mindfulness, reliability, pre-emptive conflict handling, customer orientation and outcomes in Malaysia's healthcare sector. *Journal of Business Research, 65*(4), 537–546.

Ndubisi, N. O. (2012b). Mindfulness, quality and reliability in small and large firms. *International Journal of Quality & Reliability Management, 29*(6), 600–606.

Ndubisi, N. O. (2012c). Relationship quality: upshot of mindfulness-based marketing strategy in small organizations. *International* Journal *of Quality & Reliability Management, 29*(6), 626–641.

Owusu-Frimpong, N., & Nwankwo, S. (2012). Service quality orientation: an approach to diffusing mindfulness in SMEs. *International Journal of Quality & Reliability Management, 29*(6), 681–698.

Ray, J. L., Baker, L. T., & Plowman, D. A. (2011). Organizational mindfulness in business schools. *Academy of Management Learning & Education, 10*(2), 188–203.

Roome, N., & Wijen, F. (2005). Stakeholder power and organizational learning in corporate environmental management. *Organization Studies, 27*(2), 235–263.

Schein, E. H. (1985). *Organization culture and leadership: A dynamic view.* San Francisco, CA: Jossey-Bass.

Sarre, R., Doig, M., & Fiedler, B. (2001). Reducing the risk of corporate irresponsibility: The trend to corporate social responsibility. *Accounting Forum, 25*(3), 300–317.

Sharma, S., Aragon-Correa, J. A., & Rueda-Manzanares, A. (2007). The contingent influence of organizational capabilities on proactive environmental strategy in the service sector: an analysis of North American and European Ski resorts. *Canadian Journal of Administrative Sciences, 24*(4), 268–283.

Sternberg, R. J. (2000). Images of mindfulness. *Journal of Social Issues, 56*(1), 11–26.

Swanson E. B., & Ramiller, N. C. (2004). Innovating mindfully with information technology. *MIS Quarterly, 28*(4), 553–583.

Taneja, S. S., Taneja, P. K., & Gupta, R. K. (2011). Researches in corporate social responsibility: A review of shifting focus, paradigms, and methodologies. *Journal of Business Ethics,* 101, 343–364.

Teo, T. S. H., Srivastava, S. C., Ranganathan, C., & Loo, J. W. K. (2011). A frame-work for stakeholder oriented mindfulness: case of RFID implementation at YCH Group, Singapore. *European Journal of Information Systems, 20*(2), 201–220.

Trevino, L. K. (1990). A cultural perspective on changing and developing organizational ethics. *Research in Organizational Change and Development, 4*, 195–230.

Trevino, L. K., Butterfield, K. D., & McCabe, D. L. (1998). The ethical context in organizations: influences on employee attitudes and behaviors. *Business Ethics Quarterly, 8*(3), 447–76.

Udayasankar, K. (2008). Corporate social responsibility and firm size. *Journal of Business Ethics, 83*(2), 163–175.

Vallaster, C., Lindgreen, A., & Maon, F. (2012). Strategically leveraging corporate social responsibility: A corporate branding perspective. *California Management Review, 54*(3), 34–60.

Valorinta, M. (2009). Information technology and mindfulness in organizations. *Industrial and Corporate Change, 18*(5), 963–997.

Veil, S. R. (2011). Mindful learning in crisis management. *Journal of Business Communication, 48*(2), 116–147.

Vogus T. J., & Welbourne T. M. (2003). Structuring for high reliability: HR practices and mindful processes in reliability-seeking organizations. *Journal of Organizational Behavior, 24*(7), 877–903.

Vogus, T. J., & Sutcliffe, K. M. (2012). Organizational mindfulness and mindful organizing: a reconciliation and path forward. *Academy of Management Learning & Education, 11*(4), 722–735.

Waddock, S. (2001). Integrity and mindfulness: Foundations of corporate citizenship. *Journal of Corporate Citizenship, 1*(1), 25–37.

Weick, K. E. (1995). *Sensemaking in organizations.* Thousand Oaks, CA: Sage.

Weick K. E., & Roberts K. H. (1993). Collective mind in organizations: heedful interrelating on flight decks. *Administrative Science Quarterly, 38*(3), 357–381.

Weick K. E., & Sutcliffe K. M. (2001). *Managing the unexpected: assuring high performance in an age of complexity.* San Francisco, CA: Jossey-Bass.

Weick, K. E., & Sutcliffe, K. M. (2006). Mindfulness and the quality of organizational attention. *Organization Science, 17*(4), 514–524.

Weick, K. E., Sutcliffe, K. M., & Obstfeld, D. (1999). Organizing for high-reliability: processes of collective mindfulness. *Research in Organizational Behavior, 21*, 81–123.

Wolf, M., Beck, R., Pahlke, I. (2012). Mindfully resisting the bandwagon: reconceptualising IT innovation assimilation in high turbulent environments. *Journal of Information Technology, 27*(3), 213–235.

Wong, C. W. Y., & Lai, K.-H. (2008). Organizational mindfulness and the development of information technology for logistics operations: the experience of an apparel company. *Research Journal of Textile and Apparel, 12*(3), 30–37.

Wong, C. W. Y., Lai, K.-H., & Teo, T. S. H. (2009). Institutional pressures and mindful IT management: the case of a container terminal in China. *Information & Management, 46*(8), 434–441.

Wood, D. J. (1991). Corporate social performance revisited. *Academy of Management Review, 16*(4), 691–718.

CHAPTER 19

THE TRANSFORMATIONS THROUGH THE TEACHING OF CORPORATE SOCIAL PERFORMANCE (CSP) UTILIZING CASE STUDIES, INTERVIEWS, VIDEOS AND SOCIAL MEDIA IN KNOWLEDGE TRANSFER IN TERTIARY SCHOOLS OF MANAGEMENT

Peter Odrakiewicz

AN EXPLANATION OF THE PROBLEM

This chapter seeks to demonstrate the innovative ways by which corporate social performance (CSP) knowledge transfer and corporate social performance teaching in universities and management colleges can improve

Corporate Social Performance:
Paradoxes, Pitfalls, and Pathways to the Better World, pp. 409–422
Copyright © 2015 by Information Age Publishing
All rights of reproduction in any form reserved.

performance. The author first examines these innovative methods of CSP knowledge transfer and their role in the teaching of CSP integrity. Second, the chapter highlights the importance of this subject in management education at institutions of higher learning, as well in business enterprises. It is an exploration of challenging learning and corporate social performance competences acquisition from innovatively defined and designed case studies, including practical examples (interviews, video-conferencing, web-based meetings, shared workspaces, wikis, virtual meeting spaces, and social and professional web networks). Impediments to CSP skills acquisition in institutions of higher learning can be the result of both poor attention to the issues of CSP knowledge transfer in educational management and can also stem from a lack of consultation with key players on the importance of this subject in colleges and universities. Additionally, owners or their representatives/CEOs, company directors, who knowingly or unknowingly perpetrate anti-CSP management environments, as they aim to implement a "bottom line profit" philosophy at all costs, lacking CSP ingredients, are impediments in this process.

There is an increased need in the world of academia and also in a wide range of industries, from small businesses to corporate giants, to cooperate together, exchange ideas and learn from each other in order for CSP knowledge transfer to be an effective tool in equipping future managers and leaders with CSP integrity competences. These CSP integrity competences will allow their firms to compete in an ever-changing, very competitive and challenging globalized multicultural environment—one that is increasingly intertwined and diverse—in order to succeed.

Lack of knowledge and poor competence transfer delivery in training and educational settings in small to medium-sized service providers, combined with personality conflicts, can result in people delaying or refusing to communicate a philosophy of CSP in the managerial process. As well, the personal attitudes of individual employees, which may be due to lack of motivation or dissatisfaction at work, can lead to insufficient or inappropriate CSP knowledge transfer while teaching this subject. This is especially problematic because stakeholders are becoming more and more concerned about the corporate social performance (CSP) of firms' operations.

DEFINING CORPORATE SOCIAL PERFORMANCE AND TRANSFER OF KNOWLEDGE

CSP can be defined as "a construct that emphasizes a company's responsibilities to multiple stakeholders, such as employees and the community at large, in addition to its traditional responsibilities to economic shareholders" (Turban & Greening, 1996, p. 658). CSP integrity knowledge transfer as defined in this chapter suggests a knowledge transfer in the process of CSP teaching that is sound, undivided and complete.

However, it is important to keep in mind that impediments beyond individual personalities may be the problem. For example, language or cultural barriers can undermine integrity (Griffith & Harvey, 2002), as can ineffective or inefficient channels of communication needed for the implementation of integrity management training and guidance. Odrakiewicz (2013) noted that cultural and social influences in various business environments may prevent students and workers from effective competence acquisition using social media in higher education. Additionally, they may impede transfer of the concept of a "construct that emphasizes a company's responsibilities to multiple stakeholders, such as employees and the community at large, in addition to its traditional responsibilities to economic shareholders" (Turban & Greening, 1996, p. 658). Awareness of such impediments is the first step in educators and managers acquiring the necessary tools for managing CSP and integrity education and training.

Studying CSP and integrity learning challenges using social media allows us to face new experiences and enables us to develop a global mindset. Self-examination of values, personal, cultural, or organizational, can come from new experiences, from our leaving the safety of what we know and experiencing something new and different. A global mindset allows us to transcend the constraints of our experiences and belief systems and to see the world for what it really is. In order to effectively approach the fast-paced global world, people need to work across disciplines and think holistically. CSP integrity competence education that prepares professionals for an increasingly global frame of reference will require educators and managers to inculcate those in their charge with adaptability and flexibility, while balancing this with the tools of instilling ethical reasoning and a commitment to one's own individual moral equilibrium. The process of refining these emerging global integrity competencies will be accomplished through the use of E-learning, blended learning, social media and personalized learning environments. Video-conference and collaborative blog-based methodology are beneficial in teaching CSP integrity in education and management, and they facilitate the acquisition of global CSP integrity competence.

Corporate social performance (CSP), integrity, ethics in management and management education are all intertwined. CSP competence acquisition is a new blood of business success in a new ultracompetitive environment. First, we can postulate that ethics is the foundation for codes of conduct. It is a branch of philosophy that addresses questions of morality. The questions can be answered by adhering to a set of behavioral guidelines. Because the workplace is the source of bread and butter for many, it can also satisfy self-actualization needs. In fact, work often provides a raison d'être beyond the simple maintenance of a standard of living. However, following ethical practices in the workplace is ultimately a personal choice. It is a choice that cannot be forced upon employees; it can only serve as a source of explanation of—as well as be a vehicle for—an overall CSP integrity management strategy. It can only be expected to form part of the overall CSP integrity management strategy.

A workplace is a cluster of individuals, and hence an amalgamation of attitudes and imaginations. This diversity can sometimes dilute the adherence to ethical standards of conduct. It takes the zeal of an evangelist to have the workforce imbibe of ethics while growing the organization in a holistic way (Gaikwad, 2010). But having integrity is not a state in which one is debilitated due to a strict adherence to a normative code; integrity is indivisible from the growth of both individuals and the organization. Modern organizations today do focus mainly on profit-making. There is, however, a new trend to resurrect integrity and ethics in the workplace.

Various multinational corporations today have incorporated ethics and integrity training for all their employees, from those working at the junior level to the CEO. Their employees understand what ethics are and how they can benefit the company in the long run. Many organizations, both in the public and private sectors, have designed their own workplace ethics training programs. These programs offer practical solutions to employees facing ethical dilemmas. Despite these advances in corporate training many employees lack business ethics awareness and knowledge about their role in integrity as an organizational philosophy. These programs focus on two core messages: first, ethical dilemmas are part of the world of work; and second, there are written policies and guidance on how to work through these ethical dilemmas, and they are available to all employees. These resources give a contextualizing framework to the employees upon which they can make ethical decisions. A rewards system for ethics and values, alongside one's performance, is another method of CSP and ethics promotion among employees. It is one that is increasingly being employed by many organizations.

THE ROLE OF EDUCATIONAL INSTITUTIONS AND TEACHERS IN THE TRANSFER OF CORPORATE SOCIAL PERFORMANCE

There are definite challenges to examining corporate social performance that is integrity oriented, and to implementing culturally sensitive (CSP) knowledge transfer in universities and in colleges of management utilizing case studies, videos, interviews, and social media because according to many studies the subject itself is hard to define. Max B. E. Clarkson (1995) stated that a fundamental problem in the field of business and society has been that there are no definitions of corporate social performance (CSP), corporate social responsibility (CSR1), or corporate social responsiveness (CSR2) that provide a framework or model for the systematic collection, organization, and analysis of corporate data relating to these important concepts. No theory has yet been developed that can provide such a framework or model, nor is there any general agreement about the meaning of these terms from an operational or a managerial viewpoint. Wood's (1991) concern that the "definition of corporate social performance (CSP) is not entirely satisfactory" is shared by many scholars and managers. CSP, together with CSR1 and CSR2, carry no clear meaning and remain elusive constructs (Clarkson, 1995).

Chen and Delmas (2010) state stakeholders are becoming more and more concerned about the corporate social performance (CSP) of firms' operations. CSP can be defined as "a construct that emphasizes a company's responsibilities to multiple stakeholders, such as employees and the community at large, in addition to its traditional responsibilities to economic shareholders" (Turban & Greening, 1996, p. 658). For example, investors are increasingly using socially responsible investing (SRI) screens to select or avoid investing in firms according to their environmental and social preferences (Chatterji, Levine, & Toffel, 2009). Chen and Delmas, 2010 quote several important studies below that similarly, a growing number of consumers purchase ecolabeled products that signal a lower environmental and social impact of corporate operations (Loureiro & Lotade, 2005). Some corporations are also developing socially responsible purchasing practices to promote more sustainable supply chains (e.g., Bowen, Cousins, Lamming, & Farukt, 2001; Carter & Rogers, 2008; Seuring & Müller, 2008). However, measuring CSP has proven to be a daunting task because it represents a broad range of economic, social, and environmental impacts caused by business operations and thus requires multiple metrics to fully cover its scope (Gond & Crane, 2009; Rowley & Berman, 2000).

How then, given these difficulties in pinning down CSP, can you successfully transfer such a broad and poorly defined concept of corporate social performance, integrity orientation and culturally sensitive (CSP) knowledge in universities, colleges of management, and through formal and informal training activities?

This chapter claims that such knowledge can be transferred much more effectively utilizing videos, interviews and social media while students study CSR, business ethics, moral principles, integrity, and CSP in order to humanize modern work and corporations. As an example, a student in a CSP class can carry out interviews utilizing local business contacts and obtain information and even conduct these interviews through social media, while class assignments may be related to joining CSR- and CSP-oriented social media groups. The teacher can act as a facilitator of learning and as a thematic blog oriented moderator. The proposed interview questions can range from simple assigned CSP-related questions such as:

- What does CSP mean for your organization at the personal, group and organizational levels?
- Can you provide specific examples how do you ensure your firm, organization/corporation is performing that you deem as the best possible CSP?
- How do you implement and develop the need for corporate social performance in your organization?

Students are to carry out these interviews in local or global companies obtained through networking contacts, or from contacts obtained using social media, and report their findings in the classroom. At the same time, they may instigate a discussion forum on line, using a social media-created interest group, with the teacher as a moderator and facilitator of learning. This can be performed without disclosing the names of the companies (they are known to researcher-student in this case and, if the company permits, to the teacher). Such activities will increase awareness about ethics and moral standards in a broad range of social interactions, including in business life, raised by schools, colleges, and universities in cooperation with the business community in the sphere of social media interactions.

The terms "ethical" and "moral," are used in two ways. First the term 'ethical' is used as a synonym for the moral quality of conduct. When, for example, we speak of people being "ethical" or "unethical," we often mean that they habitually or intentionally act, or fail to act, in "good faith"— that they consistently do, or fail to do, what is right. "Ethical" may also refer to a "class" of judgments pertaining to morality, distinguishable from other classes such as factual, perceptual and logical judgments: Here the terms "ethical" and "moral" do not denote that which is unethical or immoral, but pertain to ethics or morality as opposed to that which is nonmoral or nonethical (Rudder, 1999). While no one seems to believe that business schools or their faculties bear the entire responsibility for the integrity and ethical decision-making processes of their students, these same institutions do have some burden of accountability for educating students with respect to these skills. The role of the faculty is to incorporate integrity teaching into the modern communications arena using social media, such as Linkedin, Facebook, and Twitter, real life case studies, work-study-internship examples, and blogs on integrity-related discussions.

Additionally, instructors can employ nonstandard approaches, such as community visits to local companies where integrity-related interviews are carried out by students. These interviews will in fact become integrity teaching materials for real life, taking the form of interview videos, interview transcripts, and portions of analytical works, such as papers, reports, or studies. To that end, the standards promulgated by the Association to Advance Collegiate Schools of Business (AACSB), require that students learn ethics as part of a business degree. However, since the AACSB does not require the inclusion of a specific course to achieve this objective, it may be satisfied by establishing a stand-alone course in ethical decision-making or by integrating ethical decision making into the existing curricula, by a combination of the two strategies, or through some alternative mechanism. The method employed notwithstanding, an institution of higher learning must ensure that it is able to demonstrate the students' study of ethics (Hartman & Werhane, 2010).

A SPECIFIC COMPETENCE TO
TEACH CORPORATE SOCIAL PERFORMANCE

The process of imbibing integrity competence that reflects high ethical standards can be facilitated by adherence to a specific competence that, as presented in this chapter, is twofold: ethics courses should be more strongly integrated into existing curricula and also the quality of teaching can be fine-tuned to better support the delivery of this code of ethics. In European Union countries accrediting and licensing governmental and nonprofit agencies, students are required to study business ethics as a part of their academic curriculum, regardless of the type of degree: business, management, or economics, as examples. However, the process is not very structured in many schools where business ethics courses are offered as electives only. Most often, the courses are not part of the overall integrity, ethics and corporate social performance education program and are not part of an institutionally-organized instructional approach and educational philosophy. Therefore, it is highly recommended that student groups do one or more of the following:

- participate in integrity CSP and ethics exercises or scenarios using role-playing or social media;
- create integrity, ethics, and CSP discussion groups on line;
- conduct and record video interviews on the topic of CSP integrity and ethics;

All of these are active methods for students to use in order to acquire a basic orientation towards and knowledge of issues related to business ethics. Students will get the feeling they are part of the solution related to the challenges of CSP knowledge transfer in educational settings (Odrakiewicz, 2014a, 2014b).

In the field of education, ethical policies are typically recognized as protecting individuals from ethnic and gender discrimination, sexual harassment, physical brutality, violations of confidentiality, nepotism, inhumane research, and other violations of civil and human rights. Policies addressing professional competence, such as the setting standards for good teaching, tenure and promotion, are not typically identified as pertaining to ethics. Both types of policies, however, typically pertain to morality in that they both attempt to direct conduct towards what is "right" or towards that which is in keeping with policies pertaining to morality. Unfortunately, our tendency to restrict professional ethics to matters pertaining to the protection of civil and human rights, and to treat issues related to competence as nonethical, obscures significant professional moral and ethical problems and dilemmas (Rudder, 1999).

Brent K. Simonds noted in his book, *Communication Teacher* that in recent years many reports have emerged that purport a widespread lack of educational excellence in teacher preparation. According to Simonds, reports from individuals, professional organizations, and national commissions have presented in-depth critiques of the state of teacher education in the United States today, and throughout the world at-large (e.g., Carnegie Forum on Education and the Economy, 1986; Goodlad, 1990; Holmes Group, 1986; Kaplan & Edelfelt, 1996; Vaughan, Edelfelt, Houston, & Arisman, 1998). Many reports and surveys strongly suggest that an important component of teacher education, that of communication skills training, is often overlooked (Hunt, Simonds, & Cooper, 2002). Those responsible for educating and training future teachers must prepare all future teachers for diversity by focusing on how to communicate with a wide range of learners (Timm & Armstrong, 2000). Many professional accreditation agencies must accommodate a wide range of learners (Timm & Armstrong, 2000).

Many professional accreditation agencies (e.g., the Association for Childhood Education International, the Illinois Professional Teacher Standards, the Interstate New Teacher Assessment and Support Consortium, and the National Council for Accreditation of Teacher Education) have realized this need and now mandate that schools prepare teachers for diversity in the classroom. (Hunt, Simonds, & Cooper, 2002).

Many associations and governing bodies in EU do not fulfil this requirement, especially in the former East Bloc countries (Odrakiewicz, 2010), negating the need for complex integrity in management teaching systems and the need for CSP-effective and interactive education. This is often due to overall societal lack of awareness of the value of CSP and integrity in management and ethical communication in educational organizations and throughout society. The challenge of addressing student diversity is exacerbated by the fact that pre-service teachers often do not receive communication skills training (Hunt et al., 2002). Communication clarity, vocal variety, presentation aids and dealing with communication apprehension are rarely a part of the teacher education curriculum. Yet, these skills are central to many classroom processes. Given the relationship between effective teaching and communication, teacher educators must begin to explore ways to integrate communication skills training into teacher education programs.

The identification of specific communication skills should be the first step in this process. One such communication skill that has been closely associated with teacher effectiveness is immediacy (Talbert-Johnson & Beran, 1999). Teacher immediacy is defined as communicative behaviours that influence the perception of physical and psychological closeness (Richmond, Gorham, & McCroskey, 1987). Research indicates that teacher immediacy is positively associated with student cognitive and affective learning (e.g., Andersen & Andersen, 1987; Chesebro & McCroskey, 2001; Christophel, 1990; Frymier, 1994; Plax, Kearney, Richmond, & McCroskey, 2012). In fact, teacher immediacy behaviours have been linked to positive attitudes toward courses and instructors, greater motivation to learn, greater achievement, and greater perceptions of control (Christophel, 1990; Frymier, 1994).

CORPORATE SOCIAL PERFORMANCE, PERSONAL VALUES, MORALS AND WORKPLACE ETHICAL PERFORMANCE

Since individuals are the instruments who carry the process of making ethical decisions, many factors influence that process. These may include things all the way from early childhood understanding of ethical behavior, through the examples set by parents, teachers and spiritual leaders, to the behavior of organizational leaders and formal organizational codes of conduct.

Even though most instances of ethical and integrity misconduct are motivated for positive business or corporate performances reasons (i.e., financial, productivity, efficiency, effectiveness, etc.), good people sometimes do bad things believing that they are acting in the corporation's best interest. Much evidence has come out in recent years indicating that many instances of executive misbehaviour have been extremely costly to the firms or institutions with which such persons were affiliated (Khera, 2010). A substantial amount of the research related to culture and business ethics has been done by Geert Hofstede himself or by others using one or more of his dimensions of cultures, that is, the concepts of power distance, individualism versus collectivism, uncertainty avoidance, long-term versus short term orientation and masculinity versus femininity particular to different cultures. Such studies include ethical attitudes of business managers in India, the Republic of South Korea, and the United States, the effects of Hofstede's typologies on ethical decision making and on sales force performance and many more studies (Khera, 2010).

We should keep in mind that the use of case studies can be highly effective. For instance, the innovative method of synchronous knowledge delivery proposed by the Global Partner Management Institute social media CSP innovative competence acquisition method (http://www.globalpmi.org/index.php?option=com_content&view=article&id=15&Itemid=9) could be a future method for bringing more interaction into the classroom by increasing discussion, participation and making learning integrity more interactive when educating people.

CONCLUDING OBSERVATIONS

Many organizations, both public and private, suffer from a serious decline in integrity and ethical standards. Colleges and universities are neglecting CSP knowledge transfer, claiming that topic that is poorly defined and very difficult to implement. They acknowledge that it is possibly important but in reality they pay only lip service to the CSP area. Yet, as the author has attempted to point out in this chapter, the adoption of integrity social performance practices among both leading business organizations and educational institutions is not only attainable, its implementation may also go a long way toward mitigating the costly individual and structural damages to the global business community caused by non ethical actions and behaviours. In tertiary educational settings, social skills-enhancing activities such as interviews, social media discussions and case studies can be adopted with minimal risk of harming the relationship between the institution and the local business community. In fact, if done tactfully and by maintaining confidentiality, they can actually help to fuse these two domains. Such activities, especially when enhanced by the creative use of social media, can achieve a second significant aim suggested by this author—that of facilitating dynamic and communicative-focused instruction because they encourage closeness between students and teachers.

Therefore, claims that such integrity competent processes are difficult or impossible to adopt appear unfounded when considered from this perspective. Further, the implementation of such standards need not be controversial, costly or undermining of either financial or social profit, as may have been suggested in the past. Tellingly, the increased awareness of the interlinked nature of the quality of supply chains, overall human well-being and profit among concerned stakeholders speaks volumes about the advantages of strongly encouraging movement in a direction that is both ethical and moral. These stakeholders want—and more and more demand—ethically conscious decisions by business organizations. Such decisions are most likely to come from professionals who have been educated in environments where CSP has been placed at the forefront, and not at the back or on the side of the curricula.

Paying attention to the vast diversity within and across nations is an especially pointed challenge now more than ever in the management of a global workplace (Bognanno, Budd, & Kleiner 2007; O'Rourke & Brown, 2003). However, if done in a culturally-sensitive manner and by using some of the techniques outlined above, an emergence of CSP-educated global business citizens can occur. In this context, business enterprises can use their ethical and moral base to service their stakeholders and societies, both within individual nations and also between them, in order to successfully transfer and interactively share CSP knowledge. The ultimate fruit of such transfer, which will be a more socially-responsible, sustainable and inclusive global business community, seems likely only to enhance the profitability of business organizations that increasingly operate in diverse cultures across the globe.

REFERENCES

Andersen, J. F., & Andersen, P. A. (1987). Never smile until Christmas? Casting doubt on an old myth. *Journal of Thought*, *22*(4), 57–61.

Berman, S., & Rowley, T. J. (2000). A brand new brand of corporate social performance, behaviour and society, *Business & Society*, *9*(4), 397–418.

Bognanno, M., Budd, J., & Kleiner, M. (2007). Symposium introduction: Governing the global Workplace. *Industrial Relations*, *46*(2), 215–221. doi:10.1111/j.1468-232X.2007.00465.x

Bowen, F. E., Cousins, P. D., Lamming, R. C., & Farukt, A. C. (2001). The role of supply management capabilities in green supply. *Production and Operations Management*, *10*(2), 174–189.

Carnegie Forum on Education and the Economy. (1986). *A nation prepared: Teachers for the 21st century*. Washington: Author.

Carter, C. R., & Rogers, D. S. (2008). A framework of sustainable supply chain management: moving toward a new theory. *International Journal of Physical Distribution and Logistics Management*, *38*, 5.

Chesebro, J. L., & McCroskey, J. C. (2001). The relationship of teacher clarity and immediacy with student state receiver apprehension, affect, and cognitive learning. *Communication Education*, *50*, 59–68. doi:10.1080/03634520109379232

Chatterji, A. K., Levine, D. I., & Toffel, M. W. (2009). How well do social ratings actually measure corporate social responsibility? *Journal of Economics and Management Strategy*, *18*(1), 123–169.

Chen, C. M., & Delmas, M. (2010). Measuring corporate social performance: An efficiency perspective. *Production & Operations Management*, *20*(6), 789–804.

Christophel, D. M. (1990). The relationships among teacher immediacy behaviors, student motivation, and learning. *Communication Education*, *37*, 323–340. doi:10.1080/03634529009378813

Clarkson, M. (1995). A stakeholder framework for analyzing and evaluating corporate social performance. *Academy of Management Review*, *20*(1), 92–117.

Drumwright, M. E. (1994). Socially responsible organizational buying: environmental concern as a non-economic buying criterion. *Journal of Marketing*, *58*(3), 1–19.

Edelfelt, R. E., & Kaplan, L. (1996) *Teachers for the New Millennium: Aligning teacher development, national goals, and high standards for all students.* Thousand Oaks, CA: Corwin Press.

Frymier, A. B. (1994). A model of immediacy in the classroom. *Communication Quarterly*, *42*, 133–144. doi:10.1080/01463379409369922.

Gaikwad, M. (2010) *Ethics in the workplace*, Retrieved from http://www.buzzle.com/articles/ethics-in-the-workplace.html, on 11.09.2013

Gond, J. P., & Crane, R. (2010). Corporate social performance disoriented: Saving the lost paradigm? *Business & Society.* Retrieved from in http://www.environment.ucla.edu/perch/resources/chen-delmas-07-05-2010-1-1.pdf

Goodlad, J. I. (1990) *Teachers for our nation's schools.* San Francisco, CA: Jossey-Bass.

Griffith, M. G., & Harvey, D. A. (2002). Developing effective intercultural relationships: The importance of communication strategies. *Thunderbird International Business Review*, *44*(4), 455–476.

Hartman, L. P., & Werhane, P. H. (2010). A modular approach to business ethics integration: At the intersection of the stand-alone and the integrated approaches. *Journal of Business Ethics*, *90*, 295–300.

Holmes Group. (1986). *Tomorrow's teachers: A report of the Holmes Group.* East Lansing, MI: Author.

Hunt, S. K., Simonds, C. J., & Cooper, P. J. (2002). Communication and teacher education: exploring a communication course for all teachers. *Communication Education*, *51*, 81–94. doi:10.1080/03634520216497

Kaplan, L., & Edelfelt, R. A. (1996) *Teachers for the new millennium: Aligning teacher development, national goals, and high standards for all students.* Thousand Oaks, CA: Corwin Press.

Khera, I. P. (2010). Ethics perception of the U.S. and its large developing-country trading partners 2010. *Global Management Journal*, *2*(1), 32–33.

Loureiro, M. L., & Latade, J. (2005). Do fair trade and eco-labels in coffee wake up the consumer confidence? *Ecological Economics*, *53*(1), 32–33.

Odrakiewicz, P. (2010) PDW seminars during Academy of Management-USA in Montreal, Canada.

Odrakiewicz, P. (2013), New technologies lectures series 2013. Retrieved Noveber 11, 2013, from https://decano.pwsb.pl/system/-Networking

Odrakiewicz, P. (2014a). Multi-dimension CSP social media competence acquisition-a New paradigm. Retrieved from http://www.en.pwsb.pl/images/WykOtw13_14.pdf

Odrakiewicz, P. (2014b). Challenges of CSP knowledge transfer in educational settings. Retrieved from http://www.en.pwsb.pl/images/WykOtw13_14.pdf

O'Rourke, D., & Brown, G. D. (2003) Experiments in transforming the global workplace: Incentives for and impediments to improving workplace conditions in china. *International Journal of Occupational and Environmental Health*, 9(4), 378–385.

Plax, T. G., Kearney, P., McCroskey, J. C., & Richmond, V. P. (1986). Power in the classroom VI: Verbal control strategies, nonverbal immediacy, and affective learning. *Communication Education*, 35, 43–55. doi:10.1080/03634528609388318

Richmond, V. P., Gorham, J., & McCroskey, J. C. (1987). The relationship between immediacy behaviors and cognitive learning. In M. Mclaughlin (Ed.), *Communication yearbook (No.10)* (pp. 574–590). Beverly Hills, CA: SAGE.

Rudder, C. F. (1999). *Ethics in education: Are professional policies ethical.* New York, NY: Garland.

Suering., S., & Müller, M. (2008). From a literature review to a conceptual framework for sustainable supply chain management. *Journal of Cleaner Production*, 16, 1699–1710.

Talbert-Johnson, C., & Beran, D. (1999). Higher education and teacher immediacy: Creating dialogue for effective intercultural communication. *Journal for a Just and Caring Education*, 5(4), 430–441.

Timm, S. A., & Armstrong, K. B. (2000). Effective communication in the diverse classroom and beyond. *Business Education Forum*, 55(1), 16–17.

Turban, D., & Greening, D. (1996). Corporate social performance and organizational attractiveness to prospective employees. *Academy of Management Journal*, 40(3), 658–672.

Vaughan, J. C., Edelfelt, R. A., Houston, W. R., & Arisman, S. (1998) *Completing the circle of education reform: The need for standards, assessments and supports for teacher educators.* Reston, VA: Association of Teacher Educators.

Wood, D. J. (1991). Corporate social performance re-visited. *Academy of Management*, 16(4), 691–718.

INTERNET SOURCES

Gaikwad, M., *Ethics in the workplace*, from http://www.buzzle.com/articles/ethics-in-the-workplace.html last accessed 11 August, 2010.

http://www.corp-integrity.com/wp-content/uploads/2011/09/Anti-Corruption.pdf (last accessed on Jan 20, 2012).

http://unglobalcompact.org/ (accessed Nov. 12, 2011).

http://www.adb.org/Documents/Policies/Anticorruption/anticorrupt300.asp?p=antipubs (last accessed Jan 23, 2012).

http://www.unglobalcompact.org/docs/issues_doc/AntiCorruption/Bali_Business_Declaration.pdf (last accessed Jan. 9, 2012).

www.amazon .com/gp/product1613505108 (accessed on Feb. 2, 2012).

United Nations (2006) http://unglobalcompact.org/ (last accessed 2011), http://www.nauka.gov.pl/ (accessed Jan. 20, 2011).

http://www.nauka.gov.pl/higher-education/degrees-and-diplomas-studies-in-foreign-languages (last accessed Aug. 13, 2011).

ABOUT THE AUTHORS

Hadil T. Al-Khatib is human resources professional, with more than 12 years' experience working within the Public Sector-Utilities and Energy Sector in operational leadership, human resources management, recruitment and resource utilization. Her main experience is in training and development, gap-analysis and enhancement of career paths, management assessment models and manpower planning. She works closely with corporate communications in several areas such as corporate relations, CSR and media training. She is a master's holder in human resource management from the British University in Dubai (University of Manchester, England) and a bachelor degree in English language and management. She is a certified psychometric assessor from the University of Cambridge, England (on campus)—British Psychological Society and a professional member of the Society for Human Resource Management (SHRM). She is currently holding the position of head of human resources and administration at the Regulation and Supervision Bureau in the Emirate of Abu Dhabi, UAE.

Manuela Brusoni, is senior professor of public management and business government relation at SDA Bocconi, Bocconi University School of Management, where she serves also as director of accreditation. She took her MBA at SDA Bocconi in 1984. She is coordinator of several research projects and executive education programs (open and custom) about business government relations, public procurement and local development. Currently she is the director of MaSan, an executive program for buyers in the public sector and member of the scientific board of FARE, the Italian Association of Buyers of healthcare organizations. As director of accreditation, she manages the relations with international accreditation bodies and networks, such as EFMD, AACSB, ENQA. She advises Italian central and local public authorities in the field of public procurement, management education and local development. She serves as chair of the accreditation committee of ASFOR, the Italian Association for Management Education, where she is also member of the research group on management education trends. She is an active member of the Academy of Management since 2004, and GBSN Ambassador for SDA Bocconi.

Athanasios Chymis is a research fellow at the Center of Planning and Economic Research (KEPE) in Athens, Greece. He holds a PhD from the University of Missouri-Columbia in Agricultural Economics. He is interested in the connection between ethics and economics and, currently, his research is focused on how social responsibility could be infused in the public administration as well as in all organizations both of the private and the public sector. His latest book is *Public Management as Corporate Social Responsibility: The Economic Bottom Line of Government* (co-editor), Springer, 2015.

Harry Costin, PhD, received his DBA in strategy from Boston University and has 25 years of academic experience. He is the author and editor of books in strategy, international business, quality improvement and management development. He currently divides his time between consulting and teaching at diverse North American and European institutions, including Boston University, United States, NEOMA in France, and Duale Hochschule Baden-Württemberg, Germany.

Niccolò Cusumano PhD candidate at SDA Bocconi and Research Fellow at IEFE (Research Center for Energy and the Environment) at Bocconi University since 2012 is attending the PhD program in management of innovation and sustainability healthcare at the Scuola Superiore Sant'Anna of Pisa. In addition to the activities of teaching and research on issues of public procurement policies to promote renewable energy, public-private partnership, has participated in several evaluation projects of European and national policies. From June 2013 he's engaged in SDA Bocconi Lab for Impact Investments.

Paolo D'Anselmi is a practitioner of management consultancy and policy analysis. He teaches corporate social responsibility at the University of Rome Tor Vergata, Italy. He is a graduate in engineering (Sapienza, Rome) and in public policy (Harvard). He is currently working on extending corporate social responsibility to Pubic Administration. His recent related publications include *Values and Stakeholders in an Era of Social Responsibility: Cut-Throat Competition?* (Palgrave, 2011), *SMEs as the Unknown Stakeholder: Entrepreneurship in the Political Arena* (co-editor) (Palgrave, 2013), and *Public Management as Corporate Social Responsibility: The Economic Bottom Line of Government* (co-editor) (Springer, 2015).

Massimiliano Di Bitetto is a senior researcher and director central at the Italian National Research Council, in Rome, Italy. His research, currently, reaches in the field of management and organizational sociology. His related publications include: *SMEs as the Unknown Stakeholder: Entrepreneurship in the Political Arena* (co-editor) (Palgrave, 2013), and *Public Management as Corporate Social Responsibility: The Economic Bottom Line of Government* (co-editor) (Springer, 2015).

Gerhard Fink is a retired Jean Monnet professor. During 2002–2009, he was the director of the doctoral programs at WU (Vienna University of Economics and Business), Austria. He was the director of the Research Institute for European Affairs during 1997–2003. His current research interests are in cybernetic agency theory, normative personality, organizational culture and cultural change in Europe. He has about 270 publications to his credit in learned journals and has authored or (co-)edited about 25 books. Among others, he is associate editor of the *European Journal of International Management* and co-editor of the *European Journal of Cross-Cultural Competence and Management.* He was guest editor in several journals, among others in 2005 in the *Academy of Management Executive,* 2006 in the *Journal of Managerial Psychology,* 2011 in *Cross Cultural Management: An International Journal,* and 2014 in the *European Journal of Cross-Cultural Competence and Management.* He is also founding member of the Organizational Coherence and Trajectory Project (http://www.octresearch.net).

Robert L. Heath, PhD, University of Illinois, professor emeritus, University of Houston, United States, has published more than 100 articles and chapters and 20 books. This body of work focuses on the public policy and social performance challenges of large organizations, and social movements. Heath has recently edited two editions of the *Handbook of Public Relations,* several other edited books, and two editions of the *Encyclopedia of Public Relations.* He has served as an area editor for the *International Encyclopedia of Communication.* He recently published a master work on public relations for Routledge. He has written on topics such as public relations, strategic issues management, corporate social responsibility, change management, social movement advocacy, as well as risk and crisis communication.

Yi-Hui Ho obtained her PhD in educational policy and administration from the University of Minnesota-Twin Cities. She is currently an assistant professor at the Department of International Business of Chang Jung Christian University in Taiwan. Her research and teaching interests are business ethics, cross-cultural management, human resources management, and financial accounting.

Stefán Kalmansson is an adjunct lecturer at Bifrost University in Iceland. Graduated in business administration from University of Iceland in 1987 (Cand Ocon) and from Aarhus Business School in Denmark in 1992 with the degree Cand Merc. Thesis: *The Integration Process in Europe and the Position of Iceland*. He worked in a private company from 1987–1990 as an accountant and chief accountant. Same company from 1992–1999 as an assistant in budgeting department and later director of financial control. Director in a municipal 1999–2002 and financial director at Bifrost University from 2002–2006. Working as a teacher in the faculty of business from 2006. Main courses corporate finance and international financial management.

Jeong-Nam Kim received his PhD in communication (public relations) from the University of Maryland, College Park in 2006 and joined the faculty at Purdue in 2007. His specialties are communication theory, strategic management of public relations, public behavior and its social consequences, information behaviors and problem solving. Jeong-Nam has constructed a communication theory called, the situational theory of problem solving, with James E. Grunig. The situational theory explains causes and processes of information behaviors in problematic life situations. He applies the situational theory to public relations, public diplomacy, health communication, risk communication, science communication, and employee communication.

Soojin Kim, an assistant professor at Lee Kong Chian School of Business, Singapore Management University, is interested in strategic management of public relations. She is looking at how organizations' behaviors or decisions along with key antecedents can affect public behaviors, organization-public relationships, and their organizational effectiveness. As strategic management of public relations starts with understanding of publics, she also explores various types of public's communication behaviors in different contexts. She received her PhD in Public Relations from Purdue University.

Kathrin Köster is a thought leader and action researcher regarding transformation of educational and business organizations. She currently holds a full tenured professorship in the field of International Management, Leadership and Organizational Studies at Heilbronn University in Germany, where she held the position of vice president for research and continuous education until summer 2012. Kathrin applies consciousness-based learning in her teaching and delivers innovative business education and research in sustainable management. She transfers her research results to business practice with her organization Köster + Partner, focusing on transformational development of individuals and organizations. She has broad working, teaching and consulting experience in Asia-Pacific, North America, Europe, and the MENA region. Kathrin obtained her doctorate on organizational change in Japan from the University of Erlangen-Nürnberg/Germany where she also studied economics, Chinese Studies, and Japanese Studies.

Chieh-Yu Lin received his PhD degree at National Cheng Kung University in Taiwan. He is now the professor at the Department of International Business of Chang Jung Christian University. He serves as the chair of the Department of International Business from 2001 to 2007. His research interests include management of technology, business ethics, and supply chain management. He has published articles in several academic journals and international conferences, and served as editors of some international journals.

Adela McMurray has extensive experience in public and private sectors and has published over 100 refereed publications. Her research is widely recognised and she is the recipient of four prestigious Australian Research Council grants, including various other grants totalling over $2.5 million. Adela Chairs the USA Academy of Management's International Theme Committee and is a member of a number of Editorial Advisory Boards. Adela's research expertise addresses: workplace innovation, organisational culture and climate, cultural diversity, risk management and sustainability. Currently Professor McMurray holds the following positions: editorial advisory board member of the *International Journal of Studies* in Thai business society and culture, editorial advisory board member of the *International Journal of Entrepreneurship Business Research*. Emerald Group Publishing, editorial advisory board member of the *Journal of Small Business and Enterprise Development*. Emerald Group Publishing, editorial advisory board member of the *Journal of Management History*. Emerald Group Publishing, Chair USA International Theme Committee USA.

Olimpia Meglio is an associate professor of management at University of Sannio. She earned a PhD in management from University of Naples "Federico II." She has been visiting scholar at Esade (Barcelona) and at

Copenhagen Business School. Her research interests cover postmerger integration, M&A performance measurement, process research methods, intergenerational transition process in small family business. She has published articles and book chapters for international journals and handbooks and she is currently editing a companion about mergers and acquisitions for Routledge.

Andrew E. Michael, PhD, is an adjunct professor in the accelerated MBA program of Hellenic American University in Manchester, New Hampshire, United States. He is on the editorial board of the *International Journal of Organizational Analysis* and serves as a reviewer for various journals. He has published and conducted research in the areas of business ethics and humanistic management, managing diversity in the workplace, person-environment fit, work-life balance, capitalism and macroeconomics.

Susan Mravlek, PhD, drawing on over 15 years experience as a HR executive in large multinational organisations across a range of sectors that include retail, IT, Finance to Utilities. Susan has held a number of senior HR leadership roles in complex and dynamic environments. In the last 4 years, Susan's has been working independently as an organizational consultant in organizational development and dynamics. Using socioanalytical elements to explore what drives systems/groups and at the unconscious level, specifically-dynamics, roles, leadership and authority. Currently undertaking her PhD candidature at RMIT University. Her research expertise addresses: organizational culture and capability, leadership and authority, managing change, workplace innovation, stakeholder engagement.

Irene Nikandrou, PhD, is assistant professor of OB/HRM at the Athens University of Economics and Business. She has a wide teaching experience both in the academic field, where she teaches management, human resource management and organizational behavior at an undergraduate and postgraduate level, and in business. She has done extensive research in the field of HRM and OB as she is a member of the CRANET and GLOBE project teams in Greece. Her work has been published in leading journals like *The International Journal of HRM, Journal of Managerial Psychology, Human Resource Management Journal, Human Resource Development International*, etc.

Peter Odrakiewicz, PhD, is the scientific director of the GPMI Research Institute, a graduate faculty adj. at Gniezno College Milenium and a visiting professor for EU Erasmus exchanges. Also, he is a visiting professor at the University of LaVerne, an Emerald Reviewer for the *Journal of Organizational Change Management* and visiting professor, postgraduate management programs, Poznan University of Technology Dr. Peter Odrakiewicz cross appointed professor economics/management and Dept. of English, dean of faculty of English-managerial linguistics-EU Program Poznan PWSB 2006-2014, member UN Global Compact www.unprme.org, visiting professor University of Debrecen, HR Academy of Management ambassador for Poland, scientific president of Global Partnership Management Institute, Author, co-author, and editor of numerous leading scientific publications including more than eight monographies, books and chapters in leading monographies. Dr Odrakiewicz motto is "to empower everyone in the process, to instill critical evaluation skills in order for everyone involved to reach the best decision potential in a globalized interconnected world," member of Polish Association for Canadian Studies, King's University College-alumni association, University of Western Ontario alumni association-London, Canada, Academy of Management-scientific member (http://www.aomonline.org/).

Claire A. Simmers, PhD, is a professor of management and department chair at Saint Joseph's University in Philadelphia, PA. She has been at Saint Joseph's University for the past 18 years and has been department chair since 2009. She received her PhD from Drexel University in strategic management. Her current research interests are in the sociotechnical interfaces in the Internet-connected workplace, including the changing workplace, human capital contributions to competitive advantage and sustainability.

Agata Stachowicz-Stanusch is a full professor of management at The Silesian University of Technology, Poland, and is the head of the Management and Marketing Department. She is the author of over 80 research papers and has 14 books published by leading houses, among them *Integrity in Organizations: Building the Foundations for Humanistic Management* (Palgrave Macmilla, 2012), *Academic Ethos Management: Building the Foundation for Integrity in Management Education* (Business Expert Press, 2012), *Education for Integrity: Ethically Educating Tomorrow's Business Leaders* (Emerald, 2011), *Effectively Integrating Ethical Dimensions into Business Education* (IAP, 2011), and *Handbook of Research on Teaching Ethics in Business and Management Education* (IGI Global, 2012). Agata manages an international research team as part of the project Sensitizing Future Business Leaders: Developing Anti-Corruption Guidelines for Curriculum Change of the UN Global Compact and the Principles for Responsible Management Education (PRME) initiative. Pro bono, she is a member of the International Fellows for the World Engagement Institute and is on the International Editorial Board for International Higher Education Teaching and Learning Association, is a member of the Anti-Corruption Academic Initiative

(ACAD), an academic project coordinated by Northeastern University and the United Nations Office on Drugs and Crime, and is a member of the Committee on Organizational and Management Sciences (Polish Academy of Sciences), Katowice. In July 2012, she was elected for the position of Chair of Emerald Best International Symposium Award, which is one of the awards granted by the International Theme Committee (ITC) within the American Academy of Management. She is Associate Editor of the Journal of Applied Research in Higher Education, (Emerald), a member of the editorial board for *Law and Social Change: An International Journal* (Springer), and a member of the editorial advisory board for the Business Strategy Series (Emerald) as well as a member of many other journal editorial boards. She was thrice doctoral dissertations supervisor and many times a doctoral dissertations reviewer.

Abubakr M. Suliman is currently the dean of the Faculty of Business, head of MSc HRM and head of the MBA program, the British University in Dubai, Dubai, UAE. He authored and co-authored over 50 publications that appear in international outlets such as Routledge, Blackwell, and Emerald. His publication address varieties of topics in HRM and general management areas, for example, conflict management, emotional intelligence, organisational justice and leadership. He is a member of editorial board, referee, ad-hoc referee, and co-editor for many journals in the Middle East, Europe and North America such as IMJ editorial advisory board (UK).

Einar Svansson is an assistant professor at the Faculty of Business at Bifröst University, Iceland. Has lectured on business ethics and sustainable management in Iceland and Austria. Best paper award in the Tourist and Travel Research Association (TTRA) conference in 2011 for his paper about the Blue Lagoon in Iceland. Previous professional carrier was 20 years (1981-2000) in the food production industry. CEO in two of Iceland´s biggest seafood organizations. In the year 1997 he implemented the first green strategy in the Icelandic seafood industry, highly praised by big customers in Europe. From 2009– has been studying for a doctoral thesis in the University of Exeter in England. Einar holds two master's degrees, in strategic management and business administration, and marketing and international business.

Laishan Tam is a lecturer of strategic communication at La Trobe University in Melbourne, Australia. She received her PhD in public relations from Purdue University in 2015, where she has been conducting research on public diplomacy, consumer nationalism, and corporate responsibility. Her master's thesis employed the intermedia agenda setting theory to study how corporations and the print media defined the newsworthiness of different CSR-related news stories differently.

Marco Tavanti is full professor and nonprofit administration director at University of San Francisco's School of Management. He is president of the Sustainable Capacity International Institute (SCII) and co-founder of the World Engagement Institute (WEI) providing international capacity trainings. He previously served as chair of the International Public Service (IPS) Graduate Program at DePaul University's School of Public Service in Chicago. He teaches and publishes in the area of responsible management education, international sustainable development and ethical leadership. He is the editor in chief of the *International Journal of Sustainable Human Security* (IJSHS) and has authored more than 30 academic publications. With more than 25 years experience in sustainable development he serves as a special consultant the United Nations and other international organizations for the promotion of indigenous rights and inclusive development in Latin America, East Africa, and Southeast Asia.

Irene Tsachouridi is a PhD candidate in organizational behavior at Athens University of Economics and Business. Her current research interests include organizational virtuousness, psychological contracts, social identity, social exchange and social comparison processes in the workplace. Her work has been presented at international conferences such as Academy of Management, European Academy of Management, and British Academy of Management.

Betty Tsakarestou works as an assistant professor and head of Advertising and Public Relations Lab at the Department of Communication, Media and Culture of Panteion University and External Lecturer at Copenhagen Business School, Department of Intercultural Communication and Management. She teaches courses on advertising and Public Relations 2.0, crisis communication with social media, CSR and social issues in management, collaborative consumption is the sharing economy era, startup and social entrepreneurship, cultural marketing and communication with a focus on city branding. She has been a visiting assistant professor of CSR and business ethics at the part-time MBA Program of the University of Cyprus (2007–2011). Her research interests expand into various interconnected areas: organizational and crisis communication with social media, co-creation, sharing and collaborative consumption and economy, living and shareable cities/ city-branding, co-creation, CSR, social entrepreneurship and startup culturesocial innovation, mobile reputations in the sharing economy, collaborative innovation and leadership, digital citizenship and activism, cultural branding/ city branding. She has conducted research on: 1. Mobile Generation and Generation Y, 2. CSR and responsible consumption, 3. social responsibility & media responsibility. She serves as BOD member of the Greek Institute of Communication and Member and on the advisory board of Impact Hub Athens. Since January 2010, she serves as a member of the BoD of Technological Educational Institute of Ionian Islands. She has been appointed the position of director of educational radio-television, ministry of education, lifelong learning & religious affairs from June 2010 to February 2012.

Lida Tsene holds a PhD on social media and social responsibility from Panteion University, Department of Communication, Media and Culture. She is researcher and teaching associate at the same department and she is also collaborating with the other academic institutions. Her research interests apply to the fields of social media, digital economy, media responsibility, transmedia storytelling, entrepreneurship, cultural management and comics. She has been working in the field of communication since 2006 and she is public relations, art and educational director of Comicdom Press. She is organizing Athens Startup Weekend University and Athens Startup Weekend Education. Her book entitled *From Media Crisis To Social Media. A New Paradigm Of Social Responsibility* has been published in 2012.

Veronica Vecchi is professor of public management at Bocconi University School of Management (SDA Bocconi) where she researches and teaches in the following fields: public management; public private partnership for infrastructure and business development; business government relations; impact investment and social innovation; public policy and management for entrepreneurial development and competitiveness; financial strategies and evaluation for public investments and infrastructures. Veronica serves as scientific coordinator of Public Private Factory, an executive education program for public and private managers on PPPs; she coordinates Bocconi MP3, the Bocconi University research initiative dedicated to Public Private Partnerships for economic development and SDA Bocconi Lab for Impact Investments. Veronica is Director of Executive Education at MISB Bocconi (Mumbai International School of Business) faculty, where she also teaches Business Government Relations and CSR. She is external faculty affiliate at Cornell University for the Cornell Program in Infrastructure Policy.

Damion Waymer, PhD, associate professor for special initiatives at the University of Cincinnati. His program of research centers on organizational rhetoric, particularly regarding PR, issues management, corporate social responsibility (CSR), and strategic communication. His research projects address fundamental concerns about issues of diversity in general and issues of race, class, and gender, specifically, and how these social constructions shape and influence the ways that various stakeholders receive, react, and respond to certain messages.

Duane Windsor, PhD, Harvard University, is Lynette S. Autrey professor of management in the Jesse H. Jones Graduate School of Business at Rice University. He has been editor (2007–2014) of *Business & Society*, founded 1960 and sponsored by the International Association for Business and Society (IABS). He served as elected program chair and head of IABS and of the social issues in management (SIM) division of Academy of Management, receiving the Sumner Marcus Award for Outstanding Service, SIM division (2009). His recent work focuses on corporate social responsibility and stakeholder theory.

Maurice Yolles is professor emeritus in management systems at Liverpool John Moores University. His doctorate, completed 2 decades ago, was in mathematical social theory, in particular, the formal dynamics of peace and conflict. He heads the Center for the Creation of Coherent Change and Knowledge. Within this context, he has also been involved in and is responsible for a number of international research and development projects in Europe and Asia. He has published three research books, with a fourth in preparation, and more than 200 papers. He is the editor of *Journal of Organisational Transformation and Social Change*, and sits on a number of editorial boards.